W9-CDB-469

Labor Market Policies in Canada and Latin America: Challenges of the New Millennium

Labor Market Policies in Canada and Latin America: Challenges of the New Millennium

edited by

Albert Berry
University of Toronto, Canada

KLUWER ACADEMIC PUBLISHERS
Boston / Dordrecht / London

Distributors for North, Central and South America:
Kluwer Academic Publishers
101 Philip Drive
Assinippi Park
Norwell, Massachusetts 02061 USA
Telephone (781) 871-6600
Fax (781) 871-6528
E-Mail <kluwer@wkap.com>

Distributors for all other countries:
Kluwer Academic Publishers Group
Distribution Centre
Post Office Box 322
3300 AH Dordrecht, THE NETHERLANDS
Telephone 31 78 6392 392
Fax 31 78 6546 474
E-Mail <services@wkap.nl>

 Electronic Services <http://www.wkap.nl>

Library of Congress Cataloging-in-Publication Data

Labor market policies in Canada and Latin America : challenges of the new millennium / edited
by Albert Berry.
    p. cm.
  Includes bibliographical references and index.
  Contains papers presented at a conference.
  ISBN 0-7923-7232-8 (alk. paper)
    1. Labor market--Canada--Congresses. 2. Manpower policy--Canada--Congresses. 3.
Labor market--Latin America--Congresses. 4. Manpower policy--Latin
America--Congresses. I. Berry, R Albert.

HD5728 .L33 2000 2001
331.12'042'0971--dc21   00-049321

Contents

Illustrations

Tables

Figures

List of Contributors

Dwayne Benjamin is Professor of Economics at the University of Toronto. His research interests concern a variety of labor market issues in Canada and the U.S. as well as in developing countries. In a Canadian context he has explored questions pertaining to immigration, minimum wages, and aging. For developing countries, his main interests concern testing various models of rural labor markets, investigating the connections between labor market institutions and household welfare.

Albert Berry is Professor of Economics at the University of Toronto and Research Director of the Program on Latin America and the Caribbean at the University's Centre for International Studies. His main research areas, with focus on Latin America, are the economics of labor markets/income distribution and of small and medium enterprise.

René Cortázar is General Manager of the state television network in Chile, having previously been Minister of Labor and a member of the research centre CIEPLAN. He is best know for his ideas on the design of unemployment insurance systems in Latin America.

María Angélica Ducci is chief of the Training Policy and Program Development Branch of the International Labor Office in Geneva. Her writings have focused on issues in vocational training in Latin America, including financing, the roles of the state and the private sector and the search for equity with effectiveness.

Morley Gunderson holds the Canadian Imperial Bank of Commerce Chair in Youth Employment at the University of Toronto, where he is a Professor at the Centre for Industrial Relations and the Department of Economics. He has published extensively on labor issues, including gender discrimination, pensions and mandatory retirement, youth employment, immigration, workers' compensation, and training.

Jon Kesselman is Professor of Economics at the University of British Columbia and Director of UBC's Centre for Research on Economic and Social Policy. His areas of specialization include the theoretical and policy assessment of taxation,

Chapter 1

DANGERS AND CHALLENGES: THE NEW CONTEXT OF LABOR MARKET POLICY IN LATIN AMERICA AND IN CANADA

by Albert Berry

1.1 The 1990s Context

Canada and the countries of Latin America are in the midst of major changes and choices in the area of labor markets and related social policy. The decisions taken are likely to be of major significance. Many labor market outcomes—levels of unemployment, wage trends and levels of inequality, have been unsatisfactory over the last couple of decades in both developed countries (including Canada) and in many developing countries, including those of Latin America. Nearly everyone is concerned about something, either the labor market outcomes or the institutions. Some blame the labor market institutions for what is bad about the outcomes: important policy reforms are being implemented or are under consideration because of the belief that a number of existing or previous institutions have been counterproductive and/or too expensive from a fiscal point of view, and that greater labor market flexibility is important in today's world of fast-changing technology. Others feel that the reforms being proposed will make the outcomes even worse, and thus argue that those reforms are pushing the system in the wrong direction. Hard evidence on which to base professional judgments is scarce.

Most of the same policy areas are involved in the reforms being planned or implemented in Latin America and in Canada. Many of the factors inducing those reforms are also the same or similar, in spite of the considerable differences in income level, economic structure and past labor policies. A number of the options now facing Latin American countries in areas like unemployment insurance have a history of experience in Canada, which can be analyzed for its lessons. Some of the directions currently under discussion in Canada have been tried somewhere in Latin America; there has, for example, been an interesting range of experiments in the area of pension systems in Latin America.[1] Accordingly, a comparison of the two experiences has much to offer for policymakers both in Latin America and in Canada.

Canada's experience is more relevant to Latin America than that of the more frequent reference point, the United States. As a relatively small economy, Canada is forced to adjust to events at the world or hemispheric level in much the same way as the countries of Latin America must do. The United States is atypical, both in the region and in the world, in being able to influence many of the rules, and in its level of independence from other countries. It is an outlier among developed countries also in the structure of its social support network—with relatively low levels of state involvement and above normal reliance on the market (e.g., in health care). Many countries of Latin America are inclined to approach these issues in the more interventionist "European" fashion. Canada tends to fall between the American and the European models in this regard and is thus a natural comparator and source of learning, both because its position in this spectrum may be more congenial to Latin American thinking and because its recent experience gives some evidence on the problems and prospects of an intermediate approach. Finally, Canada's federal system, under which the provinces play a large and increasing role in social policy, provides an interesting model for those Latin American countries presently pursuing decentralization of government activities in one form or another (Berry, 1995).

This chapter provides a general overview of major labor market issues which confront Latin America and Canada. The remainder of this section reviews the current context, shaped in both cases by fiscal crisis, increasing openness to the world economy, rapid technological change, modest growth rates, and labor market outcomes which in various ways give cause for concern. The second section considers in a little more detail how the context shapes the labor market issues and the options available to policymakers. The next four sections summarize evidence for Canada and Latin America on four labor policy instruments: unemployment insurance, minimum wages, payroll taxes and training programs. They provide a general introduction to the chapters making up the rest of the volume.

Labor Market Outcomes and the Worries They Give Rise To

Though output per capita and per worker has been rising over the last couple of decades in most developed countries, including Canada, that growth has not always brought with it the elements of performance more directly linked to welfare—rising wages, improving income distribution, lower unemployment, greater job stability

---

[1] As witness the recent conference at the International Development Research Center in Ottawa on "Pension Systems in Crisis: What Can Canada Learn from Latin America?," Ottawa, November 10, 1997.

and in general fewer economic worries on the part of the population. Instead there have been for the most part continuing high levels of unemployment, stagnant or falling wages for important categories of workers—especially those toward the lower end of the skill hierarchy—, increasing inequality, and less job stability than before as the prevalence of part-time and temporary employment rises.

Canada's particular case has involved a progressive slowdown in per capita income growth from very high levels of the 1970s (an average of 3.8% per year) to only marginal gains during most of the 1990s. Some observers blame allegedly stagnant productivity levels for the weak growth performance and for the widespread perception that Canada's standard of living has been increasingly slipping behind that of the United States. Such productivity problems are often attributed to weak R&D and/or innovation practices and to a rigid labor market which constrains the employer more than is the case in the U. S. It is not yet clear what has in fact lain behind the tendency to slip behind the U.S. growth rates of both per capita income and per worker productivity.

Slow growth of per capita output, together with a 12% negative shift in the terms of trade between 1980 and 1996 (World Bank, 1999, 228), a more rapid increase in consumer prices than of the GDP deflator, and an increase in the tax burden as a share of GDP has meant that per capita disposable incomes have risen significantly less than in the U.S. and, according to some calculations, have fallen in the 1990s. The marked increase in U.S. inequality means, however, that a comparison of average family or personal incomes can misrepresent what happens to the majority of the two populations, and recent (1995) Statistics Canada estimates suggest that the middle class in Canada (defined by the median after tax family income) has a little more purchasing power in Canada than in the U.S., though the top quintile or a little more of the population clearly does better in the U.S. (*Globe and Mail*, December 21, 1998).

Whatever the relative situation in Canada vis-à-vis the United States, the trends of the last decade or more do contain many worrisome elements. Some authors have focused on the implications for societal welfare of the widening earnings gap between younger and older workers observed in the 1990s vis-à-vis earlier decades, and of the greater job insecurity associated with higher unemployment rates and lower job permanence. Thus Osberg *et al* (1998, 57) conclude that Canada's young workers in the 1990s can expect greater economic insecurity, as well as lower average earnings compared to older workers or to the youth of previous decades. They judge that the 1971-94 revisions to unemployment insurance (UI) in Canada, implying a substantial reduction in the generosity of the system, produced decreases in economic well-being for all deciles of the income distribution, with these declines especially large in percentage terms for youth and for the poorest deciles. Latin America's recent economic history has of course been much more traumatic than Canada's. The debt crisis of the 1980s had disastrous macroeconomic effects in the region, such that per capita income in

1990 was just 86.5% of the 1980 level and per capita GDP 91.8% of that level (ECLAC, 1995, 14). Growth over 1990-97 recovered to 3.5% per year, pulling per capita GDP back to 4% above the 1980 level and per capita income to about the 1980 figure. Open urban unemployment had risen in most countries at the height of the crisis, though the regional average was only 7.5% in 1985, up from 6.2% in 1980, partly because the two largest countries, Brazil and Mexico, registered no increase between those two years (in fact Brazil's rate fell a little) and partly because the phasing of the crisis varied from country to country. The regional average had eased down to 5.8% by 1990, but has since risen again to more than 7.5% in 1996-97 (Table 1.1). Wage behavior has varied widely across countries, again because their crisis cycles have been quite different. But the average, when country figures are weighted by population, shows continuing stagnation during the 1990s after a decline of 15% or so in the 1980s (Table 1.2). Though the region's recent (say, 1990s) performance is clearly unsatisfactory, optimists see in the rapid growth and lowered unemployment in Chile the model for what might happen in the region as a whole when the sorts of economic reforms pioneered by that country have been successfully implemented region-wide. Others are less confident, arguing that Chile's is an atypical economy, with its strong natural resource base and small population, and that it has benefitted from a series of unusually positive conditions.

Related to employment problems and to the failure of wages, especially those of the relatively unskilled, to rise has been a general tendency for household income inequality to rise. This pattern has been especially marked in Latin America, but has also plagued the U.S., a number of other industrial countries, and in lesser degree (thus far) Canada. Most advanced countries have seen a worsening of both primary and secondary income distribution[2] from around the mid-1970s, reversing the previous trend toward equality. Primary income distribution in developed countries has been affected negatively by several factors, a major one being an increased variance of wage and salary earnings. According to Corry and Glyn (1994, 214) the increase in earnings inequality was largest in the U.S., but "Sweden saw a reversal of strong earlier declines in inequality and in the U.K. a century of near stability in earnings dispersion gave way to a sharp increase." Other factors contributing to the worsening distribution trend were a tendency toward a rising share of profits and a falling share of wages; rising unemployment, which affected every OECD country; and the changing age-profile of the population, as the share of households with heads above retirement age increased. The net effect of these changes was a worsening of household primary income distribution in every country for which there is evidence. In the U.S. the top quintile of the population received ten times the average income of the bottom

---

[2] The primary distribution of income is that which emerges from the functioning of the market, before the impacts of taxes and transfers are taken into account. The secondary distribution includes the effects of those taxes and transfers.

Table 1.1
Latin America and the Caribbean: Urban Unemployment, 1982-1997

Country	Coverage of Survey[1]	1982	1983	1984	1985	1986	1987	1988	1989	1990[1]	1991	1992	1993	1994	1995	1996	1997[2]
Latin America		n/a	n/a	n/a	n/a	n/a	n/a	n/a	n/a	n/a	5.8	6.2	6.2	6.3	7.2	7.7	7.5
Argentina	Urban areas	5.3	4.7	4.6	6.1	5.6	5.9	6.3	7.8	8.6	6.5	7.0	9.6	11.5	17.5	17.2	14.9
Barbados	Total nation-wide	n/a	8.5	n/a	n/a	n/a	n/a	n/a	n/a	n/a	17.2	23.0	24.3	21.9	19.7	16.4	14.0
Bolivia	Depart. capitals	8.2	6.7	6.9	5.8	7.0	7.2	6.7	7.0	7.0	5.8	5.4	5.8	3.1	3.6	4.2	n/a
Brazil	Six metrop. areas	6.3	6.7	7.1	5.3	3.6	3.7	3.8	3.3	4.3	4.8	5.8	5.4	5.1	4.6	5.4	5.8
Chile	Metropol. region	20.0	19.0	18.5	17.0	13.1	11.9	10.2	7.2	6.6	9.3	7.0	6.2	8.3	7.4	7.0	7.5
Colombia	Seven metrop. areas	9.1	11.7	13.4	14.0	13.8	11.7	11.5	9.6	10.2	10.2	10.2	8.6	8.9	8.8	11.2	12.6
Costa Rica	Total urban	9.9	8.5	6.6	6.7	6.7	5.9	5.5	3.8	5.4	6.0	4.3	4.0	4.3	5.7	6.6	6.1
Cuba	Total national	n/a	n/a	n/a	n/a	n/a	n/a	n/a	n/a	n/a	7.7	6.1	6.2	6.7	7.9	6.0	6.5
Ecuador	Total urban	6.3	6.7	10.5	10.4	12.0	12.0	12.3	14.3	n/a	8.5	8.9	8.9	7.8	7.7	10.4	9.3
El Salvador	Total urban	n/a	n/a	n/a	n/a	n/a	n/a	n/a	n/a	14.0	7.9	8.2	8.1	7.0	7.0	7.5	n/a
Guatemala	Total national	6.0	9.9	9.1	12.0	14.2	12.1	9.6	7.2	n/a	4.0	1.5	2.5	3.3	3.7	4.9	6.4
Honduras	Total urban	9.2	9.5	10.7	11.7	12.5	11.4	12.0	13.0	13.8	7.4	6.0	7.0	4.0	5.6	6.5	n/a
Jamaica	Total national	n/a	n/a	n/a	n/a	n/a	n/a	n/a	n/a	n/a	15.4	15.7	16.3	15.4	16.2	16.0	n/a
Mexico	Urban areas	4.2	6.6	5.7	4.4	4.3	3.9	3.5	2.9	2.8	2.7	2.8	3.4	3.7	6.2	5.5	3.9
Nicaragua	Total national	n/a	n/a	n/a	n/a	n/a	n/a	n/a	n/a	n/a	14.2	17.8	21.8	20.7	16.4	14.8	13.9
Panama	Metropol. region	10.1	11.7	12.4	15.6	12.6	14.1	21.1	20.0	20.8	19.3	17.5	15.6	16.0	16.6	16.7	15.8
Paraguay	Metropol. Asuncion	5.6	8.3	7.3	5.1	6.1	5.5	4.7	6.1	7.0	5.1	5.3	5.1	4.4	5.3	8.2	n/a
Peru	Metropol. Lima	6.6	9.0	8.9	10.1	5.4	4.8	7.9	7.9	n/a	5.9	9.4	9.9	8.8	9.3	8.8	9.1
Dominican Rep.	Total national	n/a	n/a	n/a	n/a	n/a	n/a	n/a	n/a	n/a	19.6	20.3	19.9	16.0	15.8	16.5	15.9
Trinidad & Tob.	Total national	n/a	n/a	n/a	n/a	n/a	n/a	n/a	n/a	n/a	18.5	19.7	19.8	18.4	17.2	16.3	17.2
Uruguay	Total urban	11.9	15.5	14.0	13.1	10.7	9.3	9.1	8.6	9.2	8.9	9.0	8.3	9.2	10.3	11.9	11.9
Venezuela	Total urban	7.8	11.2	14.3	14.3	12.1	9.9	7.9	9.7	10.6	10.1	8.1	6.8	8.9	10.9	12.3	12.8

Notes: [1] Coverage changes over time in some countries; for details see "Source." [2] Preliminary figures.

Source: ECLAC (1990, 26) for 1982-1990 and ECLAC (1997, 52) for 1991-1997. Additional details with respect to the data are given in these two sources. Although it is not clear from those notes that there are non-comparabilities between the period up to 1990 and that from 1991 on, the sudden drops observed in Ecuador and in Honduras suggest that this may be the case; accordingly no meaning should be attached to the change between these two years without going back to the original sources for these countries.

Table 1.2
Average Real Wage Rates in Latin America,[1] Selected Years, 1980-1997
(1990 = 100)

Country	1980	1985	1990	1995	1997
Argentina	130.0	135.7	100.0	100.9	100.0
Bolivia	n/a	64.9	100.0	114.2	n/a
Brazil	87.8[2]	101.9[2]	100.0	88.0	95.4
Chile	95.4	89.3	100.0	123.6	132.2
Colombia	85.0	97.4	100.0	105.4	109.6
Costa Rica	115.8	106.8	100.0	114.4	111.6
Mexico	128.3	97.4	100.0	111.5	98.1
Paraguay	102.1	90.1	100.0	114.2	115.7
Peru	309.3	250.2	100.0	116.7	111.0
Uruguay	108.5	95.5	100.0	109.0	109.8
Latin America[3]	116.4	112.0	100.0	100.7	100.8

Notes: [1] The available wage series varies by country. For Argentina and Mexico it corresponds to the manufacturing sector, presumably those in the formal sector whose employing firms report; for Colombia it is manual workers in manufacturing; for Brazil and Costa Rica, workers covered by legislation; for Chile, non-agricultural workers; for Paraguay and Peru the capital cities only, and in Peru just private sector manual workers. [2] The two figures in the 1980s refer only to Rio de Janeiro and Sao Paulo, to which weights of 0.4 and 0.6 respectively were assigned. [3] Figures based on weights given by 1995 population; Bolivia is excluded for lack of data in some of the years.

Sources: ECLAC, 1995, p. 75 and ECLAC, 1997, p. 52.

quintile in 1989 compared with a ratio of seven in 1967. In the UK this ratio rose from four at the beginning of the 1980s to nearly six in 1991.

In a number of industrial countries the secondary distribution of income was affected by a fall in welfare expenditure as a percent of GDP—by at least 1% of GDP in the U.K., Germany and several other countries, though a number of other countries did show a continued upward trend in social expenditure. There was a general move toward means-tested provision of benefits. Though taxes continued to increase as a proportion of GDP in most of these countries, there were large declines in the ratio of direct to all taxes in several countries including the US, and most direct tax systems becoming less progressive as every OECD country except Switzerland cut the top rate. Boltho concluded that "despite continual increases in public expenditure, the combined effects of shifts in spending away from major social programs and in tax policy toward a broadly regressive position meant that in the 1980s most OECD countries spurned or severely moderated the concept of the generous welfare state that had been current during the 1960s" (Boltho, 1992, 18).

Blackburn and Bloom (1993, 260) report that changes in family income distribution were substantially different as between the U.S. and Canada between 1979 and 1987, with inequality among families clearly increasing in the U.S. while in Canada there was no clear change, perhaps a small decrease. One factor lay in the composition of families by type; in the U.S. but not in Canada, there was a shift toward female-headed families with children. But inequality also increased within all categories of families in the U.S. except one and only increased in one in Canada. The category female-headed households with children relates a striking contrast; their economic welfare increased dramatically in Canada while staying constant or declining in the U.S. This suggests that income transfers played an important role since this group is a principal recipient of such transfers and such income increased much faster over this period in Canada than in the U.S.

Blackburn (1998) reports that, judging by the coefficient of variation of per-adult equivalent disposal household income, as of 1984-87 the level of inequality in Canada was relatively low (0.57)—higher than in Sweden (0.53) and the Netherlands (0.55) but lower than Germany (0.62), the U.K. (0.64) the U.S. (0.68), Australia (0.75) and France (0.76). Over 1981-87 Canada's level of inequality was essentially unchanged by this measure, while that of a number of the other countries had increased (though France's had fallen).

Subsequently, Canada's pre-tax and transfer distribution record has weakened, as some of the same factors at work in the U.S. and other industrial countries have made their presence felt. The Gini coefficient of the distribution of income among households rose from 0.388 over 1987-89 to 0.400 over 1992-94 (Statistics Canada, 1998a). Despite the country's moderate rate of growth since the recession of the early 1990s, poverty rates seem not to have responded as might have been hoped, indicating that the poor have not shared in this economic expansion. In 1996, when the federal government replaced the Canada Assistance Plan with Canada Health and Service Transfer and cut almost three billion dollars from transfer payments to the provinces for health, postsecondary education and welfare, the incomes of the poor dropped while for the top 40% of families the trend was upward. Over this more recent decade, then, the worsening pattern seems to have been shared by Canada, the U.S. and many other countries.[3] The fact that

---

[3] There remains some ambiguity, however. Beach and Slotsve, for example, argue that nearly all of the observed increase in inequality is explained by cyclical factors and comes along with rises in the rate of unemployment. They also note that the Gini coefficients of family income indicate an increasingly equalizing effect of the progressive income tax system, since although income before transfers became less equal over 1971-1992—the Gini rose from an average of 0.383 in 1971-72 to an average 0.421 in 1991-92 (Beach and Slotsve, 1996, 103)—that of total money income (which includes transfers) became slightly less so and income after taxes did as well. Ranking of households by total rather than per capita income may produce a negative bias also; the Canada-U.S. comparisons of Blackburn and Bloom (1993, 41) suggest that this does matter, with the Canadian trend more positive (lower inequality) using the per capita measures and the U.S. trend more negative.

An even more direct challenge to conventional wisdom on inequality trends has been mounted by Slesnick (1994, 678; 1993), who argues that in the U.S. inequality in the distribution of expenditures per household equivalent member has behaved quite differently from that of family incomes, showing a net decrease over the post-war period with most of this occurring before 1970 and little change from that point up to the early 1990s. Much of the difference is related to changes in household structure and is sensitive to the equivalence scales used to calculate the number of equivalent members in a household. Cutler and Katz (1992), however, conclude that the family income Gini rose by three points and that of consumption by two between 1980 and 1988. Pendakur (1998, 259) concludes that both income inequality and consumption inequality showed an upward

increases in inequality are widespread in the industrial countries suggests a common set of factors at work.

The long period of increasing inequality in the U.S. has focused much attention on its underlying causes, and in the process led to a lively debate. This debate has in part pitted those who attribute the increase primarily to technological change against those who argue that increased trade (especially with low wage countries) is substantially to blame. The steady, marked increase in relative wages of higher skilled to lower skilled workers since 1975 has been attributed to changes in demand within industries that likely reflect skill-biased demand shifts [e.g., Berman, Bound and Griliches (1994), Levy and Murnane (1993), Katz and Murphy (1992)]. In the recent literature on trade and relative wages the Hecksher-Ohlin-Samuelson (HOS) framework has been used to link trade with relative wage changes. The increased level of imports of labor intensive goods from low wage countries is at the core of this view.

As for Latin America, the macroeconomic downturn/stagnation of the last couple of decades was accompanied in most countries by increasing inequality, with the result that the overall level of poverty rose markedly since 1980. After falling from about 65% in 1950 to about 25% in 1980 (using a poverty line suggested by Altimir, 1982) it jumped back to about 35% during the 1980s under the combined influence of falling average incomes and increasing inequality and has probably not fallen much from that level. The economic reforms—trade liberalization, labor market reforms, etc. have coincided systematically with severe accentuation of (primary) income inequality; the "normal" observed increase in inequality accompanying reforms is 5-10 percentage points as measured by the Gini coefficient of primary income; among Latin American countries for which the statistical evidence is adequate to reach conclusions on this issue, the only probable exceptions to this generalization seem to be Costa Rica, Jamaica and Peru (Berry, 1997). As with many industrial countries, it seems that the increases in inequality are typically the result of a jump in the share of the top decile, with most of this accruing to the top 5% or perhaps the top 1% (as in the cases of Colombian and Ecuadorean households) while most of the bottom deciles lose. Insufficient data are available to judge whether the distribution of secondary income (after allowing for taxes, transfers, and public provision of goods) has moved differently from that of primary distribution. Effective targeting has made a positive impact in some cases, but the reduction of government activity may have had a regressive effect, as may

trend between 1978 and 1992 and that both distributions also moved counter cyclically (rose in recessions). Between the recession years 1978 and 1990 the Gini of family income inequality rose by more than three percentage points while that of consumption rose by less than one point. The contrast between the substantial difference in these two trends in Canada and the small difference in the U.S. would seem consistent with the fact that the tax burden has risen more for Canadians and the tax and transfer system appears to have a greater equalizing effect.

All in all, it is clear that the meaning of the changing income and expenditure patterns in countries like Canada and the U.S. is far from completely understood or uncontroversial.

the changes in tax systems toward the greater use of indirect taxes.

Too little research has thus far been done on the experience of Latin America to establish causality between the increases in income concentration and specific reforms or other, exogenous changes (such as rapid technological change) coming along with them. The economic cycle appears to have played a role but it cannot in any obvious way be held accountable for the bulk of the large, lasting (at least to date) shift toward inequality. Other possible factors include both technological change and the elements of globalization—more open trade regimes and increasing foreign investment, together with the associated market-friendly reforms—the dismantling of labor institutions, and the "socialization" of debts (whereby the state makes itself responsible for certain private debts which might otherwise threaten macroeconomic or financial stability). Trade and labor market reforms have been consistent elements of the reform packages instituted in the Latin countries where distribution has worsened significantly. Among the alternative theories put forward to explain the association between the removal of trade restrictions and increasing inequality, several (e.g., Wood, 1994) assume that the labor involved in producing exports is relatively skilled, with the result that intensification of trade widens earnings differentials by level of education. Others involve "skill-enhancing trade" (Robbins, 1995); increased capital goods imports associated with trade liberalization can increase the returns to skilled labor, which is complementary to capital goods (Hamermesh, 1993, Stokey, 1994). It has also been widely noted that globalization tends to favor the "large-scale sector" of the economy—large firms, large cities, the more developed regions within the economy, etc. The dominance of large firms in the production of manufactured exports implies less employment creation than would otherwise be expected (Berry, 1992). Since earnings differences associated with firm size (including those across the formal-informal sector divide) and with region are often large in developing countries, an accentuation of this tendency constitutes a real risk. Although optimists have argued that the opening up of trade should raise the relative incomes of agricultural workers, the evidence on this point is also unencouraging. In a number of countries (including Mexico) it appears that a significant part of the agricultural sector cannot compete easily with an onslaught of imports and that its labor resources are not easily mobile to other sectors. Some policies which countries choose as complements to liberalization (of trade and foreign investment) may also contribute to increased inequality; three such are privatization, financial reform and labor market reform.

The Macroeconomic and Other Contexts

Several common points of context stand out between Canada and Latin America for the period when these labor market outcomes were emerging: fiscal stringency (real or perceived or implicit in the greater weight now placed on avoiding inflation); the already-mentioned trend toward globalization and freer trade and investment,[4] and the associated weight placed on achieving international competitiveness; the high level of dependence on one main, powerful trading partner—the United States, although this dependence varies considerably among the countries of Latin America and is less marked for some of those in South America; and the recognition/belief that the world is in the middle of an important wave of technological change, of which information technology is a key aspect. Partly underlying some of the above trends in policy and partly a separate contextual factor is the neoclassical revival in economics and in national and international institutions; its presence and effects on policy are clearly apparent both in Canada and in Latin America.

For Latin America as a region the 1980s was a very difficult period—often referred to as "the Lost Decade"; though the timing varied somewhat from country to country, nearly all suffered a major economic downturn/crisis at some time since the mid-1970s. The Southern Cone countries (Argentina, Chile and Uruguay) were already in difficulty by the mid-1970s, while for most of the others the onset was signaled by the international debt crisis of the early 1980s. For the region as a whole per capita national income fell by about 13% over 1980-85, fluctuated with no clear trend over the rest of the decade, then eased up by a few percent over the first half of the 1990s. With this sort of macroeconomic performance it was obvious that there would be many "losers" during this period. In most cases workers fell into that category; in Peru real wages fell by more than 50%.

Canada's economic fluctuations in the 1980s and 1990s have been much less marked than those of Latin America, but notable nonetheless. The recessions of the early 1980s and the early 1990s were both relatively severe and both left a legacy of high unemployment and other potentially worrisome labor market outcomes, such as an increasing prevalence of part-time employment. Growth during this period was also somewhat weaker than in earlier decades—GDP grew at about 2.75% over 1980-97 and GDP per capita at 1.5% (Table 1.3), but a combination of factors produced a situation in which in spite of a reasonably decent growth performance, albeit a slowing one, the wages of many categories of workers and the mean earnings of all males no longer rose though those of females

---

[4] The debt crisis provided the push to induce and/or oblige Latin America to jettison its trademark import-substitution strategy for a more liberalized trading system, as well as to move towards adoption of the other elements of what is now a standard package of reforms to labor markets, financial markets and the public sector. Some countries, including Colombia and Brazil, had already taken significant steps away from the traditional combination of protectionism and overvalued exchange rates and the resulting bias against trade. Chile went much farther in the mid-1970s as the Pinochet regime introduced the most free-trade free-market system in the region. Other countries moved sharply in this direction in the two decades which followed, some as early as the 1970s, others as recently as the 1990s. In nearly all cases significant labor policy reforms were part of the package implemented or considered.

Table 1.3
Average Annual Growth Rates, Canada and the United States
(1970-80, 1980-90 and 1990-97)

	1970-80	1980-90	1990-97	1970-97	1980-97
Canada, GDP	5.1	3.4	1.8[1]	3.6	2.7
Canada, GDP per capita	3.8	2.2	0.5[1]	2.4	1.5
U.S., GDP	2.9	3.0	2.6[1]	2.9	2.8
U.S., GDP per capita	1.8	2.1	1.6[1]	1.9	1.9
Canada, GDP per employed worker	0.8	1.4	0.8	1.0	1.2
U.S., GDP per employed worker	0.5	1.3	1.3	1.0	1.3

Note: [1] These figures differ from those of Table 1.4 due to the use of different sources. Though they are probably less accurate than those of Table 1.4, they are used for consistency with the rest of the table.

Source: World Bank, various issues of *World Development Report* and *World Tables*; IMF (1999).

did (Beach and Slotsve, 1996, 58). Unemployment, normally relatively high in Canada, partly for structural and institutional reasons, showed an upward trend, which took the form of an increase in each recession with limited decline in the intervening periods of growth. As a result there has been widespread dissatisfaction with labor market performance in Canada, albeit for somewhat different reasons than in Latin America. One source of concern is the increasing prevalence of part-time and temporary work; a cliché of the times is that the typical person can no longer aspire to a stable well-paid job. Students of higher education no longer have the relaxed expectation that they will quickly find such attractive jobs as before. Graduates anxiously expect that technological change will cost them their jobs or force them to learn more than used to be the case in order not to. The earnings of male youth under the age of 35 have fallen over the last couple of decades, with the gap between them and older males widening substantially (Statistics Canada, 1998b).

A number of the above features constitute parallels with many Latin countries. In both cases there has been a general perception that the labor market is either performing inadequately or not reflecting good performance on the part of the economy as a whole. One manifestation of this is an increasing concern with the training system, both as an adjunct to avoiding chronic unemployment and also as an important aspect of keeping human capital aligned with the changing technology. Pessimism with the existing success and performance of the training systems has been accentuated in most countries over the last decade or so; some, including a number of Latin countries, have initiated major reforms.

In the common regional experience of crisis and stagnation during the last couple of decades, Latin America's recent history differs from Canada's (see Table 1.4). In spite of this striking contrast, it is worth noting that the postwar period as a whole has witnessed convergence in a number of respects, some of which lay the grounds for a useful comparison of experiences and mutual learning between the two. Although it was truncated during the 1980s, the post war period as a whole

Table 1.4
Comparative Economic Data:
Latin America and Major Countries, Canada, United States

	Latin America	Brazil	Mexico	Canada	United States
Annual GDP growth:					
1950-80	5.5	7.3	6.3	4.5	3.4
1980-90	1.8	12.8	11.1	3.4	2.9
1990-97	3.3	3.1	1.8	2.1	2.5
Annual GDP per capita growth:					
1950-80	2.8	4.4	3.2	2.5	2.0
1980-90	-0.2	0.8	-1.2	2.2	2.0
1990-97	1.6	1.7	0.0	0.9	1.5
Employment structure by sector (1950):					
Primary	56.2	52.0[2]	55.0[2]	24.8	14.0
Industry	18.1	15.0[2]	20.0[2]	33.6	28.9
Services	25.7	33.0[2]	25.0[2]	41.6	57.1
Employment structure by sector (1980):					
Primary	35.9	36.7	36.3	6.7	3.5
Industry	25.9	23.9	29.1	33.5	31.1
Services	38.2	39.4	34.6	59.9	65.4
Employment structure by sector (1997):					
Primary	20.0	15.6	23.1	1.0	2.3
Industry	22.0	22.4	20.7	19.3	22.0
Services	58.0	62.0	56.2	79.7	75.6
Share of population urban:[3]					
1960	n/a	46.0	51.0	69.0	67.0
1980	65.0	66.0	66.0	76.0	74.0
1994	74.0	77.0	75.0	77.0	76.0
Annual rate of population growth:					
1950-80	2.6	2.8	3.0	2.0	1.4
1980-90	2.0	2.0	2.3	1.2	0.9
1990-97	1.7	1.4	1.8	1.2	1.0
Incidence of poverty:[4]					
1950	65.0	n/a	n/a	n/a	n/a
1980	25.0	n/a	n/a	n/a	n/a
1994	32.0	n/a	n/a	n/a	n/a

Notes: [1] In some sources mining is included with agriculture *et al* in "primary" and in other sources it is included with "industry." [2] Figures refer to 1960 (*World Development Report 1960*).[3] Since the definition of urban varies somewhat from country to country, comparisons across countries are not reliable. [4] Estimate from Berry (1997) who applies (roughly) the poverty line used by Altimir (1982) to compare the countries of the region.

Sources: Employment structure in Latin America, 1950 and 1980, PREALC (1982, 34); for 1997, Berry and Méndez (1999, 29) based on ILO data. Other data are from various issues of World Bank, *World Development Report* and *World Tables*, and of *Canada Yearbook* and the *Statistical Abstract of the United States*.

saw considerably faster growth and structural change in Latin America than in industrialized countries like Canada or the United States. Over 1950-1980 per capita income grew at 2.5% per year in Canada and 2.0% in the United States compared to 2.8% in Latin America (Table 1.4). Though Canada's employment structure—in terms of sectors and occupations—changed rather rapidly and considerably faster than that of the United States, Latin America's was altered more radically, in line with its rapid sectoral change.

Latin America's level of urbanization advanced markedly over this period to reach 74% by 1994 compared to 77% in Canada (although the definitions of "urban" are not comparable). Finally, and quite relevant to our present interests, the social structure of the two societies converged markedly, especially since about the 1950s. At that time Latin America was characterized by the fastest population growth in the world, at about 2.6%, compared with Canada's 1.95%, nearly a third of which was by the 1950s attributable to the country's high rate of net immigration. Latin America's population became notoriously young at this time. Since then, the birth rate and population growth have fallen radically. Although the current age structure still reflects the large families of previous decades, the region is now well into a fast socio-demographic transition (Magno de Carvalho, 1995) in which the small, urban nuclear family becomes the norm, female-headed households become much more common and, eventually, the age structure moves to one in which the social net for the elderly becomes important because families no longer play such a dominant role and the elderly are a much larger share of the population than before.[5] The major demographic transition and the rapid change in population structure which will occur soon,[6] together with a social transition which is moving rather fast—female-headed households, etc., suggest that in some respects the need for the social net will increase in Latin America, even though poverty should continue to fall in most of its dimensions. By 1990-95 Latin America's rate of population growth, at 1.7%, remained somewhat but not dramatically higher than Canada's (1.2%), with the latter now even more dependent on immigration.

A new aspect of their trading relationships for Canada, the U.S. and Mexico, and eventually for some of the other Latin countries is entry into a free trade area which includes both developed and developing countries and thus raises both the opportunities and the perceived dangers of such arrangements.

Interest in, expectations of and concern for small and medium enterprise (SME) has risen both in Canada and in most countries of Latin America. There is the same concern, awareness, and uncertainty as to whether this sector will get more important, as suggested by the flexible specialization ideas and the push factor from downsizing of government and large private institutions. The recognition of the employment role of this sector has raised its profile in the eyes of policy makers around the world. At the same time there is widespread concern

[5] Estimates of the total fertility rates for the region presented in CELADE (1994) show a dramatic drop from 5.6 in 1965-70 to 3.4 in 1985-90 and a further predicted fall to 2.5 by 2006-10. Magno de Carvalho (1995, 7) points out that the decreases now occurring in Latin America are much more condensed in time than the parallel historical declines in England and Sweden. Between 1970 and 2010 the child (0-14 years) dependency ratio is predicted to fall as their share of population declines from 42.4% to 28.2% while that of the elderly (65 and over) will rise from 4.1% to 6.5%. The major increase of the latter ratio will occur over the following 20 years, to reach 11.2%.

[6] The many impacts of rapid demographic change in the Canadian context are analyzed by Foot (1996).

that SMEs will have difficulties in the new more competitive international marketplace and the transition to it. Any loss of GDP share by the SME sector could provide another mechanism pushing inequality up. The recent Canadian experience with SMEs provides several results of special interest from the Latin perspective. The widespread expectation, common also in developing countries, that freer trade would bring a size structure tilted more toward the large end of the spectrum, has not been borne out (Baldwin, 1996; Berry, 1996a, 69-70). The continuing tendency for much growth to occur in SMEs may suggest an important potential role for this sector in other countries as well. It may be, however, that absence of some of the factors contributing to that growth in Canada—such as access to credit and sources of technological information, a generally stable economy, gradual policy change—will seriously impede a similar outcome in Latin countries. A fuller understanding of the roles they have played in Canada would be very valuable for the latter countries. It is not yet known in detail how SMEs have fared in the context of crisis and structural adjustment in the countries of Latin America.

1.2 How the Context Shapes Labor Policy Issues

Table 1.5 summarizes some of the major factors affecting the consideration of labor policy issues in Canada and Latin America. Some of these relate primarily to specific labor issues, while others have sweeping, general effects on all or nearly all of the details of labor and social policy. Among the latter, four or five interrelated issues/areas appear to stand out: the need for fiscal prudence; the desirability of international integration together with the difficult challenges of competitiveness which it poses; the importance of taking advantage of the major technological changes occurring and the challenges which these pose; the importance of well-functioning markets and the presence of many policy-induced impediments to that functioning (highlighted in the strong neo-liberal drift of economic thinking in the past couple of decades); and a concern with employment and income distribution given various types of evidence to the effect that there are problems in these areas. It is useful to review briefly the nature of the discussion in each of these areas.

Fiscal Prudence

Most industrialized countries have seen their debt to GNP and debt service to GNP ratios move up over recent decades. Social security systems, whose revenues and expenditures are often not treated as part of the fiscal accounts, have also moved inexorably toward crisis, many having been designed in a pay-as-you-go format

Table 1.5
Elements of the Context for Labor Market (and Related Social) Policy

Contextual Element	Relation to Policy
Fiscal Condition	1. Limits possible expenditures on unemployment insurance, training/ retraining, and other potentially expensive elements of labor policy. 2. Puts premium on the sort of pension system which most benefits the budget, which may be pay-as-you-go in the short-run but will eventually be fully funded system. 3. Puts pressure to avoid large fiscal drains through money-losing public enterprises, as well as to control wasteful public activities and make-work hiring.
International integration and competitiveness	1. Possibility that competitiveness depends on maintaining low labor costs, and guarantees against strikes and other forms of labor action. As part of this, possible need to keep labor taxes low. Level of labor costs may, however, not be relevant as long as the real exchange rate can be used to achieve balance in international payments. 2. If outward orientation inevitably worsens income distribution through pushing unskilled wages down, other policies to benefit workers may take on greater significance.
Technological Change	1. Where it threatens wages of broad groups and hence the country's income distribution, it may put a premium on encouraging firms which have employment generating capacity, usually smaller ones (microenterprise and SMEs). 2. Attempts to prevent use of specific technologies have not been common in Canada or Latin America, except on environmental grounds in the former.
Adequacy of Market Functioning	1. If the labor market, when unintervened, can function well in terms of its labor allocation and income generating functions, the grounds for such intervention are weak. Some interventions are commonly believed to be beneficial to workers on one count (usually labor income) even when damaging on the allocation/efficiency count. But careful analysis is usually necessary to identify such impacts. Often interventions help some groups of workers at the expense of other groups, the latter usually being the poorer. 2. Some labor market imperfections are generally accepted as the basis for interventions, in the form of unemployment insurance of some sort, constraints on certain behavior by employers, etc.

which is open to the possibility (likelihood) of crisis when the age structure changes (a higher share of people retired and receiving benefits) and/or the growth of the economy slows down. The natural course of the political process with respect to deficits may be taken as one in which the political benefit/cost calculus of letting things slip a little longer is often preferred to that of attacking the problem frontally. In the case of Canada and its provinces the external signals from bond raters had a bracing effect (McQuaig, 1998). Eventually governments come along claiming they will confront the issue; sometimes they do so, as with the last couple of administrations at the national level but especially the current Liberal government, and several of the provincial governments, including the Liberals under Frank McKenna in New Brunswick, the Conservatives under Ralph Klein in

Alberta and the Conservatives under Mike Harris in Ontario.[7]

Recent economic literature has featured a number of estimates purporting to show the serious negative effects of high levels of taxes. The Laffer curve (built on the idea that in some cases lowering tax rates can increase the total tax take) and supply side economics (whose central idea is that demand tends to take care of itself when the supply side is performing well) are the natural reverse images of the more simplistic versions of Keynesian economics. The Keynesian proposition that achieving growth, stability and full employment was mainly a matter of demand management was built on the (often implicit) assumption that the supply conditions for growth tended to take care of themselves; thus technological change could be considered exogenous to most economic policy (certainly to macroeconomic policy) while investment was either endogenous or influenced by demand management. Keynesian policymakers were not of course denying (or did not need to deny) that there were important supply conditions to be met; their essential position was that it was effective management on the demand side which mainly determined how well the economy would perform, i.e., that the demand conditions were not as easily or automatically met as the supply conditions. The extent to which many industrial economies corresponded to these assumptions over an extended period of time is an empirical question. Some Keynesian views were no doubt excessive in their disregard for supply issues, for the costs of high budgetary involvement, for the lack of flexibility in the management of the demand instruments and so on. It may also have been true that structural trends in the economy and diminishing policy flexibility made effective demand management less feasible over time (Bruno and Sachs, 1985).

The more extreme versions of supply side economics seem to have had more to do with wishful thinking related to strong ideological proclivities than to empirical evidence. Based on the accumulated experience thus far it appears that the Laffer curve proposition has seldom if ever been borne out. Probably the real argument for slowing the growth of the public sector as a share of GDP lies more with the facts that (i) a considerable amount of public spending may have low social value (though much private spending no doubt does also), (ii) some activities are administered less efficiently by the state or by parastatals than they would be in the private sector, (iii) a heavy debt overhang diminishes policy flexibility, and ultimately (iv) the argument for further borrowing from the future appears weak. It is of course unfortunate if reduction of public spending leads to

---

[7] The politics of this process is, perhaps not surprisingly, complex. In Canada, where the federal system of government has involved high levels of fiscal transfers from the central to the provincial governments and from these to the municipal ones, the overall process of expenditure cutbacks involved the slashing of these transfers (downloading) with the level cutting back its transfers naturally taking maximum credit for fiscal responsibility when in fact to a large degree it was just shifting the burden of adjustment to the next level down. The pattern of quiet collaboration among levels of government has been under much pressure during this process. In this respect the process seems to have been simpler in cases like the United Kingdom under Margaret Thatcher.

unemployment and recession through smaller public sector employment and the inability to stimulate certain private sectors quickly. To the extent that this becomes a serious problem, it will be increasingly important for economies to learn how to lower wages rather than cutting employment. There is no reason to believe at this time that there would be a serious employment problem if wages and salaries were sufficiently downward flexible. The problem with that approach to resolving fiscal/recession problems, however, is the possible implications for income distribution, which in any case has been moving in the wrong direction in most industrialized countries, as in most of Latin America.

The argument for combating major deficits (i.e., those big enough to keep debt/GNP ratios rising when they are already high) is strong. The question is whether a society can find efficient ways to combat them, ways which do not give up growth, employment or equity. This appears to be a tall task. One of the possible tradeoffs may be between the degree of price stability and an economy's capacity to adjust smoothly (e.g., in the context of exogenous changes in international prices). One of the functions of a moderate level of inflation (say 5-20%, thinking in terms of Latin America) is that it appears to facilitate changes in relative prices, which under such inflation are less likely to require falls in absolute prices (e.g., of labor).

International Integration and Competitiveness

The trend of recent times toward increasing openness of economies has been worldwide and has touched both Canada and the Latin American countries, albeit in different ways. The logic of this shift may be more political than economic, just as European integration was more political in origin than economic. A few serious estimates of the gains from closer economic integration do exceed the "small Harberger triangle" dimensions[8] but the imprecision of prediction in this area is impressive. In the case of Canada's entry into a free trade area with the United States (over a decade ago) most estimates of gain were a few percent (e g. a couple) of GDP. Economic science could not discount the possibility that the net effects would be negative, e.g. if enough firms elected to move from Canada to the U.S. since it was better to be nearer the big market and no longer important to be located in Canada in order to access that market. In any case the best guess with respect to developed countries like Canada is that the degree of openness is not one of the major determinants of medium and long-run performance.[9]

---

[8] Named for Arnold Harberger, on the basis of his treatment in Harberger (1954).

[9] If it were, one might have expected the natural large free trade areas constituted by big countries, especially the U.S. with by far the biggest economy in the world, to have grown faster than those which by not being fully integrated into a really large economy must be suffering from the corresponding losses. Over the last several decades Canada has fairly systematically grown a little

In the case of the Latin American countries both neoclassical economic theory (at a simplistic level) and political expectations have supported the view that entry into free trade areas (NAFTA, MERCOSUR) would have a larger impact than in the case of Canada, which was already a quite open economy, judging by trading ratios, and one with relatively good access to the U.S. markets. Here the debate is complicated and impossible to summarize in a way which does justice to the various positions and at the same time comes to anything approaching a conclusion. The pro-outward orientation view is that the main drag on the economic performance of the region in the post-war period and an important contributing factor to the economic crash/crisis of the 1970s/80s was the set of inefficiencies related to the inward-looking import substituting industrialization (ISI) policy (Corbo, 1988). On this basis it would be reasonable to expect that a major shift to the outward oriented approach to development would lead to a big increase in growth. Analysts like Krueger (1988) have argued that the distributional impact of such a shift would also be positive, something which is apparently consistent with the American fear that freer trade with Mexico and with lower wage developing countries in general would push wages down in the U.S. and thus worsen distribution there. The strong growth performance of Chile since the early 1980s recession is the most supportive empirical evidence for these optimistic expectations. The most serious competing views rest on the argument that the ISI regimes could not have been as damaging to growth as their critics often portray them, since regional growth over 1950-80 was an impressive 5.5%; that other factors than the "running out of the ISI model," and in particular the international debt crisis, accounted as much or more for the debacle of the 1980s; and that the optimistic expectations for the more open regimes are not being fulfilled very quickly or very generally around the region (average growth over 1990-99 being just 3.5%).

Though growth was strong from the end of World War II until the 1980s and was strongest in Brazil, the most closed of the region's economies,[10] various cross-country analyses have shown a correlation between export growth and overall economic growth. The degree to which this relationship provides support for an outward-oriented policy is unclear. Much evidence points to the key variable in trade success being the exchange rate; it is also important to note that encouraging exports is not the same as trade liberalization. The great success stories of East

---

faster than the U.S. The point is not that such a simple comparison indicates that there are no fairly important gains from more open trade and investment, but rather that the additional gains which might come from complete as opposed to partial integration are apparently not important enough relative to other determinants of economic performance to show up clearly in comparative growth figures.

[10] In the early 1970s the export/GDP ratio was around 6.5% and the import/GDP ratio around 8% (World Bank, 1987, 64). It may be that the sort of ISI strategy implemented in the region was most congenial in Brazil because of the size of the economy.

Asia did not open their markets.[11] Growth in the 1990s, with nearly all countries now having shifted strongly in that direction remains well below that of the pre-1980 ISI phase and unsatisfactory in absolute terms. One of the issues at this time is the extent to which that performance will improve when the governments "get some of the wrinkles" out of the new design for growth, in particular when they learn how to live more successfully with surges of short-term international capital, a phenomenon which they did not have to confront under the old regime. The other concern now taking on greater weight with respect to the effects of more open economies is the timing coincidence of worsening distribution in most of the Latin American countries which have opened their economies, or more precisely, which have undertaken the modern package of economic reforms, including those to the labor market. Only after more time has passed will the net payoff to the new model become clearer.

The debates around openness and international competitiveness bear on the labor policy issues which are the focus of this volume in two main ways. First, the concern with income distribution trends and whether they are causally related to opening of the economy provides a worrisome backdrop to policy decisions. Second, it is accepted by all that labor policy affects firm competitiveness; often SME are recognized to be in a particularly delicate situation in this regard. The most worrisome view with respect to how the current drift in economic policy affects labor issues holds that the decision to go international removes from national governments various instruments for improving the lot of their labor forces and their populations (in terms of social policy), since excessive wages or social expenditures wreck a country's international competitiveness. The "need to compete" policy syndrome can affect fiscal policy, all types of labor policy, and social expenditures; according to this view the key is to leave business as unfettered as possible to get on with the task of competing. Both supporters of an outward-orientation and many critics tend to accept the view that high labor costs damage a country's competitive performance. For the former group it is something to be accepted if the benefits of globalization are to be reaped; among the latter there is a fear that competition will have a tendency to pull all countries down to the lowest common denominator in terms of labor protection, etc. In Canada this issue was debated vigorously during the lead-in period before the signing of the

---

[11] The policy implications of the cited correlation between export growth and overall growth are unclear since, among other things: (i) direction of causation could be from overall growth to export growth rather than the opposite, and formal intra-country tests find unidirectional causality from exports to output in only a minority of cases (e.g. Bradford, 1994, Sharma and Dhakal, 1995); (ii) the cited correlations do not take account of the fact that export growth by one developing country can hurt others (through downward pressure on the product's price). The extensive discussion around the "East Asian Miracle" includes both the World Bank's interpretation (World Bank, 1993), in which outward-oriented policies come in for much praise, and quite different views which put the emphasis elsewhere, e.g. Rodrik (1995) who stresses the high level of investment, and Wade (1990). Too much of the literature (e.g. World Bank, 1996) has been at an unacceptably low technical level.

CAFTA (Canada-United States Free Trade Agreement).

The most intriguing aspect of the competitiveness discussion is the questionable economics which underlies much of it, including the failure to take due account of either the basic principle of international trade theory, comparative advantage,[12] or of the dominant role of the exchange rate in determining the international competitiveness of a country's industries. While this frequent major misunderstanding has been identified clearly enough by some economists (e.g., Krugman), it has not received nearly the recognition that one might expect of such an obvious flaw in the popular thinking on the issue.

Canada and Latin America share much in the context of this integration/competitiveness question, since the countries are "smaller partners" in their main trading/investment relationships. Whatever the truth about the ways in which doing well in the international economy impacts on feasible and optimal labor market and social policy, such smaller partners are always in a different position from the "center country," in this case the U.S. For the latter, the question is not whether its trading partners will push its labor and social policies strongly in a particular direction. As a relatively closed economy even after the surge in trade over the last years, it is not in a situation where adjustment to the ways of other countries is likely to be in the cards.[13] (Even if it were, a strong American predilection would be to close up again rather than give in to those foreign ways.) The market itself generates a certain amount of aggressive proselytizing for the American way of doing things, as where American health care companies claim equal rights with Canadian firms to operate in the Canadian market. Both Canadian and Latin companies are and will be expressing concern when any social levy puts them at a disadvantage vis-à-vis the American competition. Canada is thus the natural parallel and comparator for Latin countries within the Western hemisphere.

---

[12] The error is to confuse what helps the competitiveness of a firm (any way to keep costs down, including low labor costs) with what mainly determines the competitiveness of a country (the exchange rate). The theory of comparative advantage implies that a country's capacity to trade and to gain from that trade does not depend on its technological level; countries low on the technological profile are in principle as likely to gain as countries high on it.

It is possible that, especially in the shorter-run during which the underlying forces and mechanisms of an economy have not had time to work themselves out, the level of any given cost or the technology in use can affect a country's success in international trade. Where management of the exchange rate has more than one objective, its capacity to maintain the balance of payments in equilibrium may be prejudiced. In many Latin American countries, for example, it has been saddled both with the latter function and that of controlling inflation through a stable price of imports, which requires a stable nominal exchange rate.

[13] Some regions of the U.S. and some industries are in situations comparable to that of the "small country" but these do not often dominate U.S. thinking or policy making.

Technological Change

It is widely acknowledged that the world is in the midst of a major burst of technological change. On the surface, this recognition may seem obvious—the layman also is very aware of such change, what with the information revolution and robotics. Paradoxically, most economic measures of the overall contribution of technological change to economic growth suggest that since the mid-1970s industrial countries have been in a period of low contribution of technological advance to growth (Bruton, 1997, 41). This apparent paradox has several possible elements. One is the lag between the first appearance of new ways of doing things and their general acceptance across potential uses—the time when their quantitative impact reaches a maximum. The fact that because technological change also creates unemployment and thus tends to push an economy below its output potential may also help to explain why for some time its beneficial impacts show up only at the micro but not at the macro (and hence not at the societal) level.

Whether and under what circumstances a wave of technological change redounds strongly to society's benefit, it is clear that business and governments have responded strongly to it, placing great emphasis on its importance if firm, industry or nation is not to be left behind in the international competition. Since technological change is one of the most unplanned processes in any economy, there must also be serious concern, as indeed there is, that it is contributing importantly to the increases in income inequality which have been so frequently observed around the world. As noted above, the debate in the U.S. in fact focuses on this as one of the two main hypotheses, the other being that imports of labor intensive goods are at fault.

Getting Markets (Including the Labor Market) to Function Effectively

Currently popular views in economics place great weight on effective functioning of markets: they correspond to an increased sensitivity to the weaknesses of governments and the possible costs of market imperfections. The expectation that interference with international trade and investment will have negative effects is a manifestation of this general concern in that particular domain, and the view that interference in the labor market will likewise drag down overall performance is similar. Ironically, at about the time that this neoclassical focus on the avoidance of imperfections was reaching a high point of popularity among many policy-oriented economists, theory was generally moving to another level of complexity (which may be loosely termed the "theory of the second-best"), within which a general recognition of the fact that most markets do not operate at close to perfectly competitive levels decreases the power of economics to say anything about the impact of any specific "distortion" (and hence of its removal) on societa welfare. Theory was thus drawing back from a simple pro-market view at the same time that the view in the trenches was shifting toward that position.

Theory, whether that of the simpler models or of the more complicated ones is always useful in providing hypotheses on how a part of the economy may function, and in suggesting empirical tests to better understand that functioning But one of the lessons of experience is that simple models often do not predict well, which suggests that they do not represent reality very well, while more complicated ones are so hard to test that it is a challenge to learn much from them As a result our understanding of economic mechanisms is very partial. This has remained true with respect to most of the key elements of labor market policy, but the popularity of the neoclassical model over the last couple of decades has led to its predictions/interpretations being taken quite seriously, probably too much so. The intellectual over-simplicity of this strand of thinking is immediately evident in those many discussions where the concept of "economic efficiency" is automatically taken as the (sole) criterion to be adhered to. What is almost always meant by this term is the maximization of total dollar value of surpluses (which a perfectly competitive economy would do in the absence of any imperfections, externalities or inefficient provision of public goods), rather than the theoretically more persuasive Pareto optimality or maximization of some more interesting social welfare function. Given the practical difficulties of claiming one is applying either of the latter two criteria, we fall back on economic efficiency, which as defined assumes implicitly the same marginal utility of income for everyone and gives no weight to considerations of income distribution. To assume that an economy is living up to the highest expectations if it maximizes total income so defined is naive, especially in the context of labor market functioning and policy which directly affects the absolute and relative incomes of groups of poor people. Theoretical oversimplicity, which often accompanies strong ideological prejudices, and thus leads to the unfortunate results just alluded to, has its counterpart in weak empirical analysis. As discussed below in the context of the various policy issues considered here, and in the chapters which relate to them, the range of conclusions from the empirical studies on most issues appears to be about as wide as the ideological or theoretical predispositions which have probably greatly affected them. This problem makes the empirical literature doubly difficult to interpret; it is often sparse to start with, and may suffer from data and specification problems; when to this is added what is all too often the greatest biasing factor of all—the expectations of the researchers—it is a foregone conclusion that the literature must be read with much care to extract the value that it has. The sorts of issues discussed here are often ideologically charged.

Major Labor Policy Issues

The four labor policy issues treated below are unemployment insurance, minimum wages, labor taxes and the social safety net, and training. For reasons noted above, the Canadian experience is of considerable relevance to the countries of Latin America because these countries share with Canada the role of signal-taker rather than signal-giver vis-à-vis their main trading partners.

Labor policy has as one objective to protect the worker from a variety of threats to his/her economic welfare through the labor market. One is against very low wages; the minimum wage is the instrument designed to guard against this outcome. Another is unemployment, for which the unemployment insurance system is designed. A third, against job-loss, involves legislated limits on the conditions under which a worker can be fired, an issue not dealt with in this chapter nor in the volume as a whole. Each of these policy areas has the challenge of achieving a good balance between the welfare of the protected workers on the one side and that of employers and unprotected workers on the other.

Worker training programs fall into a different category. While they help workers, they also directly help employers. In addition, they interface with unemployment insurance systems; a good retraining program should and is perceived as alleviating the problem of unemployment, from both the workers' and from society's point of view (the latter represented in part by the fiscal costs). Such programs are considered to be especially relevant in periods of fast technological change like the present one. Large firms, especially in industrial countries, do a great deal of in-house training and other firms do a fair amount of it too; but, for various reasons, SME do not have the same chance to take care of training or retraining needs as much as they might like. Thus an effective external (to the firm) system is likely to be important in a country where the SME sector has significant weight and especially when it too is confronting rapid change. In Latin America many large firms still underinvest in training, so there remains a significant role for the state in that sector as well.

Another aspect of labor policy interfaces with social policy more generally. Labor taxes on workers and employers finance various worker benefits including retirement pensions. More generally, the most complicating aspect of labor market policy is a result of the fact that it is, inevitably, part of the battery of social policies. One objective is to make the labor market work better, improving labor mobility when that is important to the functioning of the economy and the long-run welfare of the workers; the other is to play a special sort of income maintenance role—holding up the incomes of low wage workers (minimum wage), holding up the incomes of those prone to unemployment (UI), raising the productivity of those whose skills are becoming obsolete (retraining) and so on. The challenge, with respect to most of the important components of labor policy is to achieve the specific goal (e.g., protection against the uncertainties associated with unemployment) while meshing smoothly with other elements of the income maintenance system (the social net) and not inducing an excessive degree of negative side-effects. Because what really matters is how well the system of labor market-social institutions works as a whole, no single component can be judged definitively without reference to the total system.

There are three essential grounds for public intervention (plus a few sometimes relevant ones) in labor markets of the sort under discussion here. One is redistribution—the main reason for public general education, for the welfare system, etc. The second is insurance against uncertainty and perhaps against risk. Unemployment insurance falls into this category. If its incidence were fairly easily predictable, it might be an appropriate object of private insurance schemes, if it were felt that the private sector could run these more efficiently than the state. Other interventions, such as minimum wages under conditions of monopsony, are essentially designed to reduce imperfections in the labor market, a third objective.[14] Other goals may be to soften the tension between employer and employee through involvement in some of the decisions; a system which regulates many wages—not just a single or a few minima, may perform this function in certain situations.

1.3 Unemployment Insurance (UI)

The experience with unemployment insurance in Canada highlights the delicate challenge of providing a good level of protection against the welfare costs of unemployment, and associated contribution to overall income maintenance, while inducing as few negative side-effects as possible. The system has recently been undergoing a process of reform in order to alleviate some of its major perceived weaknesses. The proposal made by Cortázar (Chapter 4) in the context of Chile is designed to skirt a number of the problems which have come to plague the Canadian system. Canada's system is an interesting case from the Latin American perspective, since it tends to fall between the spare U.S. system and the generous European ones (in terms of the income replacement rate, duration of benefits, conditions for benefits, etc.)

As described in detail by Gunderson and Riddell (Chapter 3), the historically generous (since 1971) Canadian system has certainly alleviated the social costs of unemployment,[15] but has at the same time:

---

[14] The term "imperfection" refers usually to any deviation from a set of conditions which collectively produce an economic optimum in the limited sense of a maximization of output. In this case the imperfection in question is the absence of competition, allowing the buyer of labor services to achieve a very low price.

[15] Including the direct income loss and associated psychological costs when unemployment occurs, the moderation of the "disciplining effect" which the fear of unemployment may have on workers, and the greater security of receiving a fairly stable income stream over time.

(i) contributed to a somewhat (perhaps 1-1.5 percentage points) higher unemployment rate,[16] with regionally extended benefits (relevant mainly to Atlantic Canada) helping to sustain chronically high levels of overall and (especially) seasonal unemployment, though perhaps not a lower employment rate;

(ii) deterred interregional movement, especially because of the regionally extended benefits;

(iii) possibly discouraged human capital formation, as where the easy availability of short-term jobs *cum* UI leads to early school leaving;

(iv) possibly slowed income convergence between the higher and lower income regions; and

(v) possibly increased significantly the extent of the underground economy in Canada, especially in the regions of high unemployment.[17]

Some of the negative side-effects of this federal system are related to the fact that it is in the narrow interests of provincial governments to shift as much as possible of the overall burden of income maintenance to the national level and to "collaborate" with local business and workers in the development of a system which "milks" the federal government. The UI system clearly encourages certain types of employment (e.g., seasonal) while also encouraging unemployment; its net effect on useful employment is thus not theoretically predictable, but authors like Gunderson and Riddell suspect that it is negative. Its fiscal dimensions are

---

[16] As noted by Benjamin (Chapter 8), another part of the systematically higher unemployment rate in Canada vis-à-vis its usual comparator, the U.S. is the result of the broader definition used in Canada. This has sometimes been credited as explaining up to half the differential, which in recent years has usually been around 4%.

[17] As usual, the theory gets us only so far, and on most of these effects there are questions of quantitative importance and/or counterarguments. These include:

i) the possibility that UI induces more total employment and that the income so generated has positive multiplier effects;

ii) the increased income (and temporary employment) in areas where unemployment is high may have more positive employment and income multiplier effects than the same amount of income would have in low unemployment regions, in which case the regional-equalization effects may have positive efficiency effects;

iii) UI can contribute to longer searches and hence to better employee-job matching;

iv) since much of the neoclassical theory of the impact of UI is based on the idea that workers can easily (without serious costs) become unemployed when it suits them, the obvious exaggeration built into this assumption may imply that the voluntary shift to unemployment is in fact not a quantitatively important phenomenon; along parallel lines, Reissert and Schmid (1994) conclude that in the EEC countries evidence does not support the contention that UIs influence employer dismissal policies except in the case of seasonal workers.

significant; between 1966 and 1993 the effective payroll rate of this charge rose from 1.11% to 5.15% of wages or from 0.54 to 2.57% of GDP (Lin, Picot and Beach, 1995). Whether this is excessive depends on the importance of the insurance function, on how distorting this tax is for job-choice and whether, to the extent that it acts as an instrument of redistribution, it is effective in that regard.[18] As a *de facto* part of the income maintenance system, this type of UI must be compared to the welfare system and other elements of that system as one reaches an overall judgment on it. Similarly with regard to its insurance function, one must ask whether there are better instruments (or better types of UI systems) to this end or not. Finally, it would help to be able to put a social valuation on the output resulting from the fact that UI induces some workers from non-participation into employment.

Since the issues surrounding UI have not been settled adequately on the basis of the microeconomic evidence, it is useful also to assess the program by keying on effects which may be measurable at the aggregate level. Such assessment is relevant given the fears that this program, perhaps together with other of the Canadian labor institutions, has serious effects on overall economic performance, e.g., they not only raise unemployment but also slow economic growth (through any of a wide variety of mechanisms which have been proposed in this connection), slow regional income convergence, and perhaps have other negative influences (like lowering educational attainment) whose impacts on growth or societal welfare may be more delayed than others. Thus far such effects have not been clearly identifiable, which may suggest that they are not large. To the extent that one uses the U.S. as a reference point, with its substantially less generous UI system and less complete social net, the fact that the Canadian economy has grown faster, e.g., since 1971, when Canada's UI system more or less took on its very generous format, is reassuring. The growth advantage has narrowed and disappeared over this period, however; after outperforming the U.S. economy in terms of GDP per capita by 3.0% per year to 1.95% per year over 1970-90, it has fallen short in the 1990s—0.5% per year over 1990-97 vs. 1.6% for the U.S. (Table 1.3), which is consistent with the idea that the efficiency and growth costs of this income maintenance system have risen, either as the total resource flow it involves has risen or with the total time it has been in place. Some studies have concluded that regional income convergence within Canada is slow and has been hindered by the income maintenance system—taking about 15 years to close half of the gap (Lee and Coulombe, 1995; Milne and Tucker, 1992), though it could equally be argued that it is impressive that the gap has narrowed at all, given various resource and location disadvantages of the lower income provinces. The impacts of the social

---

[18] I.e. how much subsidy is passed from the workers who do not make use of the insurance to those who make extensive use of it. Premiums are adjusted so that the system is self-financing, with government funding having ceased in the 1990 amendments so that there is now no subsidy from the general tax payer (see Chapter 3).

net will no doubt remain somewhat speculative, since it is not possible to identify them among the large number of factors which affect economic efficiency, growth and distribution. Perhaps the only fairly firm conclusion is that, if the convergence and efficiency costs of the system have been significant at all, they have not been important enough to greatly slow national growth or to prevent what others might consider to be a reasonably fast income convergence.[19]

Another major question, unfortunately not yet answered very fully in the literature, is the extent to which the differential shifts in income distribution between the U.S. and Canada since the late 1970s are related to the social net and the way it has functioned. As noted above there was a striking contrast over the period 1979-87 in that the economic welfare of female-headed households with children increased markedly in Canada while staying constant or declining in the U.S., suggesting a significant role for income transfers.

The process of retrenchment of the social security system under fiscal pressure in Canada in the 1990s provides insight into the potential for and the limitations on effective changes to such programs (Hale, 1998, 429), and hence the importance, noted by Gunderson and Riddell, of avoiding the most questionable features right from the start. The 1994-95 reforms to Canada's UI system are an example of the complexities of structural change to one of Canada's largest entitlement programs. Such social benefits become widely considered as entitlements and are energetically defended by their beneficiaries and often also, as in this case, by the government agencies which administer them. Regional advocates of the UI were strong; its seasonal worker and repeat beneficiary maintenance functions are much more prominent in these regions than elsewhere, so the discussion of UI reform quickly became focused on the regional implications of cutting back on this single largest federal transfer program to individuals in the eastern provinces. Though changes were made to the system, these were substantially less than both the framers of the first proposals and many other analysts would have liked to see.

Cortázar points out in Chapter 4 that the traditional approach in most Latin American countries to protecting workers against the negative effects of unemployment is by restricting the firm's freedom to fire them, through a combination of tight regulations on dismissal and high severance payments.[20]

---

[19] Over the period 1964-95 gross product per capita grew by 93% in Canada but by 152% in the transfer-receiving Atlantic region. As a result the ratio of average earned income in that region to the national average rose from 55% to 72% (Berry, 1996b, 60).

[20] As Adriana Marshall notes (personal communication), employer contributions to UI were a little over 4% of the wage bill in Canada after the 1994 reform, whereas in Latin America the contributions to the termination fund tend to be twice that. One of the benefits of some severance systems is the forced saving element of it; the resulting "nest eggs" have financed the start-up of many small firms. In principle Cortázar's personal savings account could have some such effect, though the "forced" element may be less, so which of the two systems is superior would appear to depend heavily on worker behavior with respect to savings, which is not well understood.

Unemployment insurance or other forms of assistance to the unemployed have not been part of the package until their recent introduction in a number of countries. Coverage remains low or modest where the systems do exist.[21] The typical system has thus provided strong protection against unemployment (at least when the legislation was vigorously enforced) for a usually relatively small "insider" group (though larger in the more developed countries of the region like Argentina and Uruguay) while providing none for what is usually the majority of workers who are outside the formal sector to which such protection is provided. This system has come under serious criticism for being regressive (protecting mainly the better off), reducing total employment in the modern sector (by increasing the employer's costs/risks in hiring, and reducing the mobility of the labor force, which may be especially damaging in middle income countries in the process of integrating themselves into the world economy.

Few in-depth studies have tried to quantify these negative effects related to the degree and manner in which formal sector workers are protected, or even to undertake a careful assessment of the *de facto* coverage of this system. The allocation of much labor to the informal sector may or may not be inefficient from a static point of view, and if inefficient it may or may not be avoidable through labor market or other policies. Increasingly the evidence seems to suggest that not much efficiency loss results from barriers to movement between the formal and informal sectors. For example, Maloney (1998), on the basis of an insightful analysis of the movement of people between the formal sector and several segments of the informal sector in urban Mexico, concludes that any impediments to movement between the formal and informal sectors do not prevent a considerable flow of economically desirable movement; that neither the earnings differentials of those who move (which go in favor of the informal sector) nor the size of the movements supports the idea of a marked segmentation between these labor market components; that labor force mobility in the formal sector (as measured by the rate of turnover) is not low, as has often been claimed, but about the same as that of the U.S.; that there is little evidence of the rigidities that the incentives implicit in the labor code would lead one to expect, and certainly no evidence that people want to stay in the formal sector until they retire—at least two thirds of those entering self-employment from formal salaried employment did so voluntarily, with a desire for greater independence or higher pay cited as the chief motivations; that paid informal sector work (often viewed as the bottom of the informal sector scale) seems to serve as the principal port of entry for the young, poorly educated workers into paid employment, but that their average wait is just

---

[21] Whereas in Canada some 90% of the workforce is covered in principle and the majority of the unemployed are UI benefit recipients, in the Latin American countries for which there are data, coverage is far smaller with the result that it is infrequent to see more than 10% of the unemployed receiving benefits (communication from Adriana Marshall).

two years before moving on, typically to other paid employment.[22] Maloney argues that the very legislation that is thought to induce rigidities into the labor market may in fact stimulate turnover and encourage workers to leave salaried formal sector employment. If the rigidities leave few opportunities for promotion and this is complemented by a general pattern in which blue collar workers hit an advancement ceiling (partly related to features of the culture) this may encourage them to go out on their own.[23]

The policy implications of this unconventional picture of labor market segmentation will depend first on whether it turns out to hold across the region; there is some possibility that Mexico's labor market is atypical. Further, the finding of considerable mobility among sectors does not imply the absence of some inefficiency-inducing barriers nor disprove the contention that the large size of the informal sector reflects an unduly low labor absorption in the formal sector related to labor-cost raising interventions.

Such contrary evidence notwithstanding, a strong enough *prima facie* case has been made to send analysts and policymakers in search of something better than the existing set of institutions. Since it seems implausible that a worker-protection system can be very effective on behalf of a large number of workers by impeding firing, it seems clear that a system must be found which gives employers greater freedom while still protecting workers against the full vagaries of the job market. Such unemployment insurance systems as do now exist in Latin America are attempts to confront this need. None has yet achieved a level of coverage anywhere near what is standard in the countries of Western Europe, the U.S. or Canada. The proposal put forward by Cortázar is designed to get around the problems of implementing standard industrial country unemployment systems in lower income countries where informal sector employment is more the rule than the exception. This fact makes it difficult to avoid serious abuse of any system where there is a private incentive to claim unemployment while continuing to work. Spain, with its very high reported levels of unemployment, may be the classic example of this problem. Cortázar's proposal involves a system which avoids these negative incentives by essentially making the worker pay for his/her own unemployment insurance through a fund which accumulates when the person is working and can be drawn on or borrowed from when unemployment strikes.[24] It is the equivalent of private insurance against any other risk. Various other proposals are also on the table or in their trial phases at this time. Most can be

---

[22] This figure is similar to that reported by Sedlacek *et al* (1995) for Brazil (which has notoriously mobile workers) and to that in the U.S.

[23] This and the next paragraph draw on Berry and Méndez (1999).

[24] The fact that there is no risk pooling across individuals in this proposal means that it is not insurance in the usual sense of the term in modern economics. How pertinent this fact is depends on the nature of unemployment risks; since no system provides more than temporary and partial income replacement anyway, this may not be a big issue.

thought of as hybrids between the Cortázar plan and the standard industrial country model, in the degree to which they combine individual self-insurance against this risk and insurance which, while pooling risks across workers, also creates incentives to abuse, and leads to the allocation of too much labor and other resources to industries in which average unemployment rates are high. With respect both to Cortázar's plan and the various hybrid systems one could think of, it is clear that only time and experimentation will allow any serious judgment as to their potential.

The choices facing countries like those of Latin America can be thought of as falling within a triangle of options defined by the three systems just described—the industrial country model, the Cortázar model and hybrids of the two. The first two have the potential to foster desirable labor mobility by reallocating the cost faced by the displaced workers—either to society (in the industrial country model) or over time (in the Cortázar model). The industrial country model can have the advantage of distributing the costs of unemployment more widely and/or acting as a progressive transfer system toward poorer workers, provided that it does not lead to too much moral hazard. In the context of labor markets with large informal sectors, it is implausible to assume that all workers can be covered, so a major issue is the extent to which the system can be selectively applied to a part of the labor force where it is useful to the workers as well as the firms.

It is tempting to conclude that the industrial country model itself holds little interest in Latin America given the level of moral hazard and the unlikelihood that it could act as an instrument to redistribute income (income maintenance for the poorer groups). On the optimistic assumption, however, that the Latin countries will proceed fairly rapidly toward the status of developed industrial countries with relatively small informal sectors (some are close to that status already) the planning of UI systems should take this into account. The best option would be one which can both serve a useful function at present but which with reasonable adjustments could in future take care of those worker needs which are more typical of an industrial economy. The Cortázar plan avoids most moral hazard problems, though there is a question of how much coverage could be extended under such a scheme. It would allow extension to workers who terminate employment voluntarily; on the other hand it is not clear how (if at all) it could incorporate informal sector workers who are not registered. One issue here is the extent to which such registration is undesirable from the worker's point of view (e.g., because it makes her liable for taxes) or desirable (because other benefits come with such registration).[25] The current pioneering attempts in the region include those of Chile, Brazil and Argentina; it will take some time before their

---

[25] As Adriana Marshall has noted (personal communication) it is necessary to assess this proposal also in the light of the recently spreading "worker capitalization funds" based on employer contributions.

performance can be fairly judged.

1.4 Minimum Wages (MW)

The main objective of minimum wage legislation in industrial countries like Canada is as a tool against poverty, by raising the labor incomes of relatively poor people, or more precisely of members of relatively poor families (Benjamin, Chapter 8). How well it may be expected to achieve this goal depends on whether it does in fact raise a significant number of incomes and whether most of the earners so affected are found in poor families. The other main issue in the evaluation of MWs as a policy tool is the extent of any negative side-effects, in particular whether it leads to fewer jobs (especially for poor family members) and slower economic growth—through its leading to efficiency (dead weight) loss. The extent of dead weight loss, if any, depends on the nature of the labor markets in which people whose incomes are around the minimum are found. If a significant share face monopsony employers (e.g., domestic workers, workers in one-industry towns, etc.) then increasing their wages via a legislated minimum can in fact reduce rather than increase this efficiency loss at the same time that it raises the workers' incomes. In more competitive markets the issue is the elasticity of the demand for the labor of the workers in question; if quite elastic, the dead weight loss tends to be large and the total income going to the poor can fall; if quite inelastic the opposite can be true—the dead weight loss low and the income gains to workers high. Since long-run elasticity is normally significantly higher than short-run elasticity, it is common that short-run gains may be achieved, but these may be followed by longer-run losses.

At a second level of static analysis is the question of whether a higher minimum wage causes an upward shift of the rest of the wage structure, or at least of parts of it. In some countries of Latin America, wages which are not at the bottom of the structure are nonetheless denominated in terms of the minimum wage, which automatically gives it a more prominent role in affecting wages in general (Riveros, Chapter 9). And even where the link is not a formal one, it is known that bargaining often occurs with the MW as the benchmark unit, and that through this mechanism it may have a greater effect, at least on the overall nominal wage structure, than would at first glance appear to be the case. If all wages move up in line with the MW, however, the main final outcome may be inflation which at the limit can cancel out any increases in real wages—for the lower income workers and everyone else, while the fact that all wages rose means that there was no redistribution within the wage system either.

Most countries of Latin America have had not just one basic MW but a number for different categories of workers. In Costa Rica, for example, this system has been very detailed (Gindling and Berry, 1992). The relationship between movements in the minimum wage structure and inflation has been widely recognized in the context of the high levels of inflation which have characterized many Latin countries. On the one hand it is clear that a nominal wage which is automatically adjusted for past inflation will tend to perpetuate the inflation; on the other hand it is clear that if this is not the case, inflation can push real wages down sharply and contribute to large increases in the level of inequality.

Canada's experience with MWs is that of a country without a high level of inflation (defined, say, by annual price increases of 25% per year or more) and with a "modern" labor force structure—few workers in agriculture, nearly all *de facto* covered by the legislation, a very small informal sector and a considerable number of families with no income earners (due to unemployment, single parent families on welfare, etc.). Against this background, Benjamin (Chapter 8) finds that minimum wages have only limited scope for improving the welfare of the lowest income households, since most of these families have no full-time earners; many of the benefits of higher minimum wages are transferred to teenagers who are distributed relatively evenly across the income distribution. Nevertheless, the benefits would flow somewhat disproportionately to poor working adults. When the estimated disemployment effects of minimum wages are also taken into account, and if estimates from the high end of confidence intervals are chosen, the loss of jobs may be great enough to actually reduce the wage bill received by low wage workers as a group. Whether this extreme outcome holds or not, it is important that this instrument be compared with others whose objective is to improve income distribution. Benjamin notes that there have been too few attempts to undertake comparisons with such alternative instruments as a negative income tax. The static economic question of how minimum wages are likely to affect welfare, redistribute income and change the total size of the pie turns on empirical issues.

Riveros observes (Chapter 9) that the minimum wage (MW) has traditionally been considered to be an important policy instrument in Latin America. Begun in the pre-WWII period, MWs were used in the 1950s and 1960s to intervene in private wage setting by providing a floor for the wage structure, in the context of protected economies. Periodic revision of its level and the maintenance of suitable enforcement machinery have been widely deemed to be crucial in the attempt to attain a better income distribution. But at present there are worries that this instrument has few if any positive effects, especially as countries strive to consolidate their trade openings and feel that wages should be flexible.

The tendency of MW laws in Latin America has been to formally include all workers regardless of gender, age, geographical context, skill or occupation, in spite of the obvious existence of labor market segmentation, and the possibly negative effects of their presence on the less skilled, through job destruction. Although the laws have stressed need as the criterion for setting MW levels, it has been rare to impose rates based on empirical studies of those needs, so that, by and large the criteria have been dominated by political assessment and expediency. The MW-setting machinery shows remarkable variation across countries, and in some cases has become very complex, with labor/management participation along with the central decision-making authorities. Automatic indexation of MWs to inflation is included in the laws of several countries, though in most, particularly those characterized by relatively high inflation, real MWs have been eroded as a result of an incomplete indexation system combined with adjustment policies aimed at lowering fiscal expenditures and labor costs.

The complexity of sorting out the determinants of wages, employment and poverty makes it a major challenge to understand how MWs have affected these variables in Latin America. Riveros notes that there have been few studies of the impact of MWs and that conclusions vary considerably across those available. It is credible, as argued by López and Riveros (1989), that the MW has little capacity to protect the poor, given the context of labor market segmentation and the resulting modest level of coverage of the instrument. This is less obvious for the more industrialized countries of the region like Argentina, however, and will hopefully be decreasingly the case with time as labor market segmentation falls and the potential coverage of the MW rises. As the economic structure of the Latin countries converges toward that of more developed economies, however, another feature may also come increasingly into play—the frequency of households with no earners. In that case, as noted for Canada, there are once again many poor families which cannot be assisted by MWs.

During the experience of the economic crises of the 1980s, real wages fell sharply in most Latin countries, partly as a direct effect of accelerating inflation. Several authors have suspected that, where implemented with vigor, MWs displayed a capacity to cushion such declines and possibly also the downward spirals of the economies as a whole. Thus, Morley (1995) suggests that a MW can be especially useful in conditions of recession where the usual tradeoff between the wage and the number of jobs in the formal sector is weakened since the job opportunities in the formal sector are declining in any case. He observes that during the 1980s in Latin America, movements of the real minimum wage were correlated negatively to movements in poverty, after allowing for the growth of per capita income.[26] The other side of this coin is that the failure of the legislation to hold up low level wages may have contributed to the sharp observed increases in inequality in such Latin countries as Chile and Brazil.

1.5 Payroll Taxes and Social Security

As of 1992-93, payroll taxes were the source of about half of the income security

---

[26] A similar result is reported by Lustig and McLeod (1997).

benefits paid to Canadians. Nakamura and Wong (Chapter 5) distinguish four basic reasons for the existence of social security programs: the inability of some people to take care of themselves at certain times (in particular children and the aged); the fact that personal risk can sometimes be dealt with in a more cost effective manner through group risk-pooling arrangements; externalities associated with keeping people healthy or out of poverty; and the importance of a broad middle class/avoidance of an underclass. The main programs constituting the social security network in Canada are the unemployment insurance system, workers' compensation programs, the Canada Pension Plan and, in some provinces, health and education taxes. Payroll taxes as a percent of GDP rose from 2.0% in 1966 to 5.8% in 1993; as a percent of wages they rose from 4.2% to 11.6% (Nakamura and Wong, Chapter 5).

Most of the controversy around payroll taxes involves their indirect costs through incentive effects, either on those who pay high marginal tax rates or via those who take advantage of the allegedly generous and "easy access" public income support program, including the UI and workers' compensation which are paid for in part with these payroll taxes. There is little dispute that the programs do provide real benefits to many people. The impact of the taxes on hours of work for those working, whichever the direction may be, is agreed to be small, especially for men. There is clear evidence that at least some workers adjust the number of weeks they work in response to changes in the number of weeks of UI-covered work that are needed to qualify for benefits (Card and Riddell, 1993). Green and Riddell (1997) conclude that many workers would not be in the labor force at all but for the UI program and that it tends to increase the weeks of work by the more poorly qualified and unemployment-prone workers. As for the demand side, estimates of the labor cost elasticity of demand tend to fall mainly in the range -0.5 to -1.0 (OECD Jobs Study, 1994). To predict the impact of lowered labor taxes on the demand for labor, however, one must allow for the fact that labor costs will fall by less than the labor taxes do, so the labor tax elasticity of labor demand could be just a fraction of the above figure (see below).

One of the trickier aspects of the question of payroll taxes relates to their impact relative to that of other ways of raising the funds used for pensions, UI, etc. In a comparison of these taxes vis-à-vis other ways of raising funds to finance social security Kesselman (Chapter 6) finds that most or all of the short-run employment effects of such taxes dissipate in the longer-run as the tax burden is shifted into lower pay, and concludes that payroll taxes are well suited to financing social security, though benefit-tax linkages may need reform in some programs. The key point is that, though in the perception of the individual employer it appears that these taxes raise the total cost of labor, that impact is smaller than it appears and could in the limit be zero. Kesselman reports empirical findings of full shifting of the taxes onto the workers. Payroll taxes are simple and easy to operate and are a relatively efficient form of taxation, at least compared to taxes on income or capital. When tied to benefits in a well-designed program of social security, they offer the additional advantage of posing minimal distortions to labor market and other economic behavior. He concludes that energies in reforming social security might best be directed at improving benefit-tax linkages, while recognizing the underlying social objectives of the program.

Payroll taxes have tended to be very high in most Latin American countries relative to both developed countries and to other LDCs (Guasch, 1998). Further, the context is different from that of Canada or other developed countries, since coverage is partial and does have the effect of creating or widening a labor cost gap between the modern and the informal sector. Thus, much of the debate on the merit of such taxes reflects differing views as to the impact of that labor cost gap. It also depends, of course, on how one sees the benefits from the social security systems. The currently ongoing reforms in Latin America are lowering these taxes and, with respect to their pension component, creating the option of the funds being invested in private sector institutions.[27] To the extent that the switch from pay-as-you-go funding of pensions in the region to the fully funded system raises national savings, this could be a major boon. Chile's fully funded system appears to have contributed importantly in this way. The impact on modern sector employment is,

---

[27] The evolution of Latin America's social security systems during recent decades reflects the triple strain of the fiscal tightness brought on by the crisis, the fact that some systems had already evolved in very expensive directions (generous conditions), and the problem that most had only modest coverage. Coverage is mainly a function of the country's level of development and the extension of the urban salaried formal sector, and ranges from a fifth or less of the population (e.g. in Colombia and Peru) to virtually total coverage in Cuba, Uruguay, and Costa Rica. Social security in Uruguay and Costa Rica alleviated some social costs of the crisis and reforms of the 1980s through their universal coverage and social assistance programs (and UI in Uruguay). Elsewhere this was not the case as social security did not cover the most vulnerable groups (Mesa-Lago, 1997, 503). Its failure led to the creation, since the mid-1980s, of various types of social safety nets in most countries of the region. Implementation of structural adjustment demanded state action to aid the most vulnerable.

Mesa-Lago (1997, 497) notes that neither of the first two major reforms of social security systems to be adopted in Latin America had much influence elsewhere in the region because of their radicalism—Cuba in the 1960s-1970s where the system was totally taken over by the state, and Chile during 1979-81 where the public system was substituted by a private one, supported and guaranteed by the state, all in line with the neoliberal framework which the government had adopted. In relatively democratic countries the negative political features of the Pinochet regime precluded any influence of its social security approach during that regime's life. The transition to democracy and the Aylwin administration's endorsement of the previous social security reform, which had by then had success in some areas, made it politically more palatable, as did IFI support of this model as a softening component of structural adjustment packages. As of mid-1996 no other country had adopted a pure Chile-style reform, though several had incorporated an important private sector component. Argentina and then Uruguay adopted mandatory private and public components, while Colombia and Peru established selective systems allowing choice between the two. Most countries still have mainly unreformed systems, though marginal private elements have been introduced, as in Costa Rica and Mexico. The trend towards democratization makes it harder for countries to choose the more radical options.

as noted above, much harder to predict and in any case the overall benefit from shifting employment from the informal to the modern sector may not raise overall economic efficiency if the modern sector continues to benefit from imperfections in the product and capital markets, imperfections which have been to date partially offset by the labor cost advantage of the informal sector.

In today's integrating world one of the issues most frequently mooted about labor taxes is their impact on international competitiveness. The perspective of the individual business is that any cost increase lowers competitiveness; when other local firms face the same cost component (such as labor taxes) it is accepted that a firm's situation vis-à-vis these competitors may not be affected, but that all of them suffer vis-à-vis competitors from other countries. This latter perception is invalid in any situation where a country's balance of payments is kept in equilibrium by the usual mechanisms—the exchange rate where it is allowed to vary, or monetary/fiscal policy where the exchange rate is fixed. Where these mechanisms are operating as they should be, tax levels should have no impact on a country's overall competitiveness in international markets.[28]

Tokman and Martínez (Chapter 7) undertake an estimate of the relative impact of labor costs (payroll taxes included) vis-à-vis other determinants of the changing competitiveness of manufactured goods in five Latin American countries over the first quinquennium of the 1990s. They note that rising labor costs would not *per se* diminish competitiveness as long as productivity rose at a comparable rate, as was usually the case. But in general the more important short-run determinants of competitiveness were macroeconomic variables, in particular the exchange rate. Thus, at least during this period, the theoretical expectation that the exchange rate would be the main factor at work is borne out, further indicating that the concern with the level of labor costs may be overdrawn. Tokman and Martinez find no general tendency for the non-wage component of labor costs to rise faster than the wage component. Still, the former costs are high in relation to wages *per se*—ranging from about 45% to 63% in 1995 in the five countries studied by Tokman and Martinez when bonuses and additional wages are treated as part of non-wage costs and 35-45% when they are treated as part of wages (see Table 7.5). The important question remains—if these costs were significantly lower, would this provide an important inducement to job creation? Here the arguments presented by Kesselman in Chapter 6 become central.

As in Canada, the recent reforms in the social benefit area have been designed to reduce fiscal strain and to encourage job creation. Unlike the Canadian situation, a relatively high share of Latin America's workers are not covered by the social benefits financed through payroll taxes; the challenge of broadening coverage has not been given much thought in these reforms and needs to be

---

[28] As noted earlier, the basic concept of international trade theory—comparative advantage—implies that a country's capacity to export is not affected by the absolute level of real or nominal costs in any or all of its industries.

addressed seriously.

1.6 Training and Retraining

Training is recognized as crucial to employers, workers and any government which is concerned with a strong performance from the economy and with avoiding the social consequences of serious mismatches between the supply of skills available and the needs of the economy. Globalization and the rapid pace of technological change are generally believed to make effective and lifelong training more important than before. In developed countries like Canada, labor markets are facing severe adjustment consequences of these and other phenomena such as the implementation of just-in-time delivery, privatization, etc. Also necessitating an increased emphasis on training are new workplace and human resource practices, together with demographic and other changes in the workforce. Despite this general recognition, it is hard to pinpoint just what needs to be done and by whom. There is logic to a certain amount being done in institutions (for more general training), some at the firm level to take advantage of inside knowledge as to the needs, and some at the industry level to respond both to knowledge of needs and economies of scale.

Canada's training system is, by most assessments, relatively small in terms of total resources expended, but at the same time rather complex. For Ontario, Canada's most industrial province, an estimate for the late 1980s indicated that about 5% of full-time permanent workers received at least two weeks of formal training over the course of the year, with 2.7% being trained in the firm and 2% in federal government-sponsored programs (Meltz, 1990, 300). These figures overstate the relative role of the firms in formal training since average duration of training episodes is much smaller for them (see Chapter 10). Around 25% or so of such workers received some training over the year, with the average weeks per worker (including also those not receiving training) about 1.5. For Canada as a whole the figures would presumably be somewhat lower.[29]

Canada has emphasized passive income maintenance programs like UI rather than active ones like training. As of 1994-95 the country was spending a little more than 2% of its GDP on *all* labor market programs, but 71% of this was on passive income maintenance programs, mainly transfers from unemployment

---

[29] Also noted by Gunderson and Riddell (Chapter 10) are the facts that about two-thirds of private firms provide some informal or formal training, with about one-third providing formal training; about 56% of employees indicated having received some informal or formal training over the previous two years, although only 7% to 19% indicated they received formal training; on average, firms spend about $250 per employee per year on formal training. Training is more prevalent in firms and industries experiencing rapid technological change.

insurance[30] (the passive component would be much larger if social assistance were included). Of the 29% of expenditures which went to active programs, most was for training, with smaller amounts channeled to employment services, job creation and subsidized employment. Canada is categorized by the OECD as one of the "weak" countries in terms of combined employer and government support for training in industry (Economic Council of Canada, 1991). It ranks as average or above for public support, implying that employer support is quite weak by international standards. This has led to statements that Canadian employers lack a "training culture"; Betcherman (1993, 22) observes that "available data offer a strong sense that Canadian firms do train less than their counterparts in other major industrialized countries."[31] Extensive reliance on immigration as a source of skilled labor may have deterred the development of an indigenous training system (Meltz, 1990). The training system in Canada is also described as not being well-linked to the education system (Gaskell, 1991), in part because of the low status attached to vocational education, a quality shared with most countries of Latin America.

Gunderson and Riddell (Chapter 10) note that there have been many task forces and Royal Commissions on this issue in Canada, reflecting, among other things, its complexity. The web of programs is difficult to understand, one reason that neither employers nor employees are typically well informed about them. The history of much wrangling and blame-shifting between the federal and provincial government suggests that divided or ill-defined responsibility may often lead to no responsibility.[32]

The measurement of benefits (whether gross or net) from training programs is notoriously difficult. Evaluation studies generally but not always find that training does pay, usually more in the form of greater employability than of higher wages. The largest estimates usually relate to employer-based training combined with work experience, rather than to basic or institutional training.[33] Gunderson

---

[30] The special development component of the UI benefits that includes training courses and supplementary allowances for training is less than 4% of such UI expenditures (Human Resources and Development Canada, 1994, 14).

[31] There is no consensus on the extent to which firms are reluctant to provide training because they are afraid that they may simply lose their trainees to other firms that do not (i.e., the poaching problem).

[32] The constitutional division of powers in Canada is such that the federal government has responsibility for the state of the economy and the provincial governments have responsibility for education. Since training relates to both the state of the economy and education, it falls under both federal and provincial jurisdiction. This joint responsibility has given rise to federal-provincial disputes over how training should be administered, with each party often blaming the other for shortcomings in this area (Gaskell, 1991; Gunderson and Riddell, 1991; Meltz, 1990).

[33] Both the periodic finding of no benefits and the smaller identified benefits associated with institutional training could easily be the result of measurement problems. In the latter case one of the problems is that benefits may be more easily identified in the immediate post-training period in the case of training which is specific and undertaken in the firm, while the benefits from the more

and Riddell also note that the measured impacts on earnings and employability have increased over time, perhaps due to better program design (as worse programs were abandoned and better ones expanded) or perhaps because the returns to training increased for other reasons, such as the speed and character of technological change. Gains from training are greatest in a more buoyant labor market, highlighting the importance of available employment opportunities.

A number of aspects of Canada's experience with training suggest a tradeoff between efficiency in raising overall productivity of the labor force and the associated distributional effects. Most notable is the fact that formal training is more likely to be received by employees who are already more highly educated and well-paid. Also, though unemployed workers are more likely to take training than others, within the unemployed those most likely to experience difficult adjustment problems are less likely to take training (Picot, 1987).

Various of the study results cited above seem to have had an impact on the re-orientation of training over time. That is, there has been a redirection from basic and institutional classroom training and toward training provided at the private sector workplace and combined with work experience. Increased emphasis has been placed on higher-level training for emerging skill shortages, and on the involvement of employers in the delivery of training. This is especially the case with respect to the recent re-orientation of UI from passive income maintenance and toward more active adjustment assistance, as UI funds are increasingly used to enable recipients to receive training at the workplace and to garner work experience.

In Latin America the training needs have also been changing significantly over recent decades, first as the economic crises—in most countries centered around the 1980s—slowed growth and cut the demand for many types of skills, then as the recovery tended to be accompanied by trade openings and a burst of imports of machinery/equipment and the associated technological change.

By the onset of the economic crises in the early 1980s, the majority of Latin countries had well-established and relatively large national training institutions which dominated much of the training scene. They shared the stage with the vocational secondary schools, technical institutes, a modest number of private training institutions, and a generally limited amount of in-house training carried out by firms. In spite of these various sources of training, it appears that most non-agricultural workers in blue collar activities had (and probably still have) received little if any training apart from informal on-the-job help from co-workers or supervisors. It is unclear how serious a failing this constituted in the past, given the generally rapid economic growth of the region during the import substituting phase of growth, led by Brazil with the highest growth rate but the lowest level of average educational attainment among the major Latin countries. A reasonable

general training imparted in institutions might well be distributed over a longer period of time and hence be harder to sort out among the other determinants of productivity or earnings.

guess, however, is that the region did suffer somewhat from its various problems and weaknesses on the training front, even during the import substituting industrialization phase of the pre-crisis period. It is likely to suffer a good deal more under the new circumstances of the 1990s and beyond, unless substantial improvements are undertaken.

Formal training still seems to be the exception rather than the rule among urban workers in most Latin countries. Arriagada (1989, 11 and 16) finds that as of 1985-86 about 20% of urban employed males in Peru had received some training, with 44% of these being job-based (on-the-job, in occupational training institutions or in the military). Perhaps 7-8% of employed urban males had their main training experience from the national training institute (SENATI) while a similar number were trained in private institutions.[34] Data from urban Colombia as of 1980 suggest that perhaps 40-50% of male workers had some structured training (Berry and Méndez, 1998, 17), with around 10% or a little more having taken SENA courses (Horn, 1987). Of those without SENA training, other institutional programs were the main source in most of the occupations, with secondary vocational important in some female activities and "practical" (i.e., in-house structured training) received by about 13-14% of males and about 6-7% of women. One may assume that the share of the labor force with some formal training is higher in Argentina, for example, than in Colombia.

As in Canada, the extent of training appears to be positively related to formal education in Latin America. Figures for urban Peru in 1985-86 show a strong association of this sort; though part of it is probably a "cohort effect" (more recent cohorts get more education and more training than older ones), there is almost certainly also a true "level of education" effect. If this pattern is as strong in other Latin countries as in Peru, the risk that unequal access to training will continue to be a significant source of earnings inequality is a very serious one. Data from Colombia on the family income levels of SENA trainees in 1992 paints a more positive picture; the distribution of the subsidies associated with SENA programs was progressive in the sense that it was less unequal than was the distribution of per capita family incomes. Though the third and fourth quintiles received the greatest per capita benefits in absolute terms, the second and fifth somewhat less and the bottom quintile the least (Molina *et al*, 1993, Cuadro 4.19), when these benefits are related to family incomes they rise from about 0.08% of income for the top quintile to about 0.52% for the bottom one. Chile is among the countries with interesting training programs for the poor, many or most of whom would normally be expected to wind up in the informal sector. The *Chile Joven* (Youth Chile) program was designed to improve the labor market access of low income youth, especially those affected negatively by the 1982-83 crisis. Many other countries have interesting experiments in this area. Careful consideration of

---

[34] The lumping together in these data of all "job-based" experiences means that one cannot deduce exactly how much training occurred in SENATI.

which ones are working better is a needed next step in this area, including the difficult question of whether they result in net positive job creation or mainly reshuffle jobs among labor force participants.

Though little quantitative information is available on in-house training, the consensus is that Latin American businesses, like their Canadian counterparts, have not been in the habit of doing much of it, and will need to do more in future. A recent World Bank study of manufacturing firms in Colombia and Mexico (Tan and Batra, 1995), providing the most detailed evidence available as of the early 1990s, confirms this surmise; it may also suggest that firms may be at least arranging for more training than has heretofore been guessed,[35] with much of it occurring outside the firm. Over 50% of Colombian small firms and about 80% of the medium and large ones indicated that they had provided formal or structured training over the past year, either in-house or externally; in Mexico the figures were somewhat lower—40-60% for all size categories (Tan and Batra, 1995). The role of internal formal training was low in Colombia—3.7% of all sampled firms vs. 48.7% providing formal training outside the firm (Tan and Batra, 1995, 14). In Mexico although slightly more firms undertook in-house formal training (5.8%) than in Colombia, very few arranged for external training (7.9% vs. 48.7% in Colombia).

The training picture in Latin America has been in a process of considerable change for some time, fueled by the macroeconomic problems and trends noted above, the increasing scarcity of public funds, and the increasing doubts about the competence of public institutions in general which have come with the neo-liberal wave of thinking about economic policy in Latin America and elsewhere. Alternative sources of training have been growing relatively fast. Varying policy responses have emerged across the region, with Chile pushing as much of the management and resource allocation decisions as reasonably possible into the private sector while other countries, though moving in the same direction, have not gone as far. As a result, there is within the region a useful range of experiments underway on the alternative ways of handling training.

Ducci (Chapter 11) highlights some of the key trends in the activities of national training institutes:

(i)   pre-employment training (including apprenticeship) has declined in importance relative to in-service training;

(ii)   training activities are increasingly organized by economic sector, either through internal compartmentalization of the VTIs (Vocational Training Institutes) or by their breaking up into sectoral VTIs;

---

[35] Lack of data on hours of training leaves some ambiguity as to the economic meaning of the figures.

(iii)   training delivery is being increasingly transferred to enterprises, with Chile the pioneer in this process;

(iv)   efforts on behalf of small enterprise focus increasingly on management training and stress the exchange of experiences and networking among these firms;

(v)   technical assistance is increasingly provided together with training.

Taken together, these trends involve a shift of focus from the individual trainee to the firms and a broadening of activities to include other productivity-related services as well as training. In terms of clientele there has been increasing recognition of the importance of small firms, though the question of just what package of services most benefits them and how it can best be delivered remains to be resolved.

As for the vocational schools, they have in most countries undergone less change than have the VTIs or the informal training systems as a whole. In Chile, however, a major experiment has transferred their management to nonprofit organizations, with interesting results which deserve the attention of other countries in the region. There is widespread recognition of the dangers of being too academic or too isolated from the business sectors which will hopefully employ the graduates.

Though organized data are usually not available, it is likely and generally believed that private and NGO involvement in the training area has been rising rather rapidly. Certainly this is the case in Colombia, noted for the strong business involvement through associated NGOs in support of microenterprise.

As Ducci argues, there is no doubt that substantial public sector involvement is needed for effective training in Latin America. The needs are changing with time and with shifts of macroeconomic context, and better training support for SMEs is pivotal. There is need for a well thought-out, activist strategy, based on a continuing reevaluation of the skill needs of the economy with focus on the unmet needs and the surpluses. The extent to which the public sector should be a funder rather than a direct provider of training is under debate.

The Latin American region faces the challenge of recovering its growth performance of the pre-1980s decades in a context where this is likely to call for a substantially improved human capital base, in order to raise productivity in a world involving increasingly complex technologies. At the same time the evidence of sharply worsening income distribution in most countries of Latin America in the wake of the 1980s crisis and the economic reforms which accompanied or followed, raises the challenge of assuring that the increases in human capital are broad-based enough to allow those who have been losing ground over the last decade or so to recover some of it or at the least not to lose more. On grounds both of productivity and of equality it is pivotal that quality and access be improved at the primary level and that training systems play an increasing role in raising and maintaining productivity potential of as large a segment of the labor force as possible. Direct evidence of the low quality and incomplete coverage of primary schooling in a number of countries (most importantly Brazil) is complemented by the views of employers and the statistical evidence indicating that most vocational training is received by people with completed primary (probably good quality primary also). The increasing pace of technological change, together with the increasing need for worker flexibility, is raising the need for systematic training over the working career, which puts a new onus on training systems.

With respect both to the overall systems and to their VTI component, a key issue is their capacity to meet the training needs of SMEs. Most have been taking this challenge reasonably seriously in the last decade or so, but the evaluations are so few and sparse that it is hazardous to even guess at performance in this regard. It is clear that most training in this area must be subsidized, especially at the start. Whether VTIs, with extensive participation in their management by employers' associations will in most cases be the best option, or whether subsidized private provision (prevalent in Chile) will be superior remains to be seen. Careful up-to-date information and assessments are needed in this area. Effective training and other support for emerging clusters involving large numbers of SMEs may be particularly important; public involvement will often come from local institutions in such cases.

1.7 A Look Ahead

Chapters 3-11 deal in detail with the four selected labor policy issues—unemployment insurance, minimum wages, payroll taxes, and training, for both the Canadian and the Latin American perspectives. Before those specific themes are addressed, Chapter 2 undertakes a comparison of Canadian with American labor markets and labor market policies. Although, as we have argued, the Canadian experience is in most ways more relevant to Latin America than is that of the United States, the latter is the heavyweight in the region and what happens there has major impacts on the rest of the hemisphere, especially on Canada but also on Latin America. It is therefore important to take note of the main similarities and differences between the Canadian and American systems and policies. Some of the differences reflect relative country size, and in these regards the Canadian experience is the more pertinent for Latin America. Others reflect policy preferences; again the Canadian case tends to be more relevant to Latin America. But the U.S. system exerts pressure on all of its neighbors, usually in the direction of doing things the American way, partly through the simple familiarity with its example, partly through conscious or less conscious proselytizing, and partly through the costs and inconveniences associated with doing things differently (as in the case of payroll taxes and overall tax levels, which are alleged to contribute to the migration of Canadians to the United States.)

Apart from these underlying reasons to keep the U.S. case in mind even as we focus on Canada and Latin America, there is a more practical reason. On many points of labor market functioning and the impact of labor market policies there are grounds to expect substantial similarity across countries; on those points it is essential to take note of the American literature since it is extensive and often of high quality. Many of the chapters in the volume thus allude to American studies in the process of trying to understand mechanisms at work either in Canada or in Latin America.

REFERENCES

Altimir, O. (1982). "The Extent of Poverty in Latin America." Washington, D.C.: The World Bank, Staff Working Paper No. 522.

Altimir, O. (1992). "Cambios en las Desigualdades de Ingreso y en la Pobreza en América Latina." Mimeo (April).

Arriagada, A. M. (1989). "Occupational Training Among Peruvian Men: Does It Make a Difference?" Washington, D.C.: World Bank, Population and Human Resources Department, Working Paper, WPS 207.

Baldwin, J. (1996). *Were Small Producers the Engines of Growth in the Canadian Manufacturing Sector in the 1980s?* Ottawa: Statistics Canada.

Beach, C. M. and G. A. Slotsve (1996). *Are we Becoming Two Societies? Income Polarization and the Myth of the Declining Middle Class in Canada.* Toronto: The C. D. Howe Institute.

Berman, E., J. Bound and Z. Griliches (1994). "Changes in the Demand for Skilled Labor within U.S. Manufacturing Industries: Evidence from the Annual Survey of Manufacturing." *Quarterly Journal of Economics*, Vol. 109, No. 2 (May), pp. 367-397.

Berry, A. (1992). "Firm (or Plant) Size in the Analysis of Trade and Development." In *Trade Policy, Industrialization and Development: New Perspectives*, Gerald Helleiner, ed. Oxford: Clarendon Press, pp. 46-88.

Berry, A. (1995). "Social Policy Reform in Canada Under Regional Economic Integration." In *Social Policy in a Global Society: Parallels and Lessons from the Canada-Latin America Experience*, Daniel Morales-Gómez and Mario Torres A., eds. Ottawa: International Development Research Centre.

Berry, A. (1996a). "Small and Medium Enterprise (SME) Under Trade and Foreign Exchange Liberalization: Canadian and Latin American Experiences and Concerns." *Canadian Journal of Development Studies*, Vol. VII, No. 1.

Berry, A. (1996b). "Selected Issues in Indian and Canadian Economic, Management and Environmental Policies." In *Perspectives on the Indian and Canadian Economies.* Ottawa: Conference Board of Canada.

Berry, A. (1997). "The Inequality Threat in Latin America." *Latin American Research Review,* Vol. 32, No. 2.

Berry, A. and M. T. Méndez (1998). "Training in Latin America: Its Impact and Potential for Growth, Employment, Equity and Poverty Alleviation." Background paper prepared for the International Labor Office's World Employment Report.

Berry, A. and M. T. Méndez (1999). *Policies to Promote Adequate Employment in Latin America and the Caribbean (LAC).* Geneva: International Labor Office, Employment and Training Papers 46.

Betcherman, G. (1993). "Research Gaps Facing Training Policy-Makers." *Canadian Public Policy,* Vol. 19, No. 1.

Blackburn, M. L. (1998). "The Sensitivity of International Poverty Comparisons." *The Review of Income and Wealth,* Series 44, No. 2.

Blackburn, M. L. and D. E. Bloom (1993). "The Distribution of Family Income: Measuring and Explaining Changes in the 1980s for Canada and the United States." In *Small Differences that Matter: Labor Markets and Income Maintenance in Canada and the United States,* D. Card and R. B. Freeman, eds. Chicago: University of Chicago Press for the National Bureau of Economic Research.

Boltho, A. (1992). "Growth, Income Distribution and Household Welfare in Industrialized Countries since the First Oil Shock." *Innocenti Occasional Papers.* Florence: UNICEF.

Bradford, C. I. (Jr.) (1994). *From Trade-Driven Growth to Growth-Driven Trade: Reappraising the East Asian Development Experience.* Paris: OECD, Development Centre Documents.

Bruno, M. and J. Sachs (1985). *Economics of Worldwide Stagflation.* Cambridge, Mass.: Harvard University Press.

Bruton, H. (1997). *On The Search For Well-Being.* Ann Arbor: University of Michigan Press.

Card, D. and W. C. Riddell (1993). "A Comparative Analysis of Unemployment in Canada and the United States." In *Small Differences that Matter: Labor Markets and Income Maintenance in Canada and the United States,* D. Card and R. Freeman, eds. Chicago: University of Chicago Press.

CELADE (1994). *Boletín Demográfico,* Vol. XXVII, No. 54, Santiago, Chile, June.

Comisión Económica para América Latina y el Caribe (CEPAL) (1997). *Crecimiento, Empleo y Pobreza: Las Transformaciones de la Estructura del Empleo Asalariado y su Impacto en la Pobreza en los Años Ochenta e Inicios de los Noventa,* prepared by Mr. Jurgen Weller. Santiago: CEPAL, Oficina de Asuntos Económicos, División de Desarrollo Económico.

Corbo, V. (1998). "Problems, Development Theory, and Strategies of Latin America." In *The State of Development Economics: Progress and Perspectives*, Gustav Ranis and T. Paul Schultz, eds. Oxford and New York: Basil Blackwell.

Corry, D. and A. Glyn (1994). "Macroeconomics of equality, stability and growth." In *Paying for Inequality; The Economic Cost of Social Injustice*, A. Glyn and D. Miliband, eds. London: IPPR/Rivers Oram Press.

Cutler, D. and L Katz (1992). "Rising Inequality? Changes in the Distribution of Income and Consumption in the 1980s." *American Economic Review*, Vol. 82, No. 2.

Economic Commission for Latin America and the Caribbean (ECLAC) (1990). *Preliminary Overview of the Economy of Latin America and the Caribbean 1990*. Santiago: ECLAC.

Economic Commission for Latin America and the Caribbean (ECLAC) (1995). *Preliminary Overview of the Economy of Latin America and the Caribbean 1995*. Santiago: ECLAC.

Economic Commission for Latin America and the Caribbean (ECLAC) (1997). *Preliminary Overview of the Economy of Latin America and the Caribbean 1997*. Santiago: ECLAC.

Economic Council of Canada (1991). *Employment in the Service Economy*. Ottawa: Supply and Services Canada.

Foot, D. K., with D. Stoffman (1996). *Boom, Bust and Echo: How to Profit from the Coming Demographic Shift*. Toronto: Macfarlane Walter and Ross.

Gaskell, J. (1991). "Education as Preparation for Work in Canada." In *Making Their Way: Education, Training and the Labor Market in Canada and Britain*, D. Ashton and G. Lowe, eds. Toronto: University of Toronto Press.

Gindling, T. H. and A. Berry (1992). "The Performance of the Labor Market During Recession and Structural Adjustment: Costa Rica in the 1980s." *World Development*, Vol. 20, No. 11 (November).

Green, D. A. and W. C. Riddell (1997). "Qualifying for Unemployment Insurance: An Empirical Analysis." *Economic Journal*, Vol. 107 (January), pp. 67-84.

Guasch, J. L. (1998). "Labor Reform and Job Creation: The Unfinished Agenda in Latin America and Caribbean Countries." Mimeo.

Gunderson, M., and W. C. Riddell (1991). *Labor Force Adaptability: Implications for Education and Training*. Victoria, British Columbia: British Columbia Task Force on Employment and Training.

Hale, G. E. (1998). "Reforming Employment Insurance: Transcending the Politics of the Status Quo." *Canadian Public Policy*, Vol. XXIV, No. 4.

Hamermesh, D. (1993). *Labor Demand*. Princeton, N.J.: Princeton University Press.

Harberger, A. (1954). "Monopoly and Resource Allocation." *American Economic Review*, Vol. 44 (June).

Horn, R. (1987). *The Economic Impact of Formal Job Training on Self-employed and Salaried Worker Earnings in Colombia: The Private Returns to SENA Programs*. Ph. D. thesis, Columbia University.

Human Resources and Development Canada (1994). *Annual Report: 1993-1994*. Ottawa: Human Resources Development Canada.

International Monetary Fund (IMF) (1999). "IMF Economic Reviews." *Public Information Notices*, January-April 1999, No. 1. Washington, D.C.: International Monetary Fund.

Inter-American Development Bank (1997). *Latin America After a Decade of Reforms*. Washington, D.C.: Inter-American Development Bank, Economic and Social Progress in Latin America - 1997 Report.

Katz, L. and K. Murphy (1992). "Changes in Relative Wages, 1963-1987: Supply and Demand Factors." *Quarterly Journal of Economics*, Vol. 107.

Krueger, A. O. (1988). "The Relationship Between Trade, Employment and Development." In *The State of Development Economics: Progress and Perspectives*, Gustav Ranis and T. Paul Schultz, eds. Oxford: Basil Blackwell.

Lee, F. and S. Coulombe (1995). "Regional productivity: Convergence in Canada." *Canadian Journal of Regional Science*, 18 (Spring).

Levy, F. and R. J. Murnane (1992). "U.S. Earnings Levels and Earnings Inequality: A Review of Recent Trends and Proposed Explanations." *Journal of Economic Literature*, Vol. XXX (September).

Lin, Z., G. Picot and C. Beach (1995). "What Has Happened to Payroll Taxes in Canada over the Last Three Decades?" Ottawa: Statistics Canada, Business and Labor Market Analysis Division, mimeo.

López, R. and L. Riveros (1989). "Macroeconomic Adjustment and Labor Markets in Four Latin American Countries." In *Towards Social Adjustment: Labor Market Concerns in Structural Adjustment*, Guy Standing, ed. Geneva: ILO.

Lustig, N. and D. McLeod (1997). "Minimum Wages and Poverty: a Cross-Section Analysis for Developing Countries." In *Labor Market Reform in Latin America: Combining Social Protection and Market Flexibility*, Sebastian Edwards and Nora Lustig, eds. Washington, D.C.: The Brookings Institution.

Magno de Carvalho, J. A. (1995). "The Demographics of Poverty and Welfare in Latin America: Challenges and Opportunities." Paper presented at the conference *Poverty in Latin America: Issues and New Responses*, University of Notre Dame, Helen Kellogg Institute for International Studies, September 30-October 1.

Maloney, W. (1998). "Are LDC Labor Markets Dualistic." Washington, D.C.: World Bank, mimeo.

Marcouiller, D. ,V. Ruiz de Castilla and C. Woodruff (1994). "Formal Measures of the Informal Sector Wage Gap in Mexico, El Salvador, and Peru." Mimeo (December).

McQuaig, L. (1998). *The Cult of Impotence: Selling the Myth of Powerlessness in the Global Economy.* Toronto: Viking Press.

Meltz, N. (1990). "The Evolution of Worker Training: The Canadian Experience." In *New Developments in Worker Training,* L. Ferman, M. Hoyman, J. Cutcher-Gershenfeld and E. Savoie, eds. Madison: Industrial Relations Research Association.

Mesa-Lago, C. (1997). "Social Welfare Reform in the Context of Economic-Political Liberalization: Latin American Cases." *World Development,* Vol. 25, No.4 (April).

Milne, W. and M. Tucker (1992). "Income Convergence Across Canadian Provinces: Does Growth Theory Help Explain the Process? *Atlantic Canada Economics Association,* Vol. 21, pp. 170-82.

Molina, C. G., M. Alviar and D. Polonia (1993). *El Gasto Público en Educación y Distribución de Subsidios en Colombia,* Informe Final. Bogota: Fedesarrollo for the Departamento Nacional de Planeación.

Morley, S. A. (1995). *Poverty and Inequality in Latin America: The Impact of Adjustment and Recovery in the 1980s.* Washigton, D.C.: Johns Hopkins University Press.

National Council of Welfare (1996). *Poverty Profile 1996.* Toronto: National Council of Welfare.

Organization for Economic Co-operation and Development (OECD) (1994). *The OECD Jobs Study: Evidence and Expectations: Parts I and II.* Paris: OECD.

Osberg, L., S. Erksoy and S. Phipps (1998). "How to Value the Poorer Prospects of Youth in the Early 1990s." *Review of Income and Wealth,* Series 44, No. 1 (March).

Pendakur, K. (1998). "Changes in Canadian Family Income and Consumption Inequality Between 1978 and 1992." *The Review of Income and Wealth,* Series 44, No. 2 (June).

Picot, G. (1987). *Unemployment and Training.* Ottawa: Statistics Canada, Social and Economic Studies Division.

PREALC (1982). *Mercado de Trabajo en Cifras 1950-1980.* Santiago: PREALC.

Reissert, B. and G. Schmid (1994). "Unemployment Compensation and Active Labor Market Policy." In *Labor Market Institutions in Europe,* G. Schmid, ed. Armonk-London: M. E. Sharpe.

Robbins, D. (1995). "Trade Liberalization and Inequality in Latin America and East Asia: Synthesis of Seven Country Studies." Mimeo, Harvard Institute for International Development.

Rodrik, D. (1995). "Trade and Industrial Policy Reform." In *Handbook of Development Economics,* Vol. 3B, Jere Behrman and T. N. Srinivasan, eds. Amsterdam: North-Holland.

Sedlacek, G. L., R. Paes de Barros and S. Varandas (1995). "Segmentaçao e Mobilidade no Mercado de Trabalho Brasileiro." Mimeo.

Slesnick, D. (1993) "Gaining Ground: Poverty in the Post-War United States." *Journal of Political*

Economy, Vol. 101, No.1.

Slesnick, D. T. (1994). "Consumption, Needs and Inequality." *International Economic Review*, Vol. 35, No. 3 (August).

Sharma, S. C. and D. Dhakal (1995). "Causal Analyses Between Exports and Economic Growth in Developing Countries." *Applied Economics*, Vol. 26.

Statistics Canada (1998a). *Canadian Economic Observer*, 11-010-XPB. Ottawa: Statistics Canada.

Statistics Canada (1998b). *Canadian Social Trends*. Ottawa: Statistics Canada.

Stokey, N. (1994). "Free Trade, Factor Returns, and Factor Accumulation." Mimeo, University of Chicago.

Tan, H. W. and G. Batra (1995). *Enterprise Training in Developing Countries: Incidence, Productivity Effects, and Policy Implications*. Washington, D.C.: The World Bank, Private Sector Development Department.

Wade, R. (1990). *Governing the Market*. Princeton: Princeton University Press.

Weller, J. (1998). "La Evolución del Empleo en América Latina en Los Años Noventa." Paper prepared for the 1998 meetings of the Latin American Studies Association, Chicago, Sept. 24-26.

Wood, A. (1994). *North-South Trade, Employment and Inequality*. Oxford: Clarendon Press.

World Bank (1987). *World Tables 1987: The Fourth Edition*. Washington, D.C.: The World Bank.

World Bank (1993). *The East Asian Miracle: Economic Growth and Public Policy*. New York: Oxford University Press.

World Bank (1996). *Global Economic Prospects and the Developing Countries*. Washington DC: The World Bank.

World Bank (1999). *World Development Report 1999*. Washington DC: The World Bank.

Chapter 2

CANADIAN VS. AMERICAN LABOR MARKETS IN A CONTEXT OF ECONOMIC INTEGRATION AND STRUCTURAL ADJUSTMENT

by Morley Gunderson, Albert Berry, and Clark Reynolds

2.1 Introduction

Canadians compare themselves in many ways with their neighbors to the south, including the functioning and outcomes of the two labor markets. The latter comparisons can be quite informative; together with the many similarities between the two systems there are interesting differences, which help analysts to understand how structural and policy differences show up in different outcomes. Many of the similarities illustrate the way advanced industrialized countries function; the differences highlight how labor market outcomes may depend on policies in areas such as income maintenance programs, adjustment assistance and legislation, and on the different size of the two economies. The contrasts may also be informative in the light of Canada's many similarities with Latin American countries (size, primary export orientation, focus of trade with a single large trading partner). As such, the Canadian experience may be of considerable relevance to Latin American countries, especially those already embarked on (Mexico) or contemplating trade liberalization with the United States (most of the rest), whether through accession to NAFTA or to other trade agreements.

This chapter outlines views from Canada and the United States on the impact of economic integration/structural adjustment on their labor markets and income distribution. Slightly more emphasis is placed on the Canadian experience because of its probably greater relevance to Latin America. With respect to income distribution, primary attention is paid to issues of wage inequality, the main avenue whereby economic integration is likely to affect labor markets. The chapter begins with a discussion of the concept of structural adjustment as it applies to countries like Canada and the United States. Similarities between Canada and many Latin American countries are then outlined, as are the similarities and differences between Canada and the United States. The focus is on features likely to have the most important implications for labor market adjustment to structural change. Those implications are reviewed both from a theoretical perspective and with illustrative empirical evidence. The chapter concludes with a brief summary and some policy observations.

2.2 Structural Adjustment in Canada and the U.S.

We use the concept of structural adjustment to refer to the process of restructuring designed (i) to recover competitiveness lost due to external shocks and (ii) to develop the capacity to adjust to new shocks and to take advantage of new opportunities. In developing countries such structural adjustment is often imposed as a condition for receiving international aid and assistance. Component policies typically include: macroeconomic stabilization (mainly inflation control); trade liberalization (lowering of tariff and non-tariff barriers, and encouraging exports); deregulation and privatization; control of "excessive" public sector expenditures while encouraging investment in public infrastructure, including education, that can enhance competitiveness.

The sort of structural adjustment called for in countries like Canada and the United States is not imposed as a precondition for international aid and assistance but rather necessitated by the imperatives of interrelated market forces, especially global competition and technological change. These forces have led to dramatic industrial restructuring, especially from manufacturing to both "high-end" services (managerial, administrative, professional, financial), and "low-end" services. They have led to massive "downsizing" as firms, especially large ones, have cut their workforces often through plant closings and mass layoffs. Pressures for structural adjustment have also emanated from the pronounced recessions of the early 1980s and 1990s, with their legacy of high unemployment. And governments have been under considerable pressure to adjust; the imperative of deficit control has given rise to spending restraint, the "taxpayer revolt" often nearly precluding the raising of taxes. Deregulation, privatization, and restraint in public sector wages and employment have all been significant aspects of the adjustment process. Thus, though the source of pressure to adjust may differ from the developing country case, the elements of the process are largely the same.

Since the demand for labor is derived from the production decisions of private firms and the size of the public sector, and is affected by aggregate economic conditions and government policies, structural adjustments have had impacts on labor markets in general and on wages and wage inequality in particular. Demand shifts have been compounded by pressures from the supply side of the labor market. Women in Canada and the United States continue to enter the labor market in large numbers; their labor force participation rate, at approximately 60%, is rapidly approaching that of men (about 75%). The two-earner family is now the norm rather than the exception. The large baby-boom population bulge (those born immediately after World War II and now middle-aged) has created adjustment problems associated with clogged promotion opportunities and skill obsolescence.

Clearly, adjustment is a key feature of the economies and of the labor markets of both Canada and the United States. While subject to similar pressures, the two countries have often responded in different ways, reflecting differences in their labor market institutions, including government policies and programs. Before analyzing these different responses and outcomes, several similarities between Canada and the Latin American countries should be noted; they highlight the potential relevance of the Canadian experience to Latin America—notwithstanding differences between snow and sunshine, and between hockey and football (soccer).

2.3 Similarities Between Canada and Latin America

Canada is a relatively small open economy, with 30% of its GNP emanating from trade, about 75% of which is with the United States. In population, economic size, and bargaining power it is dwarfed by its neighbor and major trading partner. The U.S. also accounts for a high proportion of the large stock of direct foreign investment found in Canada, investment that occurred in large part to "jump the tariff walls" by producing in Canada when that option was more profitable than exporting over Canadian tariffs and quotas. It has tended to take the form of a proliferation of small branch plants of large U.S. multinationals, producing for the small Canadian market. When subject to more open competition, these sometimes inefficiently small-scale plants have incurred significant adjustment costs as they attempt to restructure to serve a more global market. The direct foreign investment also has engendered nationalistic responses, especially in the form of concern over U.S. domination of Canadian cultural and financial matters, a concern which prompted the exclusion of cultural industries from the Canada-U.S. Free Trade Agreement. Both in the motivation and the nationalist reactions, the foreign investment experience in Latin America has had much in common with that in Canada.

Canada is rich in natural resources, with the extraction rents fostering much of its earlier growth. There have been pressures to diversify away from the "hewer of wood and drawer of water" mode. As labor costs increase they also encourage a shift toward higher value-added production as a survival strategy under global competition. Canada's economy, and especially its manufacturing base, developed under a protective tariff, and is now adjusting rapidly to trade liberalization and international competition.

    While the country is huge in area, the vast majority of its population lives in the more densely populated areas close to the border with the United States. For the most part that border is not a natural one in "economic terms"; most geographic structures and many trade flows naturally run North-South. Canada's internal trade, in contrast, has essentially developed on an East-West axis, often through the conscious design of infrastructure—especially railroads, highways and communications links.

    Immigration has been an important source of labor supply, and has contributed to increasing ethnic and cultural diversity. Canada's political development has been heavily influenced by the presence of the two "founding nations" (with English and French roots), as witness the high degree of decentralization. Government policies consciously foster multiculturalism. The phrase "vertical mosaic" contrasts to the "melting pot" stereotype often used to describe the pressure to assimilate in the United States. In spite of official bilingualism and support for multiculturalism, ethnic and regional tensions are pronounced, involving especially the indigenous people, the strong separatist movement in the province of Quebec, and the considerable disaffection in parts of the West.

    Clearly, many of these and other features of Canada have their parallels in Latin America and Canada's recent experience of tighter economic integration with the U.S. is highly relevant. Latin American countries may be particularly informed by Canada's experience in adjusting to structural change, especially as the region embarks on the road to greater trade and economic integration with the United States. The Canadian experience on the labor front is our focus here.

2.4 Similarities and Differences in Canadian-U.S. Labor Markets

Similarities

Both Canada and the U.S. are advanced industrialized economies in transition to the "information-age" with its greater emphasis on knowledge-based technology. Their conventional manufacturing base with its middle income jobs is being displaced by service jobs tending more often to occupy the polar ends of the wage spectrum—the high-wage "good jobs" in managerial, administrative, professional and financial activities on the one hand, and low-wage "bad jobs" in the personal service sector on the other. There is considerable concern in both countries about the possibility of downward wage convergence as they expand trade with low-wage countries (Reynolds, 1992). Relative to Latin American countries, both are high-wage economies. On a global basis, however, their exchange rate-adjusted labor costs are more or less "in the middle," close to Japan, slightly higher than France and Italy, but considerably below the higher cost Scandinavian and other European countries, especially Germany (Gunderson and Verma, 1992, 67).

In both countries labor adjustment is primarily through the external labor market, involving worker layoffs into unemployment followed by recall, move to another firm or departure from the labor force. Much less adjustment occurs internally to the firm—for example through transfer to different jobs or retraining during downturns. Adjustment of the wage bill tends to be through employment reduction more than through wages or hours. Although both countries have female labor force participation rates approaching those of men, women still tend on average to occupy the lower wage jobs. Both also have increasing amounts of nonstandard, precarious employment associated with sub-contracting, temporary help agencies, fixed-duration employment contracts, and permanent part-time work.

Canadian and American collective bargaining tends to be decentralized, focused at the enterprise level. There is little corporatism or trade union involvement at the higher political levels, although unions are one of the important interest groups.

The bulk of recent job creation in both countries is alleged to be due to the growth and creation of small firms, although some controversy has emerged on this point (Brown, Hamilton and Medoff, 1990; Davis, Haltiwanger and Schuh, 1993; Audretsch, 1998.) Since small firms have high death rates as well as birth rates, they are also the source of considerable job destruction. Their *net* job creation is thus considerably less than their *gross* job creation.[1] Further compounding this issue is the fact that the distinctions between small and large firms are becoming increasingly blurred. Some formerly vertically integrated firms are essentially becoming "holding companies" forming quasi-permanent alliances with a host of small "downstream" suppliers and "upstream" distributors. In many circumstances, these small firms hire the employees of the restructured large firms. Job churning of this sort would be associated statistically with job losses from the large firms and job gains for the small firms. In such circumstances, however, the large firms are still an important "ultimate" source of job creation, through their alliances and joint ventures. Such qualifications notwithstanding, recent studies

[1] Small firms may also be "credited" with more job creation and large firms with more job destruction than they should. In the case of a firm that is normally large but has a temporary reduction in employment, that job loss will be attributed to a large firm. After the employment reduction it will appear in a smaller firm category and when its employment returns to normal, that growth will be attributed to the category of smaller firms. Overall, temporary employment fluctuations are such that the job losses are disproportionately associated with large firms and the gains with small firms, and this must be taken into account when one assesses the validity of the claim that the small firms are the main source of employment creation.

seem to confirm the major role of small firms, both in Canada (Baldwin and Picot 1995; Amit, 1998) and the United Sates (Audretsch, 1995 and 1999).

Differences

Their considerable similarities notwithstanding, the U.S. and Canadian labor markets have notable differences, many of special interest to Latin America since they give evidence on the extent to which independent labor market and social policies can be followed by small countries substantially integrated with larger dominant ones. Of prime importance, Canada tends to have a more extensive state-supported social safety net of income transfer programs, legislative protection, and labor adjustment programs.[2] Income maintenance programs (e.g. social assistance or welfare) tend to have easier eligibility requirements and more generous income support. Canada's unemployment insurance tends to be more generous in various dimensions: greater coverage, easier eligibility, longer duration, and higher income replacement rates. Both countries have state-supported employment information and job matching agencies, labor adjustment programs that provide training, counseling, mobility assistance, and wage subsidies for employing particular disadvantaged groups.

Differences between the training and labor adjustment programs are difficult to establish with precision given the complexities of these programs and the fact that they are often operated differently from how they appear on the books.[3] Both countries are currently decentralizing implementation toward the local level, training is increasingly emphasized over income maintenance, and disadvantaged groups are favored. The U.S. has a special program component for workers whose jobs have been lost due to trade liberalization, but it has been ineffective either because of excessively stringent eligibility requirements or, when this has not been the case, because many workers displaced by other forces have claimed damage from import competition (McCleery and Reynolds, 1991)[4]. Overall, Canada appears to allocate a larger portion of its GDP to training and labor adjustment

[2] There is no single comprehensive source that systematically documents the differences in such policies and programs between Canada and the U.S., or their cost implications. Sources that provide information on different subsets of these programs include: Betcherman and Gunderson (1990), Card and Freeman (1993); Gunderson (1993a); and Rosen (1993).

[3] Details of the specific labor adjustment programs, in the context of their relevance to the effects of trade liberalization, are given in Rosen (1993) for the United States, and in Finbow (1993) and Gunderson (1993a) for Canada.

[4] Assessments of specific trade adjustment assistance as opposed to more general adjustment assistance are cited in Gunderson (1993b, 25). Main concerns with the former are the difficulty or impossibility of determining whether the displacement is due to trade liberalization or some other source, and the logic of treating workers adversely affected by trade liberalization differently from those hurt by other phenomena.

programs than does the U.S., though both rank low compared to most other industrialized countries (OECD, 1990). General education programs also tend to be somewhat more "egalitarian" in Canada than in the U.S. as evidenced by a higher proportion of the population that completes high school or basic vocational education, and a smaller portion that completes university.

With respect to legislated labor standards, minimum wages in Canada tend to be higher relative to the average industrial wage and hence apply to a larger segment of the workforce. Regulation of work conditions is more extensive, as are requirements for unpaid maternity leave (often supported from unemployment insurance funds). Comparable-worth legislation (providing equal pay for work of equal value between men and women) is more prevalent in Canada, whereas in the U.S. it is largely "on hold" and limited to a small number of state governments. Canada also has more extensive requirements for severance pay and advance notice in case of mass layoffs or plant closings; more protection for workers who are fired without "just cause," in contrast to the "employment at will" doctrine that tends to prevail in the United States; more extensive occupational health and safety laws, often requiring joint labor- management health and safety committees at the workplace and granting workers the right-to-refuse unsafe work, and more generous compensation for those who are injured. Canada's universal health care system contrasts with the more market-driven system of private insurance carriers that prevails in the United States.

Collective bargaining law in Canada is much more conducive to the formation and retention of trade unions (reflected in much higher unionization rates—see below) through such features as: certification through the signing of cards without a vote; stricter enforcement against unfair labor practices engaged in by firms; the possibility of mandatory first-contract arbitration; requirements for employers to collect union dues and remit them to the union; prohibitions on the use of strikebreakers during a strike; and more frequent granting of the right to strike to public sector workers.

Finally, while neither country is corporatist, organized labor in Canada is more involved politically, trying to influence social policies and hence the "social wage." Canada has a left-leaning, union supported, social democratic party (New Democratic Party) that has often held power at the provincial level, and has been influential at the federal level. Consensual decision making via tripartite cooperation among labor, management, and government is attempted more frequently. Unlike the President in the United States, who has a party affiliation but is independently elected, the Canadian Prime Minister and the provincial premiers are simply the leaders of the party in power. Whereas President Reagan had sufficient independent power to fire the striking air traffic controllers in the PATCO strike and put permanent replacements in their stead, under the Canadian system, Parliament would have to make that decision and would be subject to more public debate and scrutiny.

In Canada, most labor matters and 90% of the workforce fall under provincial jurisdiction. In the United States, by contrast, the federal government sets uniform labor laws; state legislation can be more stringent but it cannot fall below these federally set standards.

2.5 Implications for Labor Adjustment

The combination of many similarities and some differences between Canadian and American economic and social structures, institutions, laws and programs, have been used as the basis for "natural experiments" to evaluate the impact of differences in such laws, policies and programs. The similarities provide a natural "control" for the potentially confounding effect of many variables that influence labor market and social outcomes and that could produce different outcomes in the two countries. The differences create the opportunity to identify *ex post* the effects of those background conditions and policy instruments that do in fact differ, crucial for determining the impact of policy changes. This approach has been applied to the analysis of immigration policies (Chiswick, 1992) as well as policies in the labor market and social areas (Card and Freeman, 1993).

The main issue for purposes of this analysis is whether the more interventionist strategies followed in Canada, compared to the more laissez-faire, market oriented strategies of the United States, have made a significant difference to labor market outcomes in general and to the labor market impacts of structural adjustment in particular. This issue has not been addressed in an overall systematic research agenda so the lack of a clear consensus is not surprising. But there are some suggestive results.

Unionization Rates

There is general agreement, for example, that differences in the laws and institutions have been important in sustaining unionization in Canada, in contrast to the dramatic decline in the United States (Riddell, 1993, and references cited therein). Unionization rates in Canada are over twice the 16% level that now exists in the United States, while both countries had identical rates of about 30% in the mid 1960s. There is no agreement, however, on the impact of the different degrees of unionization on labor market responses to structural adjustment, or on how unions have affected productivity and overall firm performance (Gunderson, 1989). Unions can slow adjustment through various mechanisms: restrictive workplace practices (e.g., restrictions on subcontracting and on who can do particular types of work); wage rigidity; seniority for promotions and layoffs; restrictions on technological change; and pattern bargaining. But unions can also be flexible in these areas, and thereby facilitate adjustment by articulating the preferences of their membership and providing information on job alternatives. While they may slow the adjustment process, they can also make it more humane by bargaining for such items as advance notice, severance pay and early retirement.

Wage Polarization, Income Inequality and Poverty

The dramatic changes affecting the labor markets of Canada and the United States over the last decade or so have led to greater wage inequality and polarization. Middle income, blue-collar manufacturing jobs are being replaced by a combination of high-wage and low-wage jobs. To a large extent their loss can be attributed to their being in the "tradeable" sector, subject to substitution by imports especially from low-wage countries. The same applies to some other lower wage jobs, where earnings are depressed by the downward pressure from workers displaced from the manufacturing sector. Many jobs at the higher end of the wage distribution (managerial, professional, administrative) are protected from import competition by being in the "less tradeable" sectors. Others are associated with high value-added exports. Wage polarization has also been fostered by technological change that happens to be biased toward skilled labor and away from unskilled labor.

In the U.S. wage polarization was especially notable over the 1980s. In Canada it has been somewhat less marked, mainly because wages at the higher end in Canada have been dampened[5] by a larger influx of higher educated individuals (Freeman and Needles, 1993) and because of the higher unionization rate, given that unions tend to compress wage differentials (Lemieux, 1993). While both trade liberalization and technological change appear to have contributed to the polarization, there is disagreement over their relative importance.[6]

Meanwhile, income inequality and poverty increased in the United States over the 1980s but declined in Canada, mainly because of the more generous income support programs (Blank and Hanratty, 1993). These events followed the near stability of family income distribution in both countries during the 1970s

---

[5] Thus between 1979 and 1987 when the earnings differential for males with completed college and those with less than completed high school (calculated from the coefficients of ordinary least squares equations also including age, age squared, marital status and regional dummies) rose from 77% to 86% in the U.S, the corresponding figure for Canada stayed about constant at 60% (see Table 1 of Blackburn and Bloom, 1993, 255).

[6] Borjas, Freeman and Katz (1992), Katz and Murphy (1992), Murphy and Welch (1991, 1992) and Leamer (1993, 1994) find that import competition from labor intensive products had its most adverse effect on wages at the lower end of the skill spectrum in the U.S. and that this contributed to the growing wage inequality that occurred especially in the 1980s. Krugman and Lawrence (1993) find trade liberalization not to be an important contributing factor, at least relative to biased technological change that reduced the relative demand for less skilled workers.

(Nelson, 1994, 30). The widening dispersion of family income in the U.S. during the 1980s reflected a growing earnings inequality, a trend common to many industrial countries at this time.[7] Though a number of studies have reported that the increased variance of earnings in the U.S. is mainly due to an increase in the variance of the pure price of labor, Haveman and Buron (1993, 129) argue that the choice (or imposition) of different work hours may have played a significant role, in which case the much-commented increases in part-time work, temporary work, etc. may be a significant, albeit not yet well understood aspect of increasing inequality. During the 1990s the level of inequality does not appear to have changed much in the U.S. Canada's pretax and transfer distribution record has weakened, though post-tax and transfer distribution appears to have changed less.

Non-Standard, Precarious Employment

A significant recent change in both Canadian and American labor markets has been the increasing variety (polarization?) in the *type* of jobs. Much new job creation has been referred to as non-standard, precarious employment: limited duration contracts; subcontracting; temporary help agencies; permanent part-time jobs; and "homeworking" done in the person's home, especially in the garment trades. These jobs tend to provide low pay, few fringe benefits, little job security, and little protection under employment standards laws. In some instances they act as a buffer to give the firm flexibility and allow it to absorb demand shocks—a "just-in-time" workforce to meet the "just-in-time" delivery pressures that have become more common. In many respects, such precarious jobs are to developed economies what the informal sector is to the less developed economies.

Systematic evidence is lacking to indicate whether the growth of such jobs has been greater in Canada or in the United States. Possibly Canada's higher degree of unionization, coupled with strong union resistance to such jobs has restrained the increase in that country. However, they may also be used by employers as a way around the higher labor costs and rigidities imposed by unions and the regulations imposed by governments—both of which are more prominent in Canada. If that has been a prime motivation of firms, growth of such jobs may have been faster in Canada.

---

[7] International earnings comparisons using the Luxembourg Income Study data show increases in earnings inequality in the early 1980s for the U.S., Canada, West Germany and Sweden (Nelson, 1994, 51-2), with the highest level of inequality that of the U.S. but with Canada second among these countries.

Changing Workplace Practices

Structural adjustments have also forced firms in Canada and the United States to make dramatic changes in their internal workplace practices. Most have been designed to improve flexibility and adaptability, as well as the quality and commitment to customer satisfaction associated with higher value-added production. The number of job classifications has been reduced and workers undertake a wider range of tasks, putting a premium on multi-skilling and general training. Employee participation has been fostered through various mechanisms including quality circles, team production, suggestion schemes, and even employee ownership schemes. Compensation has become more flexible in various ways: wage concessions; piece rates; profit sharing; pay for performance; and two-tier contracts where new employees are hired at lower rates. Working hours have become more varied to include: flexible working hours where start and end times can vary across individuals; compressed workweeks where for example 40 hours is compressed into four 10 hour days; early retirement, often induced by pension enhancements; job sharing where two individuals share the same job at different times and each on a part-time basis; and worksharing, where all employees agree to reduce their working time in return for no layoffs.

Though systematic evidence does not exist on the extent of each of these different workplace practices, it is clear that they have increased over time and are more prevalent in the United States than in Canada (Long, 1989). This is consistent with the more laissez-faire, market-oriented nature of the U.S. labor market relative both to Canada and to most industrialized countries.

Growth and Productivity

Structural adjustment to meet new competitive challenges requires productivity growth to ensure that real wages can rise, thereby sustaining improvements in the standard of living, while prices remain competitive. A key element of competitiveness in high labor cost countries is high productivity—essential to allow them to compete with countries where labor costs are in the neighborhood of one tenth of those of Canada and the United States.

Canada's per capita income, measured in purchasing power parity (PPP) terms has been systematically a few percentage points below that of the United States. During the 1970s Canada's growth of GDP and of GDP per capita was considerably the faster of the two (see Table 1.3); by the 1980s the gaps had almost disappeared and during the 1990s performance has been stronger in the U.S. Much of the difference in overall growth was related to differences in the rate of expansion of employment. Thus GDP per employed worker grew a little faster in Canada during the 1970s and the 1980s, but markedly faster in the U.S. during

1990-97 (1.3% per year vs. 0.8% per year).

While it is growth in labor productivity that is most closely linked to increasing earnings and per capita incomes, growth of total factor productivity (TFP)[8] is often the subject of special attention since it measures how extensively and effectively the economy is incorporating new technologies. At the aggregate level it also reflects how effectively the economy allocates resources among sectors. TFP growth can be, but is not always, more important in overall economic growth than the complementary source, increases in the quantum of factor inputs.

Throughout most of the 1970s and early 1980s, productivity growth was stagnant or even negative in the major industrialized countries.[9] However, after the recession of the early 1980s, it rebounded substantially in most of these countries, especially the United States, a fact which is reflected in the accelerating growth of labor productivity (Table 1.3). Canada appears to have been an exception, with relatively stagnant productivity.[10] This is blamed for significant increases in unit labor cost (wages adjusted for productivity and the exchange rate) in Canada relative to the United States, just as and after Canada entered into the Free Trade Agreement with that country in 1989. Though differences in productivity growth can in principle be offset by devaluation vis-à-vis a country's major trading partners, Canada's policy space in this regard is limited by the need to avoid the major outflows of capital which devaluation can lead to. A similar constraint is now faced, albeit in lesser degree by Mexico since its entry into NAFTA and will be faced by other entrants to a regional trading bloc including the United States. Until quite recently, Canada's interest rate has habitually been maintained at a level higher than that of the United States in order to avoid capital outflows (and/or foster inflows) and to restrain inflation; both these complications will become more important in Latin American countries which enter such trading arrangements.

Unemployment

A similar negative picture of Canadian economic performance relative to the United States emerges with respect to unemployment rates. These rates generally differed little between the two countries from the 1950s through the 1970s, but

---

[8] Total factor productivity refers to the ratio between output and inputs. To measure changes over time it is necessary to choose a system for weighting the various inputs which are distinguished; normally these weights are the market prices of the inputs. The TFP concept can refer to one product or industry or to the economy as a whole; whenever more than one product is included, the output measure also involves aggregation similar to that undertaken for the inputs.

[9] Data for this paragraph are discussed in Gunderson (1993b, 39), Prosperity Secretariat (1991, 9), and Porter (1991).

[10] It should be noted that the accurate measurement of total factor productivity change is difficult, and there are varying views on just what has happened to Canada's productivity growth, both in absolute terms and relative to the U.S.

they began diverging systematically during the 1980s; both the recession of the early 1980s and that of the early 1990s pushed the rate up in both countries but by more in Canada and there was less post-recession decline in Canada. The mid-1999 rate of 8% in Canada was nearly twice that of the U.S. —a seemingly dramatic difference for countries whose economies are fairly similar in many other respects. Card and Riddell (1993) provide empirical evidence that part of the growing gap can be attributed to the more generous unemployment insurance scheme in Canada, although they also indicate that most of it remains unexplained. The highest levels of unemployment in Canada are found in the Atlantic provinces, where the impact of that scheme is most marked. Note that the employment (to population) ratio is about the same in the two countries, suggesting that people who appear in the Canadian data as unemployed would in the Unites States appear as nonparticipants. This outcome is consistent with Canada's institutional context being one which encourages people falling in the grey area of unstable jobs or unstable desire to work to get short-term jobs in order to qualify for unemployment insurance.

2.6 Concluding Observations

While the Canadian and American labor markets are similar in many respects, they differ in other important dimensions. This is especially the case with respect to government policies in such areas as income maintenance, adjustment assistance, labor standards and collective bargaining laws. These in turn can have important implications for how labor markets respond to structural adjustments.

In general, Canada follows a more interventionist route, compared to the more laissez-faire, market-oriented strategy followed in the United States. Although a systematic analysis of the effect of these different strategies is not available, a limited number of studies suggest that they have led to a "softening" of the adverse consequences from structural adjustment in Canada compared to the United States. For example, Canada appears to have a more extensive social safety net, more protection provided through labor standards and unions, and less wage and overall economic inequality. This may come at a price, however, in such forms as lower productivity and higher unemployment. These in turn could have negative feedback effects on long-run income growth. It would however be premature to make a judgement as to whether the comparison between the two countries reflects a classic tradeoff between issues of efficiency and equity, with the U.S. labor market operating more efficiently but with more adverse distributional consequences. Over the period 1970-97 (but not over 1980-97) Canada's economy has grown more rapidly than the U.S. one, as has output per worker. Since 1990, however, the U.S. economy has grown faster, with both labor productivity and TFP increasing more than in Canada. In general, the suggestion that Canada may be paying a price in terms of labor market inefficiency and resulting loss of growth does not meet obvious support from the longer-run record, but could be an evolving problem. What the comparison of the two cases does show is that alternative policy choices are possible, and that they can affect how labor markets respond to structural change.

Whether such policy choices will be circumscribed by global market forces in the long-run remains an open and interesting question. With greater trade liberalization and capital mobility, countries (and regions and cities within countries) may find it more difficult to establish costly policies and programs that have only an equity oriented rationale and that conflict with efficiency and competitiveness. Countries may increasingly find themselves competing for business investment and plant location decisions—and the associated jobs—on the basis of providing a low-cost regulatory environment, including labor laws, policies and programs.

In many areas, this may be desirable, getting rid of "excessive" regulations that have no efficiency rationale and that serve only to protect the rents created by such regulations. Policies that have an efficiency rationale, for example, that provide a human capital infrastructure or that facilitate the operation of markets should not only survive but thrive under such jurisdictional competition. The same is true of policies that have an equity rationale but that also enhance efficiency, perhaps by reducing resistance to change, or by providing a more stable political environment.[11] In other cases, the jurisdiction may be willing to pay the price for policies that have a pure equity rationale and that conflict with efficiency—that price is now simply more explicit in the form of lost business investment and the associated jobs.

Whether this will lead to a "race to the bottom" in terms of social policies and legislative regulations, or to a decrease in inefficient rent seeking policies, remains an interesting and important question. The provision of answers will benefit from more research on several factors: the extent of different labor market regulations and policies across countries; the degree to which their equity and efficiency objectives conflict and they impose costs and conflict with competitiveness; the extent to which business investment and plant location decisions are affected, positively and negatively, by such programs; and the degree to which different jurisdictions alter their policy initiatives in response to such investment decisions. These will be important areas for further research in Canada and the United States as well as in Latin America. It is important to know not only how labor market institutions and policies affect labor market outcomes, but also how labor market institutions and policies themselves are shaped by the forces of

---

[11] In commenting on the reasons for the success of Costa Rica's adjustment strategy of the 1980s, Gindling and Berry (1992, 1612), for example, indicate: "Perhaps the most general has been a relatively satisfactory sharing of the burden of crises/ adjustment such that no groups remained so disgruntled as to pursue highly disruptive tactics."

global competition and economic interdependence.

REFERENCES

Amit, R. (1998). "The Dynamics of Canadian SMEs." Paper presented at the conference on *Small and Medium Enterprise, Labor Markets, and Income Distribution in Latin America and the Caribbean*, Buenos Aires, August 24-25.

Audretsch, D. B. (1995). *Innovation and Industry Evolution*. Cambridge, Mass.: MIT Press.

Audretsch, D. B. (1998). "The Economic Role of Small and Medium-Sized Enterprises: The United States." Paper presented at the World Bank workshop on *Small and Medium Enterprises*, Chaing Mai, Thailand, August 10-11.

Baldwin, J. and G. Picot (1995). "Employment Generation by Small Producers: A Profile of Growing Small and Medium-Sized Enterprises in Canada." *Small Business Economics*, Vol. 7.

Betcherman, G. and M. Gunderson (1990). "Canada-U.S. Free Trade and Labor Relations." *Labor Law Journal*, Vol. 41 (August), pp. 454-460.

Blackburn, M. L. and D. E. Bloom (1993). "The Distribution of Family Income: Measuring and Explaining Changes in the 1980s for Canada and the United States." In *Small Differences that Matter: Labor Markets and Income Maintenance in Canada and the United States*, D. Card and R. B. Freeman, eds. Chicago: University of Chicago Press for the National Bureau of Economic Research.

Blank, R. and M. Hanratty (1993). "Responding to Need: A Comparison of Social Safety Nets in Canada and the United States." In *Small Differences that Matter: Labor Markets and Income Maintenance in Canada and the United States*, D. Card and R. Freeman, eds. Chicago: University of Chicago Press, pp. 191-232.

Borjas, G., R. Freeman, and L. Katz (1992). "On the Labor Market Effects of Immigration and Trade." In *The Economic Effects of Immigration in Source and Receiving Countries*, G. Borjas and R. Freeman, eds. Chicago: University of Chicago Press.

Brown, C., J. Hamilton and J. Medoff (1990). *Employers Large and Small*. Cambridge, Mass.: Harvard University Press.

Card, D. and R. Freeman, eds. (1993). *Small Differences that Matter: Labor Markets and Income Maintenance in Canada and the United States*. Chicago: University of Chicago Press.

Card, D. and W. C. Riddell (1993). "A Comparative Analysis of Unemployment in Canada and the United States." In *Small Differences that Matter: Labor Markets and Income Maintenance in Canada and the United States*, D. Card and R. Freeman, eds. Chicago: University of Chicago Press, pp. 149-190.

Chiswick, B., ed. (1992). *Immigration, Language and Ethnicity: Canada and the United States*. Washington, D.C.: AEI Press.

Davis, S., J. Haltiwanger and S. Schuh (1993). "Small Business and Job Creation: Dissecting the Myth and Reassessing the Facts." National Bureau of Economic Research, Working Paper No. 4492 (October).

Downes, A. (1993). "Trade Unions and a Sustainable Labor Market Response to Structural Adjustment Programs in the Caribbean." *Caribbean Labor Journal*, Vol. 3 (June), pp. 23-27.

Finbow, R. (1993). "Free Trade and Labor Market Adjustment in Canada: The Training Imperative." *North American Outlook*, Vol. 4 (September), pp. 39-66.

Freeman, R. B., and L. F. Katz 1991). "Industrial Wage and Employment Determination in an Open Economy." In *Immigration, Trade, and the Labor Market*, J. Abowd and R. Freeman, eds. Chicago: University of Chicago Press, pp. 235-259.

Freeman, R. and K. Needles (1993). "Skill Differentials in Canada in an Era of Rising Labor Market Inequality." In *Small Differences that Matter: Labor Markets and Income Maintenance in Canada and the United States*, D. Card and R. Freeman, eds. Chicago: University of Chicago Press, pp. 45-68.

Gindling, T. and A. Berry (1992). "The Performance of the Labor Market During Recession and Structural Adjustment: Costa Rica in the 1980s." *World Development*, Vol. 20 (November), pp. 1599-1616.

Gunderson, M. (1989). "Union Impact on Compensation, Productivity and Managing the Organization." In *Union-Management Relations in Canada*, J. Anderson, M. Gunderson and A. Ponak, eds. Toronto: Addison-Wesley, pp. 347-370.

Gunderson, M. (1993a). "Labor Adjustment Under NAFTA: Canadian Issues." *North American Outlook*, Vol. 4 (September), pp. 3-21.

Gunderson, M. (1993b). *Labor Market Impacts of Free Trade*. Vancouver: Fraser Institute.

Gunderson, M. and A. Verma (1992). "Canadian Labor Policies and Global Competition." *Canadian Business Law Journal*, Vol. 20 (March), pp. 63-89.

Haveman, R. H. and L. Buron (1993). "The Growth in Male Earnings Inequality, 1973-1988: The Role of Earnings Capacity and Utilization." In *The Changing Distribution of Income in an Open U.S. Economy*, J. H. Bergstrand, T. F. Cosimano, J. W. Houck and R. G. Sheehan, eds. Amsterdam: North-Holland.

Katz, L. F., and K. Murphy (1992). "Changes in Relative Wages, 1963-1987: Supply and Demand Factors." *Quarterly Journal of Economics*, 107 (February), pp. 35-78.

Krugman, P. and R. Lawrence (1993). "Trade, Jobs and Wages." National Bureau of Economic Research, Working Paper No. 4478.

Leamer, E. (1993). "Wage Effects of a U.S.-Mexican Free Trade Agreement." In *The Mexico-U.S. Trade Agreement*, P. Graber, ed. Cambridge, Mass.: MIT Press, pp. 57-125.

Leamer, E. (1994). "Trade, Wages and Revolving Door Ideas." National Bureau of Economic Research, Working Paper No. 4716.

Lemieux, T. (1993). "Unions and Wage Inequality in Canada and the United States." In *Small Differences that Matter: Labor Markets and Income Maintenance in Canada and the United States,* D. Card and R. Freeman, eds. Chicago: University of Chicago Press, pp. 69-108.

Long, R. (1989). "Patterns of Workplace Innovation in Canada." *Relations Industrielles/ Industrial Relations,* Vol. 44, No. 4, pp. 805-824.

McCleery, R., and C. Reynolds (1991). "A Study of the Impact of a U.S.-Mexico Free Trade Agreement on Medium-Term Employment, Wages and Production in the United States: Are New Labor Market Policies Needed?" Paper presented at the Conference on *North American Free Trade,* Washington, D.C., June.

Murphy, K. M., and F. Welch (1991). " Wage Differentials in the 1980s: The Role of International Trade." In *Workers and Their Wages: Changing Patterns in the United States,* M. Kosters, ed. Washington, D.C.: American Enterprise Institute.

Murphy, K. M., and F. Welch (1992). "The Structure of Wages." *Quarterly Journal of Economics,* Vol. 107 (February), pp. 285-326.

Nelson, C. T. (1994). "Levels of and Changes in the Distribution of U.S. Income." In *The Changing Distribution of Income in an Open U.S. Economy,* J. H. Bergstrand, T. F. Cosimano, J. W. Houck and R. G. Sheehan, eds. Amsterdam: North-Holland.

Organization for Economic Co-operation and Development (OECD) (1990). *Labor Market Policies for the 1990s.* Paris: OECD.

Porter, M. (1991). *Canada at the Crossroads: The Reality of a New Competitive Environment.* Ottawa: Business Council on National Issues.

Prosperity Secretariat (1992). *Canada's Prosperity: Challenges and Prospects.* Ottawa: Government of Canada.

Reynolds, C. (1992) "Will a Free Trade Agreement Lead to Wage Convergence? Implications for Mexico and the United States." In *U.S.-Mexico Relations: Labor Market Interdependence,* J. Bustamante, C. Reynolds, and R. Hinojosa-Ojeda, eds. Stanford, CA: Stanford University Press.

Riddell, W. C. (1993). "Unionization in Canada and the United States." In *Small Differences that Matter: Labor Markets and Income Maintenance in Canada and the United States,* D. Card and R. Freeman, eds. Chicago: University of Chicago Press, pp. 109-148.

Rosen, H. (1993). "Assisting U.S. Labor Market Adjustment to Freer Trade Under NAFTA. *North American Outlook,* Vol. 4 (September), pp. 22-38.

Chapter 3

UNEMPLOYMENT INSURANCE: LESSONS FROM CANADA

by Morley Gunderson and W. Craig Riddell

3.1 Introduction

As countries engage in greater economic integration, programs like unemployment insurance (UI) become subject to increased public scrutiny and policy analysis. This is true both in countries that have an extensive history and involvement with UI, and in countries that have little or no history with such programs, or that are contemplating their implementation.[1]

In Canada, the policy attention to UI stems from a variety of sources, many of which are associated with the greater economic integration and trade liberalization that is occurring. Concern over government deficits, and a reluctance to raise taxes to reduce the deficit, has focused attention on government expenditure reductions, with transfer programs like UI being an obvious target. Economic restructuring from declining to expanding industries and regions (much of which is induced by trade liberalization and technological change) has raised questions about the viability of passive income maintenance programs like UI, that may encourage people to stay in declining industries and regions. Emphasis is increasingly placed on "active" adjustment assistance programs, like training and mobility, that may encourage the reallocation of labor from declining to expanding industries and regions. The increasing average duration of unemployment raises questions about the viability of conventional UI, designed as it is to assist people during short periods of temporary unemployment. In many cases, the

---

[1] As indicated in Storey and Neisner (1995) and the U.S. Department of Health and Social Services (1994), slightly less than half (i.e., 75 of the 163) of the countries examined have some form of legislation requiring the compensation of unemployed workers. Of these, 12 (including Bolivia, Colombia and Mexico) required only severance pay. Argentina, Chile, and Venezuela had UI as part of compulsory social insurance, as is the case with Canada and other major industrialized (G7) countries.

questioning—indeed some would label, attack—on UI is simply part of the more conservative market-oriented agenda that is prominent in many developed countries. Even in circumstances where that agenda is not embraced, however, there is general concern that UI has a number of undesirable incentive effects in various areas: work decisions; human capital formation; mobility; occupational choice, especially with respect to self-employment; and artificial job creation geared to the ultimate receipt of UI rather than sustainable market opportunities. As well, there is increasing concern that the payroll taxes that are used to finance programs like UI may discourage job creation. For developed countries like Canada, the policy concerns associated with UI are reflected in the fact that reform of the UI system has been the subject of a wide range of recent reform initiatives in Canada.[2]

With trade liberalization and greater economic integration, the above issues have taken on increased importance. On the one hand, there is greater demand for policies to deal with the adjustment consequences of the associated restructuring. This is especially the case if the policies can assist those who are most adversely affected by such restructuring and thereby reduce the resistance to the efficiency-enhancing changes. On the other hand, the greater competitive pressures that exist increase the resistance to the cost of such programs. With increased capital mobility, greater flexibility in multinational plant location decisions, and lower tariffs, employers can more easily locate to countries with lower labor costs (including those costs that are enhanced by regulations or programs like UI) and then export into the countries with the higher labor costs. Accordingly, governments feel an urgency to reduce such costly programs.

For developing countries, programs like unemployment insurance are also of increased policy interest. As larger portions of their workforce enter the formal sector that tends to produce tradeable goods, more attention is being paid to programs that can mitigate the adjustment consequences associated with formal labor markets. Some of this is prompted by pressure from the more developed trading partners who are trying to prevent downward harmonization of their own labor regulations by encouraging upward harmonization in their less developed trading partners so as to develop a more "level playing field."[3] Some of the pressure within the developing countries is also prompted by a desire to find alternatives to other labor regulations that may be regarded as even more detrimental to competitiveness, such as the high costs of terminating employees in the formal sector. If this cost is reduced, and terminated employees enter the formal

---

[2] MacDonald (1985), Forget (1986), House (1986), and Human Resources Development Canada (1994a, 1994b). Whether this constant evaluation of UI is a sign of an intent to reform, or a sign of the difficulty of dealing with an intractable problem, is an interesting question.

[3] The extent to which this reflects a genuine concern for workers in the less regulated country, or simply thinly disguised protectionism to raise labor costs among their competitors is an open question.

labor market to search for new jobs, then UI is often regarded as a possible form of assistance for the unemployed.

In spite of the fact that Latin American countries trade and interact more with the U.S. than with Canada, and the U.S. is a more dominant economy, Latin American countries often look to Canada as an alternative to the U.S. model. In most areas of labor regulation and social policy, Canada is "in between" the more market-oriented, laissez-faire approach followed in the U.S. and the more regulated approach of Europe and many Latin American countries. As such, the Canadian experience is often of particular interest to developing countries that are establishing labor regulations and adjustment programs for their formal labor markets.

The purpose of this chapter is to highlight the Canadian experience with one labor market program—unemployment insurance. It begins with a basic description of Canadian UI—its history and evolution, its current structure, and the recent and proposed changes. The incentive effects of UI are then analyzed with respect to various dimensions: work decisions; human capital formation; mobility; occupational choice; and job creation. Concerns over Canada's UI program are dealt with throughout the analysis, and the chapter concludes with a discussion of the lessons to be learned from that program, emphasizing those that may be most relevant to countries that are considering instituting or expanding UI. One such lesson is that a UI system can evolve away from its original purpose, and once established can alter incentives and entrench institutional arrangements favorable to the continuation of the program. Hence, it is important to "get it right" from the start, and to be aware of the unintended effects it can have.

3.2 Basic Description of Canadian UI

Understanding the history and evolution of UI in Canada, its current structure, and recent and proposed changes, is important in deriving a clear picture for the lessons to be learned from the Canadian UI experience.

Establishment of UI[4]

Formal unemployment insurance schemes were first established in the early 1900s in countries like the United Kingdom (1911), Italy (1919) and Germany (1927). Largely in response to the sustained high unemployment rates of the Great

---

[4] See Dingledine (1981), Green and Riddell (1993), Human Resources Development Canada (1994a), Organization for Economic Co-operation and Development (1994), Storey and Neisner (1995), and references cited therein.

Depression of the 1930s, these were substantially expanded, and UI programs were added in countries like the United States (1935) and Canada (1940). In Canada, an earlier proposal in 1935 was declared unconstitutional since labor matters fall under the provincial and not federal jurisdiction. The importance attached to the matter is reflected in the passing of a constitutional amendment, an unusual step but required for the provinces to cede their normally jealously guarded jurisdiction in this area to the federal government.

As the name unemployment insurance implies, the program was initially set up to provide temporary assistance against the risk of income loss associated with becoming unemployed. As such, the program followed certain basic principles of insurance designed in part to deal with the common problems of insurance markets pertaining to adverse selection and moral hazard. Adverse selection occurs when individuals who have private information on the fact that they have above-average risk tend to buy more insurance because the premium is based on the average risk of the group. This problem was to be minimized by excluding persons with no previous labor market experience and who otherwise might simply enter the labor market to collect UI. Furthermore, for those who were eligible, a fixed mandatory premium was set so that high-risk individuals could not buy more insurance nor could low-risk individuals opt out.

Moral hazard occurs when an individual's behavior influences the probability of the risky event, and their having insurance makes that event more likely. This challenge was to be confronted in various ways. Recipients were required to be searching for work and willing and able to accept employment in order to maintain eligibility. When UI was first established in Canada, a low benefit (i.e., income replacement) rate and short benefit duration period were set (discussed in more detail subsequently) so as to discourage people from voluntarily becoming unemployed, and to encourage them to look for work. The self-employed were excluded since they could obviously "lay themselves off" and collect UI. In the initial phases certain occupations were also excluded (e.g., agriculture, forestry, fishing) if the seasonal nature of the work meant that a period of unemployment was predictable, and not a risky, unforseen event.

Other insurance principles were also applied. The program was to be actuarially sound and self-financing in the long-run, paid mainly by employers and employees, with some contribution from the government into the fund. Following insurance principles, payment was largely independent of family income or other measures of wealth (albeit payments were about 18% higher for persons with a dependent). Furthermore, long lists of groups were excluded if they had little risk of becoming unemployed. This included persons whose earnings were more than $2,000 per year, and who therefore could presumably absorb the risk of a temporary bout of unemployment.

Current Structure[5]

Unemployment insurance schemes have a number of design features or program parameters that can be changed to achieve the objectives of the program in a fashion that is cost effective and that minimizes its adverse consequences. To a large degree, the search for an optimal UI scheme involves the search for an optimal combination of these policy parameters.

The main policy parameters or design features are: (1) eligibility rules that determine *coverage*;[6] (2) the *qualifying* period or minimum weeks of previous insurable work necessary to qualify for UI; (3) the *benefit rate* or income replacement ratio that reflects the percent of previous earnings that get replaced; and (4) the *benefit duration* period, or the length of time a recipient can remain in UI. The Canadian UI system described here is as of the amendments made in the federal budget of 1994. They have applied throughout 1995.

Almost all of the paid workforce is covered by UI. The main exclusions are persons aged 65 and over, the self-employed,[7] part-time employees who work less than 15 hours per week, and persons who earn less than 20% of maximum weekly insurable earnings ($156 per week in 1994). Overall, slightly more than 90% of the Canadian labor force is covered by UI in that they could collect UI if they were unemployed and met the eligibility criteria.

The qualifying period, or minimum number of weeks of previous insurable employment necessary to qualify for UI ranges from 12 to 20 weeks. The lower qualifying period of 12 weeks applies to persons whose regional unemployment rate is 13% or higher. The higher qualifying period of 20 weeks applies to persons whose regional unemployment rate is 6% or less. For persons whose regional unemployment rate is 9% to 10% (which was typical in 1994) the qualifying period is 16 weeks of previous insurable employment.

The income replacement or benefit rate is 0.55; that is, 55% of the claimant's previous earnings are replaced by UI. This is increased to 0.60 for persons with low earnings and having dependents. The low-earnings cutoff ($390 per week in 1994) is half of the maximum insurable earnings.

The benefit duration period is more complicated to summarize since it depends upon two components: the number of weeks worked in the past year, and the regional unemployment rate. With respect to the work component, there are two phases. For the first 40 weeks of insurable employment in the previous year, the recipient can collect *up to 20 weeks* of subsequent benefits, on the basis of one week of benefits for every two weeks of work. For the remaining 12 weeks of

---

[5] See Human Resources Development Canada (1994b), Organization for Economic Co-operation and Development (1994).

[6] As indicated previously, eligibility can be associated with such factors as work experience, industry and age.

[7] Except for the notable exception of self-employed persons in the fish-harvesting industry.

work beyond the 40 weeks, the recipient gets *up to 12 weeks* of benefits based on an additional week of benefit for every week of work (i.e., 1.0 for 1.0). With respect to the regional extended benefit component, the recipient gets *up to 26 weeks* of benefits, based on two weeks of benefits for every percentage point by which their regional unemployment rate exceeds 4%. The maximum benefit period from all of these components is 50 weeks.

Thus, individuals who met minimal work history qualifications in that they had only 20 weeks of previous employment (based on their regional unemployment rate being 4% or less) and who therefore also were not eligible for any regionally extended benefits, would have a maximum benefit duration of 10 weeks (0.5 weeks for every week of previous employment, and no augmentation for regionally extended benefits). If their regional unemployment rate were 17% (i.e., 13 percentage points beyond the 4% floor), they would be eligible for the additional maximum 26 weeks of regionally extended benefits (two weeks of benefits for every percentage point beyond 4%).[8] Thus persons who minimally qualified for UI would be eligible for from 10 to 36 weeks of benefits depending upon their regional unemployment rate.

Individuals who worked for 26 weeks of the previous year in a region with 10% unemployment would be eligible for 25 weeks of benefits (13 weeks from the regular work component based on 0.5 weeks of benefits for every week of previous work, plus 12 additional weeks of regionally extended benefits based on two weeks of benefits for each of the 6 percentage points that their regional unemployment rate exceeded the 4% floor). An individual who had worked for 52 weeks of the previous year would be eligible for 44 weeks of benefits (20 from the first 40 weeks of work based on 0.5 weeks of benefits for each week of work, 12 from the next 12 weeks based on 1.0 weeks of benefits for each week of work, and 12 from the regionally extended benefits as before).

Special benefits are also available for sick leave (up to 15 weeks) and for maternity leave (up to 15 weeks for women plus an additional 10 weeks of parental leave that can be shared between the mother and father). Up to 10 weeks of parental benefits are also available to adoptive parents, and an additional five weeks are available for natural or adoptive parents in cases which require additional care on account of the child's health. The extent to which these benefits are a substitute for firms providing such benefits is empirically unknown.

Recipients are allowed to earn up to 25% of their UI benefits without forgoing UI. After that they forgo a dollar of UI for every dollar earned (i.e., there is a 100% tax back). UI benefits are taxable as income.

Approximately 10% of UI funds are devoted to "developmental uses" designed to help claimants become re-employed, a use determined by decisions of the department responsible for administering UI—currently Human Resources

---

[8] They would also be eligible to qualify with only 12 weeks of previous employment because their regional unemployment rate is greater than 13%.

Development Canada. The increased share of UI outlays going to these "development" uses represents a reallocation from passive UI to more active adjustment assistance, and exemplifies a process of marginal adjustments to the system, short of total restructuring. The development uses usually take the form of training allowances, mobility assistance, self-employment support, and worksharing. In the worksharing component, for example, all eligible employees in an establishment can receive UI for a day-off per week if it can be demonstrated that this would avoid layoffs that otherwise would occur to 20% of the establishment's workforce.[9] In essence, the reduced employment is shared amongst all employees in terms of reduced worktime rather than layoffs.

UI in Canada is financed by a payroll tax with premiums of approximately 3% on employees and 4.3% on employers (as of 1994). The payroll tax is subject to a ceiling but does not differ according to UI usage by industry, firms or individuals (i.e., there is no experience rating).[10] Premiums are adjusted so that the system is self-financing, with government funding having ceased as of amendments undertaken in 1990. As Nakamura, Cragg and Sayers (1994) point out, this lack of government funding means that UI no longer acts as an automatic stabilizer, infusing more government funds into the system when unemployment is high.

Evolution of UI[11]

The current structure has evolved considerably from the more insurance-based structure established in the 1940's. Table 3.1 highlights how many of the key policy parameters have changed over time.[12] Clearly, in the early years of the program, its "magnitude" was fairly limited: less than half of the labor force was covered; a fairly extensive qualifying period of 30 weeks of previous insurable employment was required; the maximum duration of benefits for an individual with the minimum qualification requirement was only six weeks; and only one-fifth of an additional week of benefit was granted for every additional week of insurable

---

[9] Reid (1985, 1986) discusses the worksharing component of UI. He also illustrates how worksharing is discouraged by the fact that UI supports layoffs but not reductions in hours, and the ceiling on the payroll tax used to finance UI encourages employers to work their existing employees long hours (to amortize the tax) rather than to hire new employees.

[10] In 1994, the ceiling for employees was $23.95 per week and $1,245 per year. For employers it was 1.4 times those amounts. A comprehensive earlier treatment of the financing of UI is given in Kesselman (1983), which includes a discussion of the extensive cross-subsidies that exist because of the lack of experience rating.

[11] See Dingledine (1981), Green and Riddell (1993) and Human Resources Development Canada (1994a) and references cited therein.

[12] For ease of exposition, the intricacies of some of the design features are glossed over. The table entries should be regarded as generalizations designed to capture the trends and main changes.

Table 3.1
Evolution of Key UI Policy Parameters in Canada, Selected Years, 1946-1994

Policy Parameter	1946	1966	1972	1989	1994
Percent of labor force covered	44	61	88	92	92
Qualifying period (weeks previous employment)	30	30	8	10-14	12-20
Benefit rate	.32-.89[1]	.50	.67[2]	.57	.55[3]
Maximum benefit duration[4] (weeks)	6	15	28-42	10-42	10-36
Additional benefit weeks per week of previous work	0.2	0.5	.5-1.0	.5-1.0	.5-1.0

Notes: [1] The benefit rates were fixed for each of 7 different earnings classes, and they were about 18% higher for persons with a dependent. The implied benefit rates ranged from 32% for a high-income earner with no dependents to 89% for a low-income earner with dependents. For a person in the middle of the middle-income earning class, they were 57% for a single person and 62% for a person with a dependent. [2] 0.75 for person exhibiting need. [3] 0.60 for person exhibiting need. [4] For claimant with minimal previous employment qualification.

Source: Dingledine (1981); Green and Riddell (1993); Human Resources Development Canada (1994a).

employment. Over the 1950s and 1960s, each of these design features was changed, usually in a fashion that expanded coverage, reduced the qualifying period, and increased benefit rates and the duration of benefits.

The most dramatic changes occurred in 1971, so that by 1972 the program was more extensive and "generous" in all dimensions: 88% of the labor force was covered; the qualifying period was only eight weeks of previous employment; the benefit rate was increased to 0.67 (0.75 for those who met certain "needs" requirements); the duration of benefits increased to between 28 and 42 weeks; and substantially more weeks of benefits were added for higher national and regional unemployment rates and for additional weeks of previous work.

Since the 1971 reforms, the modifications have generally been in the direction of reducing (but not reversing) the generosity of the program changes that were made in 1971. The reforms of 1989 and 1994, for example, generally increased the qualifying period, reduced the benefit rate, and reduced the maximum duration of benefits. The cost savings from these reforms have been distributed in a variety of ways: increased allocation to training and job creation measures; reductions in the payroll taxes used to finance the program; and reductions in the amount of government funds that go to supplement the employer and employee contributions.

Future Reform Proposals

The recent reforms (1994-96) that have occurred are generally regarded as only a partial step in a broader set of reforms that are going on in Canada in connection with the whole social security system of which UI is one part. Other aspects include workers' compensation, public pensions, welfare or social assistance, and health programs. Unemployment insurance is drawing particular attention, in part because it is completely under the federal jurisdiction and hence can be reformed without difficult jurisdictional disputes with the provinces.

Two main reform options were presented in the mid-1990s (Human Resources Development Canada, 1994a). The first involved a fundamental restructuring, designed especially to deal with "repeaters" or "frequent users," who repeatedly access UI on a fairly regular annual basis to supplement their income, usually from seasonal employment. In 1991, for example, 38% of claimants had three or more claims, and 26% had four or more claims in the past five years. Overall, 80% of UI recipients had previously received UI, with almost 50% having five or more previous claims (Corak, 1993). In the reform proposal, the benefits going to repeaters would be reduced based on their past history of claims, and they may be tied to measures of family income.[13] As well, there would be increased emphasis on developing a customized, individualized system of Employment Development Services to help the repeat users find alternative employment that is not dependent upon UI.

The second alternative involved marginal adjustments to the basic policy parameters, especially an increase in the qualification period and a reduction of the benefit rate and benefit duration period. These would be in line with the trend that has occurred, especially in the late 1980s and early 1990s, to make UI less generous and to reallocate from passive income maintenance programs like UI and toward more active labor adjustment programs like training. As well, consideration would be given to reducing the regional extended benefit period and the lower qualification period for regions of high unemployment.

Which, if any, of these alternative reform options will be followed remains an unknown. Hybrids are also obviously possible. The political dilemma is that while there is general support for reform of UI, there is also recognition that the reforms will have different regional and distributional consequences. While the reforms are designed in part to get at the problem that "teachers, auto-workers and wealthy lobster and crab fishermen regularly milk the system after earning above-average wages working less than a full year,"[14] the fact remains that a large number of seasonal workers are low-paid and they are disproportionately in Canada's poorest regions, such as the Atlantic provinces. Rightly or wrongly they have often built up a dependence on UI, a dependence that is often fostered by a lack of full-time jobs or other forms of income support.

Reform proposals have often involved issues surrounding the financing of UI as well. Concern was spurred in part because of the belief that the payroll taxes

---

[13] For example, in one proposal, the benefit rate would be reduced by one percentage point for every 15 weeks of previous UI usage in the previous five years. Therefore, a claimant who was on UI for 75 weeks over the previous five years would have their benefit rate reduced by five percentage points, from 0.55 to 0.50.

[14] *Globe and Mail*, June 10, 1995, p. A10, citing the Minister of Human Resources Development Canada.

used to finance UI often "killed job creation." One option is to average payroll tax premiums over the business cycle to avoid having to raise them (and thus kill even more jobs) during recessions. Premium increases have often occurred in recessions because the account has been in a deficit since more UI payments were being disbursed and lower payroll tax revenues were being collected. Alternatively, premiums could be put on an hourly rather than the current per-employee basis, which encourages employers to hire part-time employees who would not be eligible for UI and hence not subject to the payroll tax; the effects of this latter practice may be mitigated somewhat if wages of participating employees are otherwise higher to compensate for the lack of UI coverage. Since there is also a ceiling on the payroll tax, it encourages employers to work their existing workforce long hours (since there would be no further payroll tax if they are at the ceiling) rather than hire new employees and incur the payroll tax.

Proposals for experience rating have also been put forth, so as to tie premiums to the use of the system. This could be done on the basis of individual workers, firms or industries or some combination. Workers' compensation systems, for example, often charge different premiums on the basis of the accident rates in the industries and sometimes the firms. Individual experience-rating is often practiced in the auto insurance industry, as premiums increase with accidents suffered or are lowered for those with good accident records. Experience-rating is a feature of the UI system in the U.S.

Premium reduction for employers who provide a certain threshold level of training was put forth as an option in a recent debate on reform of the system. Of course, this would give rise to difficult monitoring issues associated with the need to define training and the appropriate threshold level—a level that may differ by industry or occupation.

Clearly, difficult tradeoffs arise among the reform proposals put forth. As well, the fact that UI reform was conducted as part of a broader review of the whole income security system highlights how the program has evolved from a simple labor market insurance program to a broader social security and income maintenance program.

The mid-1990s reforms involved four main changes (Human Resources Development Canada, 1995). First, eligibility is based on working a certain minimum number of hours in the previous year (e.g., 400 to 700 hours), with the lower requirement for areas of high unemployment) rather than the previous requirement of 12 to 20 weeks of at least 15 hours per week. The new hours requirement was designed to accommodate persons with irregular work patterns and to discourage employers from providing jobs of less than 15 hours per week to avoid paying UI premiums. Second, benefits are based on average insurance earnings over a fixed period (16 to 20 weeks depending on the regional unemployment rate) rather than the last 12 to 20 weeks. This change is designed to discourage people from refusing some lower paying work that may otherwise reduce their average earnings, or to discourage reporting earnings as earned over a shorter period so as to inflate weekly earnings. Thus for repeat beneficiaries who have used the system more intensely in the past, the benefits rate is reduced from 55%, by one percentage point for every additional 20 weeks of benefits collected in the past five years, to a minimum rate of 50%. Furthermore, the clawback of benefits from high-income earners is based on previous usage of UI. Fourth, a family supplement is to be given to claimants with children and family income under approximately $26,000.

Usage and Importance of UI[15]

Before analyzing the incentive effects of UI and the broader concerns over UI, it is informative to provide some background information on its usage and its relative importance as an income maintenance scheme in Canada.

UI is currently the largest single income security program in Canada. As of the early 1990s it accounted for slightly more than 20% of total income security expenditures (see Table 3.2), though if federal and provincial cost-shared social assistance is combined with the provincial and local welfare programs into an overall social assistance/welfare program, then it would be the largest, at about 27%. Note that this income security figure does not include health care spending (the largest item in social security expenditure, broadly defined) nor does it include tax expenditures (expenditures made implicitly through reduced tax revenue).

The liberalization of UI that occurred in 1971 pushed the share of UI as a component of income security expenditures up sharply from around 10% in the mid 1960s to around 20%. Since then the importance of UI in total income security expenditures has fluctuated considerably, reaching peaks during recession years of high unemployment like 1982-83 and dropping in periods of recovery, but has shown no clear trend.

Total income security expenditures (including UI) have increased substantially as a percent of Gross National Product since the mid 1960s, from approximately 5% of GNP in the mid 1960s to more than 13% in the early 1990s. Here too there have been substantial cyclical fluctuations, the ratio rising in periods of recession and high unemployment (e.g., early 1980s and early 1990s) and falling in periods of cyclical expansion (e.g., much of the 1980s, late 1970s, mid -1960s). A sound economy is thus the "first line of defense" in containing income security spending, especially its major components—social assistance and UI.

In 1992, the average claim was approximately $6,500, based on about $250 per week for 26 weeks. Claimants had on average 36 weeks of prior employment.

---

[15] Human Resources Development Canada (1994a), Picard (1994), Statistics Canada (1995).

Table 3.2
Distribution of Income Security Expenditures, Canada, 1992-93

Program	Percent of Total
Unemployment Insurance	20.7
Old Age Security/Guaranteed Income Supplement /Spouse Allowance	20.5
Canada/Quebec Pension Plans	18.45
Cost-Shared Social Assistance	16.27
Provincial and Local Welfare	11.12
Workers' Compensation	5.06
Family Allowance & Child Tax Credit	4.31
Training and Employment Programs	1.42
Veteran's Programs	1.35
Registered Indian Programs	0.08
Total Income Security	*100.0*
Total Income Security ($millions)	*93,004*

Note: Income security does not include health care spending. The figures are on a fiscal year basis, April 1, 1992 to March 31, 1993.

Source: Human Resources Development Canada, 1994d.

In 1993, UI benefits were received by 3.4 million Canadians, representing approximately 23% of the labor force. Overall, UI benefits amounted to 3.7% of disposable income, but that rate was more than 11% in Newfoundland and Prince Edward Island. On a regional basis, UI involves net transfers from Ontario and provinces West of Ontario to provinces East of Ontario, especially the Atlantic provinces. Newfoundland and Prince Edward Island, for example, respectively received $3.58 and $3.37 for every $1.00 they paid into the fund, while Ontario and Alberta respectively received $0.72 and $0.74.

As illustrated in Table 3.3, more than 90% of UI expenditures are in the form of benefit payments, with regular UI benefits being the most important category. Among the special categories, maternity, parental, and adoption benefits make up 7% of expenditures, with sickness and the special fishing benefits program making up an additional 3%. Developmental uses on special programs constitute an additional 10% of expenditures, mostly for training. Worksharing is a very small component of UI expenditures.

Relative to their share of the labor force, younger workers under the age of 20 and workers over the age of 40 tend not to draw on UI, and females draw on it slightly less than males. Low income individuals tend not to draw much on UI (because they often have no labor market attachment) and higher income people tend not to utilize it since they are less likely to be unemployed.

On an international basis, Canada's UI program seems to be "in the middle" in terms of generosity with respect to one key program parameter—the benefit rate or income replacement rate. At 0.55 (down from 0.67 in the early 1970s) this rate

Table 3.3
Distribution of UI Expenditure, Canada, 1993
(Percent of Total Expenditure)

Type of UI Expenditure	Percent of Total
UI Benefits	*90.26*
Regular	79.35
Maternity	4.43
Parental	2.70
Sickness	2.32
Fishing	1.43
Adoption	0.03
Developmental Uses\ Special Programs	*9.74*
Training-Income Support	5.15
Training-Course and Program Costs	2.72
Training-Supplementary Allowances	0.45
Job Creation	0.58
Self-Employment Assistance-Income Support	0.46
Self-Employment Assistance-Project Costs	0.09
Work Sharing	0.29
Total UI Benefits and Developmental Uses (%)	*100.0*
Total UI Benefits and Developmental Uses ($million)	*17,988*

Source: Human Resources Development Canada, 1994c, p.56.

is below that of France (0.80), Spain (0.80), Belgium (0.79), Denmark (0.73), and Germany (0.63), but slightly higher than that of the U.S. (0.50) and Japan (0.48), and considerably higher than those of Italy (0.26) and the United Kingdom (0.23).

Of the 22 countries listed in Table 3.4, Canada ranks sixth in terms of percent of Gross National Product spent on UI—usually labeled a "passive" income maintenance program. And Canada ranks highest among the G7 industrialized countries (the others are France, Germany, the United Kingdom, Italy, the United States and Japan). In contrast, Canada ranks low in terms of "active" income support measures such as employment services, training, youth programs, subsidized employment and measures for the disabled, albeit substantial reallocations from passive to active labor adjustment programs have occurred in Canada recently (Chapter 10). This is important, since active programs are generally regarded as facilitating adjustment from declining to expanding sectors, while passive programs can deter such adjustment by providing income support to those who stay in declining sectors (Organization for Economic Cooperation and Development, 1990).

Of the industrialized countries in Table 3.4, the United States, Japan and especially Switzerland are clearly outliers in that they are low on all dimensions of UI, both total active and total passive. All three have low unemployment rates, although it is unclear whether low unemployment rates have reduced the need for such labor market programs, or have in fact been the result of the small size of such programs.

Table 3.4
Public Expenditures on UI and Other Labor Market Programs, Selected Countries
(Percent of GNP)

Country	UI	Total Passive[1]	Total Active[2]	Total Both
Ireland	3.42	3.42	1.45	4.88
Denmark	3.24	4.51	1.20	5.71
Netherlands	2.64	2.64	1.13	3.77
Spain	2.33	2.36	0.78	3.14
Belgium	2.25	3.05	1.18	4.23
Canada	*1.58*	*1.58*	*0.51*	*2.09*
France	1.34	2.08	0.80	2.87
Germany	1.30	1.33	1.00	2.32
New Zealand	1.06	1.06	0.65	1.71
Norway	1.05	1.05	0.91	1.96
Australia	0.99	0.90	0.30	1.29
United Kingdom	0.94	0.94	0.68	1.62
Austria	0.83	0.96	0.28	1.24
Finland	0.66	1.22	1.03	2.26
Sweden	0.69	0.69	1.70	2.38
Italy	0.40	0.72	0.80	1.52
Greece	0.39	0.39	0.54	0.93
United States	0.38	0.38	0.24	0.62
Japan	0.36	0.36	0.15	0.52
Luxembourg	0.31	1.06	0.51	1.57
Portugal	0.31	0.31	0.60	0.91
Switzerland	0.19	0.19	0.17	0.36

Notes: [1] UI plus early retirement for labor market reasons. [2] Active includes employment services, training, youth programs, subsidized employment and programs for the disabled.

One of the starkest contrasts in UI payments is between Canada and the United States (Green and Riddell, 1993, 112-115). Even though the U.S. population is approximately 10 times that of Canada, its *total* expenditures on UI are only slightly higher than those in Canada. This reflects a variety of factors: the higher unemployment rate that has prevailed in Canada; the higher benefit rate; the longer benefit duration; and most important, the fact that an unemployed worker is more than three times more likely to collect UI in Canada than in the U.S. While the reasons for this last difference are not well understood, it likely reflects the lower coverage, lower take-up and more stringent eligibility requirements in the U.S.

3.3 Incentive Effects of UI

Whether its purpose is to provide insurance in the form of temporary income replacement to reduce the risk associated with being unemployed or to provide longer-term income maintenance, UI can have important incentive effects on various dimensions of behavior. These include: work decisions; human capital formation; mobility; wage determination; and occupational choice. The theoretically expected effects are first discussed, followed by the evidence on some of the effects.

Work Incentives

The basic, static, partial-equilibrium income-*leisure*[16] choice framework of labor economics predicts that unemployment insurance schemes reduce work incentives, to the extent that the cost of not working is offset in part by the UI payments. Alternatively stated, the net economic returns to working are reduced by the UI support. Without UI, the economic return to an additional unit of work is the wage rate. With UI, it is the wage rate less the income one would have received under UI. For example, if the benefit rate under UI were 2/3, then the "net wage" would be 1/3 since one would be forgoing the UI support by working. On balance, the recipient would be getting only 1/3 more by working than by collecting UI;[17] the additional income associated with UI support could enable the recipient to be able to afford not to work.

There are design features of UI that can have positive work incentive effects. For example, individuals may participate in the labor market, or shift from part-time to full-time work, to build eligibility for UI. Alternatively, they may be more willing to engage in labor market activities knowing that some of the risk is offset by UI. The feature of granting additional weeks of benefit duration for additional weeks of previous work can encourage longer spells of work in order to be eligible for the subsequent longer benefit period; this feature acts like a wage subsidy in that the return to an additional unit of work is not only the wage rate, but also the additional future UI benefits. Ultimately, however, for this to be "cashed-in" a period of unemployment must follow.

Effects on Human Capital Formation and Mobility

While the effects of UI on work incentives receive the most attention, UI can also affect the incentives to engage in human capital formation such as education, training, labor market information, mobility and job search. Adverse effects would occur if UI increased the cost or reduced the economic benefits of human capital formation; the latter could result any time that the UI has adverse work incentive effects which in turn reduce the period of employment during which the benefits of human capital formation would normally accrue. If, for example, a worker

---

[16] The term leisure is italicized here because it is essentially a catch-all phrase for all non-labour market activities including household production, education, retirement and pure leisure.

[17] The payroll tax used to finance UI would also reduce the return to work by a slight amount.

regularly alternated between half of the year on labor market work and half on unemployment insurance, then the benefit period for recouping the costs of education or training or geographic mobility is effectively reduced by half. Furthermore, a considerable amount of human capital formation occurs informally through on-the-job training and experience, both of which are reduced by shorter periods of employment. On the other hand, to the extent that one of the benefits of human capital formation is a reduced risk of unemployment, then the fact that UI also reduces this risk implies that human capital formation is less necessary to reduce the risk.

The costs of human capital formation could also increase under UI. One of the main elements of those costs is the income forgone while engaging in education, training, job search or mobility. In periods of unemployment, this forgone income is obviously low and this may induce people to return to school, to enter a training program, or to undertake a geographic move. If UI is available then the (opportunity) cost or forgone income from the human capital formation is increased, assuming that UI is not given to persons engaged in such human capital formation. This is one of the reasons that consideration is increasingly being given to the idea of allowing recipients to retain their UI if they return to school or engage in training, although attention must also be paid to the possibility that UI could simply become a subsidy for these activities.

Regional mobility may also be reduced when UI effectively mitigates the influence of unemployment rate differences as an inducement to relocation. There is less economic incentive to move from regions of high unemployment to ones of low unemployment (a process that should also reduce the unemployment differences) if the costs of remaining in the high unemployment rate region are offset somewhat by UI. This is especially true if UI provides regionally extended benefits and shorter qualification periods in regions of high unemployment as is the case in Canada.

Effect on Market Wages

UI can have a complicated set of indirect effects on market wages, depending largely on how it affects the aggregate supply and demand for labor. Reduction of aggregate labor supply by the adverse work incentive effects tends to push market wages up.[18] Furthermore, in the case of seasonal or other periodic jobs where UI may be regarded as a regular earnings supplement (if workers regularly alternate

---

[18] This is analogous to the complaint by employers that they have to "compete" with UI and other income support schemes to hire labor. Obviously, one way to "compete" is to increase market wages. Depending upon one's perspective, this can be regarded as a desirable by-product of UI—it puts more bargaining power in the hands of employees and raises what otherwise would likely be low wages.

between the job and UI) there may be an incentive for employees to work long hours when employed in order to achieve high earnings since that maximizes the receipt of externally-paid-for UI which is a percent of weekly earnings on the previous job. Employers may cooperate in maximizing weekly earnings providing it is not costly for them to do so, or if there is a *quid pro quo* for the employer. Working in the other direction, if compensating wages were otherwise paid to offset the risk associated with unemployment or seasonal jobs, then this risk is reduced by unemployment insurance and the compensating wage premium should dissipate. Furthermore, the employers' portion of the payroll tax used to finance UI may be shifted back, in whole or in part, to workers in the form of lower wages in return for the benefits derived from the payroll tax.

From the demand side of the labor market, to the extent that the payroll tax is not shifted back to labor, then the associated increase in labor cost should reduce the employers' demand for labor. This can lead to a reduction in employment (the job destruction concern discussed previously) and in wages, depending upon the elasticity of supply of labor. Kesselman discusses this issue in detail in Chapter 6.

Clearly, market wages can be affected in a complicated way by the availability of income support programs like UI. To the extent that these effects exist, they are more likely to be felt by the portion of the workforce that disproportionately uses UI.

Effects on Occupational Choice, Including Self-Employment

To the extent that UI reduces the risk of unemployment associated with particular occupations, it may affect occupational choice. In particular, it is likely to encourage seasonal work or jobs that are geared to the regular receipt of UI. In the Atlantic provinces, for example, it can encourage entry into, and discourage exit from, the fishing industry. It also reduces the risk of cyclically sensitive jobs or jobs that are otherwise displaced by changes like trade liberalization or technological change; this can have the positive side effect of reducing resistance to otherwise efficient changes, albeit the short-term nature of UI is likely to be insufficient to compensate for permanent restructuring.

Since UI is not available for the self-employed, its existence can discourage self-employment, especially because such employment is often subject to considerable income fluctuations. In that vein, UI may also discourage entrepreneurship that starts in the form of self-employment. This effect can be compounded if such entrepreneurs feel they have to "compete" with the UI system for hiring labor, although it is also the case that some entrepreneurial activity can utilize the UI system to supplement labor market payments.

Household production is likely enhanced by UI since the periods of UI supported unemployment can usually be used to engage in it. The informal or "cash" underground economy may also be enhanced by UI, since such unrecorded work may enable recipients to work illegally and accept UI at the same time.

Empirical Evidence

While UI obviously can affect a wide range of behavior and labor market outcomes, most of the empirical evidence pertains to the work incentive effects.[19] The empirical evidence from Canadian studies generally supports the predictions of basic economic theory that UI encourages individuals to move from employment to unemployment and to remain unemployed for longer periods of time. Overall, during the period of the 1970s (after the substantial 1971 liberalization of UI) the unemployment rate was probably increased by about one to 1.5 percentage points as a result of the liberalization (Grubel *et al.*, 1975; Maki, 1975; Green and Cousineau, 1976; Lazar, 1978; Riddell and Smith, 1982). Some studies find that the natural rate of unemployment is increased by UI (Cousineau, 1985; Kaliski,(1985), although others argue that the estimates of the natural rate are so sensitive to model specification, sample period, and definition of variables that such a conclusion is unwarranted (Phipps, 1993; Setterfield *et al.*, 1992). Furthermore, there is evidence that UI induces labor force participation in order to build eligibility for the benefits and because the risk of unemployment is reduced (Green and Cousineau, 1976; Rea, 1977; Sharir and Kuch, 1978). There is also evidence that when the UI standards became more stringent, both unemployment and labor force participation decreased (Beach and Kaliski, 1983; Kaliski, 1985; Green and Riddell, 1993). The large "spike" in the probability of leaving unemployment and becoming re-employed at the point when benefits elapse (Belzil, 1995a and 1995b; Corak, 1994; Ham and Rea, 1987) clearly reflects the incentive for individuals to remain unemployed as long as UI benefits last; it also reflects the fact that UI supports firms and industries whose seasonal or cyclical pattern of production matches (or adjusts to) the maximum allowable benefit period.

For workers who obtain re-employment through a recall, UI not only increases unemployment duration but in turn reduces the length of the subsequent re-employment spell. For displaced workers who obtain a new job, the longer period of unemployment may actually help them find jobs that give them a longer subsequent re-employment spell (Belzil, 1995a).

Canada's regionally extended benefits have also had a substantial effect of sustaining high unemployment rates (Milbourne, Purvis and Scones, 1991; Card

---

[19] Summaries of the Canadian evidence are given in Corak (1994), Cousineau (1985), Green and Riddell (1993), Gunderson and Riddell (1993, 666-671), Hum (1981), and Phipps (1993).

nd Riddell, 1993; Jones and Corak, 1995),[20] as well as inducing large "spikes" in mployment, for example, at the 10-week period required to be eligible for 42 veeks of regionally extended benefits (Baker and Rea, 1998; Card and Riddell, 993; Christofides and McKenna, 1993; Green and Riddell, 1997). This further ndicates that employers are also responding to the incentive system by providing uch "10 week jobs." Empirical work by Phipps (1990, 1991a, and 1991b) finds hat the incentive effects of UI are strongly affected by the availability of jobs as vell as by the parameters of the UI system. If the economy is demand-constrained o that there are few jobs, then changing those parameters to encourage work ncentives will have less impact. Good labor market outcomes depend both on the availability of jobs and on the preservation of incentives.

Evidence on other behavioral effects of UI (e.g., human capital formation, nobility, wage determination and occupational choice) is less systematic, and often anecdotal. Certainly concern has been expressed in provinces like Newfoundland hat youths leave school early in part to get short-term jobs that enable them to ollect UI (House, 1986; May and Hollett, 1995). There is some evidence that UI deters employed job searches by, in effect, supporting unemployed job searches Kaliski, 1985). There is considerable evidence that interregional mobility is deterred by UI, especially because of the regionally extended benefits (Courchene, 978; Copithorne, 1986; Maki, 1977; Mansell and Copithorne, 1986; Vanderkamp, 1986; Winer and Gauthier, 1982). In effect, the incentive to move rom regions of high unemployment to ones of low unemployment is blunted by JI. There is also some evidence that transfers like UI have slowed the regional onvergence of productivity and wages in Canada (Lee and Coulombe, 1995; Milne and Tucker, 1992).[21] UI is believed to blunt the impact of market forces in eallocating labor that would normally reduce disparities of productivity,[22] wages and income. Although they do not directly estimate its effects on regional onvergence, Lee and Coulombe (1995, 15) suggest that:

> The key to reducing regional disparities in regional living standards
> in Canada is to reduce regional disparities in unemployment rates.
> There are many possible solutions for this. We suggest the best way
> to do it is to facilitate adjustments in the labor market by eliminating
> regional distortions such as regionally extended unemployment

---

[20] Card and Riddell (1993) and Jones and Corak (1995) emphasized, however, that the umber of such recipients of regionally extended benefits were not likely to be sufficient to explain he increased level and persistence of the Canadian unemployment rate during the 1980s.

[21]The methodology these authors employ involves regressing, for example, growth in per apita regional income over a period of time, on the initial level of income. Convergence is reflected by a negative relationship; that is, the poor regions have a higher growth rate. The evidence suggests han convergence is slow, taking about 15 years to close half the gap.

[22] As discussed subsequently, it is possible that migration could exacerbate disparities if the nost qualified leave and the least qualified stay.

benefits and the perverse subsidy to seasonal employment that comes out of the UI system.

It may be tempting to link the faster growth that has recently occurred in the United States compared to Canada, to the much smaller use of UI (with its associated distortions) in the United States. To our knowledge, however, the link and its timing have never been established. Furthermore, the aggregate impact of UI on growth is likely to be small, albeit the cumulative impact of fewer labor market regulations in the United States in general may have contributed to this higher growth and job creation (as well as to greater wage inequality). Empirical evidence does suggest that UI has enhanced the seasonal employment that is already a natural part of the Canadian economy (Kaliski, 1976; Wilson, 1982 Card and Riddell, 1993). UI also increases the reservation wages of recipients, by a greater amount the farther they are from the end of their benefit period (Belzil 1995b). Furthermore, the fact that market wages are fairly high in Newfoundland (Copithorne, 1986), in spite of its having Canada's highest unemployment rate could reflect the effects of UI. It is unknown, however, as to how much the high wages can be attributed to UI as opposed to other factors such as high unionization, "isolation" pay, or federal government pay practices that tend to be uniform across the country.

The extent to which UI has fostered the "underground" economy (so that people can work for "cash" and collect UI) is obviously difficult to document given that this does not show up in regional accounts. Newfoundland, the province with the greatest dependence on UI, does have a high level of household production as well as a high degree of home ownership for a poor province (May and Hollett 1986, 209 and 1995, 53); although this may be artificially sustained by UI, it need not reflect illegal work for "cash."

Perhaps the greatest concern over the impact of UI, one that is most difficult to document empirically, is whether it has distorted the decision margins of all participants in the system toward dependency on UI benefits as opposed to the creation of viable jobs.[23] Employees may want short-run seasonal jobs that enable them to build UI eligibility for the rest of the season.[24] Employers may gear their production decisions to provide such jobs, often rotating different family members through them in a form of community worksharing. Full-time workers run the risk of being called "scabs" for taking the job of someone else who could otherwise use it to get eligibility for externally funded UI. There may be strong pressure not to lower wages in these jobs as a way of expanding employment, because this would

---

[23] This is illustrated for the province of Newfoundland in Gunderson (1999), House (1986), and May and Hollett (1995).

[24] The extreme version of this is the so-called "lotto 10-40" work pattern whereby people could work for 10 weeks and collect UI for the remaining 40 weeks in the year (given the 2 week waiting period for benefits) in areas of regionally extended benefits.

reduce the benefits forthcoming from the federal government (since UI benefits are a fixed percent of earnings). Provincial governments have little incentive to curtail abuse because it brings transfers into the community from elsewhere, and it saves on their own social assistance (welfare) payments. Indeed, the provincial governments and sometimes even the federal government are willing to use job creation funds to create artificial jobs (so-called "make-work" projects) in such communities to enable people to build eligibility for UI.

The negative side of UI, thus, lies in the fact that under some conditions the decision margins of all participants become geared to maximizing the receipt of externally funded UI rather than to the creation of sustainable jobs. A dependency on UI is fostered as income and job creation become geared to UI rather than to market forces. Weighed against these costs of UI are the benefits it provides in terms of the insurance against income losses during periods of unemployment—its *raison d'être*. The fact that reform of the system has been difficult and elusive suggests that many of the undesirable features cannot be altered simply without jeopardizing the benefits that go to many. As with most policy initiatives, difficult tradeoffs are invariably involved.

3.4 Alternative Perspective: More Positive Effects

The previous discussion has highlighted worries about possible negative effects of UI, based both on theory and on empirical evidence. Alternative perspectives view it in a somewhat more positive light.

For one thing, the balance on work incentive effects may not be very negative. Though UI may distort the decisions margins of some individuals, most are infra-marginal with respect to the effects of UI; they would not jeopardize a stable job if they had one by shifting to UI even if they were eligible. Most individuals would prefer a stable job to bouts of unemployment, especially given the negative psychological consequences and stigma of being unemployed. And UI does have features that encourage work, at least for the periods of time to build up eligibility. In regions that are demand constrained with few jobs, this may be a viable form of worksharing and hardship sharing, with household production filling the void left by lack of jobs in the formal sector. Though it may encourage informal work in the "underground" economy while UI is being collected, it may also encourage work in the formal sector to build eligibility for UI. UI can also foster job searches by providing support that can yield a better, longer-run job match rather than having to take the first job that becomes available. This, in turn, can reduce subsequent voluntary quits or involuntary terminations. If it compels employers to raise wages to compete with the generosity of the UI system, this may have the desirable byproduct of putting bargaining power in the hands of otherwise low-wage labor. This may simply offset the bargaining power they lost from the fact that they have to compete with the pool of unemployed labor—a pool that some would argue is artificially created by restrictive monetary and fiscal policy.

Even if the UI system does deter mobility, this need not always be negative. Such mobility could otherwise increase rather than decrease disparities if the "best" leave, and this leads to cumulative decline. By reducing the risk associated with unemployment, UI may also reduce employee resistance to efficiency enhancing changes and restructuring. And when UI deters pools of unemployed labor from depressed regions flooding to other regions that are also experiencing difficulties in providing jobs for their own population, some may consider this a "cheap bribe" to "keep them out of my back yard."

Even if the system has evolved unintentionally from an insurance into an income maintenance scheme, that does not automatically make it undesirable. It could be filling a void in income maintenance schemes. The fact that it was not designed as an income maintenance scheme could be at least partially rectified with design changes, such as payments based on family income or need (Osberg, 1979). As well, because benefits are taxable, the tax system claws back some of the benefits on the basis of need. Perhaps "UI is the worst possible system . . . except for all others." If UI did not exist, it would likely mean that other programs would in part take its place, and they also have their problems. Social assistance or welfare has even stronger adverse work incentive effects; negative income tax systems have their own adverse incentive effects. Termination policies to inhibit employers from laying off workers who would otherwise go on UI, can create quasi-fixed costs at the hiring stage and thus deter new hiring and lead to costly retention of redundant workers. Even the so called "active" labor market policies like training, mobility and job creation can simply be thinly disguised subsidies, crowding-out private activities in these areas. An imperfect policy like UI must be compared to other imperfect alternatives, not to a world of no policies. The adverse effect of UI may simply be the price that society is willing to pay for its beneficial insurance and income maintenance features. The adverse effects may simply be the inevitable byproduct of achieving other social objectives. It is thus possible to portray UI alternatively as embodying "the best of times, and the worst of times." These alternative perspectives should be kept in mind in considering the lessons to be learned from the Canadian experience.

3.5 Lessons from the Canadian Experience with UI

Subject to the numerous caveats raised previously, the Canadian experience with UI provides a number of lessons that may be relevant, especially for countries considering the adoption of programs like UI. These include:

• Even if it is designed initially as an insurance program to mitigate the income losses associated with temporary and unanticipated bouts of unemployment, UI can easily evolve into an income maintenance program, often to supplement earnings from employment.

• If it is not designed as an income maintenance program, UI is unlikely to have the desirable features of a good income maintenance program. For example, it is not based on family need and it does little to help those without labor market experience, although it may encourage some to acquire experience in order to build eligibility for UI.

• UI tends to be a "passive" income maintenance program encouraging people to stay in declining sectors and regions, rather than an "active" adjustment assistance program that would encourage the reallocation of labor from declining to expanding sectors and regions. As such, it tends to work against basic market forces rather than complementing them.

• UI was designed with the blue-collar, male, industrial workforce in mind, where temporary bouts of short-duration unemployment were prominent. It may be ill designed for the new workforce characterized by contingent and part-time work, self-employment, two-earner families, fundamental restructuring, and a significant level of long-term unemployment.

• UI has adverse work incentive effects and increases the unemployment rate. It reduces mobility and thereby likely perpetuates the unemployment rate and income differences that otherwise encourage mobility. As such, it probably slows the pace of regional convergence. UI is likely to encourage some school leaving and deter some training and accumulation of continuous labor market experience. It encourages seasonal work and discourages self-employment. It probably discourages downward wage flexibility that might reduce unemployment.

• Once it has been in place for some time, UI can create a dependency on the system, making it difficult to change and even harder to dismantle. It can alter the decision margins of all parties (employees, employers and governments) toward the receipt of UI instead of sustainable job creation.

• UI has a wide range of design features or policy parameters (e.g., coverage, qualifying periods, benefit rates, benefit duration) each of which can be used to achieve the goals of the program and affects behavior and program costs in different ways. To a large extent, the search for the best UI system involves identifying the optimal combination of these design features so as to achieve program goals with minimal negative behavioral consequences. Since tradeoffs are invariably involved, this is a difficult and elusive search.

● While trade liberalization and greater economic integration increases the demand
for such programs in order to deal with the adjustment consequences, these trends
also increase the political resistance to their cost consequences and to the fact that
they may deter competitiveness by slowing the reallocation of labor from declining
to expanding sectors and regions. Strong resistance also exists to the payroll taxes
used to finance such systems, since payroll taxes are often regarded as
discouraging job creation.

● While UI has these numerous imperfections, the alternatives also have their
problems.   Imperfect policies must be compared to imperfect alternatives
Knowledge of the intended and unintended consequences of the policy alternatives
can facilitate informed choices about the difficult tradeoffs that invariably are
involved.

● In spite of its problems, UI obviously has benefits in terms of the insurance it
provides against the income loss associated with unemployment. Recent reforms
in Canada have generally been in the direction of trying to mitigate the adverse
incentive effects of UI, while preserving the essential benefits. Such reforms have
involved increases in the qualifying period and reductions in the benefit rate and
the duration of benefits, with much of the cost saving reallocated toward more
active labor market programs like training and mobility. Other reforms under
consideration include use of experience rating, relating benefits to family income,
restrictions on persistent repeat users, and reconsideration of the viability of
regionally extended benefits and qualification periods. Our assessment is that these
reforms are generally in the right direction so as to preserve the essential benefits
of UI while mitigating its more adverse effects. The fact that dramatic changes are
unlikely to occur, however, highlights the difficulty of changing programs to which
all parties—employees, the unemployed, employers and governments—have
adjusted their behavior.

REFERENCES

Baker, M. and S. Rea Jr. (1998). "Employment Spells and Unemployment Insurance Eligibility
    Requirements." *Review of Economics and Statistics*, Vol. 80 (February), pp. 80-94.

Beach, C. M. and S. F. Kaliski (1983). "On the Design of Unemployment Insurance: The Impact of
    the 1979 Amendments." *Canadian Public Policy*, Vol. 9 (June), pp. 164-173.

Belzil, C. (1995a). "Unemployment Insurance and Unemployment Overtime: An Analysis with
    Event History Data." *Review of Economics and Statistics*, Vol. 77 (February), pp. 113-126.

Belzil, C. (1995b). "Unemployment Duration Stigma and Re-Employment Earnings." *Canadian
    Journal of Economics*, Vol. 28 (August), pp. 568-585.

Boadway, R. and A. Green (1981). *The Economic Implications of Migration to Newfoundland.* Ottawa: Economic Council of Canada.

Card, D. and W. C. Riddell (1993). "A Comparative Analysis of Unemployment in Canada and the United States." In *Small Differences that Matter: Labor Markets and Income Maintenance in Canada and the United States*, D. Card and R. Freeman, eds. Chicago: University of Chicago Press, pp. 149-189.

Christofides, L. and C. McKenna (1993). "Employment Flows and Job Tenure in Canada." *Canadian Public Policy*, Vol. 29 (June), pp. 145-161.

Christofides, L. and C. McKenna (1994). "Employment Patterns and Unemployment Insurance." Ottawa: Human Resources Development Canada, Unemployment Evaluation Series.

Copithorne, L. (1986). *Newfoundland Revisited.* Ottawa: Economic Council of Canada.

Corak, M. (1992). "Repeat Users of the Unemployment Insurance Program." *Canadian Economic Observer,* (January), pp. 1-25.

Corak, M. (1993). "Unemployment Insurance Once Again: The Incidence of Repeat Participation in the Canadian UI Program." *Canadian Public Policy,* Vol. 19, pp. 162-176.

Corak, M. (1994). "Unemployment Insurance, Work Disincentives and the Canadian Labor Market: An Overview." In *Unemployment Insurance: How To Make It Work*, C. Green *et al.* Toronto: C. D. Howe Institute.

Courchene, T. (1978). "Avenues of Adjustment: The Transfer System and Regional Disparities." In *Canadian Confederation at the Crossroads*, M. Walker, ed. Vancouver: Fraser Institution.

Cousineau, J.-M. (1985). "Unemployment Insurance and Labor Market Adjustments." In *Income Distribution and Economic Security in Canada*, F. Vaillancourt, ed. Toronto: University of Toronto Press.

Dingledine, G. (1981). *A Chronology of Response: The Evolution of Unemployment Insurance from 1940 to 1980.* Ottawa: Employment and Immigration Canada.

Forget, C. (Commissioner) (1986). *Commission of Inquiry on Unemployment Insurance.* Ottawa: Supply and Services Canada.

Green, C. and J. M. Cousineau (1976). *Unemployment in Canada: The Impact of Unemployment Insurance.* Ottawa: Economic Council of Canada.

Green, D. A. and W. C. Riddell (1993). " The Economic Effects of Unemployment Insurance in Canada: An Empirical Analysis of UI Disentitlement." *Journal of Labor Economics,* 11 (January).

Green, D. A. and W. C. Riddell (1997). "Qualifying for Unemployment Insurance: An Empirical Analysis." *Economic Journal,* Vol. 107 (January), pp. 67-84.

Grubel, H., D. Maki and S. Sax (1975). "Real and Insurance Induced Unemployment in Canada." *Canadian Journal of Economics,* Vol. 8 (May), pp. 174-191.

Gunderson, M. and C. Riddell (1993). *Labor Market Economics: Theory, Evidence and Policy in Canada*, Third Edition. Toronto: McGraw-Hill.

Gunderson, M. (1999). "Income Transfers Under Increased Economic Integration: The Case of Newfoundland." In *Integrating Cities and Regions: North America Faces Integration*, J. Wilkie and C. Smith, eds. Los Angeles and Guadalajara: University of California and Universidad de Guadalajara, pp. 393-422.

Ham, J. C. and S. A. Rea, Jr. (1987) "Unemployment Insurance and Male Unemployment Duration in Canada." *Journal of Labor Economics*, Vol. 5 (July), pp. 325-353.

Health and Welfare Canada (1987). *Social Security Statistics: Canada and the Provinces, 1960-61 to 1984-85*. Ottawa: Health and Welfare Canada.

Health and Welfare Canada (1988). *Social Security Statistics: Canada and the Provinces*. Ottawa: Health and Welfare Canada.

House, D. (Chair) (1986). *Building on Our Strengths*. St. John's: Report of the Royal Commission on Employment and Unemployment.

Hum, D. P. J. (1981) *Unemployment Insurance and Work Effort: Issues, Evidence and Policy Directions*. Toronto: Ontario Economic Council.

Human Resources Development Canada (1994a). *From Unemployment Insurance to Employment Insurance*. Ottawa: Supply and Services Canada.

Human Resources Development Canada (1994b). *Proposed Changes to the Unemployment Insurance Program*. Ottawa: Human Resources Development Canada.

Human Resources Development Canada (1994c). *Annual Report, 1993-94*. Ottawa: Human Resources Development Canada.

Human Resources Development Canada (1994d). *Social Security Statistics: Canada and the Provinces, 1968-69 to 1992-92*. Ottawa: Human Resources Development Canada.

Human Resources Development Canada (1995). *A 21st Century Employment System for Canada*. Ottawa: Supply and Services Canada.

Jones, S. and M. Corak (1995). "The Persistence of Unemployment: How Important Were Regional Extended Benefits?" *Canadian Journal of Economics*, Vol. 28 (August), pp. 555-567.

Kaliski. S. (1976). "Unemployment and Unemployment Insurance." *Canadian Journal of Economics*, Vol. 9 (November), pp. 705-712.

Kaliski, S. (1985). "Trends, Changes and Imbalances: A Survey of the Canadian Labor Market." In *Work and Pay: The Canadian Labor Market*, W. C. Riddell, ed. Toronto: University of Toronto Press.

Kesselman, J. R. (1983). *Financing Canadian Unemployment Insurance*. Toronto: Canadian Tax Foundation.

Lazar, F. (1978) "The Impact of the 1971 Unemployment Insurance Revisions on Unemployment Rates: Another Look." *Canadian Journal of Economics*, Vol. 11 (August), pp. 559-569.

Lee, F. and S. Coulombe (1995). "Regional Productivity: Convergence in Canada." *Canadian Journal of Regional Science*, Vol. 18 (Spring).

MacDonald, D. (Commissioner) (1985). *Royal Commission on the Economic Union and Development Prospects for Canada*. Ottawa: Supply and Services Canada.

Maki, D. (1975). "Regional Differences in Insurance-Induced Unemployment in Canada." *Economic Inquiry*, Vol. 13 (September), pp. 389-400.

Maki, D. (1977) "Unemployment Benefits and the Duration of Claims in Canada."*Applied Economics*, Vol. 9, pp. 227-236.

Mansell, R and L. Copithorne (1986). "Canadian Regional Economic Disparities." In *Disparities and Interregional Adjustment*, K. Norrie, ed. Toronto: University of Toronto Press, pp. 1-51.

May, D. and A. Hollett (1986). *The Causes of Unemployment in Newfoundland*. Background Report for the Royal Commission on Employment and Unemployment, Newfoundland and Labrador.

May, D. and A. Hollett (1995). *The Rock in a Hard Place: Atlantic Canada and the UI Trap*. Toronto: C. D. Howe Institute.

Milbourne, R. D., D. D. Purvis and D. Scoones (1991). "Unemployment Insurance and Unemployment Dynamics." *Canadian Journal of Economics*, Vol. 24 (November), pp. 804-26.

Milne, W. and M. Tucker (1992). "Income Convergence Across Canadian Provinces: Does Growth Theory Help Explain the Process?" *Atlantic Canada Economics Association*, Vol. 21, pp. 170-82.

Moorthy, V. (1989). "Unemployment in Canada and the United States: The Role of Unemployment Insurance Benefits." *Quarterly Review*, (Winter). New York: Federal Reserve Bank of New York, pp. 48-61.

Nakamura, A., J. Cragg and K. Sayers (1994). "The Case for Disentangling the Insurance and Income Maintenance Roles of Unemployment Insurance." *Canadian Business Economics*, (Fall), pp. 46-53.

Organization for Economic Co-operation and Development (OECD) (1990). *Labor Market Policies for the 1990s*. Paris: OECD.

Organization for Economic Co-operation and Development (OECD) (1994). *Economic Surveys: Canada*. Paris, OECD.

Osberg, L. (1979). "Unemployment Insurance in Canada: A Review of the Recent Amendments." *Canadian Public Policy*, (Spring), pp. 223-235.

Phipps, S. (1990). "Quantity Constrained Responses to UI Reform." *Economic Journal*, Vol. 100

(January), pp. 124-140.

Phipps, S. (1991a). "Equity and Efficiency Responses of Unemployment Insurance Reform in Canada: The Importance of Sensitivity Analyses." *Economica*, Vol. 58 (May), pp. 199-214.

Phipps, S. (1991b). "Behavioral Response to UI Reform in Constrained and Unconstrained Models of Labor Supply." *Canadian Journal of Economics*, Vol. 24 (February), pp. 34-54.

Phipps, S. (1993). "Does Unemployment Insurance Increase Unemployment?" *Canadian Business Economics*, Vol. 1 (Spring), pp. 37-50.

Picard, A. (1994). "Who Gets UI?" *Perspectives*, (Summer), pp. 29-35.

Rea, S. (1977). "Unemployment Insurance and Labor Supply: A Simulation of the 1971 Unemployment Insurance Act." *Canadian Journal of Economics*, Vol. 10 (May), pp. 263-278.

Reid, F. (1985). "Reductions in Work Time: An Assessment of Employment Sharing to Reduce Unemployment." In *Work and Pay: The Canadian Labor Market*, W. C. Riddell, ed. Toronto: University of Toronto Press, pp. 141-170.

Reid, F. (1986). "Combating Unemployment Through Work Time Reductions." *Canadian Public Policy*, Vol. 12 (June), pp. 275-285.

Riddell, W. C. and P. M. Smith (1982). "Expected Inflation and Wage Changes in Canada, 1967-81." *Canadian Journal of Economics*, Vol. 15 (August), pp. 377-94.

Setterfield, M. A., D. V. Gordon and L. Osberg (1992). "Searching for a Will o' the Wisp: An Empirical Study of the NAIRU in Canada." *European Economic Review*, Vol. 36 (January), pp. 119-136.

Sharir, S. and P. Kuch (1978). " Contribution to Unemployment of Insurance-Induced Labor Force Participation: Canada 1972." *Economic Letters*, Vol. 1, pp. 271-4.

Statistics Canada (1995). *Unemployment Insurance Statistics*. Ottawa: Statistics Canada, Catalogue No. 73-001.

Storey, J. and J. Neisner (1995). *Unemployment Compensation in the Group of Seven Nations: An International Comparison*. Washington, D.C.: Report for Congress.

U. S. Department of Health and Social Services (1994). *Social Security Programs Throughout the World—1993*. Washington, D.C.: Social Security Administration.

Vanderkamp, J. (1986). "The Efficiency of the Interregional Adjustment Process." In *Disparities and Interregional Adjustment*, K. Norrie, ed. Toronto: University of Toronto Press.

Wilson, L. (1982). *Seasonal Unemployment in Newfoundland*. Ottawa: Economic Council of Canada.

Winer, S. and D. Gauthier (1982). *Internal Migration and Fiscal Structure: An Economic Study of the Determinants of Migration*. Ottawa: Economic Council of Canada.

Chapter 4

UNEMPLOYMENT INSURANCE SYSTEMS FOR LATIN AMERICA

by René Cortázar

4.1 Introduction

The traditional way in which most Latin American countries have protected the unemployed is through a combination of high severance payments and low unemployment insurance or unemployment assistance, the latter typically having low coverage. The high severance payments contribute to create "job security" for those that benefit from them, the salaried workers of the formal sector. But such workers obtain their "job security" at the cost of reduced employment creation, less capacity by firms to adapt to change and engage in technical innovation, and an increase in "atypical" contracts and informal jobs. A system of low unemployment benefits coupled with low coverage, also concentrates the risks of the job market on those workers who lose their jobs. These risks are shared through a strong segmentation between the insiders in the formal sector who enjoy strong "job security," and the rest of the workers, who in most cases constitute the majority of the labor force, and who have fewer jobs, "atypical" contracts or no contracts at all, and limited access to the very unsatisfactory unemployment protection which exists.

The first section of this chapter describes the unemployment insurance systems in three countries: Argentina, Brazil and Chile. We chose these countries not only because of their importance but also because they are fairly representative of the type of institutions that exist in the region (Márquez, 1994). The second section discusses the unintended problems of these institutions. The following sections propose an alternative way of dealing with the issue of unemployment insurance.

4.2 Three Latin American Examples

Unemployment benefits reduce the economic difficulties inherent to unemployment and permit a better and longer search period. The worker is thus able to gather more information about conditions on the labor market and make a more informed decision. This should lead to a better eventual match in the labor market.

Argentina and Brazil have unemployment insurance (UI) whereas Chile has unemployment assistance (UA). All of them are paid to dependent workers that have been dismissed without "just cause."[1]

Argentina: Unemployed workers receive, 60 days after losing their job, 50% of their wage,[2] with a minimum of two thirds of a minimum wage, and a maximum of one and a half times a minimum wage, for a period of four months, if they have made contributions for at least 12 months in the last three years.[3] If they have made contributions for at least 24 months in the last three years, they receive 85% of the previous amount, for another four months. If they have made uninterrupted contributions over the last three years, they receive, for yet another four months, 70% of the amount received in the first four months. This system is financed by a 1.5% wage bill tax.

Brazil: Unemployed workers receive a portion of their wage for the last three months, which on average is 50%.[4] The minimum level is one minimum wage and the maximum 2.5 minimum wages, for a period of four months, if they have made contributions during the six months prior to dismissal and have had a formal job for at least 15 of the last 24 months. This is financed by part of the revenues from a tax on the wage bill.

  Chile: Unemployed workers receive, for the first three months, unemployment assistance (UA) amounting to about one third of the minimum wage. For the next three months they receive about two thirds of the previous amount, and finally, for the following three months, about half the initial sum. To receive these payments workers must have contributed to social security for 12 of the last 24 months. This is financed out of general government revenues.

4.3 The Unintended Effects of Unemployment Benefits

Unemployment benefits have several unintended effects (Blondal and Pearson, 1995; Bean, 1994; OECD, 1994; Atkinson and Mickelwright, 1991). The first is their expected tendency to raise the rate of unemployment. The cause lies in the high moral hazard associated with this type of insurance. First, they allow a longer job search. Second, they favor a higher flow into unemployment. They influence wage-setting (i.e., the existence of unemployment benefits would induce unions to

---

[1] In Chile, workers dismissed due to economic redundancies are also entitled to UA.

[2] Best normal and permanent wage of the last six months.

[3] Workers dismissed from the public sector or from agriculture, and household workers (personal services) are not covered by the UI.

[4] Lower income workers receive about 80% of their wages.

press for higher wages), and favor layoffs by employers.[5]

Second, unemployment benefits would, especially in less developed countries, increase informality. The cause lies in the cost of acquiring information about the occupational status of a worker. The cost of ascertaining whether a worker is actually unemployed is very high, and therefore fraud or abuse of the system is quite likely, particularly the emergence of informality, that is, people who work without a contract but claim joblessness so as to collect unemployment insurance. There is an incentive to look for informal jobs, and to prevent the job from being detected by the regulatory system, which would involve termination of benefits. The misuse of UI tends to subsidize "bad jobs" and diminish formality in labor markets.

Finally, unemployment benefits would increase the labor supply. They would increase the level of labor force participation. These benefits would encourage people to join the labor force. If increased labor force participation does not affect wage-setting it will be reflected in higher unemployment.

To avoid these problems, or at least to diminish them, three partial solutions have been put in place in many countries:

- Co-insurance, i.e., having the insured cover part of the cost of the occurrence. This has resulted in clauses involving waiting periods for a given number of days immediately following dismissal, during which an unemployed worker does not receive any income. From a conceptual standpoint, these clauses operate as deductibles during the first days of unemployment. Furthermore, under this system, unemployment benefits are lower than the net wages received prior to becoming jobless and are only guaranteed for a given period of time.

- Linking of payments to the UI system (whether on the part of employers or workers) with the unemployment record, i.e., with the number of times the benefits were used in the past. This method has been implemented in the United States, based on experience-rating formulas that vary from state to state, but which fundamentally subject payroll contributions made by employers to the degree to which their former employees have resorted to the system. A firm's tax rate depends on its layoff history.[6]

- Requiring UI beneficiaries to be "available for work," demanding that they "actively look for a job," or that they "accept job offers in line with their

---

[5] Unemployment benefits would subsidize unstable employment patterns in firms.

[6] State experience-rating systems take many forms. The two most common are reserve ratio and benefit ratio experience-rating. In reserve ratio systems, a firm's tax rate is a decreasing function of the difference between the taxes paid and benefits accrued divided by average covered payroll. In benefit ratio systems a firm's tax rate depends on the ratio of benefits paid to taxable wages.

qualifications." The intention is to separate individuals who cannot work but want to, from those who really do not want to work. This system only faces the moral hazard inherent to the problem of exiting joblessness, and not--at least directly--the one posed by the possibility of entering into unemployment.

Some of these attempts to solve the moral hazard problems are not only partial but also costly. They give rise to major administrative costs related to supervision and management. The cost of observing the event of unemployment itself, in order to thus prevent frauds against the system, is very high. Finally, the deficits commonly generated by the system must be shouldered by the state, and in some countries have reached several percentage points of the GDP.

At present, the reforms to UI systems most frequently proposed in order to tackle such problems are:

- improve experience rating;

- counseling programs for the unemployed to help them find work; and

- cash bonuses which are paid out if the person finds a job before the benefit termination date (re-employment bonus).

All these proposals are relatively marginal changes to currently active mechanisms. Here we propose a radical reform which, in our view, would either solve or strongly diminish the basic problems that affect traditional UI designs: moral hazard and informality. The system proposed does not create disincentives to finding a job, nor does it eliminate disincentives to losing a job. It does not tend to increase informality either, and it does not require the costly administrative apparatus needed to control fraud under traditional UI methods. Lastly, it does not require state intervention to deal with the crisis.

4.4 A New Proposal for Unemployment Protection: A Savings-Loans Scheme

A new set of rules of the game is needed to avoid the strong segmentation between insiders in the formal sector who enjoy strong "job security," and the rest of the workers, who in most cases constitute the majority of the labor force, and who hold fewer wage jobs, have "atypical" contracts or no contracts at all, and have limited access to very unsatisfactory unemployment protection. These new rules of the game would help to better distribute the risks involved in volatile labor markets. We propose a shift from strong "job security" in the formal sector, guaranteed by high severance payments, to a protection of "job mobility," through some form of unemployment insurance. We also propose an increase in the UI coverage. More than a debate on whether protection is necessary, we argue that "what" and "how" to protect has to be revisited.

The Conceptual Justification

In the absence of an insurance market, the private solution to unemployment protection would be self-insurance, for example through personal savings. The problem is that personal savings are very often much lower than what is needed to offer adequate risk coverage, whether due to liquidity constraints, i.e., if the worker has been hired only recently, or to "shortsightedness," i.e., the voluntary savings rate to cover such an event is too low--the latter being the rationale which has traditionally justified mandatory contributions to social security.

The alternative proposed in this chapter is to set up mandatory savings, ensuring adequate coverage, to which employers and workers would contribute. This would then be supplemented with loans in case the savings accumulated up to the time of unemployment are below a certain amount. In other words, an insurance that guarantees access to liquidity--rather than a permanent transfer of income--during unemployment.[7]

In traditional systems, the problems of "moral hazard" and the danger of abuse (and specifically of informality) emerge because there is a net transfer of income made to the worker whenever he or she is unemployed, and while that situation lasts. There is no such transfer in a savings-loans system, and thus the equilibria would be less distorted than under traditional systems. When workers remain unemployed, they draw against their own capital, against their present or future savings (the latter in case of taking out a loan). This means that the likelihood of becoming unemployed does not increase to the same extent as in traditional systems, and entrepreneurs would be unable to use the unemployment insurance as a way of temporarily cutting back on costs, as is the case even under a system that directly punishes such behavior, i.e., the United States. Hence, the flow into unemployment would not increase as much as with traditional UI.

Something similar occurs with respect to the likelihood of exiting unemployment. Abandoning unemployment does not mean, as in the case of traditional unemployment insurance, a loss in terms of state transfers. Hence, the length of the job search would be shorter. Finally, for the same reasons, this proposal would also lack the drawback of increasing informality.

Better access to liquidity can undoubtedly increase the number of workers who become or stay unemployed, when compared to a situation where no

---

[7] To the extent that savings are not used, they may be withdrawn when the worker retires.

unemployment benefits exist. However, the change is related to a more adequate job search. Insofar as market interest rates reflect the social discount rate, the fact that the individual discount rate is higher than the latter implies that, when UI is not in place, job-searching decisions are distorted. This point is very relevant, as it implies that the savings-loans system, by matching the social and individual discount rates, tends to solve an inefficiency in the economic system.[8]

It should be noted that this proposal could "over-insure" workers who have a low risk of unemployment, but such an effect is less important than under traditional UI systems because the tax component in the new system relates only to the postponement of income flows (savings will be used when unemployed or upon retirement). In a perfect capital market this could be offset by equivalent dissavings. The distortions that mandatory savings could introduce are thus directly related to pre-existing imperfections in the capital market, which prevent a thorough smoothing-out of the consumption path.

Another problem with the UI is the risk of cyclical fluctuations. The best response is to diversify the risk of the cycle on an inter-temporal basis, e.g., by surcharges on contributions during economic bonanzas and setting up a fund to cover deficit periods linked to recessions. This is achieved in the proposed savings-loans system by setting up a "Loan Fund for the Unemployed." Its purpose is to grant loans to jobless individuals who were somehow unable to save enough to adequately cover a given period of unemployment. This Fund would be operationally akin to a "stabilization fund," which unblocks funds during recessions and accumulates them during periods of expansion. Creating the "Loan Fund for the Unemployed" is imperative for the system--at least during the start-up period--because the unemployed are almost never deemed credit-worthy in the formal financial market.

The Institutional Design of the New Unemployment Insurance

This section describes the specific proposal of a new UI for Chile.[9] The institutional framework of social security in Chile is particularly well-suited for creating a system such as the one proposed here, at a low cost.[10] A savings-loans system needs personal accounts where the savings and dissavings of each worker can accumulate. This is coupled with the need to generate investment capacity in the funds thereby built up, plus a customer service infrastructure. Fortunately,

---

[8] In other words, the change that a savings-loans UI could have on the likelihood of entering or exiting unemployment --which only occurs if the social and individual discount rates differ-- tends to correct a pre-existing distortion.

[9] The proposal was first made in 1993, when the author was the Minister of Labor and Social Security of Chile (Cortázar, 1993).

[10] This is also true for other countries, such as Argentina, Colombia and Peru.

such elements exist in Chile under the private pension system run by the Pension Fund Management Agencies (AFP); hence, an entirely new institutional structure is not needed but, rather, merely an expansion of the functions of institutions that already exist.

The proposal has the following three elements:

- An unemployment benefit is established which will guarantee 50% of net wages of the previous months plus 7% for health coverage, for a four-month period, following those months that are protected by severance payments (SP).[11] For example, in the case of a worker who receives three months as SP, the unemployment benefit will start on month four.[12]

- The state supplements the unemployment benefits for the lowest wage groups, thereby ensuring that no one receives less than 75% of the net minimum wage.[13]

- To finance this benefit, workers and employers alike contribute 2% of wages, over a maximum period of three years, to a personal "unemployment account" at the AFP, that belongs to the worker.

- The first six monthly contributions made by workers, or on their behalf, to the system will be deposited in a Loan Fund for the Unemployed; these deposits are expressed in fund shares and are redeemable upon retirement.

- In case the contributions made to the system do not suffice to fully finance the unemployment benefit, there is guaranteed access to a loan from the Loan Fund for the Unemployed, which the workers will repay once they are employed again.[14]

[11] In the case of economic redundancies, severance payments amount to one month per year of work, up to a maximum of eleven months. In dismissals for reasons other than "just cause," severance payments are increased by 20% to 50% of that amount.

[12] The amount of the benefits and the number of months of unemployment protection could be modified in accordance with the reality of the different countries.

[13] This is the main element of direct transfer in the system. It is justified from the standpoint of redistribution. However, the amount is modest because workers who require the highest transfers --i.e. those who earn exactly the minimum wage upon losing their jobs-- will receive 20% of a gross minimum wage as a direct transfer. The second transfer element is the interest rate on loans which, due more to social than technical reasons, would be somewhat below the average market interest rate.

[14] Once a worker is earning a salary again, both the employer's and the worker's contributions are used primarily to pay the worker's debt to the system. Only after the debt is fully repaid will the contributions increase the personal "unemployment account" at the AFP. Debtors will maintain their own 2% contribution --which for non-debtors is canceled after 36 months of uninterrupted contributions to the system-- for a longer period. The access to a loan is guaranteed to workers that have made contributions for at least 18 months in the previous two years. The

Maximum coverage under the system proposed would be determined by the amount paid as SP plus the four months covered through UI benefits. For example, a worker with three years of seniority who is laid off will receive as SP three months of gross wages, which would be roughly equal to 3.6 months of net wages.[15] Under the proposed system, workers should use this payment to cover the first three months of unemployment. If a worker finds a job before the three months are up, the unspent SP balance will remain in his/her favor, thereby offering a strong incentive to find work as soon as possible.[16] If the worker has not found a job once the first three months are up, the unemployment benefit will be activated to finance 50% of net wages plus 7% of legal health care contributions.[17] This benefit may be received for up to four months. In case the amount accumulated in the personal "unemployment account" does not suffice to cover the entire four months and the worker is unable to find a job before the balance is depleted, he or she becomes eligible for an unemployment loan to prolong the benefit over the maximum pre-established period.

The number of months covered by the system seems enough for a frictional unemployment situation. Recent surveys for Chile indicate that more than 80% of the unemployed found another job in less than four months, which is the minimum coverage guaranteed by the system.

UI is not the appropriate policy instrument to deal with long-term unemployment. If an unemployed worker depletes his/her benefits without having found a job, the issue is probably not a temporary lack of income while a job suited to the worker's human capital is found. Rather, the problem is the worker's lack of sufficient skills or qualifications required to meet the demands of the labor market and/or an overly high reservation wage (minimum acceptable income), e.g., because the market value of that worker's human capital has dropped. There are two options open for such workers to find a job:

- training to increase "hireability." The new UI initiative was complemented by the proposal of creating a National Training Fund, so as to allow unemployed people to take up training courses and apply for maintenance scholarships, addressed particularly to long-term unemployed individuals and workers from sectors undergoing a restructuring process.

- a reduction in the reservation wage. Evidence shows that reservation wages undergo major adjustments once unemployment benefits cease. The Ways

unemployment benefit can be received every two years.

[15] SP is accrued for each year of seniority on the job or fraction thereof in excess of 6 months.

[16] This role of SP creates a strong co-insurance element in the UI proposal.

[17] The monthly sum for solving the liquidity problem follows a downward trend, going from 1.2 to 0.5 of the net monthly wages.

and Means Committee (1991) in the United States and Bjorklund (1990) in Sweden summarize direct evidence of this phenomenon. Moreover, Alba-Ramírez and Freeman (1986) and Katz and Meyer (1990a, 1990b) find that the average rate at which the jobless exit such status grows about the time when they are no longer entitled to UI benefits.

The Economic Costs

Experiments carried out indicate that for a company with a seniority-based structure such as the one used as reference point in recent surveys for Chile (Programa de Empleo y Trabajo, 1991), the higher nominal cost of the proposed system is 1.3% of the payroll if the probability of dismissals is 50%, and 1.5% or 1.1% if such probability is 40% and 60% respectively (Cortázar *et al.*, 1995). However, economic cost is the relevant concept for companies, which will ultimately depend on the relative elasticities of the supply and demand for labor, and on how workers value the contribution made on their behalf. If workers fully value the deposits made in their AFP, the greater cost for companies would tend to disappear.

The economic cost of the proposal must be compared with the increase both in the capacity of firms to adapt to change and in labor productivity. The latter can be achieved through better work relations in companies, and through a mechanism that makes the search for jobs more efficient, closer to the preferences and true productivity of the worker. This cost should also be weighed against the greater social legitimacy of the necessary labor mobility, which can be perceived less as a threat to the economic security of workers and their families and more as a window of opportunity.[18]

4.5 Conclusions

The traditional way in which most Latin American countries have shared the risks of volatile labor markets is through the combination of high severance payments and low unemployment insurance or unemployment assistance that has low coverage. These rules of the game have created a strong segmentation between the

---

[18] The amount of the contributions to the Loan Fund for the Unemployed was established so that, if the new system is put in place during a period of moderate economic growth (5%) with unemployment at 7%, it could satisfactorily tolerate (without running a deficit) a crisis like the one experienced in 1982-83, i.e. with open unemployment rates at over 20%. Three mechanisms have been set up to prevent excessive accumulation of debts with the Fund: maximum individual indebtedness with the system of up to two months of wages (four months of benefits), a real but slightly subsidized interest rate, and payroll deductions.

insiders in the formal sector who enjoy a strong "job security," and the rest of the workers, who in most cases constitute the majority of the labor force, and who hold fewer remunerative jobs, have "atypical" contracts or no contracts at all, and have limited access to very unsatisfactory unemployment protection.

On the other hand, the fact that most Latin American countries are well integrated to the world economy, and that there is a greater need than in the past for firms to adapt to change and for workers to have mobility, also suggests the convenience of changing the way in which risks are shared in the labor market. Here we have argued that there is a need to:

• reduce the emphasis on protecting "job security" in the formal sector to increase protection of "job mobility" for all workers (less protection for jobs and more protection for people);

• create a new unemployment insurance system based on "savings and loans." Mandatory savings, ensuring adequate coverage, to which employers and workers would contribute, would be supplemented by loans in case the savings accumulated up to the time of unemployment are below a certain amount. This scheme would guarantee access to liquidity--rather than a transfer of income--during unemployment. This would have the advantage over traditional unemployment insurance of avoiding moral hazard and the well-known effects of unemployment insurance on informality.

All the policies suggested here include the idea of changing the concept of "what" needs to be protected, and "how" that protection should take place, in the new economic setting that is faced by all of the Latin American economies.

REFERENCES

Alba-Ramírez, A. and R. Freeman (1990). "Job Finding and Wages When Long Run Unemployment is Really Long: The Case of Spain." Cambridge, Mass.: National Bureau of Economic Research, Working Paper No. 3409.

Anderson, P. and B. Meyer (1993). "Unemployment Insurance in the United States: Layoff Incentives and Cross Subsidies." *Journal of Labor Economics*, Vol. 11, No. 1 (January).

Atkinson, A. and J. Mickelwright (1991). "Unemployment Compensation and Labor Market Transitions: A Critical Review." *Journal of Economic Literature*, Vol. XXIX (December).

Bean, C. (1994). "European Unemployment: A Survey." *Journal of Economic Literature*, Vol. XXXII (June).

Bjorklund, A. (1990). "Unemployment, Labor Market Policy and Income Distribution." In

Generating Equality in the Welfare State: the Swedish Experience, I. Person, ed. Oslo: Norwegian University Press.

Blondal, S. and M. Pearson (1995). "Unemployment and Other Non-employment Benefits." *Oxford Review of Economic Policy*, Vol. ll, No. l.

Buechtemann, C. (1993). "Introduction: Employment Security and Labor Markets." In *Employment Security and Labor Market Behavior*, C. Buechtemann , ed. Ithaca: ILR Press.

Cortázar, R. (1993). *Política Laboral en el Chile Democrático*. Santiago: Dolmen Ediciones.

Cortázar, R. (1995). "Fairness, Flexibility and Growth." In *Social Tensions, Job Creation and Economic Policy in Latin America*, D. Turnham, C. Foy and G. Larraín, eds. Paris: OECD.

Cortázar, R., P. González and C. Echeverría (1995). "Hacia un Nuevo Diseño de Sistemas de Protección a los Cesantes." *Colección Estudios*, (March). Santiago: CIEPLAN.

Hausmann, R. and M. Gavin (1995). "Overcoming Volatility in Latin America." Mimeo.

Katz, L and B. Meyer (1990a). "The Impact of the Potential Duration of Unemployment Benefits on the Duration of Unemployment." *Journal of Public Economics*, Vol. 41 (February).

Katz, L. and B. Meyer (1990b). "Unemployment Insurance, Recall Expenditures and Unemployment Outcomes." *Quarterly Journal of Economics*, Vol. 105 (November).

Márquez, G., ed. (1994). *Regulación del Mercado de Trabajo en América Latina*. Caracas: Ediciones IESA.

North, D. (1990). *Institutions, Institutional Change and Economic Performance*. Cambridge: Cambridge University Press.

Organization for Economic Co-operation and Development (OECD) (1994). *The OECD Jobs Study*. Paris: OECD.

Programa de Empleo y Trabajo (1991). *Encuesta de Empleo*. Santiago: PET.

Chapter 5

CANADA'S SOCIAL SECURITY PROGRAMS AND PAYROLL TAXES

by Alice Nakamura and Ging Wong

5.1 Introduction

Economic and political adjustments associated with globalization and North American economic integration, government deficit problems, and persistent high levels of unemployment here in Canada have stimulated vigorous debate on the costs and the financing of our social programs. High Canadian taxes are alleged to be contributing to the employment deficit problem. Some see the payroll taxes that help fund our social programs as a special threat in this regard. Yet social programs must be paid for. The real issues are whether the benefits of the programs are worth the costs, and whether the cost of the programs—including any negative effects on employment—could be reduced by altering the means by which the programs are paid for or other program features.

Weighing benefits and costs is difficult without good measures of the program benefits. With most services, costs of production are easier to identify and place dollar values on than many of the benefits. In fact, it is often suggested that one reason the measured productivity of the service sector has been found in many studies to be less than for manufacturing is because service outputs are generally difficult to fully identify, let alone to measure. For many of the wide range of benefits which are funded by payroll taxes, plausible dollar measures are very hard to come up with. Though direct costs of social programs are potentially observable, it is widely believed that there are indirect costs as well and these cannot be easily measured. We discuss below the mechanisms by which these indirect costs can arise, and approaches that have been taken to try to measure some of them.

In section 5.2 we review the logic of mandatory social programs—the hoped-for social benefits, against which the program costs must be weighed. Even if we have no satisfactory measures of the value of these benefits, it is still important to keep the benefit side of social programming in mind when thinking about the costs and financing issues. As an aside, we note ways in which the affluence of a society can affect the value of these benefits and hence can affect political choices about social programs. Such level-of-affluence considerations could have implications, in turn, for how lessons from the Canadian experience apply for other countries now presently contemplating reform of their social programs, including several Latin American countries.

Section 5.3 provides a descriptive overview, as of 1994/95, of the four Canadian social program areas for which at least part of the funding is from payroll taxes. These program areas are: (1) Unemployment Insurance, referred to as UI; (2) the Canada and Quebec pension Plans, referred to as CPP/QPP; (3) the provincial workers' compensation programs, and (4) the provincial health care and education programs. For each program, the direct services provided and the funding arrangements are noted.

Section 5.4 discusses program costs, with an emphasis on certain indirect costs, notes some of the concerns which have been raised about the use of payroll taxes for funding social programs and reviews empirical evidence relevant to the hypothesized costs discussed in Section 5.4. Some of the concerns and costs discussed in this section were among the reasons for changes that were made to the old UI program with the passage of Bill C-12 in 1996, whereby that UI program was replaced by Employment Insurance, referred to as EI. A number of the EI reforms were designed to deal with incentive problems discussed there. Section 5.5 concludes the chapter.

5.2 Why Do Mandatory Social Programs Exist?

Each public sector program requires a reason for its being offered by the public rather than the private sector, and if it is also *mandatory*, an explanation for that as well. In this section we outline various risk pooling and externality reasons for the existence of social security programs, and note as well some of the main reasons for them to be mandatory.

Gains from Risk Pooling

Many social programs offer individuals protection from or compensation for such hazards as insufficient income due to job loss, injury, or retirement. When individuals band together to set aside contingency funds against such hazards, there can be risk-pooling benefits. Consider, for example, a personal hazard for which the true probability of occurrence in a year for an individual is p and the loss to the individual in that case is L dollars. A self-insuring individual acting in isolation must have a reserve fund (or credit line) of L dollars to be certain of always being able to cover such a loss. But if a large group of N such individuals form an insurance pool to deal with this personal hazard the expected annual loss for the pool is pLN.[1] Ignoring fine points such as accrued interest on the fund, this group could always have sufficient funds to cover their annual expected losses if each member paid an annual premium of pLN.[2] If the hazard for which a social program could offer protection or compensation has a fairly low probability of occurrence in any one year for each individual, then pL will be small relative to L. Insurance programs allow individuals to substitute a regular but smaller payment (pL in our example) for an uncertain but larger expense (L for our example). This is the risk pooling benefit of insurance. Many social programs provide risk pooling benefits against certain personal hazards. Notice that as p increases from 0 to 1 in our simplified example, the risk pooling benefits to individuals shrink, and if p were equal to 1, there would be no risk pooling benefits at all. The implication of this is that there will be less gain of this sort from social programs in circumstances, or in countries, where the feared personal hazard has a very high probability of occurrence.

Most public programs that provide risk pooling benefits are mandatory. A key reason for this is to avoid problems of *moral hazard,* i.e., the danger that individuals who know they face an above average risk of the hazard for which an insurance program has been established will be more likely than others to join the program if participation is voluntary.

The Human Lifecycle

There are periods in the lives of people when they cannot take care of their daily needs without help from others, most notably early childhood and old age. Others—usually the parents—must be relied on during childhood. Social programs can mitigate the risk for individuals when others prove unwilling or unable to provide the care needed in periods when full self-sufficiency is impossible. In addition, these programs can help protect the more fortunate members of a society from the negative externalities of having to view the suffering of the destitute.

---

[1] If the group is large enough, the actual annual losses will eventually equal the expected losses.

[2] As Bernstein (1999) notes, accrued interest is actually an important revenue source for insurance programs, including those run by the private sector. Notice that pL is also the expected average annual loss to an individual over a large number of years if the annual probability of the hazard remains constant at p. However, over a lifetime the number of years is quite small, so the realized average annual losses over any one individual's life (or working life) could differ considerably from pL. Moreover, an individual may lack the financial capacity to come up with the L dollars needed all at once if the hazard occurs. For a fuller discussion of the risk pooling benefits of the Canadian Unemployment Insurance program, see Nakamura, Cragg and Sayers (1994). See Atkinson (1991) on the concept of social insurance.

Manifestations of poverty such as malnourished children and infirm persons begging on the public streets lessen the quality of life of those who have empathy for others or who are socialized to feel that something should be done to help. Assistance programs for needy persons have, in fact, grown largely because those not in need have pushed for them. Those unable to care for their own needs are rarely in a position to campaign for social security programs to provide help.

The expansion of social programs to assist those unable to fully provide for their own needs and without family able and willing to do so, has accompanied the rise in national prosperity. In more impoverished countries or times, affordable social programs could not protect the better-off from the psychological costs of witnessing the suffering of the poor. This, in addition to ability to pay, helps to explain why poorer countries typically have had little in the way of public social security programs. Two other types of change accompanying economic development may also partially explain the growth of such programs: people tend to become more mobile, which attenuates family support networks, and female labor force participation increases, reducing the number available to provide care for dependents within their families.

Income Distribution Considerations

Many better-off people fear the growth of an impoverished underclass for social and political reasons. The better-off also have an economic interest in maintaining the spending power of those temporarily thrown out of work by layoffs, injuries, accidents or illness. Maintaining the spending power of those who are temporarily unable to work helps to maintain the economic stability of other businesses and of the regional economies of which these are a part. Many poor countries have large impoverished underclasses that could only be marginally reduced through feasible levels of spending on social programs; thus this benefit too is more important in wealthy than in poor nations.

Public Goods and Other Societal Externalities

Economists use the term 'public good' to refer to any commodity or service which cannot be supplied to one without it becoming available to all in a group. Quality of life and income distribution benefits of social programs are examples of public goods. There are many ways in which individuals or even families are powerless to protect themselves and those they love, solely by acting on their own. For instance, business capital is attracted by a skilled workforce, not by scattered numbers of skilled individuals. Infectious diseases are held at bay by widespread public health measures, not by the health care measures wealthy minorities could adopt for themselves alone. Similarly, history has shown that a broad-based unemployment insurance program offers better protection against the possibility of a downward spiral toward economic depression than do the precautionary savings that individuals can build up on their own.[3] Social programs provide individuals with a way of cooperating to achieve social benefits that cannot be obtained through individual action. Many of these benefits will be generally available to all residents of the country, regardless of who pays for them. If formal participation *cum* financial contribution in the programs were voluntary, many people might opt to use the services without such participation. Making the programs mandatory deals with this "free rider" problem.

Ethics, Norms and Matters of Political Choice

Finally, some of the support for social programs is rooted in ethical beliefs, and norms about right and wrong. Principles, of course, can be costly to uphold.

5.3 Institutional Basics for Four Program Areas

In Canada, there are four social program areas funded in part at least by payroll taxes: EI (formerly UI), CPP/QPP, workers' compensation, and the provincial health care and education programs (see Table 5.1). The institutional services, costs and financing basics for these programs are outlined in this section.

The Old UI Program

The old UI program, discussed in some detail in Chapter 3, provided short term supplemental income support for unemployed workers. Under the regular benefits component of the program, those who became unemployed and who applied for and who had accumulated sufficient weeks of UI-covered employment to qualify for benefits, could receive partial income replacement at the rate of 55% of their insured weekly earnings (60% for low income earners with dependent children) for a maximum of 10 to 50 weeks depending on the number of weeks worked in the previous year and regional unemployment conditions. Those who exhausted their weeks of UI benefits without finding work were eligible for income support and

---

[3] For an evaluation of the macro stabilization effects of Canada's UI program, see Stokes (1995) and Dungan and Murphy (1995).

Table 5.1
Payroll Taxes in Canada

Tax Component	Type	Authority	Effective Year
Unemployment Insurance (UI)	Federal	Federal Government	1940
Canada/Quebec Pension Plan (CPP/QPP)[1]	Federal	Federal Government	1966
Workers' Compensation	Provincial	Worker Compensation Board	1910s
Health and Education	Provincial		
Health Services Fund		Quebec Government	1970
Health and Post-Secondary Education Tax		Manitoba Government	1982
Employer Health Tax[2]		Ontario Government	1990
Health and Post-Secondary Education Tax		Newfoundland Government	1990

Notes: [1] Employees in the province of Quebec are covered by the Quebec Pension Plan. [2] Ontario charged health care insurance premiums from 1959 to 1989. Although approximately 65% of premiums were paid by employers on behalf of their employees as fringe benefits, these payments by employers were non-legislated supplementary labor income and not employer payroll taxes.

Source: Picot, Lin and Beach (1995).

other assistance from the provincial welfare programs.[4] The old UI program also paid for education and training and other employment services for some of those collecting UI income support benefits. To qualify for UI benefits, 12 to 20 weeks of UI-covered employment were needed, depending on regional unemployment conditions. Excluded from UI program coverage were jobs involving less than 15 hours per week or that paid less than $163 per week, hours of work over the UI cap on covered earnings which was $815 per week, and self employment.

The program was paid for entirely by employer and employee payroll taxes on gross employee wage and salary earnings from UI-covered employment. Table 5.2 shows the UI tax rates (often called *premiums*) as well as the benefit rates for the period 1960 through 1994. In 1995, the UI employee tax on covered earnings was $3.00 per $100 of earnings up to the weekly maximum of $815 per week and the annual maximum contribution of $1,271. The UI employer tax was 1.4 times the employee tax, with maximum annual contributions of $1,780 for each employee.

By law, the UI tax rate was adjusted periodically to try to ensure that the program was self financing. What is called the statutory UI tax rate was based on the financial state of the UI fund over the previous three years. This lengthy base period was used for determining the statutory UI tax rate so that the insured earnings base for the UI program would cover the expected benefit payments and administration costs and to ensure that the program had positive, rather than negative, externalities in terms of its smoothing impact on aggregate demand. The statutory rate could be overridden by legislative amendment for specific purposes;

---

[4] The welfare programs were and are family means tested. Since they are funded out of general federal and provincial tax revenues rather with payroll taxes, they are not dealt with in this paper.

Table 5.2
UI Premiums and Benefit Rates, Canada, 1960-1994

| Year | Weekly Benefits | | Average Weekly Earnings | Maximum Weekly Insurable Earnings | Contributions | |
	Maximum	Average			Maximum Per Week	Per $100 Insurable Earnings
1960	36	22.32	69.30	69	0.94	
1961	36	23.82	71.57	69	0.94	
1962	36	24.17	73.67	69	0.94	
1963	36	24.45	76.17	69	0.94	
1964	36	24.57	79.12	69	0.94	
1965	36	24.54	83.25	69	0.94	
1966	36	24.52	88.09	69	0.94	
1967	36	25.46	94.02	69	0.94	
1968	53	26.57	100.54	100	1.40	
1969	53	31.71	107.78	100	1.40	
1970	53	35.08	115.97	100	1.40	
1971	100	39.35	125.90	150	1.35	0.90
1972	100	61.79	136.49	150	1.35	0.90
1973	107	68.45	146.77	160	1.60	1.00
1974	113	74.89	162.89	170	2.38	1.40
1975	123	84.64	185.99	185	2.59	1.40
1976	133	92.89	208.58	200	3.30	1.65
1977	147	101.00	228.63	220	3.30	1.50
1978	160	109.71	242.71	240	3.60	1.50
1979	159	108.63	263.72	265	3.58	1.35
1980	174	120.92	290.31	290	3.92	1.35
1981	189	130.45	324.97	315	5.67	1.80
1982	210	141.88	357.47	350	5.78	1.65
1983	231	152.72	382.10	385	8.86	2.30
1984	255	161.42	398.10	425	9.78	2.30
1985	276	171.05	412.02	460	10.81	2.35
1986	297	181.07	424.25	495	11.63	2.35
1987	318	190.26	440.26	530	12.46	2.35
1988	339	202.75	459.75	565	13.28	2.35
1989	363	215.88	483.31	605	11.80	1.95
1990	384	231.18	505.14	640	14.40	2.25
1991	408	243.91	528.60	680	17.15	2.53
1992	426	254.72	547.01	710	21.30	3.00
1993	431	260.20	556.76	745	22.35	3.00
1994	437	258.07	567.11	780	23.95	3.07

Sources: Lin, Picot and Beach (1995).

it was being kept as high as it was in 1995 in order to build up a UI fund surplus that could be drawn on in the next recession.[5]

The Canadian UI program was not always paid for entirely with payroll tax revenues. Until 1990, the federal government helped support the program out of general federal tax revenues. In the 1971 UI Act by which this federal support was

---

[5] The intent was to build up the UI fund so that UI premium rates would not need to be raised during, or immediately following, the next recession.

instituted, the federal contribution to the UI fund was justified as helping to cover costs of unemployment above and beyond frictional unemployment—more specifically, unemployment above 3%—and also the fishing benefits and the regionally extended UI benefits introduced in the 1971 Act. The program was a more potent automatic stabilizer then, though it has continued to play a role in that regard. Prior to the 1971 revisions there was also a closer relationship between tax payments into the program fund by participants and the benefits they could draw when unemployed. Of special importance, those workers with UI-covered jobs that were seasonal could *not* collect UI benefits in the *off* seasons for their jobs. They could only collect benefits for weeks of layoff during the usual season. After the passage of the 1971 Act, a laid off seasonal worker might potentially be able to collect UI benefits for the rest of the year. In addition, that Act allowed those in higher unemployment regions to qualify for benefits with fewer weeks of covered employment and to receive benefits for longer than those in lower unemployment regions.

The 1971 changes greatly increased the moral hazard problems inherent to UI programs because those at greater risk of becoming unemployed were not charged higher rates for a given level of coverage; in fact they could qualify at lower cost in terms of total premium payments.

The Canada and Quebec Pension Plans

In Canada, the public provision of retirement income is made through two major programs: Old Age Security (OAS) and the Canada and Quebec Pension Plans (CPP/QPP). OAS is an income transfer program that insures a minimum level of income for older Canadians. It is funded through general tax revenues, and hence is outside the scope of this chapter. CPP/QPP provides earnings-related pension benefits for retired workers, and is funded through payroll contributions.[6]

[6] Under the Old Age Security Act, there are three benefits payable: the basic OAS pension, the Guaranteed Income Supplement (GIS) and the Spouse's Allowance (SPA). The basic OAS pension provides a monthly benefit to Canadians who are 65 or older and meet the residency requirements. The OAS entitlement is at the rate of 1/40th of the maximum OAS pension for each year of residence after 18 years of age, and with at least 10 years of Canadian residency after the age of 18. This basic pension benefit is not income-tested but is taxable, with provisions for a special surtax applied to higher-income beneficiaries for part of all of the benefit. On the other hand, OAS pensioners with little income from other sources are also eligible for a Guaranteed Income Supplement (GIS), which is income-tested but not taxable. The GIS benefit supplements a partial OAS pension to provide the same minimum income guarantee as is provided to full OAS recipients. The third benefit, Spouse's Allowance, is also an income-tested, non-taxable monthly allowance paid to OAS pensioner's spouses and widows/widowers who are between 60 and 64. The SPA benefit guarantee for partial OAS pensions is calculated in a similar manner as for the GIS. In combination, the OAS benefits are intended to provide seniors with a minimum level of income security. In 1991, OAS/GIS payments accounted for 31% and 39% of the gross income for senior single males and

The Canada Pension Plan is a federal-provincial plan established in 1966 as a mandatory contributory social insurance program. It provides premium payers with basic income protection against the loss of earnings due to retirement, disability or death. The plan operates throughout Canada with the exception of Quebec where the Régie des Rentes du Québec manages the QPP program. Reciprocity between CPP and QPP as well as comparable eligibility criteria, benefits and financing ensure continuity of coverage for contributors who move between Quebec and other provinces. CPP/QPP retirement, disability and survivor benefits are all related to the level of insured earnings on which contributions are paid. Retirement income replacement is equal to 25% of average career earnings up to the Year's Maximum Pensionable Earnings (YMPE), which approximates the average industrial wage. In 1991, CPP/QPP payments accounted for 15-18% of the gross income of seniors 65 years and over.

CPP/QPP also provides ancillary benefits, including a disability pension, a surviving spouse's pension, a disabled contributor's child benefit, an orphan's benefit, and death benefits. These ancillary benefits take the form of flat-rate plus earnings-related income paid to beneficiaries. The flat-rate benefits ($318 for disability, $160 for child's benefits, $124 for survivor benefits in 1994) introduce an income redistributive element into the otherwise earnings-related nature of CPP/QPP benefits. Considering both the flat-rate and the earnings-related portions, the 1994 maximum monthly amount was $839 for a disability pension, $385 for survivor benefits for a spouse under 65 and $417 over age 65, and $160 for a disabled contributor's child or orphan benefits. The maximum death benefit was $3,440.

CPP/QPP is funded equally by employee and employer payroll taxes; in 1995 each contributed 2.7% of pensionable earnings minus the basic exemption of $3,400, up to the annual maximum on pensionable earnings of $34,900. The annual maximum for employee and employer contributions for an individual worker was $850.50 each. Unlike the UI program, the self employed are required to participate in the CPP/QPP program. However, their tax rates differ from those for wage and salary earners. In 1994, the self employed paid a combined employer-employee tax rate of 5.9%, up to a maximum annual CPP/QPP tax contribution of $1,701 per person.

The Provincial Workers' Compensation Programs[7]

The provincial workers' compensation programs provide benefits for individuals who suffer on-the-job injury accidents or other health problems that are determined

females, respectively, and 29% for senior couples.

[7] Much of the following material on the provincial workers' compensation program comes from Thomason and Chaykowski (1995).

to be a consequence of their jobs. There are important province to province variations in program provisions, but the common element is that the programs provide needed medical and rehabilitation services, both physical and vocational, beyond what is covered by provincial health care. They provide taxable cash benefits that depend on whether a worker's disability is classified as temporary-total, temporary-partial, permanent-total, permanent-partial, or deceased. Total disability means that the person cannot work at all, partial disability that he/she can work some but with lower earnings than in the pre-disability period. Disability benefits are paid to recovering workers under a *temporary* designation up to the date of what is called *maximum medical improvement*. At that point, if the person can return to his or her previous job or to a new job with no earnings loss, the workers' compensation benefits end. Workers who have regained some earnings capacity but who cannot work as much, or who must take a job that pays lower wages than their pre-disability job, are reclassified from their original temporary-total or temporary-partial designation to that of permanent-partial. Those who still cannot work at all are given a permanent-total designation. Both the permanent-partial and the permanent-total designations are, in fact, reviewed periodically to ascertain whether they remain appropriate. The surviving spouse and dependent children of workers who die of work-related causes are eligible for survivors' cash benefits, including monthly cash benefits equal to what the deceased worker would have received if permanently and totally disabled.

The workers' compensation cash benefits, which begin without any waiting period in all provinces and territories except New Brunswick, depend primarily on weekly earnings. The 1993 benefit rates were typically about 75% of the person's gross, pretax, pre-disability CPP/QPP or 75% to 90% of their net, after tax, pre-disability CPP/QPP covered weekly earnings up to the provincial maximums. Those maximums on covered earnings in 1993 ranged from a low of $389 per week in Prince Edward Island to a high of $727 per week in British Columbia. In all of the provinces and territories except New Brunswick there are also minimum benefit levels which, in 1993, ranged from a low of $60 per week for Prince Edward Island to a high of $317 per week for Saskatchewan. For workers on permanent disability, the benefit amounts are automatically adjusted over time for changes in the cost of living. Partial disability benefits are determined as a worker-specific proportion of what the benefits would be for total disability, with the proportion depending on the medically determined extent of disability and the difference between pre- and post-disability earnings.

Workers' compensation in principle is financed entirely by provincial levies on worker wages and salaries, up to the given maximums on covered earnings. (The qualification of 'in principle' is added because several of the provincial programs have been running considerable deficits.) The tax rates vary between the provinces and territories, and by industry; firms in industries with higher per worker claims histories are assigned to higher rate groups. In some provinces, firms are also partially experience-rated within industries, with a view to providing a monetary incentive for employers to make the workplace safer for their employees.

Based on information obtained from the Workers' Compensation Board of Canada, Di Matteo and Shannon (1995, 7, Table 2) report that the average tax assessment rates for workers' compensation in 1993 ranged from a low of $1.60 per $100 of weekly covered earnings in Saskatchewan to a high of $3.23 for Newfoundland. These average employer payroll tax rates on the portion of earnings that are treated as covered for workers' compensation as well for CPP/QPP compare with the UI employee payroll tax rate of $3.00 per $100 of earnings insured under that program, the employer UI tax rate of 1.4 times the employee rate, and with the employer and the employee tax rates for CPP/QPP of $2.50 per $100 of CPP/QPP insured earnings in 1993 and $2.60 in 1995. The share of workers claiming benefits rose to a peak of 11.5% in 1974, then fell gradually to 7.5% by 1991, but the real benefit per claimant rose sharply beginning in the mid-1970s from under $1,600 to over $5,000 by 1991 (Thomason and Chaykowski, 1995, 21; both figures in 1991 dollars).

Health Care and Education

Some of the provinces impose additional premiums for covered individuals or payroll taxes on employers for the stated purpose of helping to fund health care and/or education (mostly post secondary education), although, as has been pointed out by Kesselman (Chapter 7), there is typically no effective linkage or earmarking of the funds raised. Access to health care is regulated by doctors on the basis of system capacity and individuals' relative needs for care. When needed medical specialists and equipment are in short supply queues develop. Those whose needs are least serious, from a medical perspective, wait the longest. Access to post secondary education is also determined by system capacity and by applicant numbers, as well as by the admission standards set by the various post secondary educational institutions. These standards tend to be raised when applicants are many, relative to capacity. Students are charged tuition fees which, in general, cover only part of the cost of the instruction they receive.

The role of payroll taxes as a source of funds for public health and education varies considerably across the provinces. In Prince Edward Island, Nova Scotia, New Brunswick and Saskatchewan they are not used in this way. In Alberta and British Columbia health care is paid for through a combination of general tax revenues and premium payments. Some employers pay the health care premiums for their workers as an employee fringe benefit; in this respect they are similar to a payroll tax. However, the premium amounts do not depend on earnings and are general user fees (paid not just by workers) for a program that also provides benefits to the general population, not just to covered workers and their families. In the four remaining provinces of Newfoundland, Quebec, Ontario, and Manitoba, health care and/or post secondary education are financed through a combination of general tax revenue funds and payroll taxes on employers. The latter range up to the 3.75% applied in Quebec.

5.4 Social Security Program Costs

As may be evident from the overview in the previous section, most of the payroll tax financing in Canada is for just three programs: (1) Unemployment Insurance which, under the new name of Employment Insurance, is still financed by payroll taxes, (2) the Canada/Quebec Pension Plans, and (3) workers' compensation. We estimate that roughly 50% of the $84 billion paid out to Canadians in income security benefits in fiscal 1992/93 was financed by the payroll taxes for the UI, CPP/QPP, and workers' compensation programs. These three programs all provide forms of income assistance. This may partially explain why concerns about possible negative economic effects of payroll taxes tend to be intermixed with, and poorly differentiated from, concerns about the economic effects of the programs these taxes support.

Each of the social programs described above provides direct benefits and involves direct budgetary costs. Recent public policy concerns about the employment effects of payroll taxes have coincided with the emerging public debate on social security reform within an environment of deficit control. Mandatory employer contributions to social insurance plans have risen in constant 1993 dollar terms from an average of $466 per employee in 1966 to an average of $2,209 in 1993. Meanwhile payroll taxes rose from 2.1% of wages and 1% of GDP in 1961 to over 11% of wages and 5.8% of GDP by 1993 (Table 5.3). Many believe there are *indirect costs* as well due to unintended and unwanted behavioral responses to the direct program benefits and the ways in which these are paid for. These responses include reductions in labor supply, employer downsizing, decreases in employer-provided education and training, and program abuse and misuse. The indirect costs have become an important focal point for claims that, as a nation, we can no longer afford the social programs we have.

Thus, the growth of social insurance income support payments is being criticized for contributing to government deficits, having a negative effect on labor supply, and increasing the cost to employers of labor relative to other factors of production, thereby stifling employment growth. In this section we try to distinguish concerns related to the payroll tax and those involving the labor supply and labor demand effects of the social programs themselves, and draw attention to some intrinsic interrelationships between tax program and social program effects.

Table 5.3
Trends in Payroll Taxes as a Percent of GDP, Federal and Provincial
Government Revenues, and Wages and Salaries, Canada, 1961-1993

Year	Payroll Tax Revenue ('000s)	Payroll Taxes as Percent of:			Payroll Taxes per Employee
		GDP	Govt. Rev.	Wages	
1961	414,163	1.0	4.1	2.1	
1962	424,965	1.0	3.8	2.0	
1963	439,124	0.9	3.7	1.9	
1964	457,722	0.9	3.4	1.8	
1965	504,625	0.9	3.4	1.8	
1966	1,295,640	2.0	7.7	4.1	803
1967	1,393,669	2.0	7.3	4.0	804
1968	1,506,280	2.0	6.9	4.0	825
1969	1,704,916	2.1	6.6	4.0	865
1970	1,775,608	2.0	6.2	3.9	862
1971	1,904,374	2.0	5.9	3.8	865
1972	2,308,813	2.1	6.4	4.1	964
1973	2,820,030	2.2	6.7	4.4	1,029
1974	3,853,701	2.5	7.0	5.0	1,181
1975	4,611,706	2.7	7.7	5.2	1,284
1976	5,943,841	3.0	8.7	5.8	1,467
1977	6,421,083	3.0	8.5	5.7	1,466
1978	7,084,836	2.9	8.6	5.8	1,475
1979	7,632,090	2.8	8.2	5.5	1,387
1980	8,502,916	2.8	8.0	5.4	1,358
1981	11,508,947	3.3	8.9	6.4	1,612
1982	12,345,384	3.3	8.9	6.4	1,649
1983	15,095,506	3.8	10.1	7.5	1,911
1984	16,678,467	3.8	10.1	7.7	1,998
1985	18,549,016	3.9	10.5	8.0	2,110
1986	20,512245	4.1	10.9	8.3	2,218
1987	22,905,774	4.2	11.1	8.5	2,300
1988	25,625,935	4.2	11.2	8.7	2,381
1989	26,110,065	4.0	10.6	8.2	2,270
1990	31,917,374	4.8	12.2	9.5	2,672
1991	34,671,035	5.2	13.0	10.2	2,881
1992	38,694,065	5.7	14.1	11.3	3,197
1993	40,531,457	5.8	14.4		3,273

Sources: Lin, Picot and Beach (1995).

Labor supply effects are considered first.[8]

An overall analysis of any social program entails a comparison of direct and indirect benefits with direct and indirect costs and a consideration of whether program reorganization could either raise benefits or lower costs. Really comprehensive studies of social programs have rarely been carried out. Where economists have focused their social program evaluation efforts is mostly on the unwanted potential behavioral responses to these programs, more specifically on the potential indirect costs, and particularly on potential reductions in labor supply.

[8] This section draws heavily on Picot, Lin and Beach (1995), Kesselman (1983, 1994, 1995a, and 1995b), and Nakamura and Diewert (1996).

In reviewing some of the main lessons that can be learned from recent research on program effectiveness, it is worthwhile to remember Atkinson's advice:

> The central issue is, in the final analysis, an empirical one since it is the *magnitude* of any adverse effects which will ultimately determine the appropriate policy stance with regard to the scale of the welfare state. The mere existence of a discouragement to work is not in itself a sufficient argument against taxes or transfers; disincentives become a matter of concern when they are sufficiently large to call into question the balance of advantage and disadvantage. (Atkinson and Mogenen, 1993, 3-4)

Perhaps the most important observation to emerge from what follows is that it is fundamentally hard to measure the indirect costs of social security programs. Unlike the direct benefits and costs, the indirect costs are not determined by the regulations of the programs themselves. Nor can they be measured by the observable monetary flows into and out of these programs. Many of the claimed behavioral responses to which the indirect costs are attributed could, in fact, be partially or wholly due to other factors. Economists have responded to this challenge, producing a large and growing body of empirical studies. In this section we try to summarize some of the main findings of this empirical research, and to comment on their relevance as one assesses the net benefits of social programs.

Labor Supply Effects

Many in the business world believe that our social programs are undermining work incentives and making it more costly and more difficult for businesses to hire needed labor. Some theoretical arguments and some empirical evidence have been interpreted as supporting this view. The central point is that payroll taxes and the income support benefits paid by the UI program, the provincial workers' compensation programs, and the provincial welfare programs alter the monetary returns to work. Economic theory suggests that changes in the returns to work can have both income and substitution effects on work choices.[9] And there are both theoretical and empirical reasons to believe that the wage rate a person does or could command has different impacts on the choice of *whether to work at all* in some time period such as a year or a week versus the choice of *how much to work.* For workers with continuing regular jobs, the choice of *how much* to work is the

---

[9] On the theoretical concepts of the income and substitution effects of a wage change on hours of work see, for instance, Gunderson and Riddell (1988, Ch. 2, pp. 16-26) and the references cited there, and Killingsworth (1983).

more relevant one. Consider a decrease in the take-home weekly wage, with a hypothetical auxiliary payment to hold total income constant. This combination would be expected to induce employed persons to work less because the opportunity cost of non-work has fallen—the hypothesized *income compensated substitution effect*. Of course, in reality, a decrease in take-home earnings per week of work will also result in a lower income for any given number of weeks of work, which is expected to reduce the amount of non-work time desired and hence increase the amount of work (the income effect), counteracting the income-compensated substitution effect. Thus economic theory implies that a decrease in take-home weekly earnings could lead to *either* a net increase or a decrease in work, depending on the relative strengths of the associated income and income-compensated substitution effects. Unfortunately, the published empirical estimates of the wage-uncompensated elasticity of work range from significantly negative to significantly positive. An honest reading of the empirical literature suggests that we do not know whether the elasticity is typically positive or negative; the regressions do imply that these elasticities are probably small in magnitude—particularly for men.

If the wage elasticities of work are *assumed* to be positive for most types of workers (say, by just choosing a positive one from among the vast number of estimates of the wage elasticity of labor supply and treating that as the truth), and if *only the tax side* of the UI and other relevant social programs is considered, the inevitable implication is that social programs paid for by taxes, and hence affecting workers' take-home earnings, will reduce aggregate work hours.[10] This accounts for the findings of some of the general equilibrium and simulation analyses of the economic effects of specific programs such as UI. Many economists do believe that the hours a worker will work are positively related to the wage change (i.e., that the *wage elasticity of hours of work* is positive). Obviously, all personal taxes on earnings—income taxes as well as payroll taxes—reduce both the average and the marginal take-home hourly wage. Less simplistic versions of this line of reasoning allow explicitly or implicitly for the possibility that the responsiveness of a worker's labor supply to a wage change will depend on the initial income level of the worker or the worker's family. Higher wage workers, or workers in higher income families, may be better able to afford to substitute more non-work for work time in response to downward adjustments in their take-home pay, whether these are due to higher taxes or any other reason. Such workers may also be better able

---

[10] Alternatively, if the wage elasticities of work were *assumed* to be negative (most of the large number of estimates of the wage elasticity of labor supply reported in Nakamura and Nakamura, 1985, and other papers of theirs, *are* negative), and if *only the tax side* of the social programs were considered, the opposite implication would emerge that the social programs increase aggregate work hours. Of course, these are overly simplified treatments of the social programs and of the available empirical estimates of wage elasticities of work. For a recent discussion of the difficulties in obtaining a realistic model representation of labor supply behavior, see N. A. Klevmarken (1997).

to change the nature of their work, or move elsewhere, in response to higher tax rates. On the lower end of the wage continuum, concerns have been raised about the returns from work falling below 'the returns' from going on to and staying on public income support programs such as UI, workers' compensation (for hard to diagnosis ailments such as lower back pain and psychological difficulties), and provincial welfare. Some economists and some employers maintain that large numbers of low wage jobs cannot be filled because the low skilled workers who might be expected to be interested in these jobs choose instead to rely on public income support.

For starting workers, and for those working barely enough to qualify for UI, the empirical literature on the choice of whether to work at all (as opposed to how much to work) is especially relevant. The dollar change in earned income that will result from any given wage change depends on the amount of work, and will be small for those not working very much. If the income effect of a wage change is small, then the substitution effect will dominate, implying that the wage elasticity of work will be positive. If this is so for the decision of *whether* to work for entering workers and those working small portions of the year, and if only the tax side of the UI program is considered, an after-tax wage decline due to a payroll tax, with other explanatory factors held constant, will unambiguously *decrease* the number choosing to work. Such a conclusion, however, conflicts with the vast body of anecdotal reports of persons looking for work, and welfare clients who are provided with work through government programs *for the primary purpose of qualifying to receive UI unemployment benefits*. It is necessary to take account not only of the taxes used to pay for the social programs but also of the social program benefits themselves. UI benefits raise the take-home *annual* wage substantially for those who only intend to work enough to qualify for UI. Consider the seasonal and other itinerant workers who collect UI benefits for more weeks per year than they work at UI-covered jobs. They receive a higher monetary return from work with, than without, the UI program. For these workers, the UI program acts somewhat like a wage supplement, for at least the weeks of work that are needed to qualify for UI benefits. There is general agreement that wage supplements that are offered to those who have not been working will increase their probability of work, i.e., the positive substitution effect is expected to dominate any negative income effect.[11] Of course, the wage supplement implicitly being offered through the Canadian UI program can only be collected by having weeks of declared unemployment following the weeks of work. Also, any weeks of work beyond the minimum needed to qualify for UI for all of the rest of the year will serve to *decrease* the weeks of UI benefits that can be collected, and will increase

---

[11] Green and Sargent (1995, 41) find statistically and economically significant evidence of this incentive effect of the UI program for seasonal workers. The authors estimate that one in twenty seasonal jobs are ended approximately when the workers have sufficient weeks of insurable earnings to obtain the maximum benefit entitlement within a 52 weeks planning horizon.

the total amount paid in UI worker premiums.

The 1971 changes to the UI Act made the program more generous in a number of ways, including the introduction of shorter qualifying periods of work and longer maximum benefit periods for high unemployment regions. Milbourne, Purvis and Scoones (1991) argue that this encouraged increasing numbers of marginal labor force participants to work just long enough to qualify for UI. Moorthy (1990) finds empirical evidence of this sort of behavior for women. Card and Riddell (1993) also provide supporting evidence. Corak and Jones (1992), too, find evidence of the existence of such a response, though their results suggest the effect is smaller in magnitude than reported by Milbourne, Purvis and Scoones (1991).

Green and Riddell (1997) examine the impact on observed employment behavior of an unexpected change that occurred in 1990 in the qualifying weeks of employment. Based on data from this 'natural experiment' they wrote:

> [We] focus on an event that is amenable to natural experimental analysis, i.e., the temporary suspension in 1990 of the variable entrance requirement. ... The analysis focuses on behavior in 'maximum entitlement regions,' UI regions with an employment rate equal to or greater than 11.5 percent throughout 1989 and 1990. In these regions, 10 weeks of employment in 1989 provided a UI claimant with up to 42 weeks of benefits, whereas from January 6 to November 18, 1990, 14 weeks of employment were required to qualify for benefits. ... Increasing the entrance requirements leads to significant increases in employment spell duration at or near entrance requirement weeks. Specifically, the sharp increase or 'spike' in the job leaving rate observed at 10 weeks in 1989 moves to 14 or more weeks in 1990. ... Low wage workers in seasonal industries are the most affected by the changes. (Green and Riddell, 1997,)

The profile that Green and Riddell provide of the characteristics of the workers who responded most dramatically to the change in the UI entrance requirements is consistent with the hypothesis that many of these workers would not have been in the labor force at all without the earnings supplement provided by the UI program, and more generally, that the UI program will tend to increase the weeks of work of more poorly qualified and unemployment prone workers.

In this overview of the empirical evidence, we have refrained from reporting the numerical values of the estimated effects. We feel the evidence only merits the conclusion that there is *some* effect on labor supply, with no firm evidence on the magnitudes of the potential effects discussed.

The above labor supply issues are relevant to the relative merits of payroll versus other forms of taxation to fund social programs, since the incidence of the various payroll taxes is different than for the Canadian personal income tax program (see Chapter 6). The latter is a progressive tax program, with the marginal rate rising with the level of taxable income, with no cap on taxable labor income, and with non-labor income also subject to taxation. For the payroll taxes in Canada, the average incidence tends to be higher at lower levels of earnings because of the caps on the income subject to these taxes, and because only labor income is taxed.

5.4.2 Labor Demand Effects; Employer Downsizing

Employer downsizing is a second negative indirect effect being blamed, in part at least, on our social programs. There was a time when established Canadian companies prided themselves on the security of the employment they provided. Even firms such as those in the automotive industry where temporary layoffs were commonplace, nevertheless tried to and did offer secure employment to large portions of their workforces in the sense that workers with sufficient seniority could count on being recalled after layoffs. Now, however, there appears to be a greater effort to economize on the use of domestic labor through greater reliance on capital equipment, buying more intermediate parts and services from foreign suppliers, and setting up their own subsidiary production facilities in foreign countries. Moreover, for many domestic workers, the terms of employment have been changing, as employers strive for just-in-time use of labor as well as materials. When more labor is needed during high activity periods, existing employees are expected to put in longer hours. Employers are also using more casual and part-time labor, and they are doing more contracting out at home as well as abroad. In short, employers seem to be less willing than before to pay labor in periods of slack demand.

Business taxes of all sorts directly raise the costs of doing business, which would encourage firms to look for ways of cutting all costs, including labor costs. In addition, however, payroll taxes imposed on employers raise the cost of covered domestic labor relative to all other productive inputs: machines, materials, foreign produced intermediate parts, and domestic labor not subject to the payroll taxes such as services provided under contract by the self-employed. Payroll taxes might therefore be contributing to job loss and to a shift toward nonstandard employment that is less satisfactory for many workers.[12]

The likely impact of a payroll tax on a specific firm or industry can be assessed through static partial analysis. It can be viewed analytically as an excise tax; the suppliers and the purchasers of the good end up sharing the tax that must

---

[12] In the longer-run, of course, payroll taxes imposed on employers may be partially or fully shifted onto workers through reductions in employee compensation. In that case, any initial disemployment effects might be expected to diminish over time (see Chapter 6).

be paid. The more inelastic is the demand for the good, the larger is the share expected to be paid by purchasers. With a payroll tax on labor, the situation is conceptually similar but more complex since the tax would be shared among the employer, the workers, and those who purchase the good.

In this situation employers have three main ways to reduce their share of the payroll tax. First, they can treat it as an added cost of production and raise product prices to cover it, thus passing the burden along to the purchasers. But if consumers respond to the higher product prices by buying much less, the firm may have to cut production and lay off workers; this outcome may be more likely since the trade liberalization agreements that Canada has entered into (CAFTA and NAFTA), since Canadian producers now face expanded competition from producers in countries where wages are lower. If firm profits suffer much in the process, the firm has more incentive to pursue a second option—to try to shift the tax burden back onto workers by reducing wages. This response is particularly likely to be successful with categories of labor for which demand has become slack, due to factors such as competition from foreign labor and technological change; workers are then less likely to try to resist employer initiatives to cut wages and less likely to succeed if they do try to resist. If unions or other constraints block reductions in wages, the firms will consider a third possibility—changing production methods so as to conserve on labor. This will typically involve substituting more of other factors of production, including machines, material inputs, and imported intermediate parts, though direct investment in foreign production operations is another option, as is the substitution of self-employed or other types of domestic labor not subject to the payroll tax.

Since payroll taxes apply to a high share of all workers in an economy like Canada's, partial analysis of their impact is less than satisfactory. In particular, it is not possible to shift the burden to buyers as a group, and it is ultimately shared between workers and firms (profits).[13]

Though payroll taxes have been of special concern for the reasons discussed above, much of the empirical research has not differentiated between them and other tax measures, changes in labor regulations (minimum wage provisions for example), and other factors that raise the costs of labor for business. It is not always clear, either, whether the analysis performed would more likely test for short-run effects of changes or longer run ones. As in the case of labor supply the empirical results are hard to interpret in an unambiguous manner.

Lin, Picot and Beach (1995) provide recent empirical estimates of tax effects on employer labor demand in Canada, using a CES production function approach with labor supply treated as infinitely elastic at the going wage level. Because of the nature of the data available to them, the approach of this study is highly aggregative. Their results suggest that payroll taxes contribute to job loss. A now-

---

[13] For a fuller discussion, see Chapter 6.

famous U.S. study by Card and Krueger (1994) reaches the opposite conclusion, based on establishment level data. They examine the observed patterns of change in employment, wages and the prices of food at 410 fast food restaurants surveyed in New Jersey and eastern Pennsylvania before and also after New Jersey changed the state minimum wage from $4.25 to $5.05 per hour. Card and Krueger are very definite in stating the employment effect implications of their study:

> Contrary to the central prediction of the textbook model of the minimum wage, but consistent with a number of recent studies based on cross-sectional time-series comparisons of affected and unaffected markets or employers, we find no evidence that the rise in New Jersey's minimum wage reduced employment at fast-food restaurants in the state. (Card and Krueger, 1994, 792)

If one accepted these results as implying that wage changes of the substantial magnitude of the New Jersey minimum wage increase will often not affect employment, this would suggest that concerns about our payroll taxes killing jobs are at the least exaggerated. We feel, however, that this case has not yet been convincingly made. The time elapsed between the two sets of interviews (from February-March, 1992 to November-December of that same year) is simply too short for most businesses—even fast food stores—to adjust their production methods and staffing. Moreover, many of the stores surveyed are part of multi-state chains that have staffing specifications. For these stores, it might be unlikely that staffing decisions would change even given more time because New Jersey is only one state out of 50.

Empirical study of employer responses to payroll taxes is difficult because employer responses are not necessarily closely related in time to the relevant payroll tax changes. More so than households, larger firms undertake explicit long-run planning, and actively collect information and speculate about probable changes in government programs and regulations that could affect their interests. Firms can and do make anticipatory plans and investments, such as pushing ahead with the development of new products and processes believed to be of future competitive importance. It seems likely, therefore, that some firms probably begin exploring ways to shift payroll tax costs *in anticipation* of the actual enactment of the taxes or tax increases. In other cases, there may be substantial delays involved in the firm responses. Undertaking major changes in business operations—such as a shift to the use of labor-saving machines like scanners at retail checkout counters, or direct foreign investment in lower wage countries—may take years to plan and implement. Moreover, since all changes in large organizations involve costs, the changes that are made in response to, or in anticipation of, higher payroll taxes will not necessarily get rolled back if and when the higher tax rates are subsequently reduced, or it becomes clear that business anticipations of rate increases were excessive.

Decreases in Employer-Provided Education and Training

A third possible negative indirect effect of payroll taxes is a reduced willingness of employers to provide education and training for ordinary workers. This could come about if such taxes lowered profits and hence the willingness either of firms to undertake these expenditures, or because the overall impact of the payroll taxes and the associated social benefits was to decrease the permanency of the labor force, this in turn lowered the direct benefits to firms from the expenditures.

Employer-provided education and training has traditionally had three important advantages for workers. First, it is usually provided in ways that fit in with the other job tasks of the workers, so that they do not have to take unpaid time off or give up their present jobs. Second, since the employers pay for, or at least subsidize, this education and training the workers do not usually have to pay its full cost. Third, workers could usually assume that the education and training provided by their employers would be relevant to their future job prospects, thus reducing worker risk in devoting resources to acquiring the job-related learning. These advantages are lost if most workers can no longer count on their employers to provide them with the education and training they need to stay employed and, perhaps, to qualify for better positions over time.

As part of the shift toward a just-in-time hiring approach, employment relationships are becoming more ephemeral. Employer-supplied education and training for workers beyond the skills needed for their immediate job tasks makes sense only when workers are likely to stay with their employers and progress over time to new job responsibilities.

Misuse of Public Social Security Programs

Many critics feel that our social security programs provide incentives for program misuse, that this misuse has been growing, and that it is one reason for the high costs of our social security programs. Program misuse, or even the allegation of it, is a serious concern in that it undermines public support for our social security programs.

Much of the empirical evidence on program misuse relates to the UI program (Wong, Laurendeau and Routhier, 1992) and the workers' compensation programs (Thomason and Chaykowski, 1995). The studies we are aware of demonstrate that such misuse is indeed present but they do not establish clear linkages between the prevalence or degree of particular types of program misuse and particular program features such as the use of a payroll tax to pay for program costs.

5.5 Concluding Remarks

Canadian public social security programs were instituted in the hope that they would increase the personal well-being of individual Canadians and Canadian families. But inadequate employment opportunities are a major cause of individual and family *insecurity*. If our public social security programs encourage behavioral responses that do seriously reduce the labor supply of individuals, render Canadian businesses less competitive, reduce domestic output, and result in employer shifts toward job arrangements which are more tenuous, the resulting indirect costs could cancel out the benefits the programs provide.

If real, the alleged negative behavioral responses to the taxation that supports the social programs, in interaction with other features of the programs themselves, might constitute grounds for cutting back or eliminating these programs or for finding new and better ways of financing them. However, the magnitudes, and in some cases even the signs, of these indirect responses have not yet been reliably ascertained. Nor is there convincing empirical evidence that payroll taxation has been more undesirable than other methods for financing the social programs.

In trying to pull together the overall economic implications of the payroll and other taxes used to finance our social programs, some researchers select figures from the diverse set of published labor supply and labor demand elasticity estimates or produce their own estimates of these elasticities, and then embed these in general equilibrium models—models that seek to capture the overall interactive effects of programs and proposed program changes. When these models are used to calculate the total costs to the economy of the tax programs that support our social security programs, including indirect effects due to labor supply and other behavioral changes, the estimates give, at least in principle, a lower limit on the returns our social programs must generate to be worthwhile for Canada. In some cases the models embed simplified versions of social programs such as UI; the resulting findings are of course no more definitive than the elasticity estimates embedded in them, though some are phrased as if they provided firm numerical conclusions on the combined indirect and direct costs and benefits of our social security programs. Even the direct costs and benefits of these programs are not appropriately captured in these models. The benefits are not related back to and assessed in terms of the basic purposes of our social programs, something which would be almost impossible to do in models based on aggregates.

REFERENCES

Atkinson, A. B. (1991). "Social Insurance." *Geneva Papers on Risk and Insurance Theory*, Vol. 16, No. 2, pp. 113-131.

Atkinson, A. B. and G. V. Mogenen, eds. (1993). *Welfare and Work Incentives.* Oxford: Clarendon Press.

Banting, K. G. (1995). "The Social Policy Review: Policy Making in a Semi-Sovereign Society." *Canadian Public Administration*, Vol. 38, No. 2 (Summer), pp. 283-290.

Barrett, G., D. Doiron, D. Green and C. Riddell (1995). "The Interaction of Unemployment Insurance and Social Assistance." Ottawa: Human Resources Development Canada, UI Evaluation Series.

Bernstein, J. I. (1999). "Total Factor Productivity Growth in the Canadian Life Insurance Industry: 1979-1989." *Canadian Journal of Economics*, Vol. 32, No. 2.

Betcherman, G. and N. Leckie (1995). "Employer Responses to UI Experience Rating: Evidence from Canadian and American Establishments." Ottawa.

Black, D. A. (1995). "Family Health Benefits and Worker Turnover." A revision of a paper for the W. E. Upjohn Institute Conference on *Employee Benefits, Labor Costs and Labor Markets in Canada and the United States*, Kalamazoo, MI.

Card, D. and P. B. Levine (1974). "Unemployment Insurance Taxes and the Cyclical and Seasonal Properties of Unemployment." *Journal of Public Economics*, Vol. 53, No. 1 (January), pp. 1-29.

Card, D. and W. C. Riddell (1993). "A Comparative Analysis of Unemployment in Canada and the United States." In *Small Differences That Matter: Labor Markets and Income Maintenance in Canada and the United States*, D. Card and R. B. Freedman, eds. Chicago: NBER and University of Chicago Press.

Card, D. and A. B. Krueger (1994). "Minimum Wages and Employment: A Case Study of the Fast Food Industry in New Jersey and Pennsylvania." *American Economic Review*, No. 857, pp. 772-793.

Corak, M. (1993). "Unemployment Insurance Once Again: The Incidence of Repeat Participation in the Canadian UI Program." *Canadian Public Policy*, Vol. 19, No. 2, pp. 162-176.

Corak, M. (1995). "Unemployment Insurance, Temporary Layoffs and Recall Expectations." Ottawa: Human Resources Development Canada, UI Evaluation Series.

Corak, M. and S. R. G. Jones (1992). "The Persistence of Unemployment: How Important Were Regional Extended Unemployment Benefits?" Hamilton, Ontario: McMaster University, Working Paper No. 92-2.

Corak, M. and W. Pyper (1995). "Firms, Industries and Cross-Subsidies: Patterns in the Distribution of UI Benefits and Taxes."Ottawa: Human Resources Development Canada, UI Evaluation Series.

Di Matteo, L. and M. Shannon (1995). "Payroll Taxation in Canada: An Overview" *Canadian Business Economics*, Vol. 3, No. 4 (Summer), pp. 5-22.

Dungan, P. and S. Murphy (1995). "The UI System as an Automatic Stabilizer in Canada." Ottawa:

Human Resources Development Canada, UI Evaluation Series.

Forton, B., P. Lanoie and C. Laporte (1994). "Is Workers' Compensation Disguised Unemployment Insurance?" Working paper.

Green, D. A. and W. C. Riddell (1997). "Qualifying for Unemployment Insurance: An Empirical Analysis." *Economic Journal,* Vol. 107 (January), pp. 67-84.

Green, D. and T. Sargent (1995). "Unemployment Insurance and Employment Durations: Seasonal and Non-Seasonal Jobs." Ottawa: Human Resources Development Canada, UI Evaluation Series.

Gruber, J. and M. Hanratty (1994). "The Labor Market Effects of Introducing National Health Insurance: Evidence from Canada." Paper presented at the *Canadian Employment Research Forum* conference, Calgary, Alberta, May.

Gunderson, M. and W. C. Riddell (1988). *Labor Market Economics: Theory, Evidence and Policy in Canada,* Second Edition. Toronto: McGraw-Hill Ryerson Limited.

Henson, H. (1995). "Payroll Taxes in Canada." Ottawa: Human Resources Development Canada, Applied Research, Strategic Policy, Analytical Note RIAN94-1.

Human Resources Development Canada (1994). "Improving Social Security in Canada: A Discussion Paper."

Jones, S. (1995). "Unemployment Insurance and Labor Market Transitions." Ottawa: Human Resources Development Canada, UI Evaluation Series.

Kesselman, J. R. (1995a). "Taxation Policies for British Columbia in the New Economy." Vancouver: University of British Columbia, Department of Economics, Discussion Paper No. DP-27.

Kesselman, J. R. (1995b). "Payroll Taxes Around the World: Concepts and Practice." Vancouver: University of British Columbia, Department of Economics, Working Paper.

Kesselman, J. R. (1994). "Canadian Provincial Payroll Taxation: A Structural and Policy Analysis." *Canadian Tax Journal,* Vol. 42, No. 1, pp. 150-200.

Kesselman, J. R. (1983). *Financing Canadian Unemployment Insurance.* Toronto: Canadian Tax Foundation.

Killingsworth, M. R. (1983). *Labor Supply.* Cambridge: Cambridge University Press.

Killingsworth, M. R. and J. J. Heckman (1986). "Female Labor Supply: A Survey." In *Handbook of Labor Economics,* Vol. 1, O. Ashenfelter and R. Layard, eds., pp. 103-204. Amsterdam: North-Holland.

Klevmarken, N. A. (1997). "Did the Tax Cuts Increase Hours of Work? A Pre – Post Analysis of Swedish Panel Data." Uppsala: Department of Economics, Uppsala University, Working Paper No. 1997-07-22.

Lin, Z. (1995). "Jobs Excluded from the Unemployment Insurance System in Canada: An Empirical Investigation." Ottawa: Human Resources Development Canada, UI Evaluation Series.

Lin, Z., G. Picot and C. Beach (1995). "What Has Happened to Payroll Taxes in Canada over the Last Three Decades?" Ottawa: Statistics Canada, Business and Labor Market Analysis Division, mimeo.

Milbourne, R., D. Purvis, and D. Scoones (1991). "Unemployment Insurance and Unemployment Dynamics." *Canadian Journal of Economics*, Vol. 24, pp. 804-826.

Moorthy, V. (1990). "Unemployment in Canada and the United States: The Role of Unemployment Insurance Benefits." *Quarterly Review*, Vol. 14, pp. 48-61. New York: Federal Reserve Bank of New York.

Nakamura, A. (1995). "New Directions for UI, Social Assistance, and Vocational Education and Training." *Canadian Journal of Economics*, Vol. 28 (November), pp. 731-753.

Nakamura, A., J. Cragg and K. Sayers (1994). "The Case for Disentangling the Insurance and Income Assistance Roles of Unemployment Insurance." *Canadian Business Economics*, Vol. 3, No. 1 (Fall), pp. 46-53.

Nakamura, A., J. Cragg and K. Sayers, (1995). "Corporate Governance and Worker Education: An Alternative View." In *Corporate Decision Making in Canada*, Ron Daniels and Randall Morck, eds. Calgary: University of Calgary Press.

Nakamura, A. and W. E. Diewert (1996). "The Canadian UI Program: Problems and Suggested Reforms." Working Paper.

Nakamura, A. and P. Lawrence (1994). "Education, Training and Prosperity." In *Stabilization, Growth and Distribution: Linkages in the Knowledge Era*, T. J. Courchene, ed. Kingston, Ontario: The John Deutsch Institute for the Study of Economic Policy, Queen's University, pp. 235-279.

Nakamura, A. and M. Nakamura (1992). "The Econometrics of Female Labor Supply and Children." *Econometric Reviews*, Vol. 11, No. 1, pp. 1-71.

Nakamura, A. and M. Nakamura (1981). "A Comparison of the Labor Force Behavior of Married Women in the United States and Canada, with Special Attention to the Impact of Income Taxes." *Econometrica*, Vol. 49, pp. 451-489.

Nakamura, A. and M. Nakamura (1985). *The Second Paycheck: A Socioeconomic Analysis of Earnings*. Orlando: Academic Press.

Nakamura, M., A. Nakamura and D. Cullen (1979). "Job Opportunities, the Offered Wage, and the Labor Supply of Married Women." *American Economic Review*, Vol. 69, pp. 787-805.

Picot, G., Z. Lin and C. Beach (1995). "Recent Trends in Employer Payroll Taxes." *Canadian Economic Observer*, September. Ottawa: Statistics Canada.

Stokes, E. (1995). "Canada's Unemployment Insurance Program as an Economic Stabilizer." Ottawa: Human Resources Development Canada, UI Evaluation Series.

Thomason, T. and R. P. Chaykowski (1995). *Research in Canadian Workers' Compensation.* Kingston, Ontario: Queen's University, Industrial Relations Centre, IRC Press.

Vaillancourt, F. (1994). "The Financing of Workers' Compensation Boards of Canada, 1960-1990." Toronto: Canadian Tax Foundation, Canadian Tax Paper no. 98.

Wong, G., M. Laurendeau and A. Routhier (1992). "Evaluation of UI Claimant Abuse." Ottawa: Employment and Immigration Canada, Strategic Policy and Planning.

Wong, G. and A. S. Roy (1997). "Effectiveness of UI Non-compliance Detection." *The Canadian Journal of Program Evaluation*, Vol. 12, No. 2, pp. 21-34.

Chapter 6

PAYROLL TAXES IN THE FINANCE OF SOCIAL SECURITY[*]

by Jonathan R. Kesselman

6.1 Introduction

Payroll taxes have been widely portrayed in Canada by the media, business leaders, policy advisors, and even at the highest levels of the political hierarchy as "job killers." In some of the more extreme rhetoric, Finance Minister Paul Martin asserted that "...there is nothing more ludicrous than a tax on hiring. But that's what high payroll taxes are" (Canada Department of Finance, 1994b, 7).[1] This view raises critical questions about the use of payroll taxes in general and in the finance of social security programs:

- Are payroll taxes guilty as charged, in whole or in part, of harming employment?

- If increased payroll tax rates have killed jobs and discouraged job creation, would cutting their rates yield large and enduring employment gains?

- Are there ways to restructure payroll taxes and the associated social security benefits so as to minimize any disadvantages or maximize any advantages of these taxes?

- Are there available other, more attractive and feasible, means of financing social security programs?

[*] A similar version of this chapter appeared in *Canadian Public Policy*, Vol. 22, No. 2 (June), 1996, pp. 162-179.
[1] For other similar views see Kroeger (1994, 18-20); "Payroll Taxes Blamed for Job Losses," *Globe and Mail*, February 10, 1994, B8; and discussion of the "business view" in Di Matteo and Shannon (1995).

- If payroll taxes are undesirable and alternative means of financing limited, must our social programs themselves be cut back?

Policy discourse on employer payroll taxes has focused almost exclusively on their short-run adverse employment effects. Indeed, most discussion appears not even to be aware that the disemployment effects are transitory and dissipate over time. What has been neglected in the public debate over payroll taxes are the longer-run economic impacts of financing social security programs. What are the comparative impacts of payroll taxes vis-à-vis other financing means on economic outcomes such as: 1) efficiency costs; 2) long-run growth; 3) long-run tax incidence; 4) the incentives of workers and firms; and 5) external effects of the programs such as social order and macro stability?

The present analysis will consider all of the major effects of payroll taxes in financing social security programs. It begins by examining general payroll taxes, where the taxes paid are not linked to specific program benefits. This general-revenue type of payroll tax is compared with other major tax sources. All taxes have undesirable effects, and the policy question is which form of tax has the least unacceptable attributes. The analysis then turns to the payroll tax's potential for benefit-tax linkages; this aspect of payroll taxes offers more efficient incentives than can be achieved with the other forms of tax finance. The analysis also considers the evidence and policy implications of the short-run disemployment effects and the longer-run incidence of payroll taxes.

This analysis uses the term "social security" to embrace public programs that have often been labeled "social insurance." Examples in the Canadian context include workers' compensation, unemployment insurance, and the Canada/Quebec Pension Plans. All these programs are financed by payroll taxes or "premiums" imposed on employers and/or employees. Additionally, the analysis at points refers to health care and/or educational programs that are financed in part by payroll taxes in several provinces. A distinction to be made at a couple of points is between social insurance and income maintenance programs. Where not otherwise indicated, the term "social security" will refer only to the former. In contrast to social insurance, income maintenance aims at *ex ante* redistribution to those at lower incomes. Pure social insurance aims to replace earnings lost due to uncertain events, and it results in redistribution across persons only after-the-fact, or *ex post*.

6.2 Payroll Taxes Versus Other Taxes

To provide a proper setting for analysis of payroll taxes in the social security context, it is useful to review what is known about the economics of general payroll taxes. That is, payroll taxes can be used to collect general revenues independent of any linkage to specific programs. As will be seen later, the Canadian provincial payroll taxes are of this general nature despite their nominal earmarking of revenues.[2] Indeed, parts of the social security programs in many countries are financed by payroll taxes but have little effective linkage between the "premiums" paid and the benefit entitlements (Kesselman, 1996a). Only after reviewing the economic properties of general payroll taxes shall I turn to the additional attributes that derive from linking the taxes to benefits within a social security program.

In the relevant public finance theory, payroll (or wage) taxes are one of three basic generic types of tax.[3] The other two are consumption taxes and income taxes. Income taxes include both the payroll base of labor income and income to capital. One might expect some similarities in the economic effects of the various bases. For example, most of all income derives from labor rather than capital, so that an income tax would share some distortions of a payroll tax base. However, the income base also imposes biases in the allocation of resources across time, mainly savings and investment choices. The payroll and consumption bases both avoid this distortion but introduce others in labor choices.[4]

Economic Efficiency

Raising an additional dollar of revenues from alternative tax bases imposes additional distortions and therefore efficiency costs on the economy. To calculate these "marginal efficiency costs," it is necessary to construct and simulate a computable general equilibrium model of the economy. This exercise has not been undertaken for the Canadian economy in a way that would cast light on the comparative efficiency costs of payroll taxes versus other taxes in any general manner. The most relevant estimates for Canada can be taken from a study for the U.S., which has tax and industrial structures that are not radically dissimilar (Ballard, Shoven, and Whalley, 1985).

In the American estimates, the tax having the lowest incremental efficiency cost is a consumer sales tax with broad coverage other than alcohol, gasoline, and tobacco (which are already sharply taxed and hence distorting). The second lowest-cost way to increase tax revenues is through labor-type taxes applied at the industry level, which includes payroll taxes. In ascending order of efficiency cost, the other major tax types are ranked as follows: output taxes, income taxes, and

---

[2] For detailed description of the Canadian provincial payroll taxes, see Kesselman (1994a); for further description of those taxes plus workers' compensation levies and the federal payroll taxes in Canada, see Di Matteo and Shannon (1995) and Picot, Lin, and Beach (1995).

[3] We do not consider here a fourth generic tax type, wealth taxes, and focus on tax bases that constitute flows rather than stocks of resources.

[4] For an early analysis suggesting a payroll tax as a replacement for the Canadian manufacturers' sales tax, see Whalley and Fretz (1990, 126-33); for a later analysis suggesting a payroll tax component in a direct consumption tax to replace the Goods and Service Tax (GST), see Kesselman (1994b).

capital-type taxes at the industry level. In these results, consumption and payroll taxes are less costly in efficiency than taxes which impact on capital accumulation, such as income and capital-type taxes.

Canadian estimates are available for the marginal efficiency costs of personal income taxes by province (Dahlby, 1994). The findings are that the added efficiency costs from raising an extra dollar of revenue range from 40 cents to over a dollar for increases in the basic tax rate. For increases in the surtax rates on higher earners, the estimated marginal efficiency costs range from several dollars to infinity per dollar of incremental revenue.[5] In contrast, the marginal efficiency cost of raising revenue from an increase in the UI payroll tax is estimated to be slightly *negative*. This result reflects the taxable ceiling in the payroll tax for UI, which acts in a lump-sum and non-distorting fashion for workers with earnings above that ceiling.[6] For a more general payroll tax without a taxable ceiling, the marginal efficiency costs should be similar to those for an income tax hike in a model that considers only distortions of labor supply and ignores effects on savings and capital accumulation.

Canadian estimates are not available to rank the relative efficiency costs of payroll and consumption taxes comparable to those for the U.S. economy.[7] However, the Canadian tax structure is closer to that of the U.S. than for most other countries. The greater openness of the Canadian economy would tend to raise the efficiency costs of taxes on capital relative to those on labor and consumption. Moreover, Canada's higher rates of tax on consumption and lower payroll tax rates than the US would also tend to raise our relative efficiency advantages from raising incremental revenues through payroll taxes. Given these factors and the lack of directly comparable Canadian studies, there is some unavoidable uncertainty in assessing the findings.

---

[5] In other words, the tax rates are estimated to lie beyond the peak of the Laffer Curve, so that further rate increases both aggravate economic distortions and depress aggregate tax revenues. Dahlby also provides estimates of the marginal efficiency costs for taxes when distributional considerations are included.

[6] The payroll tax rate increase is still distorting for workers with earnings below the taxable ceiling, but the lump-sum tax effect on higher earners causes them to work more (leisure is a normal good) and hence produce more output while also paying more payroll and income taxes. See Dahlby (1994, 68).

[7] Of course, the methods that underlie all of these studies may be open to critique based on the models' structures or parameter values. For example, the Dahlby (1994) estimates hinge critically on the assumed responsiveness of labor supply to tax rates. Yet those findings are supported by estimates for efficiency costs of the U.S. income tax that use a completely different methodology (Feldstein, 1995).

Long-Run Growth

The cited studies for efficiency costs of various taxes used static models that do not incorporate the full dynamics of economic adjustment over time. Hence, they ignore the impacts on savings and capital accumulation, which influence labor productivity and real wages over the longer run. To obtain insight into the "dynamic efficiency" of alternative taxes, we need to consider analytical and simulation exercises that include these factors.[8] The outcomes of interest include long-run economic growth, which is measured here as the utility levels of representative persons, and the long-run incidence of various taxes, which in this context has both a capital-labor aspect and an intergenerational aspect.

Both the consumption tax and the payroll tax avoid the distorted resource allocation over time that arise with a tax on income or capital. Hence, they will induce greater savings and aggregate capital accumulation. Because a consumption tax postpones the timing of tax payments over individuals' lifetimes relative to a payroll tax, it will also induce them to save more. Additionally, a consumption tax will tap some of the resources from dissavings by the elderly, so that it can collect the same revenues with a lower effective tax rate on current labor earnings than a payroll tax. For that reason a consumption tax imposes less distortion of labor market decisions than a payroll tax that collects the same total revenue.

The implications of these comparative tax properties are several, though the precise conclusions depend upon the model specification and assumed parameter values. Long-run economic growth will be higher under a consumption tax than a payroll tax and under a payroll tax than an income tax. The lifetime utility level for a representative individual will also tend to be ranked in the same order, although under some conditions a payroll tax can be ranked inferior to an income tax. Moreover, shifting from one type of tax to another affects the generations differently. For example, moving from a tax on consumption or income to a payroll tax is adverse to current workers and favorable to current retirees.

The cited ranking of the tax types can be very sensitive to the assumptions that are made about various aspects of the economic model. In particular, the established literature assumes that individuals' consumption rises continuously over their lifetime. Survey data on family expenditures, in contrast, shows that consumption levels exhibit an inverted U-shaped pattern, with declines in the later part of the life cycle. Using this more realistic consumption-age profile, it is possible for the payroll tax to yield a higher steady-state level of utility for a representative individual than a consumption tax.

---

[8] Major studies include Summers (1981), Auerbach, Kotlikoff, and Skinner (1983), Auerbach and Kotlikoff (1987), and Fullerton and Rogers (1993).

Long-Run Incidence

Shifting from income taxes toward greater use of payroll taxes, whether imposed on employers or employees, will reduce the economic well-being of the current generation of workers. In the long-run, though, the associated capital deepening will raise the level of real wages for future cohorts of workers. Hence, the long-run incidence of payroll taxes will not fall on labor, but rather on capital via a lower rate of return. For Canada's relatively small open economy, international capital mobility will retard a decline in the return to capital and the deepening of capital that raises real wages. Still, imperfect mobility of equity capital for smaller businesses will leave some scope for real wage increases. Gains to domestic well-being will also arise through decreased foreign indebtedness with increased savings.

Policy choices are also concerned with the interpersonal aspect of tax incidence in the long-run. The relevant comparisons here are the lifetime tax burdens borne by different groups, not simply the annual tax burdens which reflect the differing lifecycle stages of various individuals in the particular year. Using a model fitted to U.S. data, Fullerton and Rogers (1993, 36-37) find that the lifetime incidence of sales/excise taxes and payroll taxes are both regressive, with payroll taxes somewhat more so at the highest incomes.[9] They also report that the long-run efficiency cost of the payroll tax "is 0.1% of income, or 1.3% of revenue, figures that are smaller than for any other tax category."

Personal income taxes applied at progressive rates, even on imperfect bases, have the most progressive incidence of all major tax types. This finding holds both for the short-term impacts and the lifetime impacts on individuals.[10] However, income taxes are already heavily used in Canada, and there are questions about whether they should be applied still more heavily, especially on those at upper income levels. Reasons for restraint include the high efficiency costs of raising income tax rates (Dahlby, 1994) and compliance problems and even limits on incremental revenues (Kesselman, 1995). Of the remaining revenue sources, payroll taxes have a more acceptable incidence than most of the alternatives (Vermaeten, Gillespie, and Vermaeten, 1995, 331-32).

Operational Considerations

Payroll taxes excel with respect to their operational characteristic—simplicity in concept and application, low compliance costs for business, low administrative

---

[9] This result likely reflects the ceilings on U.S. social security taxable earnings more than any inherent property of a general payroll tax.

[10] See evidence and sources cited in Vermaeten, Gillespie, and Vermaeten (1995).

costs for government, and low vulnerability to abuse.[11] A well-designed payroll tax presents few of the complexities of valuation, measurement, or verification that arise for almost all other forms of tax, particularly the income tax. A payroll tax may include or exclude supplementary benefits of employees, but usually it includes only items that are also covered by the direct personal tax system. Floors or ceilings to covered earnings add some complications to payroll tax compliance, but these pale in comparison to the progressive rates of income tax withholding[12] or to the exemptions common under indirect consumption taxes.

Payroll taxes are further distinguished from many other taxes in that they can be applied in a broad and neutral fashion across all sectors of the economy. Payroll taxes can be levied on employees in public and non-profit entities as well as private firms, and they can also be levied even on the smallest firms. These attributes minimize the tax distortions across sectors and types of economic activity. However, extending a payroll tax to self-employment earnings requires special provisions, which can complicate the tax and face compliance problems similar to those in taxing incomes of the self-employed.[13] Relatively simple forms of tax have been applied to self-employed workers by the Canada/Quebec Pension Plans and the Quebec provincial tax; the Ontario levy is more complex.

6.3 Payroll Taxes for Social Security

Payroll taxes have in some cases been used for general revenue purposes, but they are most widely used around the world for financing social security programs.[14] A critical element in the use of payroll taxes to finance social security relates to the linkage between earnings and benefits, with payroll taxes or "premiums" based on earnings. It is useful to examine more closely the reasons for using payroll taxes to finance social security and the economic functions of having linkages between benefit entitlements and payroll taxes paid by the individual worker. Earmarking of payroll taxes for social security, general revenue finance, and the comparison

[11] These points are based on evidence in Kesselman (1994a, 1994b, and 1996b) and Pope, Fayle, and Chen (1993).

[12] Flat tax plans are often critiqued for assuming that the rate progessivity introduces much complexity into their operation. Yet, the interaction between rate progressivity and many features of the income tax (such as the taxable unit, accounting periods, averaging of taxes, capital gains, etc.) does substantially complicate the tax (see Kesselman, 1990).

[13] To make a payroll tax apply purely to labor earnings of the self-employed, some allowance should be made for the returns to tangible capital included in their net earnings. This refinement has not been included in the Canadian payroll taxes on the self-employed, but it has been done in Denmark.

[14] The most prominent examples of general-revenue payroll taxes are those of the Australian states and four Canadian provinces; see Kesselman (1994a and 1996b) for detailed treatment.

with income maintenance also warrant our consideration.

Reasons for Payroll Tax in Social Security

Several factors explain why payroll or employee compensation is used as the tax base for financing most social security programs.[15] These include: 1) the relative administrative and operational ease of payroll-type taxes, as discussed above; 2) the ability to link benefits to the worker's earnings and tax payments, with desirable incentive effects as discussed below; 3) a desire to confine the costs of the program to those who will benefit, as well as to confine the benefits to those who have been working; 4) the relative security and stability of a program that has its own earmarked funds and does not have to compete in the annual budget allocation process; and 5) related to the last factor, the political support for programs where the public can see what it is receiving for what it is paying, at least relative to the many public expenditures financed out of general revenue sources.

Yet another factor is also vital in explaining the use of payroll taxes to finance social security programs. A major objective of such programs is to replace a part of the worker's accustomed earnings in the event of the covered contingency. This earnings-replacement objective of social security programs differs from the income-maintenance   objective   of   welfare-type   programs.   Earnings replacement—where benefits rise with the individual's accustomed (and "insured") earnings—would be unacceptable in a program financed out of general revenue. Even if the overall tax system were substantially progressive, paying out larger benefits to higher earners would not likely pass the test of public acceptability.[16]

Benefit-Tax Linkages and Incentives

The primary objective of most social security programs is to cushion the individual's or family's income against earnings loss from specified risks. This earnings-replacement goal is typically achieved by structuring benefits to yield a strong benefit-earnings linkage. However, from the standpoint of incentives— both for workers and employers—it is the linkage between *expected* benefits and *taxes paid* that matters. If all covered workers faced the same risk or frequency of drawing benefits, then a payroll tax would intermediate these two concerns well. Premiums in the form of a proportional payroll tax (up to a specified ceiling) would simultaneously achieve both the social objective of a tight benefit-earnings

---

[15] This discussion draws on Kesselman (1996a); also see Messere (1993, 174-176) and, for a more critical view of payroll tax financing of social security, Dahlby (1992, 125-131).

[16] Moreover, paying a high standard benefit to all claimants so as to replace a reasonable portion of average earnings would pose strong disincentives for lower earners.

linkage and the economic concern of a close benefit-tax linkage.

When the expected risk or frequency of claims differs systematically across workers, it is no longer possible to achieve both the social and economic goals with a proportionate payroll tax. This arises when the risk of earnings loss differs by industry, occupation, region, skill, experience, age, or other characteristics of workers. In that case, one can still satisfy both goals by varying the premium or payroll tax rates to reflect the differential risks and probabilities of drawing benefits. Alternatively, one can structure the eligibility for benefits or the benefit rates inversely with the individual worker's risk. This would satisfy the incentive concern but at the cost of weakening the earnings-replacement objective. For programs financed by means other than a payroll tax or earnings-related premiums, the benefit-tax linkage is much looser, even if there is a good benefit-earnings linkage.

Before examining the incentive implications of having a tight benefit-tax linkage, it is useful to consider the key Canadian social security programs. The relevant "benefits" here are the *expected* level of benefits—the nominal benefit level times the probability of it being claimed.[17] The programs can be ranked from tightest to loosest linkages as follows:

- Workers' compensation has the tightest benefit-tax linkage, because of the variation of premium rates by the industry of the employer and, in some provinces for some industries, the experience-rating of individual firms based on their claims;

- The Canada/Quebec Pension Plans have the next tightest linkage due to their structure for retirement benefits (their largest benefit component) in relation to lifetime earnings and premium payments; however the massive intergenerational transfers from the start-up of the program compromise the linkage;

- Unemployment insurance displays a highly variable benefit-tax linkage on account of regional and other features of the benefit structure, social benefits in the program, lack of experience rating of premiums, and other provisions;

- Health care benefits partially financed by premiums in Alberta and British Columbia show very little benefit-tax linkage because they are levied at flat rates per person or family independent of age or health risk and further because persons who have not paid the premiums are not always excluded from benefits;

---

[17] Probability of claims includes the frequency of claims and the duration of benefits for each claim.

- Health care and/or post-secondary education partially financed by payroll taxes in four provinces have no benefit-tax linkage, both because real earmarking is absent and because the public services are provided irrespective of whether the beneficiary has worked in employment covered by the tax.

Worker-side Incentives A close linkage between benefits and taxes paid by the individual worker will remove almost all of the distortions and disincentives that have been noted for social security programs.[18] When some workers can obtain benefits that are far out of proportion to the taxes that they pay to finance the program, this can affect their choices about whether to seek work, what jobs to take, how long and how hard to work, and how much to save for old age. Notable impacts of poor linkages include stimulus to seasonally and cyclically unstable employment and intermittent participation in the labor market to qualify for benefits. For workers whose payroll taxes exceed their expected benefits, the customary disincentives and distortions to work choices also arise.

With a tight benefit-tax linkage, each individual in effect pays for their own benefits over the long-run. This is much like purchasing insurance at a fair, risk-adjusted premium rate that reflects the individual's past claims. In this case, the individual should make work and other choices that are undistorted by the program financing (Browning, 1975). Of course, this outcome hinges not only on the formal linkage of taxes to benefit entitlements but also requires that individuals value the benefits at their full costs.[18] It further requires that individuals have confidence that benefit provisions will be stable in the future. Public opinion polls indicate doubts about the long-term security of Canada Pension Plan benefits, so that premiums used to finance the program may be unnecessarily distorting.

Employer-side Incentives A close benefit-tax linkage can also serve important purposes from the standpoint of employer incentives. Imbalances between payroll taxes paid and benefit entitlements will distort the allocation of resources across the sectors of the economy. Industries that are more cyclically or seasonally unstable, and therefore generate more UI benefit claims for their workers, will expand relative to the more stable industries. This in itself will raise the economy's aggregate unemployment rate even if there is no response by workers to the increased net attractions of taking unstable work combined with periodic benefits. At the level of the individual firm, moreover, there will be implicit subsidies for using temporary layoffs to smooth demand fluctuations rather than stabilizing employment through means such as shortened work weeks or producing for inventory.

[18] In Chapter 5 Nakamura and Wong provide a comprehensive assessment of the unintended secondary effects of social security programs.

If a tighter benefit-tax linkage were pursued entirely through benefit-side changes, it might unduly penalize workers in the most unstable types of employment. If the average construction worker, for example, claims ten times as much UI benefits as the average hospital worker, the benefit rate for the former group would have to be cut to one-tenth that for the latter group if premium rates are uniform across industries. That would gut the program's fundamental objectives. Partial moves toward "experience rating" of individual benefit rates were proposed for the Canadian UI program in late 1995, and other reforms of the past decade have limited repeat claimants' access to or duration of benefits.

The other approach is to experience rate the premiums of individual employers, which has been a feature of the American state UI programs since their inception. This approach has been discussed in Canada but repeatedly resisted for UI, although it is common in the provincial workers' compensation programs.[19] Substantial variations in the payroll tax rates by employer would correct both the inter-industrial distortions of resource allocation and individual firm decisions to use temporary layoffs as a cheap means of accommodating demand fluctuations. By relying at least partially on experience rating in the financing of a social security program, it is possible to avoid excessive use of experience rating on the employees' side that would undermine the program's primary objective.[20]

Floors and Ceilings Frequent claims have been made that the insurable floors and ceilings in Canadian social security programs induce employers to work their employees either part-time or overtime.[21] The logic is that employers will attempt to minimize the premiums they pay for a given amount of work. Yet, to the extent that the programs have tight benefit-tax linkages, distorted employment patterns should not arise. If workers value the incremental social security benefits to which additional work entitles them, they will demand a higher wage for working hours that are not insured—either part-time hours below the floors or over-time hours above the ceilings. These higher wages will exactly offset the tax savings that firms enjoy from using uncovered employment.

To the extent that social security programs depart from tight benefit-tax linkages, the asserted employment distortions may arise. They can still arise even

---

[19] For a description of the potential application of experience rating to Canadian UI and a critique of the arguments against its use in Canada, see Kesselman (1983, Chapter 9).

[20] To some extent, though, higher premiums for industries that access UI benefits disproportionately would be shifted into lower gross earnings for their workers. However, within any given industry, firms that are less adaptable in smoothing their employment patterns to reduce their experience-rated UI premium rates would have to absorb those higher rates rather than passing them along to workers, since they compete with other firms in the same industry for labor.

[21] UI and CPP/QPP both have ceilings on insurable earnings. CPP/QPP has an exempt level of earnings per year, and UI has a threshold level of weekly earnings and work hours below which the employment is not insured. After the planned reforms are implemented, the UI lower threshold for coverage will be eliminated.

with good linkages in markets with wage rigidities (such as bargained, social, or uniform wages) or with high unemployment. The commonly prescribed solution is to remove the floors and ceilings for payroll taxes. However, this approach would further weaken the benefit-tax linkage unless the ceilings on benefit rates were also lifted and the qualification criteria for benefits were reduced. An alternative approach is to tighten the linkages through reforms on both the financing and benefit sides of the program.

Earmarking of Payroll Taxes

It is important to distinguish between benefit-tax linkage of payroll taxes and the case where payroll taxes are applied and earmarked for a specific program but without any clear linkage to an individual's benefit entitlements. With only nominal earmarking, all of the potential economic advantages of linkages are lost. Three Canadian provincial payroll taxes—those of Ontario, Manitoba, and Newfoundland—exhibit an even more extreme form. Although their statutes have titles such as "health and post-secondary education tax," these revenues are in fact paid into provincial general revenues and are not earmarked for the stated purposes.[22] Only Quebec's payroll tax has any legal earmarking with expenditures, through a Health Services Fund. Yet that Fund also draws heavily on general revenues, so that the earmarking is more symbolic than substantive.

General Revenue Finance of Social Security

To the extent that a social security program provides benefits that are not linked to the previous earnings and tax payments of the individual worker, the "linkage" arguments for using payroll tax finance are absent. This can arise under several circumstances: 1) benefits are tied to earnings but with a ceiling amount, whereas payroll taxes are levied without any ceiling (common in Europe); 2) the conditions for claiming, the amount of, or the duration of benefits have little relationship to a claimant's past earnings or past tax payments; and 3) the social returns to the cash or in-kind benefits provided to individual beneficiaries are large, such as with a) macroeconomic stabilization; b) reduced crime or improved social order; and c) improved functioning of labor markets.

If the linkage basis for payroll taxes is absent or attenuated, or if the external benefits of social security programs are significant, then partial finance by general

---

[22] See Kesselman (1994a) for description; Dahlby (1993, 154) argues that on the basis of "truth in advertising" Ontario's Employer Health Tax should be renamed to remove any mention of health.

revenues may be appropriate. In that case the general taxation criteria of efficiency and equity are relevant in choosing tax instruments. Those considerations do not *per se* rule out the use of general payroll taxes to collect the requisite funds. Partial finance by general revenues is common in many countries' social security programs. However, the general-revenue portion is typically earmarked to features such as flat-rate benefits or provisions targeted at the needy rather than enhancing the earnings-related portion of benefits.[23]

Macroeconomic effects have on occasion been used as an argument explicitly against payroll tax finance and in favor of general revenue finance. This has particularly been the case for the Canadian UI program, where the premium rates are adjusted annually and in a way that may reduce or thwart macro stabilization. Yet payroll taxes *per se* do not have any less stabilizing properties than some other major types of taxes such as consumption taxes; both are less stabilizing than income taxes. The issue here is simply how rapidly premium rates are adjusted to macro-induced funding needs of a social security program and the level of reserves held (Kesselman, 1983, Chapter 8). Recently announced changes to the setting of UI premium rates should help to address this issue.

Social Insurance versus Income Maintenance

Social security programs often contain important redistributive elements in addition to the *ex post* type of redistribution associated with social insurance. This fact has been cited as an argument against using payroll taxes to finance social security (Boadway, 1992). An alternative view is that the social insurance and income maintenance objectives should be separated by program.[24] The reasons for reducing or removing the vertical equity elements from social insurance programs is not that vertical equity does not matter. It is also not simply to improve the efficiencies that result from payroll-tax finance combined with strong benefit-tax linkages. After all, shifting the redistributive functions to programs of income maintenance—whether direct cash payments, tax-transfers, or public services—requires additional general revenue finance with its own efficiency costs.

The most compelling reason for stronger differentiation between payroll-tax financed social insurance and general-revenue financed income maintenance is

---

[23] This point is well illustrated by features of the Canadian unemployment insurance program prior to its conversion to full finance by "premiums" in recent years. Large general revenues went into the program in the 1970s and early 1980s, but those funds were tied to benefits paid at high national unemployment rates, extended benefits in regions of high unemployment, and various benefits provided for social reasons. For description and analysis, see Kesselman (1983, Chapters 4-5).

[24] This view is consistent with the recommendations of the Macdonald Commission, especially with respect to UI, and with more recent analyses such as Nakamura, Cragg, and Sayers (1994).

based upon political economy. *Ex ante* redistributive elements are much less simple, transparent, and effectively targeted in social insurance programs than in income maintenance. Any targeting in social insurance is typically based on individual rather than family income.[25] The redistributive elements in social insurance programs often take on unanticipated forms (cross-industry, cross-occupation, cross-region, cross-generation) or perverse forms (poor kids or spouses in well-off families, seasonal workers with high annual earnings). Such effects would not be tolerated in income maintenance programs on account of their greater transparency.

One might argue that entwining redistributive elements in a social security program can increase total transfers to the poor—even if the program contains some perverse or low-priority forms of redistribution. This argument would hinge on the greater popularity of social insurance vis-à-vis income maintenance and the lesser opprobrium of "premiums" vis-à-vis taxes. There is no way to assess this hypothesis with any certainty. Yet, it is less likely to be valid in today's environment where the public feels pressed by taxes of all kinds including payroll taxes. If that is the case, lower-priority forms of redistribution are being achieved at the expense of the currently destitute and the lifetime poor.

6.4 Payroll Tax Incidence and Policy

In the simplest economic theory, the incidence of a payroll tax hinges on the relative elasticities of the aggregate supply and aggregate demand curves in the labor market.[26] If labor supply is very inelastic relative to labor demand, the impacts of a payroll tax on employers will be shifted onto workers in the form of lower wages. However, this simple partial equilibrium approach ignores other channels that can also lead to tax shifting. The most obvious alternative is that higher employer payroll taxes, which raise unit production costs, get translated into higher product prices. Eventually this works its way into the cost of producing capital goods as well, so that both labor and capital have increased prices.[27] Then

---

[25] For example, the Canadian UI program has had a partial benefit recapture on higher earners (through an income surtax) for many years. Recent moves to toughen this recapture for frequent claimants at high incomes will still be based on individual incomes, as is appropriate in a social insurance program where premiums are also levied on an individual basis.

[26] Almost all the empirical literature on the incidence or employment effects of payroll taxes assumes that there is a single market for labor and that all labor services are homogeneous. These assumptions may miss important effects on the composition of labor demand or employment and wage rates.

[27] If substantial amounts of capital goods are imported, this process works as follows. The higher price level on domestic output causes the exchange rate to depreciate, which in turn raises the domestic currency price of capital good imports. All of this process requires monetary accommodation for a higher price level.

any initial substitution in production away from labor is offset, and the payroll tax is borne by workers through lower purchasing power of their unchanged nominal wages.[28]

To reflect the presence of downward wage rigidities, the adjustments to a payroll tax increase have been set within macroeconomic models.[29] The theory connecting payroll tax rates to employment or unemployment is based on the effects of a "tax wedge" between gross wage costs paid by employers and the real purchasing power of the employees' net wages. Three tax components enter this wedge—payroll taxes on employers, payroll and income taxes on employees, and retail sales or value-added taxes. Employer payroll taxes include mandatory social security premiums as well as general revenue levies.

In the macro models of taxation and employment, several characteristics are notable. First, *changes* in the total tax wedge may affect the gross cost of employing labor and thereby the demand for labor and total employment. Second, in the very long-run changes in the tax wedge will be borne mostly or entirely by labor through lower real net earnings. Hence, the actual magnitude of the wedge has little if any effect on the ultimate employment level. Third, increases in employer payroll tax rates are likely to have a faster and larger impact on gross wage costs and employment than are increases in employee payroll tax rates. And fourth, payroll taxes are not unique among taxation forms in causing temporary job losses. Taxes on employees or their consumption also can affect employment because workers may resist the fall in their real living standards by raising their wage demands.

Empirical Evidence

The body of empirical studies of employer payroll tax incidence has been reviewed in three recent papers.[30] Dahlby's (1993, 133) extensive critical review concludes that "These empirical studies ... suggest that labor bears over 80 per cent of the employer payroll tax burden in the long run." Hamermesh (1993, 172-173) reaches a similar conclusion:

---

[28] Dahlby (1992, 114-115) describes yet another channel of causation which can yield full shifting of the payroll tax onto workers; it is based on the general equilibrium elasticity of demand for labor, which can become perfectly elastic for a small, open economy with internationally elastic supply of capital.

[29] See Layard, Nickell, and Jackman (1991), Lindbeck (1993), and Phelps (1994), which take a similar approach. For Canadian analyses, see Keil and Symons (1990) and Fortin, Keil, and Symons (1995).

[30] Estimates of the employment impacts of payroll taxes need to distinguish the effects of tax changes from benefit-side incentives. Reduced-form methods are generally weak on this count, and even macro-based estimates that attempt to model benefits may fall short because of the complexity of benefit structures.

... the lack of convincing direct estimates of payroll tax shifting and the well-established values of the labor supply and demand elasticities suggest that there is only small scope *in the long run* for a payroll subsidy to increase employment, or for a payroll tax to reduce it. Barring substantial improvement in empirical studies of tax incidence, we must tentatively infer that most of the burden of payroll taxes is on wages.

Marchildon, Sargent, and Ruggeri (1996, 16) similarly find:

In the short run, empirical studies indicate a significant effect on employment and unemployment: employers will bear from 50 to as much as 100 percent of the tax ... However, as expected, in the long run these effects diminish as the tax burden is shifted onto employees. In the long run employees bear almost the full burden of payroll taxes.

A recent study using Canadian employer payroll tax data reached a finding "... that is more consistent with full shifting of the tax back onto labor than with no or partial shifting" (Beach, Lin, and Picot, 1995, 38).

Empirical findings from the numerous macro adjustment studies of payroll and other taxes are quite varied depending upon their data sets, countries, time periods, and methodologies.[31] In most cases the employment impacts of increases in employer payroll taxes are largest at the outset and decline over time. In some of the studies there remain significant job reductions even five or ten years beyond the change. For many studies the job losses decline more rapidly and mostly or entirely dissipate in the long-run. The extent of real wage resistance is important in these outcomes, and Canada appears to fall intermediate between the highly flexible US economy (for which most of the non-macro studies of payroll tax incidence have been undertaken) and the more rigid labor markets of Europe.

Perhaps the most striking empirical study of payroll tax incidence was undertaken for an unusually large, discrete cut in Chilean tax rates (Gruber, 1995). The entirety of the cut in employer tax rates was reflected quickly in higher gross pay for employees, so that there was no employment expansion as a result. In an economy with more extensive collective bargaining than Chile, the shifting of this tax windfall would undoubtedly be delayed and some extra jobs would be created

---

[31] See the studies cited in note 30, Stokes (1993), and the reviews in Organization for Economic Co-operation and Development (1994, Chapter 9 and 1995). Symons and Robertson (1990, 169) report that "Cross-country evidence is consistent with the view that employer taxation is shifted on to contractual wages in the long run," though there is not unanimity on this finding in the other studies.

in the transition.[32] Nevertheless, in this most ideal social experiment for examining payroll tax incidence and the employment effects, the results supported 100% shifting onto employee compensation.[33]

Benefit-Tax Linkage and Incidence

Gruber (1995, 27) states that his empirical finding of full shifting of payroll taxes onto wages does not distinguish between two competing hypotheses: "… that employees value these benefits highly, so that an outward shift in labor supply is 'undoing' the inward shift in labor demand; or that labor supply is very inelastic, so that employers are able to pass the full costs of taxation on to workers regardless of their valuation of benefits." Distinguishing between these two hypotheses is crucial to assess the incidence of payroll taxes used to collect general revenues or to finance programs without a benefit-tax linkage.

Three studies provide insight into this issue, though they focus on the distinction between uniform payroll tax rates and firm-specific (rather than benefit-linked) payroll tax rates. Using data at the aggregate level for Quebec (Vaillancourt and Marceau, 1990) and at the firm level for the U.S. (Anderson and Meyer, 1995 and 1996), uniform payroll taxes are found to be shifted fully into lower wages but firm-specific variations in payroll tax rates are born by the employer or produce changes in employment or layoff patterns.[34] Both results support the relevant economic theory, since a firm is not able to shift into lower wages a tax rate that is higher for itself than for other firms operating in the same market.

Policy Implications

The findings on payroll tax incidence carry important implications for public policy. Since the incidence of employer payroll taxes falls mostly or entirely on workers in the long-run, the disemployment effects diminish over time. Hence, the adverse effects of existing payroll tax rates may be minimal if those rates were first

---

[32] These changes occurred in a high-inflation environment, though that should not affect the outcome for an employer payroll tax cut; with downwardly rigid nominal wages, the inflation context could affect the speed of tax shifting for an *increase* in employer payroll tax rates.

[33] Anderson and Meyer (1996) estimate payroll tax incidence for another natural experiment that arose in 1985 when Washington state moved from a uniform UI tax rate to an experience rated system. They also found full shifting of the "market-level" tax component into workers' wages.

[34] Note that the firm-specific payroll tax for Quebec was workers' compensation premiums and for the US was unemployment insurance premiums in selected states. Hence, for Quebec one interpretation of the higher wages associated with higher tax rates is a compensating differential for riskier employment.

imposed many years ago. Only recent hikes in the rates might be expected to depress current employment. Moreover, payroll taxes are similar to other taxes, including income and consumption taxes, in placing a wedge between employers' labor costs and workers' real take-home earnings and thereby reducing employment. To the extent that the other tax forms strike capital incomes or retirement assets, they create smaller wedges in the labor market and thereby impose somewhat smaller short-run disemployment effects.[35]

The apparent asymmetry in labor market responses to upward versus downward changes in employer payroll tax rates has further policy implications. Raising these rates can depress employment over a period (up to a number of years) whose duration hinges on institutional factors affecting wage rigidity. These include the extent to which wages are determined by collective agreements, the intervals between such agreements, and the rate of inflation. Reducing employer payroll tax rates may yield much less boost to employment than the employment lost from a comparable size of tax increase. The reason is that there is much less resistance to wage hikes than wage cuts, making the adjustment process more rapid for the former. Hence, hopes for large or sustained stimulus to jobs from cutting the rates of payroll taxes may be misplaced, or at least the benefits may be short-lived.

My interpretation of the evidence suggests that the reliance on payroll tax finance of social security programs should hinge mainly on long-term factors of efficiency, growth, and equity rather than transitory employment effects. But once we have decided either to decrease or increase the relative use of payroll taxes, the short-run effects should be heeded in the timing of changes.[36] Payroll tax cuts should be applied as the economy begins its decline so that their (transitory) employment stimulus will cushion the trough. Payroll tax hikes should be applied during cyclical expansions so that their (transitory) disemployment effects will arise as the economy hits its peak. One application of this point would be to raise the CPP/QPP premium rates by larger amounts in boom periods rather than following a scheduled program of gradual rate hikes independent of the state of the economy.

One could also consider variations in the employer and employee shares of payroll taxes or social security contributions for countercyclical purposes. That is, payroll taxes would be shifted from the employer side to the employee side as the economy declines and conversely during economic expansion. However, this approach goes against the current distaste for fine-tuning stabilization policies. It

---

[35] The Organization for Economic Co-operation and Development (1994, 251-256 and 275) considers ways that the tax burden could be shifted away from labor to reduce the labor market wedges and concludes that "... large shifts in the tax burden are difficult."

[36] These recommendations are consistent with findings that premium rate changes for Canadian UI have acted to reduce the macro-stabilizing properties of the program (Dungan and Murphy, 1995; Stokes, 1995).

would also be complicated by the uncertain lags in response to payroll tax changes, similar to other macro policy lags.[37]

A permanent shift in the employer and employee shares of payroll taxes could be exploited for the one-time transitory employment stimulus. For example, the current ratio of 1.4 between employer and employee UI premiums could be converted to equal shares; this would entail a 20% hike for employee premiums and about a 14% cut for employer premiums. Such a move, though, would reduce the scope for any subsequent experience rating of the employer premiums. Alternatively, policies could shift away from employer payroll taxes and toward greater reliance on income taxes to capture employees' earnings. To avoid heavier taxes on capital-source incomes, this shift would also require provisions for exempting or sheltering such incomes from higher personal tax rates.

Yet another reason could be cited for shifting the balance of payroll taxes from levies on employers to employee levies. The visibility of these taxes and hence the accountability of governments to most voters is increased by imposing the taxes on employees. Indeed, a country such as Sweden that has traditionally relied heavily on employer payroll taxes (at 30% of gross payrolls in 1995) is in the process of shifting more of the contributions to employees to raise their visibility.[38] Similarly, in the 1980s Chile eliminated employer payroll taxes while instituting employee charges as part of its radical social security reform.

Finally, by linking payments to valued social security benefits, well-structured payroll taxes can eliminate most tax distortions for both employers and workers. In effect, social security premiums that reflect the expected value of benefits for each worker become like a price on a privately supplied good. This mutes any transitory disemployment effects of tax increases, if benefits are expanded at the same time. It can also avoid the static and long-run efficiency costs of this form of taxation, since it becomes a user charge.[39] Yet it should be stressed that this approach limits the potential for using social security programs to promote social goals such as redistribution across income groups, industries, or regions.

[37] Changes in payroll tax rates or employee-employer shares would also have to consider the other public finance reactions that arise through differential tax treatment of the payroll taxes paid by employers and by employees (see Kesselman, 1996a).

[38] Sweden imposed only a 5% rate on employees (through the income tax) in 1995 but planned to increase the employee contributions to half of the total payroll tax by the year 2000. Note that even higher total payroll tax rates are imposed in other European countries including Belgium and Germany; they rise as high as 60% in France and Italy (see Kesselman, 1996a).

[39] This analogy between the benefit-linked portion of payroll taxes and user charges (and the associated economic efficiencies) has also been noted by Marchildon, Sargent, and Ruggeri (1996).

6.5 Closing Thoughts

One can readily understand why many members of the business community would believe that payroll taxes are "job killers." At any point in time the payroll levies add to the total costs of hiring additional workers, just as higher wages would. What this view neglects is that market wage rates would also be higher in the absence of the payroll taxes, after all economic adjustments have taken place. Opposition to payroll taxes may also stem from a confusion between the effects of those taxes and the effects of poorly structured benefits financed by those taxes.

If the empirical findings of full shifting of employer payroll taxes onto workers are correct, the total cost of employing workers would be the same with or without payroll taxes, or at higher or lower tax rates. Even the Finance Department has acknowledged that it is the shock of increases in payroll taxes that inhibits hiring rather than the levels of the tax rates; it recommended only "a reversal of the steady rise of payroll taxes" and not a slashing of their rates.[40] Hence, a key conclusion is that the use of payroll taxes in the finance of social security should be based on their long-term economic effects as compared with other means of finance.

Payroll taxes in general are a relatively efficient form of taxation in the long-run, at least compared with taxes on income or capital. They can also be simple and low-cost to operate for both governments and taxpayers. When tied to benefits in a well-designed program of social security, payroll taxes offer the additional advantage of posing minimal distortions to labor and other economic behaviors. This potential is unlike most other forms of taxation, which have unavoidable efficiency costs. Energies in reforming social security might best be directed at improving benefit-tax linkages, while recognizing the underlying social objectives of the programs.

Two concrete examples illustrate this approach to reform. Experience rating the UI premiums—preferably by individual firm but at least by industry/occupational groups—would complement the limited experience rating of individual workers that has already been done. This would also be consistent with financing practices for the provincial workers' compensation plans. It has been estimated that moving the American UI programs from partial to full experience rating would reduce temporary layoffs by more than one quarter (Topel, 1983, 555). For the Canadian UI program, which lacks any experience rating on its financial side, this reform could bring even larger gains.

Reforms to improve the credibility of workers' future Canada/Quebec Pension Plan benefits would tighten the perceived benefit-tax linkage and thereby reduce any disincentives of the premiums. This might be achieved by shifting the

---

[40] Canada Department of Finance (1994, 26); also see discussion of payroll taxes on pp. 21-22 and 52-53.

program to a funded basis or by more radical moves toward forced savings in the form of individual retirement accounts.[41] In view of the inevitable increases in CPP/QPP premium rates over future years, this reform could improve incentives simultaneously with higher payroll tax rates.

Some redistributive elements might best be removed from social security programs and installed in existing or new income maintenance or tax-transfer programs. This would produce better benefit-tax linkages in social security and hence improve incentives. More fundamentally, this change would make redistribution more effective and better targeted, because the transparency of income maintenance would avoid the perverse and low-priority forms of redistribution that can be camouflaged within the complexity of social security programs. Hence, the total volume of effective vertical redistribution to the neediest groups might actually be increased.

It is time to end the misguided rhetoric about payroll taxes, so that serious analysis of the real options for reforming social security and its finance can proceed. Payroll taxes will undoubtedly continue to play a major role in financing these programs, for reasons that have been examined here. The structure of those taxes, the balance between employer and employee levies, and the benefit-tax linkages for social security are all important matters for inquiry. The mix of payroll taxes and general revenues in financing social security may also warrant review. But we should not be impelled to greater general revenue finance or smaller social security programs based on hopes for large or enduring employment gains.

REFERENCES

Anderson, P. M. and B. D. Meyer (1995). "The Incidence of a Firm-Varying Payroll Tax: The Case of Unemployment Insurance." Cambridge, Mass.: National Bureau of Economic Research, Working Paper No. 5201 (revised April 1996).

Anderson, P. M. and B. D. Meyer (1996). "Using a Natural Experiment to Estimate the Effects of the Unemployment Insurance Payroll Tax on Layoffs, Employment, and Wages." Mimeo, Dartmouth College, Northwestern University, and National Bureau of Economic Research, January.

Auerbach, A. J. and L. J. Kotlikoff (1987). *Dynamic Fiscal Policy*. Cambridge: Cambridge University Press.

Auerbach, A. J., L. J. Kotlikoff and J. Skinner (1983). "The Efficiency Gains from Dynamic Tax Reform." *International Economic Review*, Vol. 24, pp. 81-100.

---

[41] The latter approach has been proposed by the Reform Party of Canada; it would require a period of substantially increased levies to cover the future costs of benefit liabilities that have already been incurred by the program. This proposal is patterned after Chile's privatization of public pensions that was tied to the cut in employer payroll taxes combined with a hike in employee payroll taxes.

Ballard, C. L., J. B. Shoven, and J. Whalley (1985). "General Equilibrium Computations of the Marginal Welfare Costs of Taxes in the United States." *American Economic Review*, Vol. 75, pp. 128-38.

Beach, C., Z. Lin, and G. Picot (1995). "The Employer Payroll Tax in Canada and Its Effects on the Demand for Labor." Kingston: Queen's University, mimeo, May.

Boadway, R. (1992) "Comment" on Dahlby (1992). In Richard M. Bird and Jack M. Mintz (eds.), *Taxation to 2000 and Beyond*, pp. 160-65. Toronto: Canadian Tax Foundation.

Browning, E. K. (1975). "Labor Supply Distortions of Social Security." *Southern Economic Journal*, Vol. 42, pp. 243-52.

Canada Department of Finance (1994). *A New Framework for Economic Policy*. Ottawa: Department of Finance.

Dahlby, B. (1992). "Taxation and Social Insurance." In *Taxation to 2000 and Beyond*, Richard M. Bird and Jack M. Mintz, eds., pp. 110-156. Toronto: Canadian Tax Foundation.

Dahlby, B. (1993). "Payroll Taxes." In *Business Taxation in Ontario*, Allan M. Maslove, ed., pp. 80-170. Toronto: University of Toronto Press.

Dahlby, B. (1994). "The Distortionary Effect of Rising Taxes." In *Deficit Reduction: What Pain, What Gain?*, William B. P. Robson and William M. Scarth, eds., pp. 43-72. Toronto: C. D. Howe Institute.

Di Matteo, L. and M. Shannon (1995). "Payroll Taxation in Canada: An Overview." *Canadian Business Economics*, Vol. 3, No. 4, pp. 5-22.

Dungan, P. and S. Murphy (1995). "The UI System as an Automatic Stabilizer in Canada." Ottawa : Human Resources Development Canada, Evaluation Brief # 5.

Feldstein, M. (1995). "Tax Avoidance and the Deadweight Loss of the Income Tax." Cambridge, Mass.: National Bureau of Economic Research, Working Paper No. 5055

Fortin, P., M. Keil, and J. Symons (1995). "The Source of Unemployment in Canada, 1967-1991: Evidence from a Panel of Regions and Demographic Groups." Toronto: Canadian Institute for Advanced Research, Working Paper No. 45.

Fullerton, D. and D. L. Rogers (1993). *Who Bears the Lifetime Tax Burden?* Washington, D.C.: Brookings Institution.

Gruber, J. (1995). "The Incidence of Payroll Taxation: Evidence from Chile." Cambridge, Mass: National Bureau of Economic Research, Working Paper No. 5053.

Hamermesh, D. (1993). *Labor Demand*. Princeton: Princeton University Press.

Keil, M. W. and J. S. V. Symons (1990). "An Analysis of Canadian Unemployment." *Canadian Public Policy – Analyse de Politiques*, Vol. XVI, pp. 1-16.

Kesselman, J. R. (1983). *Financing Canadian Unemployment Insurance.* Toronto: Canadian Tax Foundation.

Kesselman, J. R. (1990). *Rate Structure and Personal Taxation: Flat Rate or Dual Rate?* Wellington, New Zealand: Victoria University Press for the Institute of Policy Studies.

Kesselman, J. R. (1994a). "Canadian Provincial Payroll Taxation: A Structural and Policy Analysis." *Canadian Tax Journal,* Vol. 42, No. 1, pp. 150-200.

Kesselman, J. R. (1994b). "Assessing a Direct Consumption Tax To Replace the GST." *Canadian Tax Journal,* Vol. 42, No. 3, pp. 709-803.

Kesselman, J. R. (1995). "Provincial Tax Policies in the New Economy: The Case of British Columbia." *Canadian Business Economics,* Vol. 4, No. 1, pp. 24-46.

Kesselman, J. R. (1996a). "Payroll Taxes Around the World: Concepts and Practice." *Canadian Tax Journal,* Vol. 44, No. 1.

Kesselman, J. R. (1996b). "Toward a Harmonized Payroll Tax for Australia." *Australian Tax Forum,* Vol. 13, No. 2.

Kroeger, A. (1994). "Governments and the 'Jobs' Issue." *The Eric Hanson Memorial Lecture Series,* Volume 7, Fall 1993. Edmonton: Department of Economics, University of Alberta.

Layard, R., S. Nickell and R. Jackman (1991). *Unemployment: Macroeconomic Performance and the Labor Market.* Oxford: Oxford University Press.

Lindbeck, A. (1982). "Tax Effects versus Budget Effects on Labor Supply." *Economic Inquiry,* Vol. 20, pp. 473-89.

Lindbeck, A. (1993). *Unemployment and Macroeconomics.* Cambridge: MIT Press.

Marchildon, L., T. C. Sargent and J. Ruggeri (1996). "The Economic Effects of Payroll Taxes: Theory and Empirical Evidence." Mimeo. Ottawa: Economic Studies and Policy Analysis Division, Department of Finance, February.

Messere, K. (1993). *Tax Policies in OECD Countries: Choices and Conflicts.* Amsterdam: IBFD Publications BV.

Nakamura, A., J. Cragg and K. Sayers (1994). "The Case for Disentangling the Insurance and Income Assistance Roles of Unemployment Insurance." *Canadian Business Economics,* Vol. 3, No. 1, pp. 46-53.

Organization for Economic Co-operation and Development (OECD) (1994). *The OECD Jobs Study: Evidence and Explanations. Part II, The Adjustment Potential of the Labor Market.* Paris: OECD.

Organization for Economic Co-operation and Development (OECD) (1995). *The OECD Jobs Study: Taxation, Employment and Unemployment.* Paris: OECD.

Phelps, E. S. (1994). *Structural Slumps: The Modern Equilibrium Theory of Unemployment,*

Interest, and Assets. Cambridge, Mass: Harvard University Press.

Picot, G., Z. Lin, and C. Beach (1995). "Recent Trends in Employer Payroll Taxes." *Canadian Economic Observer*, Cat. No. 11-010 (September), pp. 3.1-3:24. Ottawa: Statistics Canada.

Pope, J., R. Fayle, and D. L. Chen (1993). *The Compliance Costs of Employment-Related Taxation in Australia*. Sydney: Australian Tax Research Foundation.

Stokes, E. (1993). "Payroll Taxes and Employment." Paper prepared for the conference on *Unemployment: What Is to Be Done?* Laurentian University, Sudbury, Ontario, March.

Stokes, E. (1995). *Canada's Unemployment Insurance Program as an Economic Stabilizer*. Ottawa: Human Resources Development Canada, Evaluation Brief #6.

Summers, L. H. (1981). "Capital Taxation and Accumulation in a Life Cycle Growth Model." *American Economic Review*, Vol. 71, pp. 533-44.

Symons, J. and D. Robertson (1990). "Employer Versus Employee Taxation: The Impact on Employment." In *OECD Employment Outlook*, pp. 153-177. Paris: OECD.

Topel, R. H. (1983). "On Layoffs and Unemployment Insurance." *American Economic Review*, Vol. 73, pp. 541-559.

Vaillancourt, F. and N. Marceau (1990). "Do General and Firm-Specific Employer Payroll Taxes Have the Same Incidence? Theory and Evidence." *Economics Letters*, Vol. 34 , pp. 75-81.

Vermaeten, A., W. I. Gillespie and F. Vermaeten (1995). "Who Paid the Taxes in Canada, 1951-1988?" *Canadian Public Policy – Analyse de Politiques*, Vol. XXI, pp. 317-343.

Whalley, J. and D. Fretz (1990). *The Economics of the Goods and Services Tax*. Toronto: Canadian Tax Foundation.

Chapter 7

THE IMPACT OF LABOR COSTS ON COMPETITIVENESS AND WORKER PROTECTION IN THE MANUFACTURING SECTOR OF LATIN AMERICA

by Víctor Tokman and Daniel Martínez

7.1 Introduction

Some of the most important labor legislation and social security reforms in Latin America over recent years have had the reduction of labor costs as a key objective. The main supporting argument is that labor costs are an important component in total production costs; hence, by lessening the former, the final cost of value-added is diminished, which in turn improves the competitiveness of enterprises.

This labor cost reduction policy has been pursued through one or both of two avenues: first, cutting the contributions and employer payroll taxes used to finance social security programs and other benefit entitlements in order to reduce the non-wage component of labor costs; and second, granting incentives (subsidies and/or tax exemptions) in order to encourage enterprises to hire specific workers. The objective of this second approach is to promote the employment especially of youths without work experience and of workers who are getting on in years.

This new orientation of labor legislation and social security systems (which naturally have other objectives as well) is open to debate. Not surprisingly, entrepreneurs generally consider that labor cost reduction, along with greater flexibility in both labor contracts and the tasks which workers can be assigned within the enterprises, does indeed improve competitiveness by permitting them to offer better prices and/or product quality and to more easily adapt the organization and the size of the payroll to abrupt fluctuations in product demand. On the other hand, workers are apprehensive that such cost reductions will affect them adversely in terms of their income and/or the extent and quality of benefits, especially those related to health and pensions.

In this context, two relevant questions arise. Is a reduction of labor costs necessary to improve competitiveness?[1] Does the present policy orientation on labor costs seriously affect the worker protection systems?

The next sections will analyze these two questions by examining the recent experience of five important Latin American countries—Argentina, Brazil, Chile, Mexico and Peru, three of which (Argentina, Chile and Peru) have recently implemented substantial labor legislation and social security reforms, while the other two (Brazil and Mexico) have, as of the date of writing, made no changes at all.[2] Due to data constraints, the analysis of competitiveness is limited to the manufacturing sector; for the same reason, the analysis of productivity relates only to labor, not to all factors.[3]

7.2 Labor Costs and Competitiveness in the Manufacturing Sector

Competitiveness has always been a challenge for countries and enterprises, even for economies where "inward-oriented" growth was and still is favored and where domestic demand is the locomotive for this growth. In the present context of greater openness, however, it is becoming increasingly important and is giving rise to questions such as: What exactly is competitiveness? Is it possible to "measure" the competitiveness of a country's economy? Are available measurements based on correct and verifiable figures and data? Can the measuring rods used for enterprises be applied at the national level?

As mentioned previously, the concerns of this chapter are, first, whether and when labor costs are a major determinant in the evolution of competitiveness and, second, how labor cost reductions will impact the welfare of workers.

Domestic Labor Costs, Labor Productivity and Competitiveness

In the following discussion, an attempt is made to compare the impacts of changes in labor costs and of the real exchange rate on manufacturing competitiveness over

---

[1] This analysis of labor costs considers changes in their non-wage component, but does not attempt to deal with subsidies and tax exemptions designed to promote the contracting of certain types of workers, since not enough empirical information is available on that phenomenon.

[2] Brazil and Mexico are still in the process of reforming their legislation on social security and the effects are unknown.

[3] Although this study reports only on labor productivity, changes in this variable are generally correlated to those in total factor productivity. Hofman (1995) reports that this was the case in Argentina, Brazil, Chile and Mexico during 1950-1992.

the early 1990s in the cases of Argentina, Brazil, Chile, Mexico and Peru. In assessing the impact of labor costs it is relevant to compare increases in that variable with increases in labor productivity. We may say that "labor competitiveness" (c) is improved when the increase of labor productivity (q) is higher than that of labor costs (e).[4]

$$c = q - e$$

A look at the performance of each country in the manufacturing sector between 1990 and 1995 reveals that productivity (constant U.S. dollars) surged in Argentina, Brazil, Mexico and Peru, while growing adequately in Chile, but did not match the increase in real labor costs (nominal values, deflated by the Producer Price Index) except in the case of Mexico (Table 7.1); therefore labor competitiveness, based on the proxy used here, fell at annual rates ranging from 1.9% in Argentina to 9.0% in Peru. Meanwhile, the increase in wages (earnings deflated by the Consumer Price Index) was less than that of labor productivity for all countries except Chile (Table 7.2).[5] If labor competitiveness were defined by

Table 7.1
Evolution of Labor Competitiveness in the Manufacturing Sector,
Five Latin American Countries, 1990 - 1995
(Annual Percent Change - Values Deflated by the
Production Price Index for Manufacturing)

Country	Real Labor Costs	Labor Productivity	Labor Competitiveness
Argentina	9.1	7.0	-1.9
Brazil	12.5	7.5	-4.4
Chile	6.9	3.2	-3.5
Mexico	4.3	5.2	0.9
Peru	17.2	6.6	-9.0

Source: ILO, unpublished statistics.

[4] Labor costs include gross wages plus non-wage labor costs. In order to estimate the 1995 labor costs, the cost increase during the first semester of 1995 with respect to the first semester of 1994, has been used. The variable c provides only a rough proxy for overall competitiveness, which is likely to depend ultimately on the rate of profit in a sector. This might not move in the same direction or by a similar amount as would "labor competitiveness" as defined here. The relation would tend to be close if the difference between the increase in labor productivity and that in labor costs were matched by the increase in capital productivity. This would be the case, for example, if the increase in labor costs measured an increase in quality-corrected labor incomes and the rest of the increase in labor productivity were due to factor-neutral technological change.

[5] Workers and employers view the importance of labor cost increases from different perspectives. For workers, what matters is the relationship between wages/social security contributions and the prices of goods and services they purchase, measured by the Consumer Price Index (CPI). For employers what matters is the relationship between wage/social security costs and the Producer Price Index (PPI) of the goods and services they produce.

Table 7.2
Evolution of Real Labor Costs, Labor Productivity, and Labor Competitiveness
in the Manufacturing Sector, Five Latin American Countries, 1990 - 1995
(Absolute Values Expressed in 1990 Prices; Values Deflated by the Consumer Price Index)

Country	Wages	Non-Wage Labor Costs	Total	Labor Productivity	Labor Competitiveness
		Real Hourly Labor Costs			
Argentina (peso)					
1990	0.95	0.60	1.55		
1995	0.94	0.49	1.43		
Annual % change	0.0	-4.0	-1.6	7.0	8.5
Brazil (real)					
1990	n/a	n/a	n/a		
1995	n/a	n/a	n/a		
Annual % change	2.9	2.9	2.9	7.5	4.5
Chile (peso)					
1990	5.65	2.52	8.17		
1995	6.98	3.10	10.08		
Annual % change	4.3	4.2	4.3	3.2	-1.1
Mexico (peso)					
1990	4.98	2.33	7.31		
1995	5.21	2.56	7.77		
Annual % change	0.9	1.9	1.2	5.2	4.0
Peru (N. Sol)					
1990	0.21	0.12	0.33		
1995	0.26	0.16	0.42		
Annual % change	4.4	5.9	5.1	6.6	1.4

Source: ILO, unpublished statistics.

the comparison of productivity growth against this measure of labor costs, it would be viewed as rising in four of the five countries. In each of the countries the increase in labor costs from the employers' perspective was significantly higher than the increase in real earnings of the workers; in some cases the gap was dramatic. Thus real labor costs rose by an annual rate of 9.1% in Argentina, while real earnings fell by 1.6% per annum. This huge difference between the evolution of labor costs and wage earnings was due to changes in relative prices between tradeables and non-tradeables as a result of macroeconomic policies: on the one hand, trade liberalization with resulting foreign capital inflows and, on the other, the use of the exchange rate to promote economic stability. Furthermore, the increase in exports (mainly primary products) resulting from trade openness, brought about local currency overvaluation. All this affected tradeables (more important for the producer) more rapidly than non-tradeables (more important to workers as consumers). Thus, while the evolution of labor costs and wages is perceived differently by the parties involved, the differences in performance were essentially due to factors beyond the labor environment.

Note that the increase of non-wage labor costs (NWLCs) was similar to that of wages (W) in Brazil and Chile,[6] lower in Argentina, and higher in Mexico and Peru (Table 7.2). These variations among the countries during the 1990-95 period reflect the differing ratios of payroll taxes or contributions to gross wages.[7]

The Exchange Rate, Labor Costs and Competitiveness

Although it is not possible without full details on the cost structure of a sector to compare the effects on competitiveness of changes in productivity, in labor costs and in the real exchange rate, a rough idea of their relative importance may be obtained with available data.

A country's competitiveness vis-à-vis others depends on relative prices expressed in a common currency. Changes reflect not only growth of productivity and of labor costs but also variations in the country's real exchange rate vis-à-vis other countries. For present purposes, the U.S. dollar has been used to calculate productivity and labor costs (see Table 7.3).

As in the case of real labor costs calculated in local currencies using the PPI as a deflator, the estimates in U.S. dollars show that in the period 1990-95 labor costs grew at higher rates than those of productivity in all the Latin countries considered, except Mexico. Therefore, competitiveness in external markets decreased in almost all the countries: -6.5% per annum in Argentina, -0.9% in Brazil, -5.7% and -4.5% in Chile and Peru respectively. In Mexico, competitiveness improved by 3.6% annually owing to the 1995 peso devaluation,while until 1994 there had been losses. As a basis for comparison, in the same period of 1990-95 competitiveness improved in the United States (1.2% annually) and in Korea (8.0%) but worsened in Germany (-0.3%).

With the performance of productivity and labor costs expressed in U.S. dollars with conversion at the actual exchange rate (as in Table 7.3), the estimates are affected by any currency over-or-undervaluation patterns among the countries. During the period under discussion, the currencies of most of these countries became overvalued (or increasingly so) owing both to the large inflow of foreign

---

[6] It is worth mentioning that Chile began reducing non-wage labor costs at the beginning of the 1980s.

[7] Note that the estimated growth rates in competitiveness may differ *slightly* from those in official publications of the countries. The explanation for these discrepancies lies in the different average wages registered according to whether the source was household or establishment surveys and also in the different methods used when calculating workers' and employers' contributions. As relates to productivity, the figures given here refer to all those employed in the manufacturing sectors (and not only large enterprises), while some official estimates only consider the workers employed in enterprises with a hundred or more workers. When calculations include those employed in large enterprises only (which in general have shrunk during 1990-95) productivity estimates become significantly higher and labor competitiveness as well.

Table 7.3
**Labor Costs and the Evolution of Labor Productivity and Labor Competitiveness
in the Manufacturing Sector, Eight Countries, 1990-1995**
(values expressed in U.S. dollars)

Country	Hourly Labor Costs			Labor Productivity	Labor Competitiveness
	Wages	Non-Wage Labor Costs	Total		
USA					
1990	10.83	4.37	15.2		
1995	12.33	4.97	17.3		
Annual % change	2.6	2.6	2.6	3.8	1.2
Korea					
1990	3.85	0.85	4.7		
1995	4.59	1.01	5.6		
Annual % change	3.6	3.5	3.6	11.9	8.0
Germany					
1990	14.17	11.13	25.30		
1994	15.40	12.10	27.50		
Annual % change	2.1	2.1	2.1	1.8	-0.3
Argentina					
1990	1.90	1.21	3.11		
1995	4.01	2.10	6.10		
Annual % change	16.1	11.7	14.4	7.0	-6.5
Brazil			7.6		
1990	1.95	1.14	3.09		
1995	2.94	1.71	4.65		
Annual % change	8.6	8.4	8.5	7.5	-0.9
Chile					
1990	1.85	0.83	2.68		
1995	2.91	1.30	4.21		
Annual % change	9.5	9.4	9.4	3.2	-5.7
Mexico					
1990	1.77	0.83	2.60		
1995	1.88	0.92	2.80		
Annual % change	1.2	2.1	1.5	5.2	3.6
Peru					
1990	1.06	0.64	1.70		
1995	1.81	1.14	2.95		
Annual % change	11.3	12.2	11.6	6.6	-4.5

Source: ILO, unpublished statistics.

capital and the use of the exchange rate as an "anchor" for economic stability. In other cases, the exchange rate was more closely linked to the performance of both local and external inflations, sometimes moving towards undervaluation.

Real gains in labor competitiveness (c) are achieved when the increase of labor productivity (q) is higher than that of labor costs expressed in terms of the price of local output (cl) by enough to offset any move in the direction of overvaluation (Tc).

$$c = q - cl - Tc$$

Macroeconomic phenomena which have little or nothing to do either with the evolution of productivity or with that of real wages can alter competitiveness of the manufacturing sector through currency overvaluation or undervaluation—defined against a benchmark exchange rate determined by relative inflation of the local currency vis-à-vis that of the main trading partners. Table 7.4 shows how the competitiveness index is affected by this factor.

As noted earlier, labor competitiveness expressed in dollars fell in four of the five countries (Mexico being the exception), at rates ranging from 0.9% to 6.5% per year as shown above in Table 7.3. If the effective exchange rates had remained unchanged, the losses in competitiveness would have been less in Argentina (2.8% annually), Chile (4.2%) and Peru (1.8%) and gains would have been achieved in Brazil (6.2%) (based on the last column of Table 7.4). The devaluation of the peso in Mexico in 1995 was responsible for the net positive shift in competitiveness in that country; until 1994, though, the trend was in the other direction, with losses of 3.8% per year. In fact, if the devaluation had not overshot in 1995, the net shift of competitiveness would still have been marginally negative.

The importance of exchange rate movements is of course not limited to Latin America. In South Korea, for example, the large gain achieved in competitiveness would have been reduced by two-thirds had the currency devaluation not taken place.

The foregoing results demonstrate that the degree of competitiveness in the countries is the outcome not only of decisions made by employers and workers on matters of labor costs and productivity, but also of macroeconomic policies. During the period 1990-95, the prevailing currency overvaluation in many countries of the region raised the labor costs in dollar terms and eroded the export earnings in local currencies, giving rise to losses in competitiveness. As of 1995, only in Mexico had the currency devaluation and the related stagnation of wages in dollar terms had the effect of allowing both earnings and competitiveness to increase.

As mentioned previously, these exchange rate policies have been influenced by the great short-term or speculative foreign capital inflows occurring in the framework of greater openness to international trade and by policies for economic stability. In the countries under study, globalization of the world economy has thus had not only the well-known positive effects, but also an "exchange-rate effect" which thus far has tended to impinge negatively on the competitiveness of the manufacturing sector.

In summary, though the evolution of labor costs in the countries under study did, indeed, have an impact on competitiveness in the early 1990s, competitiveness also depends on the evolution of productivity and on the effects of macroeconomic

Table 7.4
Factors Affecting the Evolution of Labor Competitiveness in the
Manufacturing Sector, Eight Countries, 1990-1995
(absolute values in U.S. dollars - Index, 1990 = 100)

Country	Labor Productivity			Labor Costs			Effective Exchange Rate		Labor Competitiveness Index	
	1990	1994	1995	1990	1994	1995	1994	1995	1994	1995
U.S.										
Level	38.6	44.8	46.5	15.2	16.9	17.3				
Index	100.0	116.0	120.5	100.0	111.0	113.8	100.0	100.0	104.5	105.9
Korea										
Level	14.3	22.4	...	4.7	5.4	...				
Index	100.0	157.0		100.0	115.0		118.4	...	115.3	...
Germany										
Level				25.3	27.5					
Index	100.0	107.4		100.0	108.7		102.0		96.9	
Argentina										
Level	17.1	25.7	24.0	3.1	5.2	6.1				
Index	100.0	150.3	140.4	100.0	168.0	197.0	78.4	82.0	113.9	86.9
Brazil										
Level	10.5	14.1	15.1	3.1	4.2	4.7				
Index	100.0	134.0	144.0	100.0	137.0	150.0	92.9	71.2	105.3	134.8
Chile										
Level	13.6	15.3	15.9	2.7	4.1	4.2				
Index	100.0	113.0	117.0	100.0	152.0	156.0	96.5	93.0	77.0	80.0
Mexico										
Level	12.3	15.9	15.9	2.6	3.8	2.8				
Index	100.0	130.0	129.0	100.0	146.0	108.0	81.9	120.5	108.7	99.1
Peru										
Level	10.8	13.8	14.8	1.7	2.7	3.0				
Index	100.0	128.0	137.0	100.0	159.0	174.0	84.4	86.2	95.4	91.3

Sources: Productivity: UNIDO; Labor Costs: ILO; Effective Exchange Rate: ECLAC.

policies, factors which turn out to have been more important for competitiveness than the performance of wages or labor taxes.

7.3 Labor Costs in the Manufacturing Sector and the Protection of Workers

As just noted, the main single factor in the trajectory of competitiveness in the manufacturing sectors under review during the period 1990-95 was currency overvaluation and the adjustment lag of relative prices within a context of trade openness and the slowing down of inflation.

As for the labor cost increases themselves, it is important to consider to what extent they are caused by higher real wages and to what extent by higher labor taxes. And with respect to labor taxes, it is relevant to distinguish between those allocated to finance social security programs and other benefit entitlements which directly favor the worker or indirectly the enterprise—as is the case of retirement pensions, health services (including insurance against occupational accidents), vocational training, etc. and those financing programs and activities which neither benefit the enterprise nor the worker, and can be considered, *strictu sensu,* as labor taxes. Increases in the latter type of labor taxes would not mean greater worker protection. This section analyzes the evolution of labor cost composition between the wage and non-wage components over 1990-95.

The Evolution of Labor Cost Structure in the Manufacturing Sector

Workers' contributions[8] rose in Argentina from 14% of the gross wage in 1980 to 16% in 1990 and to 17% in 1995; in Peru they climbed from 6% in 1990 (before the reform of the pension system) to 11% in 1995, though having peaked at 19% in 1994. In Brazil, Chile and Mexico they remained at 9%, 21% and 5% respectively over 1990-1995 (Tables 7.5a-7.5e). The high workers' contributions in Chile and the sharp increase in Peru can be attributed to the reform of these pension regimes on the basis of exclusive financing of pensions from workers' contributions. The previous workers' and employers' contributions were transferred to the new system. The shift of pension contributions from employers to workers was compensated by a proportionate gross wage increase.

Employers' contributions to social security programs and other benefit entitlements (bonuses and vacations) as a percent of gross wages varied across countries (Tables 7.5a-7.5e). In Argentina this ratio was reduced from 67.4% in 1980 to 63.7% in 1990, remaining unchanged until 1995, when it declined more significantly to 51.8%. In Brazil and Chile the ratio remained unchanged at 58.2% and 44.5% of the gross wage respectively. In Mexico it increased from 40.6% in 1980 to 46.8% in 1990 and to 49.0% in 1995 while in Peru it eased up from 60.8% in 1990 to 62.9% in 1995. Currently, employers' contributions to social security and other benefit entitlement as a share of total labor costs (gross wage plus contributions) are 39% in Peru, 37% in Brazil, 34% in Argentina, 33% in Mexico and 31% in Chile.

---

[8] "Workers' contributions" refers to the deductions from the workers' gross wages to finance social benefits and "employers' contributions" refers to the additional contributions corresponding to the employer for the same purpose.

Table 7.5a
Components of Labor Costs, Argentina, Selected Years, 1980-1995

	1980	1990	1994	1995[1]
A. Gross Wage	100.0	100.0	100.0	100.0
Average monthly net wage[2]	97.1	95.1	94.1	94.6
B. Worker's Contributions	14.0	16.0	17.0	17.0
Pensions	11.0	10.0	11.0	11.0
Social Programs[3]	4.0	6.0	6.0	6.0
C. Employer's Contributions	67.4	63.7	63.7	51.8
1. Contributions	*43.9*	*40.4*	*40.4*	*30.4*
Retirement	15.0	11.0	16.0	9.6
Social Programs[3]	4.5	8.0	8.0	8.0
Family Allowance	12.0	9.0	7.5	4.5
Unemployment Fund	0.0	0.0	1.5	0.9
IPD[4]	5.4	5.4	5.4	5.4
Accidents	2.0	2.0	2.0	2.0
Housing	5.0	5.0	0.0	0.0
2. Other Employer's Costs	*23.5*	*23.3*	*23.3*	*21.4*
Complementary Income[5]	11.6	11.6	11.6	10.5
Vacations	11.9	11.7	11.7	10.9
D. Total Costs (A+C)	167.4	163.7	163.7	151.8
Worker's Contributions/Total Cost	8.4	9.8	10.4	11.2
Employer's Contributions/Total Cost	40.3	38.9	38.9	34.1
Non-Wage Costs/Total Cost	48.6	48.7	49.3	45.3

Notes: [1] During the first quarter of 1995 in Buenos Aires, employer's contributions were slashed by 80% in the poorest provinces, yielding an estimated average reduction of 40%. In April of 1995 the rates were replaced by those of 1994, except Social Programs. [2] Net wage = gross wage - worker's contributions + complementary income. [3] Health, including PAMI in 1980. [4] Indemnity for dismissal. The 1994 rate was applied for 1980 and 1990. [5] Bonuses and additional wages.

Source: ILO, based on official figures.

Workers' and Employers' Social Security Contributions and Labor Market Policies

Since as far back as the last century countries have implemented policies designed to support and protect those in the labor market. Such policies have had three basic components. The first involves worker protection against occupational accidents and death, as well as old age (pensions); financing is derived from workers and employers (including the state as an employer) via the non-wage component of labor costs. The second includes active policies to create jobs for the unemployed or to improve the productivity of those who are employed—programs to generate and promote work for specific types of workers, vocational training programs for the employed and unemployed, etc. Finally, unemployment insurance is designed to ensure an income for those unemployed for more than some minimum period of time.

Table 7.5b
Components of Labor Costs, Brazil, 1990, 1994, 1995

	1990	1994	1995
A. Gross Wage	**100.0**	**100.0**	**100.0**
Average monthly net wage[1]			
B. Worker's Contributions	**9.0**	**9.0**	**9.0**
Pensions	9.0	9.0	9.0
C. Employer's Contributions	**58.2**	**58.2**	**58.2**
1. Contributions	*35.8*	*35.8*	*35.8*
Retirement	20.0	20.0	20.0
Ind. Social Services	1.5	1.5	1.5
Ind. Training Services	1.0	1.0	1.0
IBCRA	0.2	0.2	0.2
Education	2.5	2.5	2.5
SEBRAE	0.6	0.6	0.6
FGTS	8.0	8.0	8.0
Accidents	2.0	2.0	2.0
2. Other Employer's Costs	*22.4*	*22.4*	*22.4*
Complementary Income[2]	11.1	11.1	11.1
Vacations	11.3	11.3	11.3
D. Total Costs (A+C)	**158.2**	**158.2**	**158.2**
Worker's Contributions/Total Cost	5.7	5.7	5.7
Employer's Contributions/Total Cost	36.8	36.8	36.8
Non-Wage Costs/Total Cost	42.5	42.5	42.5

Notes: [1] Net wage = gross wage - worker's contributions + complementary income. [2] Bonuses and additional wages.

Source: ILO, based on official figures.

Table 7.5c
Components of Labor Costs, Chile, 1990, 1994, 1995

	1990	1994	1995
A. Gross Wage	**100.0**	**100.0**	**100.0**
Net wage[1]	103.9	103.9	103.9
B. Worker's Contributions	**9.0**	**9.0**	**9.0**
Pensions	9.0	9.0	9.0
Health			
Accidents			
C. Employer's Contributions	**44.5**	**44.5**	**44.5**
1. Contributions	*10.4*	*10.4*	*10.4*
Indemnity for dismissal	8.3	8.3	8.3
Accidents[2]	2.1	2.1	2.1
2. Other Employer's Costs	*34.1*	*34.1*	*34.1*
Complementary Income[3]	25.0	25.0	25.0
Vacations	9.1	9.1	9.1
D. Total Costs (A+C)	**144.5**	**144.5**	**144.5**
Worker's Contributions/Total Cost	14.6	14.6	14.6
Employer's Contributions/Total Cost	30.8	30.8	30.8
Non-Wage Costs/Total Cost	45.4	45.4	45.4

Notes: [1] Net wage = gross wage - worker's contributions + complementary income. [2] Average, maximum rate: 3.9%. [3] Profit sharing: estimated to be equivalent to 25% of gross wage.

Source: ILO, based on official figures.

Table 7.5d
Components of Labor Costs, Mexico, Selected Years, 1980-1995

	1980	1990	1994	1995[1]
A. Gross Wage	100.0	100.0	100.0	100.0
Net wage[1]	105.9	105.9	105.9	105.8
B. Worker's Contributions	5.1	5.1	5.1	5.2
Pensions	2.1	2.1	2.1	2.1
Health[2]	3.0	3.0	3.0	3.1
C. Employer's Contributions	40.6	46.8	48.7	49.0
1. Contributions	*19.0*	*25.2*	*27.1*	*27.4*
Retirement	3.8	4.2	5.7	6.0
Health[2]	5.6	8.4	8.8	8.8
Nurseries	1.0	1.0	1.0	1.0
Retirement for non-age reason	0.0	2.0	2.0	2.0
Accidents	2.6	2.6	2.6	2.6
Housing	5.0	5.0	5.0	5.0
Income tax	1.0	0.0	0.0	0.0
Payroll tax	0.0	2.0	2.0	2.0
2. Other Employer's Costs	*21.6*	*21.6*	*21.6*	*21.6*
Complementary Income	11.0	11.0	11.0	11.0
Vacations	10.6	10.6	10.6	10.6
D. Total Costs (A+C)	140.6	146.8	148.7	149.0
Worker's Contributions/Total Cost	3.6	3.5	3.4	3.5
Employer's Contributions/Total Cost	28.9	31.9	32.8	32.9
Non-Wage Costs/Total Cost	32.5	35.4	36.2	36.4

Notes: [1] Net wage = gross wage - worker's contributions + complementary income. [2] Mexican Institute for Social Security: Private Sector.

Source: ILO, based on official figures.

In the OECD countries, significant resources are allocated to such social security programs; in the European Union, for example, 20.5% of the GDP was budgeted for this purpose in 1991. In 1992, The OECD countries destined almost 0.6% of the GDP to finance active labor market policies (1.1% in the European Union and 0.3% in the United States) and nearly 1.2% of the GDP to fund unemployment insurance (2.1% in the EU and 0.6% in the United States). Labor market policies taken together absorbed 1.7% of GDP in all the OECD countries (3.2% in the EU). Spending on social benefits, active intervention in the labor market, and income protection of the unemployed together consumed resources equivalent to 24% of the GDP in the European Union.

In Latin America, social security absorbs approximately ten to twelve percent of the GDP. Government expenditure allocated to social security in 1991 represented 5.9% of the GDP in Argentina and 6.0% in Brazil. Few resources are allocated to active labor market policies. The scarce data available show that Argentina in 1993 spent approximately 0.06% of the GDP this way, Bolivia in 1990—including the Emergency Social Fund (FSE)—0.04%, Honduras in 1993—with the Honduran Fund for Social Investment (FHIS)—0.03%, and

Table 7.5e
Components of Labor Costs, Peru, 1990, 1994, 1995

	1990	1994	1995
A. Gross Wage	**100.0**	**100.0**	**100.0**
Net wage[1]	113.0	100.0	107.6
B. Worker's Contributions	**6.0**	**19.9**	**11.4**
Pensions[2]	3.0	16.0	11.4
Health	3.0	3.0	0.0
C. Employer's Contributions	**60.8**	**56.9**	**62.9**
1. Contributions	*30.8*	*26.9*	*32.9*
Retirement	6.0	0.0	0.0
Health	6.0	6.0	9.0
Accidents[3]	3.0	4.0	4.0
Housing	6.0	6.0	9.0
SENATI (Training)	1.5	1.2	1.2
CTS (dismissal)	8.3	9.7	9.7
2. Other Employer's Costs	*30.0*	*30.0*	*30.0*
Complementary Income	11.0	11.0	11.0
Vacations	19.0	19.0	19.0
D. Total Costs (A+C)	**160.8**	**156.9**	**162.9**
Worker's Contributions/Total Cost	3.7	12.1	7.0
Employer's Contributions/Total Cost	37.8	36.3	38.6
Non-Wage Costs/Total Cost	41.5	48.4	45.6

Notes: [1] Net wage = gross wage - worker's contributions + complementary income. [2] Average, maximum rate: 3.9%. [3] Workers affiliated to the AFP. [3] Average. Rates fluctuate between 1.2% and 12.2%.

Source: ILO, based on official figures.

Mexico—Solidarity National Program (PRONASOL)—0.1%. Finally, unemployment insurance is unavailable in most Latin American countries. Argentina, which probably has the best coverage, allocates approximately 0.2% of the GDP in this direction. In total, the amount which the countries of the region allocate for the financing of social security and labor market policies taken together represents a little more than 12% of the GDP, half the amount designated by the European countries.

Resources generated from contributions and labor taxes are designated to finance social security and labor market programs virtually in their totality. Hence, changes in the amounts of these contributions and of labor taxes would be expected to have a major impact on all national policies oriented to workers.

Contributions and labor taxes also have a macroeconomic impact. Public pension systems are legally obliged to build up reserves by means of investing part of the funds received while the private pension systems invest practically all their funds in equity and debt markets. Therefore, all pension fund systems contribute to savings and investment in the country. In Chile for example, investment based on the annual contributions to private pension funds (AFPs) is approximately US$ 2.3 billion annually, or roughly 5.0% of the GDP. With an investment to output ratio of around 23%, these resources would account for almost 20% of total investment. The accumulated funds of all the private pension systems in said country now stand at approximately US$ 25 billion, equivalent to 40% of the GDP. These large resources strengthen the capital market. However, as the fund grows, AFPs find it increasingly difficult to invest their funds due to the limited size of the market.

Workers' Benefits

The labor cost increases in U.S. dollar terms reported above (Table 7.3) were not primarily a result of increased contributions to finance social security benefits. The reforms on pension fund systems, and in some cases on health care, were primarily oriented to improve operational and financial efficiency. They created no upward pressure on wages, though neither was there an expansion of coverage (except in Mexico).

As yet it is not clear whether in the medium term these reforms will contribute to a reduction of the fiscal burden. Although the financial problems faced by the private pension and health systems have been solved, it is also evident that a large sector of the population—i.e., the poorest—continues to depend on the public systems. As the latter no longer provide for a mechanism of subsidy from the higher to the lower income groups, they could be compelled to draw increasingly on general fiscal revenues to fund their services (especially health care). Therefore, the positive effects which the social security reforms are supposed to accomplish in terms of alleviating the burden on the state remain to be demonstrated.

Without foregoing a steady increase in revenues to the public systems, there could have been a redistribution of contributions which would have implied a restructuring of workers' benefits. As will be seen in the last section, this did not occur. Although important modifications were made to the pension regimes in the early 1990s, this has neither given rise to an increase in the cost of benefits nor to extended coverage (except in Mexico). The same results emerged in the case of health services. Contributions not directly related to workers' benefits (i.e., labor taxes) are only present in Mexico and Peru. In Peru they increased, raising the share of non-wage labor costs in total cost.

In summary, the recent social security reforms have neither changed significantly the share of non-wage labor costs in total labor costs nor expanded the coverage. Furthermore, the anticipated fiscal benefits need to be reevaluated; it is possible that in the middle-run, public health systems which cater for the lower income-level groups may require more funds, since resource transfers are no longer available to them.

The next sections will analyze the pension fund and health care systems for workers and their families.

Pension Fund Systems

Recent reforms in most countries of the region have brought about significant changes in the pension fund systems as well as in their financing, with resulting effects on their coverage.

The different systems At present, there are at least six pension fund systems in Latin America, the main distinguishing feature being whether they are based on individual capitalization or not. Table 7.6 provides a classification. In two countries, Chile and Peru, the private system is now the only option for new workers, though workers already affiliated to the old system have not been obliged to switch. Those who choose to move to the private pension system (AFP) cannot later revert to the old system. In Argentina and Colombia there are two options, public and private, and it is obligatory to be affiliated to one of them. In Uruguay, affiliation to the public system is obligatory for workers who earn less than US$ 770 per month (August 1995). In this case, the worker has the option to also be affiliated to the private system which is based on individual capitalization, but the law stipulates a maximum of 50% of the worker's contributions may go to this system. When income is over US$ 770 but less than US$ 2,300 affiliation to the private system is compulsory. In this case the total of a worker's contributions are saved in a private pension fund (AFP) and the employers' contributions are deposited in the public system. Finally, if a worker's income is higher than US$ 2,300 per month, affiliation to the private system is obligatory under the same conditions as for the above-mentioned range, but contributions made from the remunerations over and above US$ 2,300 are optional. In the rest of the countries it is still compulsory to be affiliated to the public system. It is understood that affiliation is compulsory for all workers who are contracted, whatever the type of contract.

Financing the system The pension systems are financed with workers' and employers' contributions and, in the case of Costa Rica, a small contribution by government (Table 7.7). The contributions are exorbitant in Argentina, Brazil and Uruguay (all over 20% of gross wages) if compared to the other countries, where they vary between 7.5% and 13.5% of those wages. As shown, the private systems of Chile and Peru are cheaper than the various public-private arrangements found in Argentina, Brazil and Uruguay, but more expensive than the public systems in Costa Rica, Colombia and Mexico. In the private systems the cost is totally covered by the worker, who assumes the burden which was covered in the old regime by the employer; to compensate for this, workers' wages were increased in

Table 7.6
Features of Pension Fund Systems, Selected Latin American Countries

Type of Program	Country	System	Condition	Characteristics
Public Reformed	Brazil Costa Rica Mexico Panama	Public	Compulsory	- Retirement age raised - Contribution increased - Privileged regimes eliminated
Private Substitutive	Chile Peru	Private	Compulsory	- Minimum pension guaranteed - Pension depends on capitalization - Credit notes for contributions to old system
Mixed	Argentina	Public and Private	One of them compulsory	- Basic pension is guaranteed in public system and complementary pension in the private
Selective	Colombia	Public or Private	One of them compulsory	- Contributor chooses system - Under certain conditions contributor can change to the other system - Credit notes for contributions to old system
Complementary	Ecuador Guatemala Mexico	Public and Private	Public is compulsory and private is voluntary	- In Mexico, to complement pension is compulsory in private sector, but not in public sector
Mixed	Uruguay	Public or Private	Compulsory one or the other depending on income	- 1st level (up to US$770) public is compulsory - 2nd level (up to US$2,300) private is compulsory - 3rd level (over US$2,300) private is compulsory, but contribution is optional for income above US$2,300

Source: Studies made available by Carmelo Mesa-Lago.

the same proportion. In Chile and later in Peru, the total contributions to the system decreased following the reforms. In Peru as of 1994, the worker totally covered the 16% cost (seven percentage points higher than all contributions in 1990), but this percent was reduced to 11.4% in 1995. Chile's reform occurred earlier, so pension financing has remained unchanged in recent years. In Argentina workers' contributions have remained unchanged while those of employers decreased from 15% in 1980 to 9.6% in 1995. In Uruguay, workers' contributions were increased to 15% from 13% in the 1995 reform while those of employers were decreased to 12.5% from 14.5%. Colombia's 1994 reform mandated an annual one percent increase until 1996, with workers financing 25% of the increase and employers 75%. In Mexico, workers' contributions have been constant but employers' contributions have risen from 3.8% in 1980 to 4.2% in 1990, and to 6% in 1995. In summary, there has been no general upward trend in pension fund contributions during the early 1990s; Mexico is an exception.

In the countries under study, contributions to the pension system amount to between 3.5% and 4.5% of GDP, vary between a third and a half of all non-wage

Table 7.7
Sources of Finance for Pension Systems, Eight Latin American Countries, 1995
(percents of salary)

Country	Year	Worker	Employer	Government	Total
Argentina[1]	1995	11.0	9.6	0.0	20.6
Brazil[2]	1995	9.0	20.0	0.0	29.4
Colombia	1995	3.1	9.4	0.0	12.5
Costa Rica	1993	2.5	4.75	0.25	7.5
Chile[3]	1995	13.5[5]	0.0	0.0	13.5
Mexico[5]	1995	2.1	6.0	0.0	8.1
Peru[3]	1995	11.4	0.0	0.0	11.4
Uruguay[6]	1995	15.0	12.5	0.0	27.5

Notes: [1] Public. One portion is transferred to the private pension system (commissions and insurance are included) and another portion to the public system. [2] Includes pensions and health care. [3] Private pension system. [4] Includes 3.5% of commissions and insurance. [5] Public and private systems. [6] After the reform of August 1995.

Source: ILO, based on official sources.

labor costs, and account for a third of all the resources which the countries allocate to social security and labor market policies.

A key question at this time is whether the private systems, apart from being less expensive, are also more effective than the public ones. This issue is still being debated, with two main issues under dispute: workers' assurance of receiving an adequate pension on retirement, and degree of coverage of the labor force. Due to the plummeting inflation and the recent arrival of the private systems, it would be premature to attempt conclusions on how well the capitalized contributions will hold up in the long-term or on the performance of the invested funds.

Coverage The share of the labor force affiliated to pension systems during 1993-1994 was only 16% in Peru, 23% in Colombia and 26% in Honduras (Table 7.8). In the remaining countries where information was available, it varied between 40% (Mexico) and 50% (Costa Rica, Chile and Panama being close to the latter figure). Coverage has been slowly increasing in all of these countries, whatever the system in operation, but the shift from public to private led to dramatic declines in Chile (from 61% to 33%) and in Peru (from 37% or perhaps higher to 13%) when these countries drastically reformed their systems.up to 47%[9].

In many countries of the region, social security coverage has never been extensive. The increase over time has been associated with the development of

---

[9] In addition to the extent of coverage, the private systems are being affected by arrears in contribution payments, as in the case of public systems. In Chile for example, this amount has been estimated at US$ 300 million a year for the last few years. The annual contributions are between US$ 3.6 and US$ 3.7 billion, thus overdue payments represent approximately 8% of the total. This problem is due to both contributions that are registered but unpaid (approximately US$ 250 million annually or 84% of total overdue) and contributions that are not registered (approximately US$ 50 million or 16% of total overdue payments).

Table 7.8
Health and Pension Coverage, Selected Latin American Countries, 1980-1994

Year	Colombia		Costa Rica		Chile		Honduras		Mexico		Panama		Peru	
	H	P	H	P	H	P	H	P	H	P	H	P	H	P
1980	24	24	80	44	92	61	n/a	n/a	44	42	n/a	n/a	17	37
1985	24	24	81	45	92	33	n/a	n/a	45	n/a	n/a	n/a	28	n/a
1990	25	21	82	46	95	42	16	22	46	42	52	42	34	n/a
1991	25	21	85	46	95	44	18	24	46	43	51	42	35	n/a
1992	27	23	86	47	95	46	19	24	43	42	53	48	36	n/a
1993	29	24	86	48	95	45	20	26	42	40	56	48	31	13
1994	29	23	86	48	95	47	n/a	n/a	42	39	59	49	27	16

Note: H = all beneficiaries of health systems as a percent of total population. P = all contributors to pension systems (public and private) as a percent of total economically active population.

Source: ILO, based on official figures.

various organizations and groups who claimed social security as one of their basic rights. Thus urban wage earners, some permanent farm workers, professionals, etc. have been incorporated into the system. However, important sectors have been little covered, especially the unemployed and those who do not have a work contract—peasants, informal self-employed, non-remunerated family workers and domestic workers. Mesa-Lago (1990) notes some of the obstacles faced by the informal sector: the fact that double contributions have to be paid by the owner of a micro-enterprise (as both a worker and an employer); generally low and unstable income of the self-employed; employment instability of wage earners in the micro-enterprises, etc. Peasants face the same problems. Although some of these difficulties have been removed or alleviated (e.g., elimination of double contributions or lower contributions) with the privatization of the pension systems, other basic factors persist, namely the low income of workers not covered by the system and their employment instability.

Some countries try to tackle the problem by having the state guarantee a minimum pension. Only in a few of them, however, is this guarantee extended to all citizens, including those who have not contributed. In the rest only those who are affiliated with the public system—even though contributing with small payments due to low income, are guaranteed a minimum pension.

The application of a model which guarantees a minimum pension to all citizens, including those who have not contributed, seems to be the most desirable strategy from a welfare point of view. However, since not all countries are in the position to finance such a model, it is necessary to explore alternative, less ambitious, models. Among these alternatives, one involves the provision of a minimum pension to special target groups who have not contributed to the system (for example, indigenous persons over the age of 65);[10] another involves the contracting of a private pension insurance on the part of the informal workers and peasants, which would generate pensions based on individual capitalization at the time of retirement.

Thus far, however, the various reformed pension systems have not achieved significantly extended coverage. The principal reason for this is probably the high cost (relative to income) of monthly payments for affiliation, which many workers are not in the position to pay.

Health Care for Workers

There have also been reforms over recent years in the health care systems for workers and their families, though they have been less far-reaching than the pension systems.

The different systems Currently there are three systems in operation in the region (Table 7.9). There is a clear difference between the private variants in Chile and Colombia and those in Argentina and Uruguay. In Chile and Colombia, the private systems are composed of enterprises which provide health services to any person who buys health insurance and contributes regularly to keep the policy valid. These enterprises are either medical institutions or, as in the case of Colombia, insurance companies which subcontract the services of medical centers, hospitals, etc. In Argentina and Uruguay the systems consist of a number of health funds which are financed by compulsory workers' contributions and administered by the representatives of workers ("Obras Sociales" in Argentina and the "Mutualistas" in Uruguay). These funds subcontract the services of medical centers.

The public systems are managed in one of three ways: directly by the public institution responsible for the service[11] or indirectly by the subcontracting of the services to health institutions, or as a combination of the two.

Financing In the six countries under study, as of 1995 the cost of health care (including occupational accident insurance) was between 10% (Chile) and 16% (Argentina, Costa Rica and Mexico) of gross wages (Table 7.10), with Mexico and Peru at intermediate levels of 12% and 13% respectively. In Brazil health and pensions together represented 29% of wages, but the amount destined to each is not preestablished.

---

[10] It is estimated that in countries such as Guatemala, Honduras, Bolivia, etc. the application of this system targeted to indigenous persons over the age of 65 would require resources equivalent to between 1% and 2% of the GDP.

[11] In some countries where this system is applied, some sectors such as the army and public servants receive health care from specially created public institutions.

Table 7.9
Features of Latin American Health Care Systems

Program	Country	System	Characteristics	Beneficiaries
Selective	Chile, Colombia	Public and private	One of them compulsory	Contributors, family, retirees
Private	Argentina, Uruguay	Private	Compulsory	Contributors, family, retirees
Public	All other countries	Public	Compulsory	Contributors, family, retirees

Source: ILO, based on official information.

In Peru, the cost is totally funded by the employer. In the others, it is shared by the worker and the employer and, in Costa Rica and Mexico by the government as well. Note however that in many countries the government also covers the deficit of the system, an amount not been reflected in Table 7.10, but which stands at between one and three percent of the GDP and is hence a very significant share of the total in some cases.

Comparing the evolution of health system contributions of the workers and employers over the last few years, Tables 7.5a-7.5e and 7.10 show that in Argentina the workers' contributions surged by nearly 50% and those of the employers by almost 100% between 1980 and 1995. In Mexico, only the employers' contributions were hiked (by close to 50%). In Chile and Peru the total contribution percentage has remained unchanged, but in Peru the employer has assumed the total cost, of which the worker previously bore a third.

The expenditure on health care for workers and their families appears, as in the case of the pension fund, to typically fall in the range 3-5% of GDP. In 1994, for example, it reached 4.8% of the GDP in Costa Rica and 3.8% in Chile and Mexico.

Coverage In the seven countries where reliable data is available, the percentage of the population benefitting from the health care system[12] has risen in recent years, with the exception of Mexico (Table 7.8). Thus, in Colombia, nearly 30% of the population was protected in 1994 by social health care, while 25% was covered in 1990; in Costa Rica, 86% was protected as compared to 80% or a little more during the 1980s; in Chile, 95% vs. 92% at the onset of the 1980s; in Honduras, 20% against 15% in 1990; in Panama, 59% as compared to 52% in 1990 and in Peru, 27% versus 17% in 1980. Only Mexico experienced a minor decline from 46% in 1990 to 42% in 1993.

Considering that slightly more than 90% of the population is covered by social health care in Argentina and Brazil, one can conclude that approximately

---

[12] Excluding certain public health institutions which provide universal coverage for limited services.

Table 7.10
Sources of Finance for Workers' Health Care, Seven Latin American Countries, Circa 1995

Country	Year	Worker	Employer	Government	Total
Argentina[1]	1995	6.0	10.0[2]	0.0	16.0
Brazil[3]	1995	9.0	20.0	0.0	29.0
Colombia	1994	n/a	n/a	n/a	12.0
Costa Rica	1993	5.5	9.25	1.25	16.0
Chile	1995	7.6[3]	2.10[4]	0.0	9.7[5]
Mexico	1995	3.1	12.4[6]	0.7	16.2
Peru	1995	0.0	13.0[7]	0.0	13.0

Notes: [1]April, 1995, after the deduction on the employer's contribution had been suspended. [2]Includes health and occupational accidents. [3]Includes pensions and health. [4]Occupational accidents. [5]Minimum contribution. Additional payments are optional for the worker. [6]Includes illness-maternity (8.75%), work hazards (2.6%) and nursery (1.0%). [7]Includes work hazards.

Source: ILO, based on official figures.

55% of the population in the region currently benefit from such health care systems. Moreover, if those covered by special government health programs are added, the rate of coverage ascends to 85%.[13]

Labor Taxes

In Argentina and Chile all contributions seem to be aimed at the financing of workers' benefits. In Mexico and Peru there are also contributions regarded as taxes, whether explicitly as in the case of Mexico (payroll taxes) or implicitly (for housing in both countries, as the contributing worker does not have the assurance that he/she will acquire a house financed by such a program). In the hypothetical case of these types of taxes being removed, it would imply a labor cost drop of slightly over 4% in the manufacturing sector in Mexico and nearly 6% in Peru. It would have a positive impact on competitiveness of enterprises.

7.4 Fiscal Implications of Health and Pension Reforms

A clear trend exists in Latin America to direct the numerous reforms on social security towards a more active participation of the private sector in the management of health and pension systems, as well as to change the basis of financing. Diverse circumstances prompted the reforms: the traditional social security model, by and large still predominant, theoretically designed under a systemic solidarity principle with the intention of providing universal coverage and having beneficiaries contributing according to their means, was not performing as

[13] According to UNDP (1994), the rate of coverage of health programs reached 88% of the population of the region.

expected; sizable groups, particularly those in rural areas and those participating in unorganized activities were excluded; and pensions and/or the quality of the health services had declined due to difficulties in financing these benefits. Therefore, the wave of reforms should be seen as a welcome initiative to confront the existing problems in these vital pension and health systems.

The social security reforms in the field related to pensions include the introduction of a system based on individual capitalization managed by private pension fund companies. This system is best illustrated in Chile and Peru; these countries have introduced this scheme without eliminating the existing one, producing, for the time being at least, mixed systems. In the case of health, again with the Chilean case as the harbinger but with less followers than in the case of pensions, privatization has brought about a self-financed sector catering mostly to the middle and higher income groups, based on medical insurance which is managed and executed by the private sector, while the lower income groups are attended through the traditional system of public health which is financed out of the wage bill.

These reforms were implemented with the intention of reducing the fiscal deficit by eliminating mis-targeted subsidies going to the rich and the expectation that private management would be more efficient than that of the government. In addition, the pressure from interest groups which did or might benefit from public service provision would diminish, while the mobilization of savings would greatly contribute to the development of financial markets.

It is too early to evaluate the results of the reforms, but one main concern, the fiscal one, clearly needs to be recognized. Resources previously directed to the public coffers are now placed in private corporations and it remains to be seen whether fiscal expenditure will be correspondingly reduced. The new emerging post-reform systems are in a fragile equilibrium.

In the case of health, the implementation of a dual system implies the forgoing of revenues which contributed to finance the deficits incurred to provide health care to lower income-level groups. Additionally, in spite of segmentation, these two health service systems are interrelated; costs and service quality are inevitably linked. The introduction of a health system for high income-level groups affects medical costs, while a system with quality of service differentiated by income level gives rise to higher expectations for those served by the public system. Additionally, subsidies from the public system to lower income-level groups cannot be entirely phased out, as illustrated by the case of Chile. This results in systems which require increasing resources, even as fiscal revenues are reduced.

The Chilean experience under a mixed system illustrates this phenomenon. The private health system based on health insurance companies (ISAPRES) caters to the medium and upper income-level groups while the public health system funded by contributions from the wage bill and fiscal transfers (FONASA) responds to the needs of the rest of the population. Both systems include a levy for services rendered. There is a clear difference in the income level of groups affiliated to each system. Of the upper and lower quintiles of the income distribution 44% and 2.5% respectively are affiliated to ISAPRES, while the public system covers 84.5% of the latter group. The cross subsidy from the higher to the lower income-level groups decreased as a consequence of the privatization, since the two upper quintiles contribute more than they claim. In 1990, for example, the surplus of the upper quintile could have financed more than half of the deficit of the lower quintile. Each newcomer to the private system represents a net loss for the public system, since revenues from contributors generally exceed expenditures. To confront this imbalance the contribution from the wage bill had to be increased from 4% to 7% in order to finance FONASA.

A similar pattern may evolve regarding pensions. The governments not only have to confront transition costs, which imply paying pensioners who are affiliated to the old system without the corresponding contributions, and transferring contributions of those who change to the new system, but also have to finance the pensions of those who, because of low incomes, might not be able to accumulate enough funds to finance a minimum level of pension. This will signify a future fiscal burden without corresponding revenues. The magnitude of such a burden would depend on the earnings of contributors as well as on the profitability of pension funds.

It is difficult to estimate the potential fiscal implications, since not all of the effects are known—for example the likely fiscal burden caused by those pensioners who cannot pass the minimum threshold and revert to the public system, or the positive fiscal impact stemming from increased savings and growth, due to better management of pension funds. In order to assess the initial impact, it is worth recalling that prior to the reform (1977-79) Chile was transferring as pensions around 6.9% of its GDP while contributions amounted to 4.5% of the GDP, resulting in a deficit of 2.4%. In 1993 the pensions inherited from the old regime were equivalent to 38% of the social expenditure and around 6% of the GDP. As contributions are no longer collected by the government, but rather made to the *AFPs*, the fiscal deficit related to social security is currently larger than before. It is expected to shrink once the new system covers all new pensions and the pensioners of the old regime die out, but the speed of this transition is difficult to predict.

In sum, the pension and health reforms, while addressing existing financial problems and introducing innovative approaches, could also lead to future fiscal commitments that would have to be financed from general fiscal revenues. Said revenues are expected to rise, due to the positive impact of the reforms on savings and tax increases, though the latter is uncertain as high taxes are envisaged as counterproductive given the need to protect profits in order to reinvest in productive activities and in turn generate employment. An in-depth discussion would be necessary in order to assess long-term financial consequences and fiscal implications.

7.5. Conclusions

Following are the general conclusions drawn from the foregoing sections:

1. Labor costs and competitiveness in the manufacturing sector of five countries.

Although real labor costs (wages deflated by the cost of living index) grew over 1990-1995 in four of the five countries examined in this document, productivity rose even more, implying that labor costs by themselves were not a serious impediment to improving competitiveness. However, in four of the countries the gap between productivity growth and real labor cost increase was more than offset by the prevailing exchange rate policies, as a result generating net losses in competitiveness.

2. The evolution of the labor cost structure.

The increase in real gross wages over 1990-95 was less than the increase in labor costs in Mexico and Peru, higher in Argentina and Chile and equal in Brazil. That is to say, in the first two countries, non-wage labor costs rose more than wages while in the other two the lowering of non-wage labor costs dampened the effect of the wage increase on labor costs.

3. Labor cost and labor market policies.

The sum of non-wage labor costs destined to finance all benefits of workers and budgeted resources which the countries of the region allocate to financing labor market policies are equivalent to approximately 12% of the GDP, half the amount which more developed countries budget for this purpose. Almost the whole amount of these resources is derived from workers' and employers' contributions. Therefore, any changes made to the latter will have a very important impact on worker protection policies.

4. Benefits.

In the selected countries, with the exception of Mexico, the early 1990s did not see a large hike in pension costs. Thus, this component was not responsible for the increases in labor costs which did occur. Reforms of pension systems have not yielded the anticipated extension of coverage, which is still inadequate. Therefore, there is a need for considering alternatives which would guarantee at least a minimum pension for everyone.

In the area of health, with the exception of Chile and Colombia, there have been practically no reforms. The cost for workers and employers has remained constant during the last five years in Argentina, Brazil and Chile. In Colombia workers' contributions increased (compensated by an increase in wages) while those of employers were reduced. In Mexico the employers' contributions were raised slightly and in Peru the same contribution also rose but it was offset by a proportionate reduction in workers' contributions. The coverage of the population benefitting from the health care system has increased somewhat over the last few years, with the exception of Mexico. It is estimated that social health care at present covers approximately 65% of the population in the region.

5. Labor taxes.

In some of the countries there are social security contributions which can be considered as either explicit (payroll taxes) or implicit labor taxes (housing). The elimination of these taxes, which in fact have swelled over recent years, would allow for a reduction in total labor costs and consequently improve competitiveness of the enterprises. This labor cost component accounts for an important part of the increase in non-wage labor costs.

6. Fiscal implications of reforms.

Although reforms on pension and health care were aimed at tackling the deficit problem with innovative ideas, they could give rise to an even greater fiscal burden since fiscal revenues would be affected by decreasing contributions as a consequence of privatization. Thus, this issue calls for more in-depth analysis.

7. Labor costs and competitiveness: Final comments.

Productivity and labor costs do have an impact on the competitiveness of firms and industries. But an increase in labor costs does not necessarily lessen competitiveness, as long as it is accompanied by a larger increment in productivity. Even more important, there is a strong correlation between national competitiveness and the performance of certain macroeconomic variables, especially the exchange rate and relative prices; these variables affected competitiveness negatively in most of the countries studied over 1990-95.

Available information does not sustain the arguments that the recent evolution of non-wage labor costs are the result of reforms of pension systems or that these reforms erode worker protection. Although coverage of the different protection systems has expanded slightly, a high percentage of workers—namely informal workers, low-wage earners and peasants—still do not enjoy any kind of protection. This situation implies a challenge which has not always been considered in the region's recent wave of reforms. The pursuit of financial and operational efficiency of the protection systems must be accompanied by a greater social impact, which calls for an increased coverage so that benefits can be extended to the great majority, ensuring a minimum protection for all.

REFERENCES

Asociación Internacional de la Seguridad Social (1994). *Desafíos de Reforma en la Seguridad Social.* Geneva: Asociación Internacional de la Seguridad Social.

Asociación Internacional de la Seguridad Social (1995). *Tendencias en la Seguridad Social.* Geneva: Asociación Internacional de la Seguridad Social.

Baez, V. S. (1989). "Experiencias Mundiales en la Privatización de los Sistemas Pensionales." *Revista Jurídica del Trabajo*, No. 544. Santiago.

Blancas, C., M. Carrillo, and J. Franco, (1993). "Constitución, Trabajo y Seguridad Social. Estudio Comparado en 20 Constituciones Hispanoamericanas." Lima: ADEC/ATC.

Bour, S. L. (1995). "Los Costos Laborales en Argentina." In *Libro Blanco Sobre el Empleo en la Argentina.* Buenos Aires: MTSS.

Bureau of Labor Statistics, United States Department of Labor (1994). *Statistics.*

Castillo Marín, L. (1995). "El Cálculo de los Costos Laborales en el MERCOSUR." *Revista RELASUR*, No. 7. Montevideo.

Cichón, M. and Gillión C. (1993). "El Financiamiento de la Atención de la Salud en los Países en Desarrollo." *Revista Internacional del Trabajo*, Vol. 112.

Comisión Económica para América Latina y el Caribe (CEPAL) (1995). "La Reforma de la Seguridad Social y las Pensiones en América Latina." *Serie Reforma de Política*, Publicación No. 28. Santiago: CEPAL.

Conferencia Interamericana de Seguridad Social (1993). *La Seguridad Social en México.* Monografía No. 5.

Conferencia Interamericana de Seguridad Social (1994). *La Seguridad Social en Colombia.* Monografía No. 7.

Conferencia Interamericana de Seguridad Social (1994). *La Seguridad Social en el Perú.* Monografía No. 12.

Conferencia Interamericana de Seguridad Social (1995). *La Seguridad Social en Brasil.* Monografía No. 16.

Cortázar, R. (1993). *Política Laboral en el Chile Democrático*. Santiago: Dolmen Ediciones.

Fernández Moreno, M. (1993). "El Gasto de Protección Social en los Países de la Unión Europea Durante el Período 1980-1991." *Revista de Economía y Sociología del Trabajo*, No. 21-22. Madrid.

Giangiacomo, G. (1995). "El Costo Laboral Argentino y su Relación con el de los Países del MERCOSUR." *Revista NOTISUR.*

Hofman, A. (1995) "Economic Growth and Fluctuation in Latin America: The Long-Run". Paper presented at the conference on *Development Strategy after Neoliberal Economic Restructuring in Latin America*, University of Miami.

Instituto Colombiano de Seguridad Social (1994). *Estadísticas del Seguro Social*. Bogota: Instituto Colombiano de Seguridad Social.

Jaramillo, H. (1994). *Reseña de las Reformas de Políticas Sociales en Colombia*. Santiago: CEPAL.

Krugman, P. (1994). "Competitiveness: A Dangerous Obsession." *Foreign Affairs*, March-April.

Mesa-Lago, C. (1990). *La Seguridad Social y el Sector Informal*. Santiago: PREALC-OIT.

Ministry of Labor and Social Security - Argentina (1997). "La Recaudación por Impuestos al Trabajo, 1950-1996." ILO/UNDP Project, ARG/90/007.

Oficina Internacional del Trabajo (OIT). (1997). *Costos Laborales y Competitividad en América Latina*. Lima: OIT.

Raczynsky, D. and R. Cominetti (1994). *La Política Social en Chile: Panorama de sus Reformas*. Santiago: CEPAL.

Rodríguez Ardila, N. (1995). "La Reforma de la Seguridad Social: Sistema General de Pensiones y Salud." *Revista de Seguridad Social.*

United Nations Development Program (UNDP) (1994). *Human Development Report 1994*. New York: UNDP.

Chapter 8

MINIMUM WAGES IN CANADA

by Dwayne Benjamin

8.1 Introduction

Canada's perpetual constitutional wrangling aside, the division of powers between the provinces and the federal government has unintended benefits for social science research: cross-sectional and time-series variation in policy. Since labor standards are in the provincial domain, the possibility for variation in minimum wage policy exists, and Canada is a potentially important "laboratory" for studying the impact of minimum wage laws on the labor market. Whether lessons learned from Canadian experience can be extended to Latin America is a different matter. The first prerequisite is that there are Canadian lessons to pass along. A second would be that the labor market institutions and minimum wage laws in Latin America bear some similarity to Canadian experience. Caveats about answers aside, the types of questions one would ask regarding minimum wages can more easily be extended from the Canadian to the Latin American context.

Stigler (1946, 358) set the terms for policy-oriented discussion of minimum wages by economists: "The popular objective of minimum wage legislation—the elimination of extreme poverty—is not seriously debatable. The important questions are rather (1) Does such legislation diminish poverty? (2) Are there Efficient Alternatives?" Following these terms, I take as a premise that minimum wage laws are one tool from a set of possible policies whose primary purpose is to reduce poverty by increasing the incomes of the poor. Given the historical objectives of these laws, it is by this benchmark that we should also judge minimum wages, rather than by the narrower criterion of economic efficiency alone. Of course, it may turn out that there are significant efficiency costs, or better tools available for increasing the welfare of the poor, but as a starting point one would want to know how much minimum wages improve the welfare of the poor. There is then a set of obvious empirical questions to be answered. Only individuals who work can get paid minimum wages. How many of the poor earn wages that might be raised by the existence of a legislated minimum wage? How many work at all? How do minimum wages affect other parts of the wage distribution, i.e., are there "ripple effects" that may benefit other low wage workers? Within the set of low wage workers, are there those who lose their jobs because of minimum wages? Finally, there is an important distinction to be made between wages and income: many low wage individuals do not come from low income households. How much might this affect the distributional efficiency of minimum wages? The answers to these questions may differ significantly between Canada and Latin America; however, the Canadian experience should place some useful bounds on the consequences of changes in minimum wages in some Latin American labor markets.

In this chapter the focus is on minimum wages in Canada, with an emphasis on the degree to which minimum wages achieve their distributional objectives. This topic is not much emphasized in the economics literature, perhaps because it is less intellectually appealing than some others. The fate of neoclassical economics does not rest in the balance; however, the usefulness of minimum wages as a policy instrument is more directly addressed. While my focus is on Canada, I draw heavily on the U.S. literature since there is a lack of Canadian evidence. To fill some of the gaps, I provide limited explorations with Canadian data. In summary, I find that the minimum wage is a very blunt instrument for helping the poor. This is the approximate consensus in the U.S. literature, and the U.S. patterns appear to hold in Canada. However, while it is true that minimum wages provide only limited benefits to the poor and many benefit who are not poor, they do primarily transfer income to the working poor. The question then is what alternative policies exist that may do the job better. Unfortunately, we have little evidence on the relative efficacy of such other policies.

The chapter proceeds as follows. In the first section I outline the institutional setting of minimum wages in Canada, by looking at their trajectory over time. Here we see that while they do vary somewhat across provinces, Canadian minimum wages are similar in level to those in many countries and have followed similar patterns over time, namely a gradual erosion of their importance in the labor market over the last couple of decades. In the next section I lay the groundwork for an assessment of the distributional consequences of minimum wages by exploring the characteristics of minimum wage jobs. Very few Canadian workers earn the minimum wage, and many of these are young. I then turn to evidence on the consequences of minimum wages in the labor market, first briefly reviewing the debate on how minimum wages affect levels of employment, then turning to the distributional evidence. While researchers differ in their overall views as to whether minimum wages should be raised, there is a broad consensus on their limited usefulness in improving the distribution of income or reducing poverty. These conclusions are reinforced by an examination of Canadian data. Most of the poor do not work at all, and cannot benefit from higher wages, and many low wage workers come from better-off families.

8.2 Institutional Background

In their review of the history of minimum wage legislation in Canada, West and McKee (1980) note that the original primary motivation at its inception after World War I was the elimination of the "sweating of labor," especially of young, single women. In the Ontario legislation, for example, the objective was "to protect the physical, moral, and intellectual well-being of female workers."[1] As with many other forms of protective legislation, there was often an intent to protect certain workers from employment altogether, since "the requirement of higher wages for minors will cause their replacement by adults," and thus keep them in school longer.[2] By mid-century (post-World War II), by which time minimum wages had been extended over most North American jurisdictions, the anti-poverty aspects of minimum wages were emphasized. While possibly overstating the motives of legislators, Stigler (1946, 363) argued that "Minimum wage legislation commonly has two stated objectives: the reduction of employer control of wages; and the abolition of poverty." Nevertheless, the anti-poverty, "living wage" aspects of minimum wages are the prime motivations for most policy makers today. As one example (hardly statistically representative), a state legislator in Oregon has on her Internet home-page arguments in favor of raising the MW that include "(1) A full-time minimum wage worker earns $9,360 a year--the poverty level for a family of four is $15,141, and (2) A higher minimum wage would increase the incentive to choose work over welfare."[3] Minimum wages are now sold with the same packaging as "workfare." It is also interesting to note that these points form the core of responses to Stigler's two questions for evaluating minimum wages.

Of course, there are a number of dimensions to minimum wage legislation beyond their mere existence: they vary by level, coverage, and distinctions by category of worker (age, sex, industry, etc.). Given the multitude of jurisdictions, a summary of the evolution of minimum wages in all these dimensions is impossible. However, a reasonable starting point is to look at the structure in Canada, whose main details are presented in Table 8.1. The first column shows the current level of the minimum wage in each province and the federal jurisdiction; the latter consists primarily of federal public sector workers, few of whom are "minimum wage" workers. The federal minimum wage is lower than all of the provincial minimums (reflecting its irrelevance), and indeed, is to be rolled into provincial minimum wages. The 1995 level of minimum wages varied significantly

---

[1] Province of Ontario (1920, Chapter 87), quoted in West and McKee (1980, 5).
[2] National Industrial Conference Board (1927, 5), quoted in West and McKee (1980, 5).
[3] Representative Avel Gordly, "http://www.portals.pdx.edu/~gordlya", District 19, Oregon.

Table 8.1
Canadian Minimum Wages by Province, July 1995

Jurisdiction	Adult Minimum Wage (MW)	Average Industrial Wage (AW)[1]	MW/AW	Youth Subminimum	Special Minimum Wage
Newfoundland	4.75	11.54	0.41		
Prince Edward Island	4.75	9.92	0.48		
Nova Scotia	5.15	10.84	0.48		4.70[2]
New Brunswick	5.00	11.12	0.45		
Quebec	6.00	13.45	0.45		5.28[3]
Ontario	6.85	14.23	0.48	6.40[4]	5.95[5]
Manitoba	5.25	12.41	0.42		
Saskatchewan	5.35	11.99	0.45		
Alberta	5.00	12.33	0.41	4.50[6]	
British Columbia	6.50	15.97	0.41		
Federal[7]	4.00	13.70	0.29		

Notes: [1]Average hourly earnings for workers paid by the hour, not including overtime for firms of all sizes. [2]Inexperienced workers (less than 3 months experience). [3]Employees who receive tips. [4]Students under 18 employed less than 28 hours per week, or during school holidays. [5]Employees of liquor serving establishments. [6]Employees under 18, attending school. [7]Federal jurisdiction is primarily federal government employees.

Sources: Minimum wages - Labor Canada (1995); Average Industrial Wages - CANSIM (Average Hourly Earnings by Industry (not including overtime, monthly, not seasonally adjusted), Employees paid by the hour, firms of all sizes).

across provinces, from $4.75 in Newfoundland and Prince Edward Island, to $6.85 in Ontario. The minimum wage in the U.S. was then $4.25, or about $5.75 in Canadian dollars, not far from that in most Canadian provinces. Another benchmark is the ratio of the minimum wage to the average industrial wage. Indeed, variation in general wage levels helps explain some of the provincial variation in minimum wage levels. The ratio varies from 0.41 to 0.48, all higher than the average U.S. ratio, which is about 0.37. Of course, there is also considerable variation of this ratio within the U.S. Some states have higher minimum wages of their own, and average wages vary across states, possibly more than in Canada.

In the U.S., one of the main sources in variation of effective minimum wages has been coverage, or the share of workers to whom minimum wage laws apply. Since the early 1970s, on the other hand, coverage in Canada has been virtually complete, with a few exceptions. The principal exclusions are farm workers and, historically at least, domestic employees.[4] Supervisory or managerial employees, apprentices, students in "job experience" programs, and straight commission salespersons are also exempt from minimum wage laws.

While coverage may be nearly complete, there are separate minimum wages for special categories of workers. Historically, exemptions have been made for young workers through the provision of youth and student sub-minimum wages.

[4] Labor Canada (1995) provides more details on both coverage, and on minimum wages for special categories of workers. Many provinces have recently extended coverage to domestic workers.

Youth sub-minima are based purely on age (usually applying to those under 17 or 18), while student sub-minima are for youth attending school. Ostensibly because of problems with the Charter of Rights (age discrimination), most provinces have eliminated their sub-minima. Only Ontario and Alberta still have student sub-minima. Another reason for their elimination may be that sub-minima are rarely used. While Baker, Benjamin and Stanger (1999) find that in some provinces sub-minima relax the adult minimum constraint for some teenage workers, few employers make full use of them. In a study of Texas fast-food restaurants, Katz and Krueger (1992) confirm the results of previous researchers that employers rarely make use of sub-minima. While they point out that this is puzzling in the context of a neoclassical interpretation of labor market functioning, for our purposes their evidence simply suggests that sub-minimum wages are not the most important ingredients in minimum wage legislation. Finally, within the adult covered sector, there exists further variation in minimum wages. For some trades, like construction, higher minima are set in some provinces. In other sectors, like retail trades where there are commissions, or in restaurants and bars where tips are important, lower minima are set. In Nova Scotia there is a training minimum wage for the first three months of some jobs, and in other jurisdictions weekly minima are set in occupations where hours of work are "unverifiable," such as logging and forestry which have significant piece-rate components.

Figure 8.1 shows the evolution of nominal minimum wages between 1975 and 1994 for Alberta, British Columbia, Ontario and Quebec. The time series resemble step functions, though in some provinces there were few steps during the 1980s. The basic patterns are similar across provinces, though the levels clearly vary (see Table 8.1). This figure also shows the levels of youth and student sub-minima, and the elimination of sub minima in most provinces.

Figure 8.2 shows the evolution of the (adult) minimum wage in real terms (deflated to 1993 prices by the CPI) and the ratio of the minimum wage to the average manufacturing wage.[5] Several points are worth noting. First, there is more variation in real minimum wages than one would guess from the nominal wage series alone; real minimum wages follow a sawtooth pattern, as a given nominal level is eroded by inflation, until it is raised by a discrete amount. In this sense, minimum wage laws are regularly repealed.[6] Some provinces have done better than others in maintaining the real value of the minimum wage, but by the mid-1990s it had generally fallen to the point that it was lower than in the late 1970s in all provinces. In 1993 constant dollars, the minimum wage was $6.50 in Ontario in 1993, versus a peak of $7.50 in the late 1970s. The decline was even larger in

---

[5] Unlike Table 8.1 where the average industrial wage is the benchmark, we are forced to use the average manufacturing wage including overtime in this figure. This is the only series that extends back prior to 1983. To convert to a different benchmark, this manufacturing wage series is about 1.03 times the series without overtime, and 1.16 times the average industrial wage.

[6] Again, I borrow this from Stigler (1946, 358).

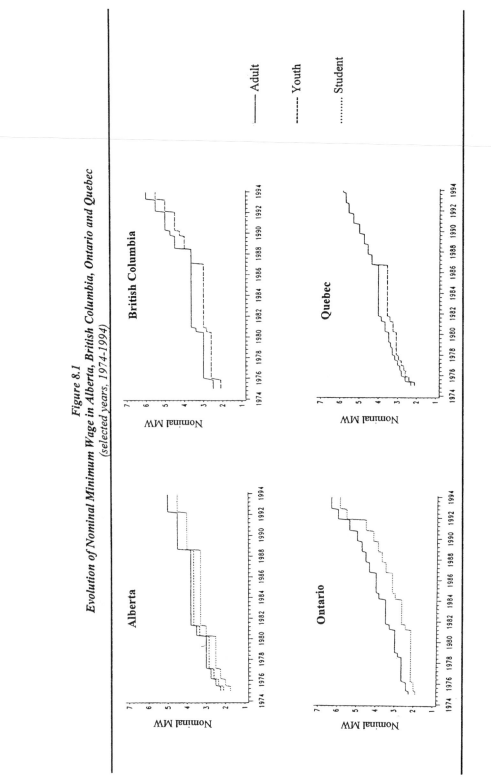

Figure 8.1
Evolution of Nominal Minimum Wage in Alberta, British Columbia, Ontario and Quebec
(selected years, 1974-1994)

Figure 8.2

Evolution of Real Minimum Wage in Alberta, British Columbia, Ontario and Quebec, Selected Years, 1974-1994

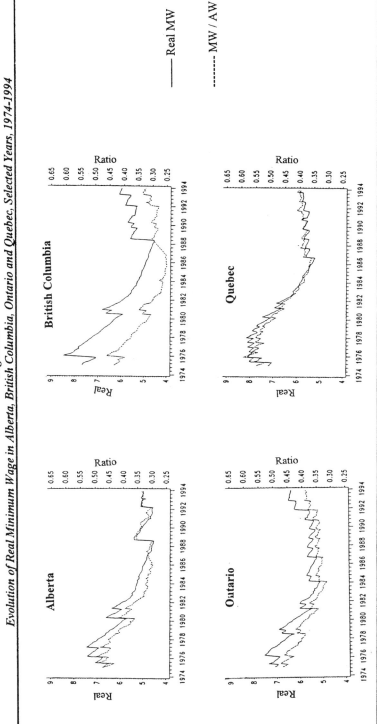

——— Real MW

------- MW / AW

Quebec and British Columbia, where the real drop was on the order of $2.00. This mirrors the trend in the U.S. over the same time period. A similar decline occurs vis-à-vis the average manufacturing wage. In Quebec, for example, that ratio was down to 0.41 from a peak of 0.56. In Ontario, the ratio was as high as 0.46 and as low as 0.32. In British Columbia, the ratio ranged between 0.26 and 0.41. Here too, the U.S. experience has been similar; the ratio of the minimum wage to the average manufacturing wage was 0.45 in 1975, reached 0.48 in the late 1970s, but fell to 0.38 in 1991, having reached as low as 0.32.[7] In France this ratio has been close to 0.50 since the late 1970s (Card, Kramarz and Lemieux, 1995), somewhat higher than the comparable Canadian ratios reported in Table 8.1. Comparison to other industrial countries is generally hampered by the lack of comparability of the average wage series.[8] For Latin America Bell (1995) reports that minimum-average wage ratios in Mexico (using "blue-collar" wages) have declined from 0.40 to 0.31 over the 1980s. In Colombia (relative to "skilled wages") the ratio has increased from 0.32 to 0.40. Obviously, the ratios are higher for unskilled labor. The ratios in these two Latin American countries are within the range of the North American experience. As an example of a quite different experience though, Castillo-Freeman and Freeman (1992) report results from Puerto Rico, where the U.S. minimum wage level has been imposed directly in the Puerto Rican labor market. In that labor market, the ratio has been as high as 0.72 to 0.74 (in manufacturing) and is now 0.63. To the extent that other Latin American countries contemplate minimum wages at higher levels (in relation to average wages) than we have seen in Canada, lessons learned in Canada will be less applicable, and those from Puerto Rico perhaps more relevant.

8.3 What Is a Minimum Wage Job?

Before turning to the impact of minimum wages on individuals, it is worth examining the importance of minimum wages in the labor market by looking at their role in the wage distribution. We are interested in two questions. First, does the minimum wage "bite" in Canada? If set sufficiently low, minimum wages can be entirely irrelevant. Second, what are "minimum wage jobs?" To address this question we look at the industrial and occupational distribution of jobs, as well as measures of the skills of workers associated with them.

An approximate idea of how important minimum wages are in each province's labor market can be obtained from the Labor Market Activity Survey (LMAS), one of the very few data sets in Canada that provides the information

---

[7] See Ehrenberg and Smith (1994) for a table listing U.S. minimum wages and their ratio to manufacturing wages.

[8] See Card and Krueger (1995), Chapter 8, Table 8.1, for the 1992 ratios of minimum wages to average manufacturing wages for a selection of other countries.

necessary to look at the distribution of wages, though it has a number of problems. The LMAS is a survey of individuals and their work history. The survey period is a year, though respondents provide detailed week by week information on their labor force status, including employment in up to five jobs per year. Though it is possible to identify an individual's job at any point in the year, the characteristics of the job and specifically the wage information are only reported on an annual basis, leaving an imperfect match between the data on employment status in any given week and the wage paid at that time. This limits our ability to fully replicate CPS-style wage distributions which are snapshots of a particular week. It becomes a more irritating problem in those provinces where the minimum wage changed over the year, since we cannot tell whether the wage reported corresponds to the reported job or is higher or lower than that wage.

In Figure 8.3, we plot histograms of hourly wage rates for jobs held in the fourth quarter (46th week) of 1990 for a slightly different set of provinces.[9] Only paid workers (jobs) are shown, so self-employed and unpaid family jobs are excluded. We are primarily interested in the size of the spike at the minimum wage, which indicates how much the minimum wage binds the wages that employers may pay. To make the graphs more presentable, I employ a log-scale.[10] In five provinces, minimum wages rose during 1990, so there is potentially an overestimate of the spikewhen one adds the two minimum wage spikes together. That caveat aside, we see considerable variation in the "bite" of the minimum wage. In Alberta, the minimum affects only 1.5% of jobs, while in Saskatchewan, 6.5% to 7.5% of jobs are affected. More typically, the range of estimates is 2.5% to 4% of jobs. Are these large or small numbers? As one point of comparison, Card and Krueger (1995) provide estimates of the minimum wage spike in the U.S. before and after the increase in the Federal minimum wage from $3.35 to $4.25 per hour in 1991. At the lower rate, the spike accounted for 1.5% of workers, but after the increase, the spike rose to 4%. At another extreme, Castillo-Freeman and Freeman (1992) show that in Puerto Rico the $3.35 minimum wage applied to 28% of the workforce in 1988.

Of course, these numbers do not fully inform us on which and how many workers may be affected by discrete changes in the level of the minimum wage. If minimum wages increase from MW_0 to MW_1, we expect all workers with wages between MW_0 and MW_1 to have their wages raised to the new minimum, so that

---

[9] Recognizing the seasonality of jobs, especially student summer jobs that may tend to be minimum wage jobs, these figures have been produced for each quarter. While conclusions about teens may be affected, the overall picture does not vary much across quarters, especially given the imprecision of the time period (week) associated with the wage of a given job in 1990.

[10] While the wage-categories underlying the histogram have equal width in logs, they do not have equal width in levels, so that the bin sizes for the histograms are not constant in dollars. The bin sizes in the range of the minimum wage are approximately 0.20 to 0.25. More precisely, the bins and the minimum wages they bracket are $4.05-$4.26 (4.25), $4.48-$4.71 (4.50), $4.71-$4.95 (4.75), $4.95-$5.21 (5.00), and $5.21-$5.47 (5.30).

Figure 8.3
Histogram of Hourly Wage Rate in Alberta, Ontario, Saskatchewan and Quebec, Fourth Quarter, 1990

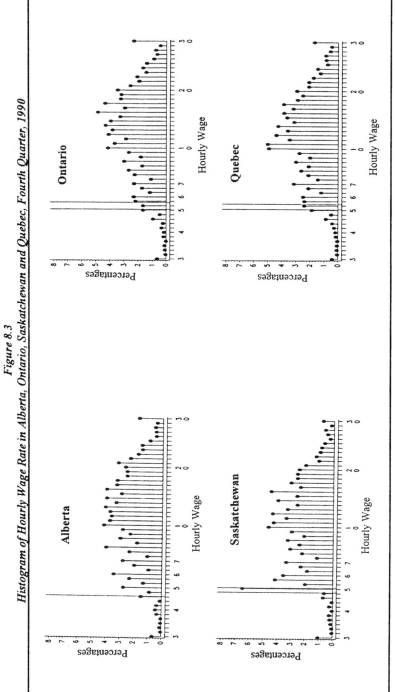

the number of jobs affected by increases in the minimum exceeds those paid exactly the minimum. Shannon and Beach (1995) use the LMAS to simulate the consequences of raising the minimum wage in Ontario from $4.75 to $6.75. While they find that only 3.3% are paid exactly the minimum wage (essentially the same as shown in Figure 8.3) a further 14.4% had wages below the new minimum, and would potentially be affected by the increase. Another consideration is that jobs are equally weighted in these figures, yet some jobs are full-time and others part-time. We might expect minimum wage jobs to be disproportionately part-time. Thus, in terms of annual-hours equivalent jobs, Shannon and Beach report only 1.6% of jobs are paid the minimum, and a total of only 10.9% of jobs would likely be affected by the increase of the minimum wage (vs. 19.2% of unadjusted jobs). Finally, we expect that the minimum wage will be atypically important in certain sub-sectors of the labor market. Thus Baker, Benjamin and Stanger (1999) report that the minimum wage spike for teenagers is closer to 15-20% in Ontario and Quebec, and closer to 40% in the lower-wage provinces.

While minimum wages seem to "dam" the wage distributions at the minimum, another obvious feature from Figure 8.3 is the "leakage" of the distribution past the minimum. A significant percentage of jobs are paid less than the minimum wage. One explanation for these below-minimum wages is non-compliance with the law. Given imperfect enforcement, one might not expect to see perfect compliance. Indeed, Ashenfelter and Smith (1979) estimated that only 60% of covered U.S. workers who "should have" been paid the minimum wage were in fact paid at least that wage. This compliance rate measures the percentage of those covered workers who were paid at (plus or minus an allowance for measurement error) or below the minimum who were indeed paid the minimum. I repeat this exercise with Canadian data. My objective is to see to what extent those workers paid below the minimum are likely to be in situations of non-compliance. I give "compliance" the benefit of the doubt by excluding below-minimum workers if another plausible explanation exists for their low wage.

The results of this exercise for the national sample are presented in Table 8.2. Here, potential minimum wage jobs are defined as those jobs that paid less than MW + $0.05. They comprise 5.89% of all jobs. Of these potential minimum wage (MW) jobs, 52.84% are paid exactly the minimum.[11] The hourly wage in the LMAS is constructed for many workers by dividing annual earnings by estimated annual hours. For salaried workers and the like, this may introduce considerable measurement error, including generating some quite low wages. Thus, following Ashenfelter and Smith (1979), I drop out of the "noncompliant" set those who are not paid by the hour. This eliminates 22.85% of the potential MW jobs. In the next category are teens, paid between the sub-minimum and the minimum, which

---

[11] "Exactly" is defined as within $0.04 of the minimum. For provinces where the minimum wage changed, I take payment below the lower minimum as evidence of potential non-compliance, and payment below the higher for defining potential minimum wage jobs.

Table 8.2
Accounting for "Non-Compliance" with the Minimum Wage, Canada, 1990

Percentage of all jobs paying less than MW + $0.05 is 5.89%

Of those jobs:	Percent:
Paid within $0.04 of the minimum wage:	52.84
Paid less than minimum, but not paid by the hour:	22.85
Paid less than minimum and by the hour, but for teens above the youth/student sub-minimum:	6.83
Paid less than minimum and by the hour, and below teen-sub-minimum for teens, but in industries with special minima (i.e. retail, food and accommodation, tips, agriculture)	13.99
Paid by the hour, but less than $0.75	1.31
"Unexplained," potential non-compliers	2.17

Notes: [1]Industries subject to special minimum wages include (from the LMAS) agriculture, forestry, fishing and trapping, wholesale and retail trade, amusement and recreation services, personal services, accommodation and food services, and miscellaneous services. [2] Health and welfare services are included in the "unexplained" category, and account for 59% of this category. In fact, this industry may belong in the list above.

Source: Labour Market Activity Survey (LMAS), 1990.

accounts for a further 6.83%. Recognizing that some industries have their own minima (such as retail, liquor servers, those working for gratuities), I then exclude those jobs, as long as the wage was greater than $2.50. This eliminates almost 14% of potential MW jobs, leaving an unexplained 3.5%. Some of these wages are certainly measured with error. It is unlikely that even non-compliers could pay less than $0.75 an hour. Excluding those whose reported hourly wage is below that level leaves just 2% of the initial set of minimum wage jobs unaccounted for and a tiny 0.12% of all jobs. Because I have erred on the side of assuming compliance, this quite small figure may well be an underestimate of the extent of non-compliance in Canada.[12] Nevertheless, I take these results as suggesting that non-compliance is not an especially important problem in Canada. This is one result that may not extend to Latin America.

What are the skill-characteristics of minimum wage employment?[13] (A more detailed description of minimum wage workers is deferred until later.) I define minimum wage jobs in two ways (Table 8.3). The first includes jobs below the

---

[12] It is not straightforward to get an upper bound on non-compliance, but a reasonable approximation is to recompute the numbers in Table 8.2, including the non-hourly paid workers, and not attributing low wages to measurement error. After a similar breakdown is conducted, 15.7% of the "at or below" minimum wage workers cannot be accounted for (just 0.92% of all jobs), and are thus possibly not being paid in compliance with the minimum wage law.

[13] As is common in the literature, I define minimum wage status by the paid hourly wage, as distinct from average hourly earnings. Hourly earnings may include tips or commissions, and thus some of these apparently low wage workers actually earn more per hour. When re-calculated using earnings information including tips, we find slightly fewer "minimum wage" workers (5.1% vs. 5.89%), with a similar breakdown in other dimensions.

Table 8.3
Characteristics of Minimum Wage Jobs, Canada, 1990
(Percentage of Jobs with Given Characteristics)[1]

	Below MW +$0.05	Below MW + $1.00	Above MW + $0.04
Percentage of all jobs:	5.89	11.99	94.1
Male	36.4	36.7	53.6
Age:			
Teen (16-19)	31.3	29.6	4.4
Young Adults (20-24)	15.8	17.9	11.3
Prime Age (25-64)	52.5	52.0	83.8
Older (65+)	0.3	0.5	0.6
Education:			
Less than High School	49.4	46.1	22.9
High School Grad	22.3	23.9	24.5
Some Post Secondary	16.9	20.1	29.1
Trade Certificate	5.9	5.2	7.0
University	5.5	4.7	16.5
Unionized	7.3	9.2	41.8
Full Time	48.6	51.1	80.8
Industry:			
Primary (except mining)	3.9	3.1	1.5
Mining	0.3	0.2	1.5
Manufacturing	6.5	9.1	18.3
Construction	1.6	1.8	5.4
Utilities	3.2	2.7	8.3
Trade	24.7	29.3	16.9
Finance	3.6	3.3	5.7
Education	2.6	2.5	8.8
Health and Welfare	8.9	7.4	11.3
Amusement and Recreation	2.9	2.5	1.1
Business Services	1.6	2.6	4.9
Personal Services	6.3	5.0	1.2
Accommodation, Food, Beverage	28.7	25.1	4.5
Miscellaneous Services	3.0	3.4	2.2
Government	2.2	1.9	8.2
Occupations:			
Administrative/management	4.9	4.9	12.8
Science/Engineering	1.8	1.4	5.7
Education/Religion	2.1	1.8	6.1
Health	1.1	1.4	5.6
Arts and Recreation	1.8	1.6	1.6
Clerical	15.4	17.0	19.1
Sales	14.7	17.4	8.2
Protective Services	1.0	1.2	2.1
Food and Beverage Services	25.9	22.5	4.4
Apparel Services	6.5	5.8	2.0
Other Services	6.8	5.8	3.0
Primary (except mining)	3.4	2.7	1.5
Mining	0.0	0.1	0.5
Beverage Processing	1.1	1.4	1.3
Other Processing	0.7	0.8	2.0
Machining	3.8	4.7	7.4
Mechanical	0.7	0.7	3.1
Construction	0.6	1.0	5.5
Transportation	3.1	3.1	3.9
Other Occupations	4.7	4.6	4.0

Notes: [1] Rows give the percentage of each wage-classified job (e.g., minimum wage or above minimum wage) with the given characteristic.

Source: Labour Market Activity Survey (LMAS), 1990.

minimum wage plus $0.05 and comprises 5.89% of all jobs. The second expands this set to include those jobs paying up to the minimum plus a dollar. This latter set, which comprises about 12% of all jobs, more accurately represents those jobs that would be affected by large minimum wage increases. As a comparison group, I take those (better) jobs paying five cents or more above the minimum wage. As indicators of skill, I look at the age and education of the workers, as well as industry, occupation, and other firm characteristics.

Before turning to the skill correlates of minimum wage jobs, we note that the incumbents are disproportionately female, with males constituting only 36% of these jobs, but well over half of the higher paying jobs. One of the most interesting skill-related variables from our perspective is age, since its relationship with earnings has further implications for our assessment of the distributional consequences of minimum wages. Minimum wage workers are often dismissed as unimportant to the family income distribution because they are teenagers. Indeed, the young are disproportionately represented in minimum wage jobs: 30% of these jobs are filled by teens, contrasted with only 4% of the higher paying jobs. Most striking, though, is that 52% of the minimum wage jobs are held by individuals over 25 years old. Thus the majority of minimum wage workers are not teenagers but rather in the age categories where they may be important contributors to family income. These Canadian results line up remarkably well with U.S. results. Card and Krueger (1995) report the age distribution of workers likely to have been affected by the 1991 increase in the federal minimum wage; 29.4% of workers paid up to $0.90 above the $3.35 minimum were teens, 19.8% were young adults, and 50.8% were 25 years and older, virtually identical to the numbers in Canada. In terms of education, minimum wage workers are disproportionately less educated, and there are few university graduates. (Note that these percentages do not adjust for age). Not surprisingly, relatively few are unionized; those who are must be represented by weak unions! As mentioned previously, the majority of minimum wage jobs are part-time, compared to less than 20% of the higher paying jobs. Turning to industry, that caricature of the minimum wage job seems more reasonable. Retail trade, and accommodation, food, and beverages account for over half of minimum wage jobs, but only 20% of the higher paying jobs. The occupational mix is commensurate with these industries, with minimum wage jobs concentrated in food and beverage, sales, and clerical occupations.

8.4 Employment Effects of the Minimum Wage

In 1946, George Stigler (1946, 358) could safely claim that on the subject of minimum wages, "Economists have not been very outspoken," but that would hardly be true 50 years later. Economists have by now spent a great deal of research effort studying the impact of minimum wages, especially the effect they have on employment. While the direct policy implications are of interest, economists have primarily focused on these employment effects as a more general test of neoclassical theory. In the standard textbook model, an increase of minimum wages above the equilibrium wage *must* reduce employment, as long as labor demand curves slope downward. In the nonstandard case of monopsony, a minimum wage increase can actually raise employment, but traditionally economists have not viewed this as particularly relevant to the low wage teen labor market. Such a dismissal may be less appropriate in a developing country context.

A negative employment effect, however, need not mean that minimum wages would not be beneficial to low wage workers. The overall welfare implications of minimum wages require knowing more than the sign of the employment effect, but also the magnitude. Consider the following simple illustrative exercise. Assume we can identify minimum wage workers, and we wish to increase their incomes. The wage bill to these workers would be given by $W_M H_M$, where W_M is the minimum wage and H_M is the total hours worked. An increase in the minimum wage would affect the wage bill as follows:

$$e_{YM} = \frac{d \ln W_M H_M}{d \ln W_M} = 1 + \frac{d \ln H_M}{d \ln W_M} = 1 + e_{HM}$$

where e_{YM} and e_{HM} are the elasticities of the total wage bill and of the total hours worked, both with respect to the minimum wage. The wage bill would increase as long as the elasticity of hours with respect to the minimum wage was less than one in absolute value. In the terminology of Gramlich (1976), we can denote this as the break-even elasticity. If we are willing to ignore the effect on hours (e.g., adjustment from full-time to part-time), then the relevant elasticity to estimate would be the elasticity of minimum wage employment with respect to the minimum wage. A break-even elasticity of one would suggest a remarkable (implicit if not explicit) consensus among economists that increasing the minimum wage transfers income to low wage workers, since few reasonable estimates of the employment effects are that large.

Unfortunately, such a characterization would be premature, since few estimates of employment elasticities measure the effect on minimum wage employment, as opposed to that on all low wage workers, many of whom are paid above the relevant minimum wage. We thus need a way to adjust the benchmark elasticity to account for the fact that many in the broader market may be unaffected by minimum wage changes, and that a small elasticity for the whole group may translate into a considerably larger one for the minimum wage employees *per se*. Assume that a given proportion, S_M, of a group G of workers (say, teens) are paid the minimum. Assume further that the remaining $1-S_M$ of these workers are paid wages that are not affected by the increase in the minimum, nor is their employment affected.[14] The break-even elasticity will then be given by S_M.

Given the sometimes small shares of minimum wage workers in the labor force categories studied in many minimum wage papers, the possibility for disagreement on whether minimum wages transfer earnings to minimum wage workers becomes much greater. Of course, there are a number of complications in treating S_M as the critical elasticity. First, as already mentioned, earnings depend on hours worked, not just employment status, and very few studies make adjustments for hours. Second, minimum wage changes are seldom really small, so that the share of affected workers is understated by the share of minimum wage workers before the minimum wage change. A more accurate estimate of the "at risk" group are those workers who have wages below the new minimum wage. Of course, for those workers whose wages lie between the old and new minimum wages, they are not receiving the same proportional increase as those being paid the old minimum wage.[15] Finally, using S_M as the break-even elasticity ignores distributional costs *within* the set of original minimum wage workers. Gramlich (1976) builds in the disutility of unemployment to his break-even elasticity to account for the fact that not all workers will receive the raise, and some will become unemployed. In the end, without specific estimates of the elasticities for minimum wage workers, evidence on the teen (or young adult) aggregates will only provide an imperfect indication of the impact of minimum wage changes on the specific minimum wage subgroup. These caveats aside, S_M provides a useful "back of the envelope" benchmark employment elasticity with which to judge the policy implications of the minimum wage-employment effect literature.

My objective is to provide a summary review of the policy implications of the available empirical evidence, rather than a comprehensive outline of the literature.[16] A capsule summary of the received wisdom in the early 1980s and reported in most labor economics textbooks, is that the teen-employment minimum wage elasticity is between -0.1 and -0.3. Using estimates from Card and Krueger (1995), the fraction of teenagers in the U.S. paid less than the minimum wage plus $0.50, was 32%, so the break-even elasticity for teens would be -0.32. Thus, only elasticities at the high end of the range would suggest that raising the minimum

---

[14] Of course, these assumptions may be wrong. As we will discuss later, minimum wage increases have small spillover effects that may lead to wage increases for non-minimum wage teens. Off-setting this, however, some in the non-minimum wage group may also lose employment, so that the net effect on the wage bill of this group is ambiguous.

[15] Indeed, an alternative way to think about the problem of using teen elasticities as the relevant elasticity for minimum wage workers, is to recognize that a 1% increase in the minimum will not lead to an increase in average wages of 1% for teens as a group, if only some of them are paid the minimum wage. This lowers the increase in average hourly earnings to teens (from a 1% increase in the minimum), and the critical employment loss that would offset this wage increase is therefore less than 1%.

[16] For excellent summaries of the empirical findings and methodologies employed, see Brown, Gilroy, and Kohen (1982) for earlier studies, and Card and Krueger (1995) for the more recent studies.

wage would not result in a net transfer of wage income to minimum wage workers. When 1980s data are added to the time-series studies (e.g., Wellington, 1991), the elasticity drops virtually to zero. Perhaps this is the consequence of including a substantial set of observations in which the minimum wage affected fewer workers (recall that the minimum wage declined significantly in real terms over the 1980s). Whatever the implications for economic theory, this result suggests that minimum wage at the levels that existed in the U.S. during the 1980s had little impact on the labor market, leading Brown (1988) to conclude that the "best guess" estimates of the minimum wage elasticity for teens are on the lower end of the -0.1 to -0.3 range, well below the break-even elasticity.

One of the unintended consequences of the neglect of the federal minimum wage over the 1980s was that it was due for significant increase in the late-1980s and early 1990s; these increases prompted several new studies of the impacts of minimum wages, studies that would challenge the "consensus" reflected in Brown, Gilroy, and Kohen (1982) even further. A first round of new studies, which appeared in a symposium on minimum wage research published in the *Industrial and Labor Relations Review* (1992), went beyond earlier efforts in trying to extract information from minimum wage variation other than the aggregate time-series fluctuations in the effective federal minimum wage. Since 1938, there had only been 11 increases in the nominal minimum wage, so most of the variation that could be used to identify employment effects reflected changes in the real minimum wage caused by inflation or changes in coverage. Katz and Krueger (1992) implemented a classic "before" and "after" study of employment in Texas fast-food restaurants, by surveying a sample of restaurants before and after an increase in the state minimum wage. Rather than finding a drop in full time equivalent (FTE) employment as expected, they found a positive, sometimes significant increase. Even if interpreted as "no effect," this result clearly challenged the "-0.1 to -0.3" consensus.

Card (1992b) also applied the "before" and "after" approach to the 1988 increase of the state minimum wage in California, finding an increase in the employment of low-wage workers relative to other states that did not increase their minimum. This result has been challenged by Kim and Taylor (1995), who use different data to study this particular episode in California and find a large significant elasticity of employment, on the order of -0.7 to -0.9 and well above the cut-off of -0.3.[17] Card (1992a) used cross-state variation in the proportion of workers "at risk" of losing their jobs due to minimum wage increases to assess the

---

[17] Kim and Taylor used the more aggregated County Business Patterns (CBP) data, whereas Card used individual level CPS data. See Card and Krueger (1995) for a response to the Kim and Taylor results. In particular, Card and Krueger investigate the sensitivity of Kim and Taylor's results to choice of sample period, as well as the correct treatment / measurement of the wage variable. In the end, they conclude that the effect of the 1988 minimum wage increase may have been negative (with these data), but is small and statistically insignificant.

impact of the increase in the federal minimum wage from $3.35 to $3.80 and $4.25 per hour. He finds that those states where a higher fraction of workers were at risk, actually saw relative increases in employment associated with the increase in minimum wages. His findings have been challenged by Deere, Murphy, and Welch (1995), who argue that cross-state variation is a flawed source of identification, since the low-wage states were otherwise fast growing. Instead, they sub-divide samples of workers in other dimensions (race, age, and sex) and show that with these sub-divisions, groups with higher fractions "at risk" indeed saw relative employment declines. The implied elasticities from their study are in the higher part of the -0.1 to -0.3 range, some even higher (not accounting for sampling error).

Neumark and Wascher (1992) use a third approach to the identification of minimum wage effects, based on cross-state time-series (i.e. panel) data which allows them to exploit cross-state differences in coverage and in state minimum wages to supplement the usual time-series variation. Depending on the chosen specification, they find elasticities for teens on the order of -0.25. While their estimates are subject to criticisms by Card, Katz, and Krueger (1994), one could still reasonably conclude that Neumark and Wascher have made a serious case for the existence of significant, negative employment effects, at least at the lower end of the range. In summary, then, the 1992 symposium saw a serious challenge to conventional wisdom in the form of positive estimates of the employment effect of higher minimum wages. At the other extreme some of the estimates were negative and high. But most of the estimated teen employment elasticities were in the range below the break-even elasticity, and in that sense did not contradict the prior consensus on policy.

The second major round of minimum wage studies surrounds the book by Card and Krueger (1995), and especially their paper, Card and Krueger (1994) which forms an important part of the book. That article uses a more extensive survey of fast-food restaurants than Katz and Krueger's (1992) Texas study. They survey restaurants in New Jersey and neighboring Pennsylvania a few months before, and 8 months after an increase in the state minimum wage in New Jersey to $5.05; the minimum did not change in Pennsylvania. In many ways, this relative increase can be characterized as a "natural experiment," so that the "before" and "after" methodology, with "treatment" and "control" groups could be fruitfully employed. They find a relatively robust, (usually though not always statistically significant) increase in employment in New Jersey relative to Pennsylvania, again counter to the prediction of economic theory. Card and Krueger also explore some of the secondary predictions of the monopsony model, since the positive employment effect is suggestive that the monopsony model may be more appropriate than initially believed.[18] Even fast food restaurants may face upward

---

[18] One such prediction is that the price of output should fall as output rises; since the increase in employment is presumed to be the result of the flattening of the labor supply curve and

sloping labor supply schedules, perhaps due to imperfect wage information and search behavior. However, the authors find no support for these auxiliary predictions, and conclude instead that whatever the theoretical interpretation, their results are inconsistent with a statistically significant adverse employment effect.

Not surprisingly, these findings too have been challenged. Brown (1995) and Hamermesh (1995) point out that the short time period may not have allowed a complete adjustment of employment in New Jersey. Some of the evidence provided in previous minimum wage studies (surveyed in Brown, Gilroy, and Kohen (1982), as well as in Baker, Benjamin and Stanger (1999)) indeed suggests that minimum wage dynamics may yield only delayed, longer run declines in employment. Nevertheless, even a short-run increase in employment may be a challenge to the conventional model of the labor market. Freeman (1995) questions the applicability of the results to larger minimum wage increases. At the extreme, surely an increase in the minimum wage to $100 would decrease employment. But in the relevant range in which we observe minimum wages, and which is therefore relevant to policy makers, the Card and Krueger results suggest that the disemployment effects are small or non-existent; the impact of $100 minimum wages may be more relevant to labor demand theorists.

Perhaps the most serious challenge to the Card and Krueger results regards their survey data. Welch (1995) has a number of specific criticisms of their survey methodology, while Neumark and Wascher (1995) use establishment pay-roll records to analyze the same New Jersey-Pennsylvania comparison. They find that Card and Krueger's data are more noisy than the payroll data, and further re-estimation of the employment effect yields a more traditional elasticity of -0.24. Since the share of restaurant workers earning the minimum wage exceeds that for teens as a group, this elasticity is still below the break-even elasticity. I doubt the dust has completely settled in this exchange. In summary, while intellectually and methodologically exciting, the debate generated by the Card and Krueger study still does not suggest that the minimum wage disemployment effects are so large as to indicate that minimum wage increases decrease the total amount of income earned by minimum wage workers. Estimates from the two sides of the debate are remarkably similar, with t-values only at the margins of statistical significance.

As might be expected, the minimum wage debate in Canada has been less heated. One benefit, already noted, of the Canadian studies is that they could exploit cross-province variation in the levels of the minimum wage, as well as the timing of changes in the minimum. One of the problems in any analysis of the impact of minimum wages is that the timing of changes is rarely exogenous to the employment situation. Legislators are often reluctant to raise wages during recessions, and instead wait until employment is growing. This pattern will tend

the cause of the increase in output, that output increase should lead to a fall in price. Instead, Card and Krueger found that the price of fast food meals increased, which is more consistent with the traditional competitive model.

to reduce the negative correlation between the minimum wage and employment. While this problem still exists when the analysis uses a cross-section of provinces, differences in political preferences should provide more variation than time-series data alone, and the simultaneity bias is likely to be smaller. Another benefit of the Canadian data is that, at least until the early 1980's, minimum wages were slightly higher than those in the U.S., at least in some jurisdictions, so that the possibility of detecting minimum wage effects was greater. Before reviewing the empirical results, it is worth considering the likely break-even benchmarks for Canada. Using the 1990 LMAS, the proportion of teens at or below the minimum was 0.33, and the share at or below the minimum plus 50 cents, was 0.47. For young adults, the figures are 0.095 and 0.143, and for older adults 0.038 and 0.053. Thus, for teens the cutoffs are a little higher, but quite close to those in the U.S.

Swidinsky (1980) presented the first set of minimum wage results. While he pooled the data across provinces, he also estimated province-specific responses to minimum wage changes. For teens, he estimated elasticities ranging from -0.04 in Ontario, to -0.79 in Quebec for males, and -0.34 to -0.93 for females. Thus, these estimates bracket the break-even elasticities, at least when the elasticities are based on 1990 data.

Schaafsma and Walsh (1983) updated the results, though using a slightly non-standard specification. They found larger elasticities of -0.6 for teens, -0.30 for young adults, and -0.15 for older adults. All of these estimates exceed the relevant break-even elasticities. However, since Schaafsma and Walsh's sample covered 1975-1979, it is possible that the break-even elasticity was higher at this time because the minimum wage was significantly higher. One might then be less likely to accept the hypothesis that the minimum wage elasticity was equal to the break-even elasticity against the alternative that it was greater. Of course, shifting one's null to the break-even elasticity (rather than zero), might result in very few elasticities being rejected in favor of the alternative that the elasticity was greater. Grenier and Séguin (1991) replicate the earlier (Swidinsky, 1980) study with data from the 1980s. As with Wellington, they find the employment elasticities reduced in absolute value, and indeed negative and statistically insignificant. Cousineau, Tessier, and Vaillancourt (1992), on the other hand, use time-series data from Ontario and find that minimum wages have an adverse effect on unemployment, and by inference, employment. In summary, these earlier Canadian studies mirror the U.S. literature in the sense that minimum wage effects estimated on data prior to the 1980s were larger than those estimated with data that included the lower wage 1980s.

Two more recent studies suggest, however, that minimum wage effects may be quite significant in Canada. Baker, Benjamin, and Stanger (1999) use pooled time-series and cross-section data covering the period 1975-1993 to estimate employment consequences of the minimum wage. They employ methodologies very similar to those used in the previous U.S. studies, such as Neumark and

Wascher (1992). They also explore the dynamic consequences of minimum wage changes in some detail, and find that dynamics were quite important. For teens, they estimate a straight minimum wage effect of -0.264, which is negative and statistically significant, but less than the cut-off elasticity (though within the traditional range in the literature). For young adults, the comparable elasticity was -0.082, which is also negative and statistically significant, and slightly less than the break-even elasticity.

However, once the elasticities are decomposed into "short-run" and "long-run" components, they find long-run elasticities of -0.413 and -0.092 for teens and young adults. These long-run elasticities are on the high end of the range reported in the previous literature, and are also very close to the break-even elasticities, at least for small changes in the minimum wage. In their study, the long-run corresponds to periods in excess of 5 years, suggesting considerable delay in the response of employment to minimum wage changes. One possible explanation would be potentially long horizons associated with adjusting the capital stock. They also find positive and insignificant short-run elasticities, consistent with the small effects found by Card and Krueger. This suggests that studies like Card and Krueger (1994) and Card (1992a and 1992b) that look at employment "before" and immediately "after" a minimum wage increase do not capture the complete adjustment process of firms, or indeed very much of it. Most studies (like the time series studies) provide estimates that essentially "average" the large long-run effects with the small short-run effects. The Baker, Benjamin, and Stanger paper thus emphasizes the importance of exploring the timing of responses to minimum wage changes, as well as providing a partial reconciliation of some of the disparate results found in the U.S. literature.

Yuen (1995) also looks at the disemployment possibilities of the minimum wage, though using an entirely different methodology. He follows Currie and Fallick (1995) who use U.S. micro (individual) panel data to estimate the consequences of minimum wage changes on specific individuals who are at risk of losing their jobs. Yuen estimates employment probability equations on a sample of teens and young adults drawn from the LMAS longitudinal file, 1988-1990. He follows individuals as they move from employment state to employment state across quarters. Given information on individual wages, he assigns them to a risk group. Those whose wages lie at or below the new minimum wage are assigned to the group at risk of losing their jobs. He finds that for teens as a whole, there is no correlation between provincial minimum wage changes and the probability of employment in the next quarter. However, focusing on those teens most "at risk," he finds that a 30 cent increase in the minimum wage is associated with a reduced probability of employment of -3% to -4%. This is remarkably similar to Currie and Fallick's result. For young adults, Yuen finds a slightly larger effect, on the order of -7% to -8%. In summary then, the more recent Canadian studies find significant disemployment effects, some close to the break-even level.

8.5 Distributional Effects of the Minimum Wage

The previous discussion emphasized the efficiency aspects of minimum wage policy. Implicit in the disemployment studies, however, are two distributional consequences. First, some low wage workers will lose their jobs, so some may gain and others lose from a minimum wage increase. Second, if the disemployment effect is large enough, fewer dollars will actually end up in the hands of low wage workers as a group. In this section, I extend the distributional focus to the effectiveness of minimum wages in alleviating poverty. I follow three different avenues, with the objective of tracing through the effect of the minimum wage, first on wages, then on individual incomes, and finally on poverty. I begin with an investigation of the impact of minimum wages on the overall distribution of wages. Next, I estimate the incremental income "transferred" to low wage workers by changes in provincial minimum wages between 1988 and 1990. Finally, I tabulate the relationship between low wages and poverty. My results mirror the small U.S. literature that directly addresses the distributional aspects of minimum wages: while the benefits of minimum wage increases are concentrated among low income households, the association with poverty is quite weak, and many besides the poor "collect" benefits.

As Figure 8.3 makes clear, a non-rigorous "eyeball" approach suggests that the minimum wage acts as an effective wage floor. The spike at the minimum, as well as the small number of wages below the minimum suggests that the minimum wage constrains firms in the wages that they may pay. This point is made strikingly clear in Card and Krueger (1994 and 1995) for restaurant employees. Thus, at least for low wage workers, conditional on employment, the minimum wage has obvious direct positive impact on earnings since they obtain higher wages than they otherwise would. Indeed, more formal studies of the overall wage distribution suggest that minimum wages have played an important role as a "backstop" in the wage distribution. DiNardo, Fortin, and Lemieux (1995), for example, show that the real decline in the minimum wage over the 1980's contributed to increasing wage inequality in the U.S. The reverse naturally follows that minimum wages have historically helped compress the wage distribution.

Minimum wages may have further effects on the wage distribution, through "ripple" or "spillover" effects. These effects may help low wage workers just above the minimum. If firms maintain their relative wage structure, however, the higher minimum wage may be "transferred" further up the wage distribution. This would offset the equalizing effect of the minimum wage, though employees as a group would be receiving more from firms (or consumers). This is essentially the finding of Grossman (1983). Card and Krueger (1995) look in some detail at the wage structure immediately following the minimum wage increases in the U.S. in 1990 and 1991. They find that spillover effects are concentrated among those workers paid just above the new minimum, rather than spreading throughout the distribution, at least in the short-run.

Previous researchers with access only to more aggregate data have conducted a more limited exercise, by looking at the impact of the minimum wage on the average wage, and indirectly inferring distributional effects. If the minimum wage affects only those workers who are paid at or below the new minimum, then the average wage should go up by approximately $S_M \times \Delta MW$, the share of these workers times the change in the minimum wage. If it rises more, it suggests the existence of spillover effects, as non-minimum wage workers also experience wage increases. Gramlich (1976) estimates a regression of average wages (AW) on minimum wages (MW), and a set of control variables, using U.S. aggregate data. In elasticity terms, the coefficient on the log minimum wage should be $S_M \times MW/AW$ if there are no spillover effects. Gramlich estimates a coefficient of 0.028, which is statistically significant, but not suggestive of spillover effects. While not presented as such, Castillo-Freeman and Freeman (1992) estimate a similar equation for Puerto Rico, where both S_M and MW/AW are higher. They estimate a coefficient of 0.21, which compares favorably to a predicted coefficient of $0.7 \times 0.3 = 0.21$.

Similar equations for Canada, based on a pooled time-series cross-section of provincial level data (the data of Figure 8.2) are presented in Table 8.4. The first column refers to the average manufacturing wage (including overtime), for which data extend farther back in time than for other series. The remaining columns refer to a variety of shorter wage series. For each equation I show the predicted coefficient on the log minimum wage term if there are no spillover effects and if minimum wages are exogenous. This latter assumption is unlikely to hold, however, among other reasons because many jurisdictions use average wages as the target variable for the minimum wage (though evidently not as much over the 1980s). If jurisdiction i chose to continually adjust its minimum wage such that $MW_i = \theta_i AW_i$, estimating these equations by OLS would be subject to a serious simultaneity bias. In logarithms: $\ln MW_i = \ln \theta_i + \ln AW_i$. This would likely lead to an overstatement of the impact of minimum wages on the average wage. Similarly, we might expect high wage jurisdictions to have higher minimum wages, or more prosperous times to lead to higher minimum wages. Controlling for province fixed effects, time trends, and other economic performance measures should help alleviate the bias associated with the endogeneity of minimum wages, but as long as θ_i is not fixed, some degree of bias can be expected. Nevertheless, many of the ln MW coefficients reported in the table are consistent with the null hypothesis of no spillover effects. Exceptions are those corresponding to the retail trade average wage and the average industrial wage. For trade, the coefficient is much smaller and not consistent with spillovers, but the coefficient for the average industrial wage does suggest spillovers. But since this is the wage most often cited as the target of minimum wage policy advocates, the coefficient may alternatively be high because of the aforementioned simultaneity bias. Nevertheless, the

Table 8.4
Regression Estimates of the Effect of Minimum Wages on Selected Average Wages,[1] Canada
(Standard Errors in Parentheses)

	1975-1993		1983-1993			
	Manufacturing Wage[2]	Manufacturing Wage[2]	Manufacturing Wage[3]	Trade Wage	Accommodation/Food Wage	Industrial Wage
Share MW workers[4]	0.022	0.022	0.022	0.084	0.285	0.058
MW/AW[5]	0.37	0.35	0.36	0.54	0.73	0.40
Predicted Coeff.[6]	0.008	0.008	0.008	0.045	0.208	0.023
Ln Minimum Wage	0.077 (0.028)	-0.007 (0.035)	-0.033 (0.035)	0.158 (0.044)	0.191 (0.091)	0.117 (0.035)
Ln CPI[7]	0.820 (0.043)	0.199 (0.111)	0.283 (0.112)	0.657 (0.139)	0.945 (0.286)	0.721 (0.112)
Ln GDP	0.216 (0.030)	0.320 (0.036)	0.301 (0.037)	0.119 (0.046)	-0.011 (0.094)	0.175 (0.037)
Unemployment Rate	1.022 (0.116)	1.393 (0.124)	1.529 (0.125)	0.939 (0.156)	0.498 (0.320)	1.184 (0.125)
Trend	-0.012 (0.002)	0.011 (0.004)	0.008 (0.004)	-0.008 (0.005)	-0.008 (0.010)	-0.010 (0.004)
Province Dummies	Yes	Yes	Yes	Yes	Yes	Yes
Test Equality to Predicted (p-value)[5]	0.014	0.672	0.254	0.012	0.850	0.010

Notes: [1] Pooled time series / cross-section data for 9 provinces (Prince Edward Island is excluded, due to small sample sizes for some key variables). Regressions are weighted by relative populations of each province. [2] Manufacturing wage is the manufacturing wage, including overtime. [3] Manufacturing wage excluding overtime. [4] Share of MW workers is estimated from the LMAS, 1990, and represents the fraction of workers at or below the minimum wage. [5] The ratio of the minimum to the average wage. [6] The predicted coefficient on ln MW, the product of the share of minimum wage workers and MW/AW. The test at the bottom of the table is a test of whether the ln MW coefficient is equal to this predicted value. [7] Consumer Price Index.

Sources: CANSIM (wages and other economic variables), Labour Canada (minimum wages).

Canadian data do not allow us to completely rule out spillover effects. Clearly, better data would be required to sort out this puzzle.

As a further input into an evaluation of the impact of minimum wages on income distribution, Card and Krueger (1995) use cross-state variation in the likely impact of minimum wages to assess the impact of the 1990 and 1991 minimum wage increases on the wage distribution. They find that in high impact states, that is in states with a high fraction of minimum wage workers, wages of the lowest deciles of workers increased relative to the higher deciles. This would suggest that minimum wage workers benefitted from the increase in minimum wages, especially given that Card and Krueger do not estimate an offsetting disemployment effect.

Ideally, of course, one would like to follow actual *minimum wage workers* over time in order to better identify the response of their earnings, which would reflect both the changes in wages and any potentially offsetting reductions in hours. Such an exercise requires panel data; fortunately, the LMAS has a panel component, though its very short duration is a real limitation to its usefulness in this dimension. Nevertheless, as a "back of the envelope" exercise, I estimate the impact of minimum wage changes between 1988 and 1990 on the earnings of *low wage workers*, whom one might predict would have benefitted. Essentially, this is an extension of the methodology of Yuen (1995), and Currie and Fallick (1995), who look at employment probabilities, though my study is conducted on a more limited scale.[19] The group of workers likely to benefit from an increase in the minimum wage include those who worked for the minimum wage during 1988 plus those with wages between the January 1988 minimum and the December 1990 minimum. Potential minimum wage workers who were not employed as such in 1988 will be missed by this methodology. Ignoring this problem, we can use cross-province variation in the increases in the minimum wage, as well as within province variation in the magnitude of the anticipated raise, to identify the role that the minimum wage plays in increasing low wage worker incomes. My basic strategy is very similar to that of Card and Krueger, except that I employ individual-level panel data: did low wage workers' earnings grow relatively faster in those provinces that saw the largest minimum wage increases? *Non-minimum wage workers* form part of the "control group" within provinces, and across-province variation in changes in minimum wages provides the remainder of the "experiment."

How much should these low wage workers gain? A very crude calculation would suggest that if hours and wages otherwise stay the same, then their earnings should grow by $\Delta MW \times Average\ hours\ in\ 1988$. Using the actual sample means, this suggests that for all low wage workers, earnings should rise by 0.89×1025, or about \$912. For teens, since their average annual hours are lower, at 594, their

---

[19] The dependent variable in my study is the change in earnings between 1988 and 1990. Earnings estimates are available for all individuals "at risk" in 1988, though earnings may be zero for those who did not work in 1990. For a more detailed study of employment itself, see Yuen (1995).

predicted increase in earnings would be $528. I thus estimate regressions of the annual earnings change between 1988 and 1990 as a function of individual characteristics, as well as the "at risk" measures. I control for low wage status, as well as an interaction of this low wage indicator with (i) the total increase in the minimum wage in the province, or (ii) the "gap" or difference in wages between the individual's wage in 1988 and the level of the minimum in 1990. It is the interaction term that identifies the minimum wage effect, since we might expect low wage workers to experience wage growth for other reasons (measurement error and mean reversion, for example).

The findings, reported in Table 8.5 for all workers as well as for teens, include specifications with and without controls for province fixed effects. As emphasized by Deere, Murphy, and Welch (1995), one criticism of the Card and Krueger approach is that there may be other sources of changes in employment or other economic conditions at the state level that are correlated with minimum wages or the level of wages; it is therefore important to test the sensitivity of the results to controls for these effects. The age and education coefficients look as one might expect: earnings grew faster for younger and more educated workers. Women's earnings also grew faster than men's. While the earnings of low wage workers did grow significantly more than those of other workers, there does not appear to be any relationship between this growth and changes in the provincial minimum wage. Only in the case of teens, when province effects are included, do we mirror Card and Krueger's results that low wage earners gained relatively more in those provinces that saw larger increases in their minimum wages. On the other hand, there is no evidence that low wage workers were adversely affected by minimum wages either. Given the simple nature of the regressions, the criticism of Welch (1995) bears repeating: just because I did not find an effect does not mean that one did not exist.

Finally, I turn to the "bottom line" evaluation of the usefulness of minimum wages in combating poverty. As first noted by Stigler (1946, 362), "One cannot expect a close relationship between the level of hourly wage rates and the amount of family income. Yet family income and needs are the fundamental factors in the problem of poverty." While minimum wages may increase the wages, and even the earnings of low wage workers, they may have limited value in combating poverty for two separate reasons: first, low wage workers may not be in low wage families, and second, for a given level of income, family needs may be the most important determinant of poverty. For this reason, critics have emphasized that the minimum wage is a very blunt anti-poverty tool. First, many minimum wage workers are teenagers, possibly from higher income families. Second, poor families are more often characterized by having no earners than very low wage earners. Gramlich (1976) showed that, at least for teens, increases in minimum wages had very little beneficial distributional effect. However, there was a closer connection between the adult low-wage earners and poverty, at least in the early 1970s, though again

Table 8.5
Regression Estimates of the Impact of Changes in the Minimum Wage
on Annual Earnings Growth, Canada, 1988-1990
Dependent Variable: Change in Annual Earnings
(Standard Errors in Parentheses)

	Full Sample				Teen			
	(1)	(2)	(3)	(4)	(5)	(6)	(7)	(8)
Male	-659.0	-661.3	-660.2	-661.9	249.6	225.4	246.3	221.6
	(141.5)	(141.5)	(141.5)	(141.5)	(278.5)	(278.3)	(278.4)	(278.4)
Age 16-19	8076.9	8099.5	8106.6	8125.4				
	(352.8)	(352.5)	(353.1)	(352.8)				
Age 20-24	7277.2	7266.2	7288.1	7271.9				
	(315.2)	(314.9)	(315.2)	(314.9)				
Age 25-34	5216.9	5203.8	5222.4	5205.3				
	(281.7)	(281.4)	(281.7)	(281.4)				
Age 35-44	5080.6	5084.2	5084.1	5085.1				
	(286.9)	(286.7)	(286.9)	(286.7)				
Age 45-54	4480.8	4485.8	4486.5	4490.4				
	(303.6)	(303.6)	(303.6)	(303.7)				
Some Secondary	-202.2	-146.9	-197.6	-140.0	533.5	706.4	520.9	743.9
	(293.2)	(292.8)	(293.3)	(292.8)	(663.9)	(662.0)	(663.7)	(662.1)
High School Graduate	-111.8	-34.4	-109.8	-23.0	561.2	673.4	497.0	678.0
	(295.8)	(292.2)	(295.8)	(292.2)	(697.0)	(689.5)	(697.4)	(690.0)
Some Post Secondary	240.1	310.6	244.1	323.4	1029.1	1201.5	983.7	1179.7
	(332.2)	(330.1)	(332.3)	(330.1)	(709.5)	(708.0)	(709.4)	(708.6)
P.S. Diploma/Certificate	973.0	995.2	974.0	1002.7				
	(309.1)	(307.8)	(309.1)	(307.8)				
University	1193.0	1228.8	1192.9	1237.3				
	(315.4)	(313.1)	(315.4)	(313.1)				
Low Wage[1]	-636.3	-728.3	1198.9	1126.1	56.3	-1727.5	1504.9	1358.6
	(1128.5)	(1098.3)	(375.5)	(374.0)	(1256.4)	(1075.6)	(407.0)	(396.6)
Low Wage / Change in Prov. Min. Wage[2]	2310.4	2303.8			1072.3	2891.7		
	(1238.8)	(1203.7)			(1350.7)	(1151.1)		
Wage Gap[3]			247.6	219.2			-666.2	-670.3
			(310.6)	(310.6)			(377.7)	(376.7)
Province Dummies	Yes	No	Yes	No	Yes	No	Yes	No
F-Test for Low Wage (p-val[ue])[4]	15.42	13.85	14.01	12.27	6.05	7.74	7.29	6.17
	(0.0001)	(0.0001)	(0.0001)	(0.0001)	(0.002)	(0.0004)	(0.0007)	(0.002)
F-Test for Provinces (p-value)	4.89		4.93		2.67		2.67	
	(0.0001)		(0.0001)		(0.004)		(0.004)	
Sample Size[5]	36,598	36,598	36,598	36,598	3,539	3,539	3,539	3,539

Notes: [1]Low wage is defined as usually being paid below the December 1990 provincial minimum wage (plus $0.05) in 1988. [2]Change in Prov. Min. Wage is the difference between the January 1988 and December 1990 minimum wage. [3]The Wage Gap is the difference between the individual's 1988 wage and the December 1990 minimum wage. [4]The F-test for Low Wage is a joint test of the significance of the low wage coefficients. [5]Inclusion in the sample is conditional on positive earnings in 1988.

Source: Labour Market Activity Survey (LMAS).

minimum wages could not help those families without any full-time workers. Burkhauser and Finegan (1989) show that, whereas in 1960 42% of low wage workers were in families below the poverty line, by 1985 the proportion had fallen to 18%. Card and Krueger (1995) also explore the distributional question in more detail. They point out that only 30% of minimum wage workers are teens, so that the typical minimum wage worker need not be a secondary worker. They also show that 43% of workers affected by the increases in the minimum wage were in the bottom 3 deciles of the family earnings distribution. When family earnings are combined with family size to construct an indicator of poverty, they find that 30% of the affected workers were in poor families. Thus, while there is certainly leakage, minimum wages do transfer income to the poor. Nevertheless, there remain many poor families who do not benefit at all from increases in the minimum wage. As a summary exercise they employ their cross-state methodology to determine whether poverty rates declined fastest in those states where the most workers would have been affected by the rise in the minimum. They found no statistically significant relationship.

In the Canadian context, Shannon and Beach (1995) present evidence consistent with the U.S. literature that low wages are only loosely connected with low family income and poverty. I extend their analysis to the entire country, and also focus on the distributional questions raised by Card and Krueger (1995). Table 8.6 provides a cross-tabulation between worker wages and family income deciles based on the family earnings measure of LMAS. The exercise is not as straightforward as one would like. The LMAS measure of family income excludes the incomes of full time students and includes only labor earnings, i.e.self-employed earnings are not reported. The latter limitation was also a feature of the CPS data used by Card and Krueger, and I adopt their solution of eliminating these households, since there is no way to impute their income decile. The LMAS also has poor indicators of the exact family structure (age of children at home, etc.), as well as no indicator of city, so only crude "poverty"indicators can be constructed.[20] I take Statistics Canada's most pessimistic definitions from 1990, based on their highest needs estimate for a family of a given size.[21] If income falls below this cutoff, families are designated as low income. Finally, I define low wage workers in two ways; first, those being paid below the provincial minimum wage plus $0.05 and second (in order to include more low wage workers who would be affected by minimum wage increases), those workers earning up to a dollar more than the

[20] An additional problem with the LMAS is the fact that income is reported as a categorical variable, with a cap at $65,000, which forces us to combine the top two deciles. However, since our focus is on the lower deciles, this is not much of a problem.

[21] The low income cut-offs are based on family size: for a family size of 1 adult, the level is $11,838; for 2 it is $16,573; for 3, $21,308; for 4, $26,044; for 5, $30,779; for 6, $35,514. The cut-offs are higher than they should be since Statistics Canada has lower cutoffs for families with children.

Table 8.6
Distributional Impact of Minimum Wage Changes, Canada, 1990

Decile¹	All Individuals		Low Income Individuals		Individuals Paid at or Below Minimum Wage						Individuals Paid at or Below Minimum Wage plus $1.00		
	%N²	%Hrs³	Incid	%N²	Incid⁴	%N²	Hrs³	%Teen Hrs⁵	%Y Ad Hrs⁵	%Ad Hrs⁵	Incid⁴	%N²	%Hrs³
1	10.8	0	100	42.5	0	0	0	0	0	0	0	0	0
2	9.1	4.5	100	35.6	17.1	29.5	25.9	20.1	20.6	29.5	31.8	26.6	21.7
3	9.1	8.7	50.9	18.3	7.0	12.3	19.0	8.9	22.7	21.0	15.4	13.0	18.6
4	9.5	10.2	8.7	3.3	4.1	7.5	8.6	5.8	10.0	9.1	9.6	8.4	9.6
5	9.7	10.5	1.1	0.4	4.6	8.5	8.8	10.1	9.6	8.1	10.0	8.9	9.1
6	10.2	11.8	0	0	4.1	7.9	7.6	9.3	9.1	6.5	9.4	8.8	9.2
7	9.7	11.7	0	0	5.4	10.1	9.7	8.7	8.0	10.5	10.7	9.6	9.3
8	9.9	12.6	0	0	5.1	9.7	9.7	12.3	6.0	10.2	9.7	8.9	8.9
9-10	22.1	30.1	0	0	3.5	14.6	10.7	24.9	14.0	5.1	7.8	15.9	13.5
Low Income			24.5				36.1	28.0	30.4	40.6			32.3

Notes: ¹ Deciles are deciles of family earnings. The top two deciles are pooled because of LMAS top-coding. ²% N refers to the percent of the designated group in a given decile (or in the low income category). ³ % Hrs. weights %N by annual hours worked, so that it gives the share of hours worked by the given group in the particular decile. ⁴Incid is the incidence within the decile of the particular group. ⁵The age breakdowns are Teen (16-19), Y Ad (young adults, 20-24), and Ad (Adults, 25-65). All results are weighted by the LMAS sample weights. ⁶Low Income is defined as having family earnings less than an "approximate" Statistics Canada Low Income Cutoff.

Source: Labour Market Activity Survey (LMAS), 1990.

minimum. This yields an estimate of low wage workers very similar to Card and Krueger's "Affected Workers" category, those who were affected by the increase in minimum wage between 1990 and 1991 (an increase of $0.95).

Table 8.6 reports the shares of the sample of individuals, as well as the share of total hours worked in each income decile.[22] As can be seen, hours worked are not evenly distributed across deciles. The poorest 3 deciles account for only 13% of hours worked (the bottom has zero), while the top two account for over 30%. Not surprisingly, the incidence of low incomes is universal for those individuals located in the bottom deciles, and most low income individuals are found in these lowest deciles. The story is different for low wage workers. (I focus on the first definition of this group—those paid at or below the minimum, since the results are only slightly different for the other definition). The bottom family income decile contains no low wage workers, since these families have no workers. Clearly, minimum wage increases will not help this group. However, 17% of families in the second decile have a low wage worker, a much higher number than the higher income deciles. In the column most comparable to Card and Krueger, we see that

[22] The deciles do not contain exactly 10% of individuals (only one individual is sampled from each household) because of the rounding of the income categories. For example, more than 20% are in the top 2 deciles because of the top coding, and more than 10% are in the bottom decile because of truncation at zero family earnings.

42% of all low wage workers and 45% of the hours worked by low wage workers, are accounted for in the bottom 3 deciles. These numbers are virtually identical to those found in Card and Krueger for the US. As emphasized by Gramlich, the anti-poverty feature of the minimum wage is somewhat distorted if we do not distinguish between teens and older workers. Indeed, only 36% of individuals, and 19% of total low wage hours are accounted for by teens. Thus, while the caricature of minimum wage workers as being relatively evenly distributed over the income distribution is true for teens, over half of the low wage hours of adults are concentrated in families falling in the bottom 3 deciles (really, deciles 2 and 3). If one looks instead at low income status, Table 8.6 shows that 41% of low wage adult hours are from poor households. Thus, confirming the findings in Card and Krueger, I find that increases in the minimum wage may have disproportionate benefits for low wage working adults, who tend to come from poor families. Of course, this does not negate the earlier insights that the link between low wages and poverty is weak, since the very bottom families cannot be reached at all by minimum wages.

The results from this strand of research also suggest that much of the focus of the minimum wage literature on employment effects has been misplaced, at least in terms of public policy analysis. In North America, the distributional evidence highlights the real limitations of minimum wages as a policy lever for helping the poor. This is one area, however, where simple extensions of the lessons to Latin America may be problematic. If minimum wage workers are primary earners (as they appear to be in Puerto Rico, for example), then subject to enforcement issues, minimum wages may have a more direct link with low household earnings. If that is true, the traditional focus on disemployment effects is better placed. In some labor markets in Latin America, however, coverage becomes an important issue; it may be the more privileged workers who earn the minimum wage, while poorer households have workers in the uncovered, informal sector. Without comparable evidence from Latin America, it would clearly be unwise to take the Canadian and US evidence as representative of the policy consequences in Latin America. This only highlights the importance of obtaining similar evidence in the Latin American context.

8.6 Conclusions

In this chapter we have explored some of the lessons that Canadian experience, placed in the U.S. context, might offer Latin America with regard to minimum wages. Our organizing principle was an assessment of the distributional effectiveness of minimum wages. We found:

1) Minimum wages, which are set by the provinces in Canada, are at a level

comparable to the U.S. The real value of the minimum wage deteriorated significantly since the late 1970s.

2) Estimated disemployment effects of minimum wages are slightly higher in Canada than in the U.S. If estimates from the high end of confidence intervals are chosen, in Canada at least, the loss of jobs may be great enough to actually reduce the wage bill received by low wage workers.

3) Minimum wages have only limited scope for improving the welfare of the lowest income households, since most of these families have no full-time earners. Similarly, many of the benefits of higher minimum wages are transferred to teens who are distributed relatively evenly across the income distribution. Nevertheless, the benefits would flow disproportionately to poor working adults.

These results provide useful background information in addressing Stigler's first question on the effectiveness of minimum wages. Unfortunately, we still come up short in answering the second, on how the minimum wage compares (and interacts) with other policies addressed to the poor. Whatever their other failings, minimum wages have the benefit of increasing the incomes of those who actually work, and may enhance incentives to do so. Given current Canadian attitudes to social programs, this is one feature of minimum wages that is often neglected. As Stigler (1946, 364) concludes his own paper:

> Incomes of the poor cannot be increased without impairing incentives. Skillful policies will, for a given increase in the incomes of the poor, impair incentives less than clumsy policies. But the more completely poverty is eliminated, given the level of intelligence with which this is done, the greater will be the impairment of incentives. This is a price we must pay, just as impairment of incentives is a price we have willingly paid to reduce the inequality of income by progressive income and estate taxes.

Stigler proposes that a negative income tax scheme would be less distortionary than minimum wages. There are very few studies that combine information on such transfer programs. Johnson and Browning (1983) simulate the distributional effects with the income tax system, while Burkhauser, Couch, and Glenn (1995) conduct a detailed comparison of minimum wages and the Earned Income Tax Credit as means of transferring income to the working poor. These studies represent an important frontier that could benefit from more research, so that the results of minimum wage research could be placed in a more informative context.

REFERENCES

Ashenfelter, O. and R. Smith (1979). "Compliance with the Minimum Wage Law." *Journal of Political Economy*, Vol. 79, pp. 333-350.

Baker, M., Benjamin, D., and S. Stanger (1999). "The Highs and Lows of the Minimum Wage Effect: A Time Series-Cross Section Study of the Canadian Law." *Journal of Labor Economics*, Vol. 17, No. 2 (April), pp. 318-350.

Bell, L. (1995). "The Impact of Minimum Wages in Mexico and Colombia." Washington, D.C.: The World Bank, Policy Research, Working Paper #1514.

Brown, C. (1988) "Minimum Wage Laws: Are They Overrated?" *Journal of Economic Perspectives*, Vol. 2, No. 2, pp. 133-47.

Brown, C. (1995). "Book Review of Myth and Measurement." *Industrial and Labor Relations Review*, Vol. 48, pp. 828-830.

Brown, C., C. Gilroy, and A. Kohen (1982). "The Effect of the Minimum Wage on Employment and Unemployment." *Journal of Economic Literature*, Vol. 20, pp. 487-528.

Burkhauser, R., K. Couch, and A. Glenn (1995). "Public Policies for the Working Poor: The Earned Income Tax Credit Versus Minimum Wage Legislation." In *Research in Labor Economics*, Vol. 15, Solomon Polachek, ed.

Burkhauser, R. and T. A. Finegan (1989). "The Minimum Wage and the Poor: The End of a Relationship." *Journal of Policy Analysis and Management*, Vol. 8, pp. 53-71.

Card, D. (1992a). "Using Regional Variations in Wages to Measure the Effects of the Federal Minimum Wage." *Industrial and Labor Relations Review*, Vol. 46, pp. 22-37.

Card, D. (1992b). "Do Minimum Wages Reduce Employment? A Case Study of California, 1987-89." *Industrial and Labor Relations Review*, Vol. 46, pp. 38-54.

Card, D. and A. Krueger (1994). "Minimum Wages and Employment: A Case Study of the Fast Food Industry in New Jersey and Pennsylvania." *American Economic Review*, Vol. 84, pp. 772-793.

Card, D. and A. Krueger (1995). *Myth and Measurement: The New Economics of the Minimum Wage*. Princeton, N.J.: Princeton University Press.

Card, D., L. Katz and A. Krueger (1994). "Comment on David Neumark and William Wascher, 'Employment Effects of Minimum and Subminimum Wages: Panel Data on State Minimum Wage Laws.'" *Industrial and Labor Relations Review*, Vol. 48, pp. 487-496.

Card, D., F. Kramarz, and T. Lemieux (1995). "Changes in the Relative Structure of Wages and Employment: A Comparison of the United States, Canada, and France." Princeton University, Industrial Relations Section, Working Paper #355.

Castillo-Freeman, A. and R. Freeman (1992). "When the Minimum Wage Really Bites: The Effect of the U.S.-Level Minimum Wage on Puerto Rico." In Borjas, G. and R. Freeman (eds.),

Immigration and the Workforce. Chicago: University of Chicago Press, pp. 177-212.

Cousineau, J-M., D. Tessier, and F. Vaillancourt (1992). "The Impact of the Ontario Minimum Wage on the Unemployment of Women and the Young in Ontario." *Relations Industrielles-Industrial Relations,* Vol. 47, pp. 559-566.

Currie, J. and B. Fallick, (1995). "The Minimum Wage and the Employment of Youth: Evidence from the NLSY." Mimeo.

Deere, D, K. Murphy, and F. Welch (1995). "Employment and the 1990-1991 Minimum-wage Hike." *American Economic Review,* (Papers and Proceedings), Vol. 85, No. 2, pp. 232-237.

DiNardo, J., N. Fortin, and T. Lemieux (1995). "Labor Market Institutions and the Distribution of Wages, 1973-1992: A Semiparametric Approach." Cambridge, Mass.: NBER, Working Paper #5093.

Ehrenberg, R. and R. Smith (1994). *Modern Labor Economics: Theory and Public Policy,* Fifth Edition. New York: Harper Collins.

Freeman, R. (1995). "Book Review of Myth and Measurement." *Industrial and Labor Relations Review,* Vol. 48, pp. 830-834.

Gramlich, E. (1976). "Impact of Minimum Wages on Other Wages, Employment, and Family Incomes." *Brookings Papers on Economic Activity,* pp. 409-451.

Grenier, G. and M. Séguin (1991). "L'Incidence du Salaire Minimum sur le Marche Travail des Adolescents au Canada: Une Reconsideration des Resultats Empiriques." *L'Actualite Economique,* Vol. 67, pp. 123-143.

Grossman, J. (1983) "The Impact of the Minimum Wage on Other Wages." *Journal of Human Resources,* Vol. 18, pp. 359-378.

Hamermesh, D. (1995). "What a Wonderful World This Would Be: A Review of Myth and Measurement." *Industrial and Labor Relations Review,* Vol. 48, pp. 835-838.

Johnson, W. and E. Browning (1983). "The Distributional and Efficiency Effects of Increasing the Minimum Wage." *American Economic Review,* Vol. 73, pp. 204-211.

Katz, L. and A. Krueger (1992). "The Effect of the New Minimum Wage on the Fast Food Industry." *Industrial and Labor Relations Review,* Vol. 43, pp. 254-65.

Kim, T. and L. Taylor (1995). "The Employment Effect of California's 1988 Minimum Wage Increase." *Journal of Economic and Business Statistics.*

Labor Canada (various years). *Labor Standards in Canada.* Ottawa: Supply and Services Canada. Selected years over the period 1976-1987.

Labor Canada (various years). *Employment Standards Legislation in Canada.* Ottawa: Supply and Services Canada. Issues for the years 1989-1995.

National Industrial Conference Board (1927). *Minimum Wage Legislation in Massachusetts.* New

York: National Industrial Conference Board.

Neumark, D. and W. Wascher (1992). "Employment Effects of Minimum and Sub-Minimum Wages: Panel data on State Minimum Wage Laws." *Industrial and Labor Relations Review*, Vol. 46, pp. 55-81.

Neumark, D. and W. Wascher (1994). "Employment Effects of Minimum and Subminimum Wages: Reply to Card, Katz, and Krueger." *Industrial and Labor Relations Review*, Vol. 48, pp. 497-512.

Neumark, D. and W. Wascher (1995). "The Effect of New Jersey's Minimum Wage Increase on Fast-Food Employment: A Re-evaluation Using Payroll Records." Cambridge, Mass: NBER, Working Paper #5224.

Province of Ontario (1920). *Statutes*. Toronto: Province of Ontario.

Schaafsma, J. and W. Walsh (1983). "Employment and Labor Supply Effects of the Minimum Wage: Some Pooled Time-Series Estimates from Canadian Provincial Data." *Canadian Journal of Economics*, Vol. 16, pp. 86-97.

Shannon, M. and C. Beach (1995). "Distributional Employment Effects of Ontario Minimum Wage Proposals: A Microdata Approach." *Canadian Public Policy*, Vol. XXI, No. 3 (September), pp. 284-303.

Stigler, G. (1946). "The Economics of Minimum Wage Legislation." *American Economic Review*, Vol. 36, pp. 358-365.

Swidinsky, R. (1980). "Minimum Wages and Teenage Employment." *Canadian Journal of Economics*, Vol. 13, pp. 158-171.

Welch, F. (1995). "Book Review of Myth and Measurement." *Industrial and Labor Relations Review*, Vol. 48, pp. 842-848.

Wellington, A. (1991). "Effects of the Minimum Wage on the Employment Status of Youths, An Update." *Journal of Human Resources*, Vol. 26, pp. 27-46.

West, E. and M. McKee (1980). *Minimum Wages: The New Issues in Theory, Evidence, Policy, and Politics*. Ottawa: Economic Council of Canada.

Yuen, T. (1995). "The Effect of Minimum Wages on Youth Employment in Canada: Evidence from the LMAS." Toronto: Department of Economics, University of Toronto, mimeo.

Chapter 9

MINIMUM WAGES IN LATIN AMERICA: THE CONTROVERSY ABOUT THEIR LIKELY ECONOMIC EFFECTS

by Luis A. Riveros

9.1 Introduction

The minimum wage (MW) has traditionally been an important policy instrument in Latin America. Periodic revision of its level and the maintenance of suitable enforcement machinery have been widely deemed to be crucial in the attempt to attain a better income distribution. But many others consider MWs a highly distorting labor market policy, with few if any positive effects. In the context of notable social and political tensions and the presence of significant stabilization-cum-adjustment programs, and with countries hoping to consolidate their trade openings through commercial trade agreements, the role of MWs occupies a prominent role in the economic debate.

The conceptual framework underlying the use of MW policies in Latin America has changed notably over time. Begun in the pre-World War II period, MWs were used in the 1950s and 1960s to intervene in private wage setting by providing a floor for the wage structure. This occurred mostly in the context of protected economies, characterized by substantial economic distortions. In the 1970s, in the middle of a growing crisis of the import substitution strategy, labor market intervention through MWs was extended to a generalized price intervention in factor and good markets, with MWs continuing to be considered a fundamental tool for improving the distribution of income. However, in the 1980s and 1990s, as a result of years of macroeconomic distortions and allocative problems, Latin America entered into a wave of privatization, liberalization and encouragement of trade, in which government wage and price intervention have no longer been considered suitable policies, and MWs have thus lost their traditional importance.

This chapter analyzes historical trends of MWs in Latin America, and reviews the controversies about their use and enforcement mechanisms. It concludes that MWs are not an important current policy instrument, due to the requirements of greater flexibility associated with adjustment policies in the context of open economies. The chapter warns about the effects of MWs in the context of an expanding economy, where labor market constraints may harm the flexibility needed to provide an adequate supply response to shifts in relative prices. This latter point is illustrated with a model of labor market segmentation, in which the MW has a double role: it may prompt real wage growth, since it constitutes the floor of the wage structure, but it may also increase quasi-voluntary unemployment, worsening the income distribution.

9.2 The Minimum Wage Issue in Latin America

Historical Trends and Purposes of MWs

The use of MWs began in the 1930s in most Latin American countries. Both in Mexico and Peru, the principle had been formulated still earlier,[1] but specific legal norms were enacted only in 1931 and 1933, respectively. Similarly, although the principle had been already stated in the Chilean Labor Code of 1924, a MW system was set up for nitrate workers only in 1934; from then on, the system was made nationally binding to cover all workers, starting with white collar workers in 1937, agricultural workers in 1953, and industrial labor in 1956. In Brazil, the legal framework was established in 1938, the first MW level being scheduled in 1940. Both in Costa Rica and Uruguay a MW system was enacted in 1943, while in Colombia the urban MW was established only in the mid 1950s. Finally, in Argentina, MW origins are found in local initiatives in the 1930s, but they took the form of a national law only in 1946.

The origins of MW regulations are primarily found in the objective of confronting a stubborn poverty problem. The financial crisis of 1929 had drastically affected most Latin American economies, particularly those, such as Chile, Mexico and Peru, which were highly vulnerable to trade and international price fluctuations. The lack of adequate fiscal conditions to permit proactive and reactive programs to alleviate poverty, in combination with low labor productivity caused by both generalized low skill levels and little investment in physical capital, led to an increase in labor market intervention. In general, the objective of MWs was not only to provide a minimum living standard for the poorest, but also to improve income distribution through holding up the floor of the wage structure,

---

[1] In Mexico, the principle was introduced in the 1917 Constitution. In Peru, MW regulations date back to 1916, when a fixed minimum pay was created for unskilled labor in Lima.

and extracting rents from capital and the most skilled labor. The rather limited scope of formal labor markets in most of these countries made the enforcement of MWs applicable to only a smallish fraction of the labor force, making the benefit quite uncertain for most of the poor.

The tendency of MW laws in Latin America has been to formally include all workers regardless of gender, age, geographical context, skill or occupation. As pointed out below, the criteria for setting MWs have operated oblivious to the existence of labor market segmentation, and to the likely negative effects on the less skilled. Few exceptions have typically been allowed with regard to coverage, as for instance in the case of workers under 16 years of age in Colombia, domestic workers in Argentina, and apprentices in Colombia, Chile, Mexico and Peru. Although laws stress "need" as the criterion for setting MW levels,[2] it has been rare to impose uniform rates based on empirical studies of "needs," so that, by and large the criteria have been dominated by political assessment and expediency.

The MW-setting machinery shows remarkable variation across countries, and in some cases has become very complex, with labor/management participation as well as central decision-making authorities.[3] Different groups of workers are distinguished for purposes of wage setting, contributing to a complex negotiating system. Mexico was a classic case in this respect, with 111 geographic regions and 86 job categories distinguished in the setting of MWs,[4] though the actual setting of the levels was done at the central level as a deliberate policy act.

Automatic indexation of MWs to inflation has been included in the law in the cases of Colombia, Costa Rica and El Salvador, although the adjustment criteria have not allowed for a complete indexing mechanism. As a matter of fact, in most Latin American countries, particularly those characterized by relatively high inflation, real MWs have been eroded as a result of an imperfect indexation system, combined with adjustment policies aimed at lowering fiscal expenditures and labor costs. Only Chile has an indexing criterion under which MWs are adjusted to expected instead of past inflation rates, while changes in labor

---

[2] In Argentina, the law states that MW is "the remuneration for work that will ensure an employee or worker and his family adequate food, healthy living quarters, clothing, education of his children, medical care, transport, pension, holidays and recreation." Similarly, the notion of "normal needs" is stressed in the Brazilian law, while in Mexico and Chile "adequate living standards" and "daily minimum consumption standards" are explicitly mentioned. Finally, in Colombia, the MW is designed to cover a worker's "normal requirements and those of his family both in the material and in the moral and cultural spheres."

[3] In the case of Brazil, for instance, committees formed by workers and employers approve certain MW schedules that must be further confirmed by a presidential decree. In Mexico MW boards function at parish levels with representation of workers, employers and the government, their recommendations going to a national committee. In Chile and Peru the system is centralized with indirect participation of workers, while in Argentina the 1991 employment law created a National Council with direct participation of workers. In Uruguay, in contrast, sectoral wage councils were until recently responsible for MW setting.

[4] This system experienced certain changes with the economic reforms of the 1980s.

productivity are also taken into account. This latter element, however, has not been successfully applied in practice, given the existence of empirical problems in the measurement of the relevant labor productivity.

As argued by Webb (1977), after about 50 years the issue for MWs has become less their existence than their level. While the basic purpose of the MW was to improve unsatisfactory living standards of the working population, this goal has often been broken up into more specific objectives, such as growth promotion by means of increased effective demand in periods of low inflation (Solimano, 1983), or (when MWs have been raised relatively little) as a brake on wages and inflation in support of stabilization and adjustment policies. Critics claim that MWs discriminate in favor of modern sector labor and against the unemployed, the informal sector and the fairly large group of self-employed workers.[5] Also, a discrimination of MWs against the less skilled (generally, women and the youth) has been empirically found (Paredes and Riveros, 1989), further evidence of their questionable distributional effects. Besides the claimed failure of MWs to exert a positive distributional impact, it is also argued that they contribute to generate inflation and may lead to significant losses of international competitiveness.

Previous Studies

In spite of the long history on MWs as an institution, an extensive theoretical discussion,[6] and many political claims as regards their likely effects, empirical analyses of those effects are anything but abundant in Latin America. Three specific areas are particularly noticeable for the lack of adequate empirical research:

(i) the effect of MWs on employment, a very central issue, but complicated by the uncertainty about actual enforcement (and even enforceability) of MWs, as well as by the absence of suitable employment data and the existence of analytical difficulties such as simultaneity and the stationary aspect of the series involved;[7] (ii) the macroeconomic effects of MWs, particularly with regard to their inflationary consequences, as well as their impact on the wage setting at firm-level. (iii) cross-country studies of the impact of the MW on the economy.[8]

---

[5] With regard to this distributional issue, Webb (1977) suggests that a large proportion of wage earners were receiving less than the MW in Mexico. Suárez (1987) for Peru and Castañeda (1983) for Chile arrive at similar conclusions; but it appears that there are few if any reliable figures on enforcement.

[6] For a review of main theoretical issues involved in MW regulations, see Rottemberg (1981).

[7] In the case of Canada, however, Benjamin (Chapter 8) has found that the disemployment effects of MWs are important, and even higher than in the case of the U.S.

[8] Exceptions to this are Paldam and Riveros (1987) and a study of the World Bank (1995).

Analyzing Argentina, Marshall (1980) reported that MWs have increased agriculture's relative wages as well as absolute wages in a number of industries and across the board. More recently, however, Sánchez (1987) showed that the effective level of MWs has been well below the legal minimum because of the inadequacy of the enforcement machinery, a fact also highlighted by Riveros and Sánchez (1994) in the context of the structural adjustment issue. Since MWs have been used in Argentina to index severance payments[9] and public sector pensions, one of their important effects in that country may be through the impact on the cost to firms, or in the case of public employees the fiscal cost, of sacking workers.

In the case of Brazil, considerable analytical effort has been expended but no firm conclusions reached as to MWs employment effects. In this country, the MW controversy has centered around the possible distributional impact. Macedo (1977 and 1986) has argued that wages for unskilled workers in the urban sector are determined by demand and supply and that, consequently, MWs cannot play an important role. In support of this view, Taylor *et al.* (1980) found that MWs are widely evaded even in the formal sector, helping to explain an elasticity of MWs to average wages of only 0.5. Similarly, Fox *et al* (1994), indicate that although the MW dropped by 10% in 1980-85, real wages in the industrial sector increased, and the formal-informal wage gap remained fairly constant, thereby suggesting the limited relevance of MWs in practice.[10] On the other hand, Souza and Baltar (1979) argued that, even when MWs do not influence wages of unskilled workers outside the formal sector, they do exert an important impact within this sector. Likewise, Drobny and Wells (1983) suggest that MWs play an important signaling role in the wage setting for unskilled workers in the construction industry and that MWs exert an important impact on the size distribution of earned income.

There has been more agreement with regard to the effects of MWs on the Chilean labor market. Gregory (1979) stated that, although little could be said in connection with their distributional impact on the basis of available data, MWs do indeed produce a slower employment growth. Along these same lines, Corbo (1981) concluded that manufacturing employment losses derived from MWs were not negligible, even when his analysis assumed no substitution between high-wage and low-wage labor. Similarly, Riveros (1984) has shown that the negative impact of MWs in employment generation in manufacturing was important in a short-run context, while Castañeda (1984), using Lineman's (1982) methodology and based on labor force surveys, showed that the potential coverage of MWs was as high as

---

[9] Whenever a worker is discharged, severance payments are determined on the basis of the number of years worked with the employer and the highest wage ever earned. The law set an upper limit to the annual payment, which is made equivalent to three times the prevailing MW at the moment of the discharge.

[10] Benjamin (Chapter 8) also finds that in Canada MWs have only limited scope for improving the welfare of the lowest income households, since most of them have no full time wage earners.

20% of the labor force. These latter results have been further explored by Paredes and Riveros (1989) using a statistical analysis based upon Heckman's selectivity bias technique, showing that the potential coverage of the MW in Chile—considering unemployed and discouraged labor— could be in the range of 40%.

Aggregate effects of MWs have concentrated the attention of Colombian researchers. In analyzing alternative policies to affect the income distribution, Bourguignon (1988) did not consider the role of MWs important enough to include. However, López (1987) found a rather strong impact of MWs upon the rate of open unemployment, as well as on aggregate investment. In Mexico the evidence is even more mixed; Isbister (1971) concluded that MWs have not been important in terms of employment effects and the observed increase in manufacturing wages, but Márquez (1982) and Casar and Márquez (1983), in analyzing this subject more extensively, concluded that the actual impact of MWs in the labor market can be considered substantial. Bell (1995) confirms these results in her study for Colombia and Mexico; she found that in Colombia the MW is closer to the average wage in the formal sector, thereby having a significant impact on employment, whereas in Mexico, low levels of compliance and ineffective levels of MWs imply negligible employment effects.

In the Peruvian case, Suárez (1987) has shown that MWs have played a small role in shifting the wage structure of the economy upwards. This result would essentially respond to the path of economic growth. The small effect of MWs on average wages is, in turn, associated with the relatively small importance of the formal labor market. In several countries a large positive effect of MW regulations has been found on unemployment and non-participation, rather than on wages directly. This has been the case, for instance, in Puerto Rico (Santiago, 1989), Costa Rica (Vargas, 1994) and Bolivia (UDAPSO, 1993). In most of them, however, the lack of coverage in the informal sector has been pointed out.

The effects of MWs on the aggregate labor market and the macroeconomy have been formally studied only in a few countries. In connection with the first issue, research has dealt with the role of MW in the context of segmentation; results for the cases of Colombia, Chile, Argentina and Uruguay indicate that the existence of an uncovered sector makes the effectiveness of the minimum wage very controversial in terms of protecting the poor (López and Riveros, 1989). With regard to the second issue, the main question involves the inflationary effects of MWs. In the case of Chile, García (1992) reports a relatively low inflation-MW elasticity of 0.17, with a nominal wage-MW elasticity of 0.28. Paldam and Riveros (1989) indicated that the reverse effect of inflation *on* MW was also important in the case of Chile, as well as in Brazil, Colombia and Uruguay. In general they found a strong causality from MW to average wages and inflation in their six countries, the only exception with regard to the latter effect being Argentina.

9.3 The Actual Use of MWs as a Policy Instrument in Latin America

There has, then, been broad concern about the use and effects of MWs in Latin America. As indicated in the literature review, emphasis has been placed on analysis of the likely distributive impact of MWs in terms of covered/uncovered labor, as well as their likely important effect on raising open unemployment, particularly in the case of the unskilled labor. At the same time, and in contrast to the practice which evolved during the 1960s and 1970s, most analysts agree that the use of MWs became more and more conservative in the 1980s.

Three developments have augured against a more active use of MW policies during the 1980s and 1990s in Latin America. First is the substantial effort toward macroeconomic adjustment that most Latin American countries have made during these decades. Second, the presence of a significant and (during the 1980s) growing unemployment problem, together with a broader recognition of the existence of a segmented labor market and the complications it creates. Third, the development of a new approach to social policy in the aftermath of the debt crisis demanded a change with regard to traditional labor market intervention.

Macroeconomic Adjustment and Labor Market Deregulation

The 1980s and 1990s have been years of stabilization and structural adjustment in Latin America. As a result of the protracted oil crises of the 1970s, and the financial crash of the beginning of the 1980s, most Latin American countries were under severe pressure to tighten fiscal policies in order to contain inflation. Similarly, there was a need to use commercial policy to reach higher productive efficiency, through opening the economy to international trade and financial flows. To a large extent, structural adjustment policies were designed to improve the supply response to external shocks, through more flexible markets in which prices could play an effective role in order to reflect the relative resource scarcity. As a result, a widespread consensus prevailed in most countries regarding the need to deregulate goods and factor markets, and to avoid active price intervention by the state. Hence, traditional labor market intervention affecting levels of employment and wages was considered contradictory to the aim of achieving a more efficient and effective supply response to price changes. It was argued that interventionist policies usually led to serious rigidity of wages and of labor allocation, thereby implying a slower productive response to price shifts. As a consequence, recent policy making has been characterized by a lower emphasis on government-guided wage adjustments, as well as on actively using MWs to achieve social objectives.

Inflation was the most serious macroeconomic problem in Latin America

Table 9.1
Indicators of the Opening of Selected Latin American Economies, 1980-1993

1. Current Account Deficit as a Percent of GDP

Year	Argentina	Brazil	Colombia	Mexico	Chile	Peru	Costa Rica
1980	6.30	5.10	0.50	5.00	8.40	0.42	15.20
1985	0.90	0.13	4.70	0.33	7.74	0.02	8.50
1990	1.50	0.14	1.40	4.10	2.80	4.90	10.40
1993	3.30	1.40	2.10	8.45	2.90	10.10	7.30

2. Exports Plus Imports as a Percent of GDP

Year	Argentina	Brazil	Colombia	Mexico	Chile	Peru	Costa Rica
1980	15.9	19.2	31.8	26.1	49.8	44.6	63.3
1985	25.9	19.3	25.8	25.7	55.4	37.4	64.5
1990	30.9	12.7	35.4	32.7	70.2	21.5	76.6
1993	14.5	17.4	38.5	29.1	55.5	24.5	84.3

Source: ECLAC.

during the 1980s.[11] Argentina, Brazil, Mexico and Peru have at various times suffered from significant hyperinflation problems, demanding highly restrictive fiscal and monetary policies. Others, such as Chile, Colombia and Costa Rica, although experiencing relatively less inflation, also had rates substantially above international levels. All these countries suffered from the financial crisis of the beginning of the decade, which bared an extremely weak and inefficient productive structure. Since then, several Latin American economies have experienced a dramatic increases in trade flows, though the picture has varied widely from country to country (Table 9.1).

As indicated by the figures in Table 9.2, the adjustment experience of Latin American countries in response to the debt crisis has taken a significant toll, with average wages and MWs typically experiencing a dramatic real drop at some point during the first part of the 1980s, to recover thereafter, while open unemployment (Table 9.3) has often reached serious levels during the adjustment period. The consequence of global macroeconomic targets, together with the perception that flexible markets are indispensable to attain better results, is that the sort of *de facto* government intervention via active wage policies in the labor market practiced by most countries during many years, has significantly declined.[12] This

[11] For the purposes of this analysis, a sample of Latin American countries is considered, which includes the larger countries in both a geographical and economic sense.

[12] In most countries—including Chile, Argentina, Mexico and Bolivia—traditional labor laws have been modified to make labor mobility less expensive (through lower dismissal costs and severance payments), wages more flexible (by reducing the government's direct and indirect intervention on wages), and the private negotiation of wages and working conditions more feasible. These legal changes have also included less restrictive regulations regarding unions, as well as the political and economic costs of strikes.

Table 9.2
Real Wage Trends¹ in Selected Latin American Countries, 1980-1994
(Index 1980 = 100)

	Argentina		Brazil		Colombia		Costa Rica		Chile		Mexico		Peru	
Year	W	MW	W	MW	W	MW	W	MW	W	MW	W	MW	W	MW
1980	100.0	100.0	100.0	100.0	100.0	100.0	100.0	100.0	100.0	100.0	100.0	100.0	100.0	100.0
1981	89.4	97.8	104.1	102.2	101.4	97.9	88.3	90.4	108.9	99.2	103.5	100.7	98.3	83.8
1982	80.1	103.6	107.2	103.2	104.8	102.7	70.8	85.9	108.6	97.2	104.4	88.7	100.5	77.6
1983	100.5	152.9	94.0	91.9	110.3	107.4	78.8	99.3	97.1	78.3	80.7	73.5	83.7	79.3
1984	127.1	167.5	96.7	85.3	118.5	112.7	84.7	104.4	97.2	66.9	75.4	68.2	70.1	61.7
1985	107.8	113.1	118.9	90.0	114.9	108.0	92.2	112.2	93.5	63.4	76.6	67.0	59.6	54.2
1986	107.5	110.0	137.3	91.0	120.2	113.9	97.8	119.0	95.1	61.3	72.8	60.6	101.9	55.8
1987	96.9	120.8	127.7	73.5	119.2	113.0	88.5	117.9	94.8	57.6	72.0	56.3	108.9	60.1
1988	93.7	93.5	138.3	76.1	117.7	108.5	84.5	114.6	101.1	61.7	71.3	49.3	82.1	45.5
1989	75.8	42.1	149.1	78.4	119.5	109.5	85.1	119.4	103.0	68.6	77.8	46.3	44.8	24.2
1990	79.4	40.2	130.8	55.4	116.0	105.7	86.5	120.5	104.8	73.3	79.4	42.0	39.1	21.4
1991	80.5	52.9	125.4	64.9	115.3	102.0	82.5	111.8	110.1	79.9	84.7	40.2	42.1	14.9
1992	81.6	45.3	138.1	56.6	117.3	102.4	85.9	111.5	115.1	83.4	92.9	38.3	41.6	17.0
1993	80.3	70.0	151.9	64.0	122.8	103.2	94.7	112.8	118.6	87.5	100.2	37.9	41.3	n/a
1994	85.7	81.1	162.7	n/a	122.2	101.5	93.0	112.8	124.6	90.8	99.4	37.8	47.4	n/a

Note: ¹ W: average wage; MW: minimum wage. In most of the countries the wage in question is that of manufacturing but in Peru and Costa Rica the coverage is more extensive.

Source: ECLAC.

led, among other things, to a drastic real decline in MWs in most countries.[13]

Unemployment and Labor Market Segmentation

The adjustment experience of the 1980s and 1990s led, in most countries, to a significant open unemployment problem (see Table 9.3). Policies aimed at providing public sector employment were no longer relied on as in the past in order to maintain labor market equilibrium. The observed open unemployment has been largely structural, derived from the reduction of the size of the public sector, which typically concealed massive unemployment associated with both the process of rural-urban migration and the existence of an ill-designed formal schooling system. However, there was also an important transitional or frictional component in observed unemployment, as relative price changes caused shifts in the structure of production across industries which in turn led to significant skill mismatches and frictional unemployment; expanding industries took a while to get moving while contraction of the losing industries tended to take place immediately following price changes. Whatever the combination of factors at work, unemployment rates

---

[13] Colombia is the only country where real MWs have remained relatively stable around the 1980 level; it is also the only country that did not experience a substantial macro problem in the 1980s, thanks to its better conditions with regard to internal balances and the external debt.

Table 9.3
The Unemployment Rate in Selected Latin American Countries, 1980-1996
(Percent of the Labor Force)

	Argentina	Brazil	Colombia	Mexico	Chile	Peru	Costa Rica
1980	2.3	6.3	9.7	4.5	11.8	7.1	6.0
1981	9.5	7.9	8.2	4.2	9.0	6.8	9.1
1982	4.7	6.3	9.3	4.1	20.0	6.6	9.9
1983	4.2	6.7	11.8	6.7	18.9	9.0	8.5
1984	3.8	7.1	13.5	6.0	18.5	8.9	6.6
1985	5.3	5.3	14.1	4.8	17.2	10.1	6.7
1986	5.0	3.6	13.8	4.3	13.1	5.3	6.7
1987	5.9	3.8	11.8	3.9	11.9	4.8	5.9
1988	6.3	3.8	11.3	3.5	10.2	7.1	6.3
1989	7.6	3.3	10.0	2.9	7.2	7.9	3.7
1990	7.5	4.3	10.5	2.7	6.5	8.3	5.4
1991	6.5	4.8	10.2	2.7	7.3	5.9	6.0
1992	7.0	5.8	10.2	2.8	4.9	9.4	4.3
1993	9.6	5.4	8.6	3.4	4.0	9.9	4.0
1994	11.2	5.1	8.9	3.7	6.2	8.8	4.3
1995	17.5	4.6	8.8	6.2	5.3[1]	9.3	5.7
1996	17.2	5.4	11.2	5.5	5.0[1]	8.8	6.6

Notes: [1] The figures for 1995 and 1996 for Chile come from a revised series which, like the original, refers to the metropolitan region of Santiago. The recent series provides figures on unemployment rates which are usually about two percentage points higher than those of the original series. The figures presented here are thus estimated as the new series minus 2.1 and 2.0 percentage points respectively for the two years.

Source: ECLAC, based on official figures.

rose significantly, helping to shift the policy concern from wage fixing—where it had traditionally been—to employment creation and production growth.

Unemployment was an important companion of the adjustment experience in such early adjusters as Chile and Bolivia, in the former of which open unemployment reached more than 25% of the labor force in the 1970s and 1980s. This has also been, more recently, the case of Argentina and Mexico where open unemployment was traditionally in the range 3% to 5% of the labor force but reached as high as 20% (Argentina) and 7.0% (Mexico) during 1995. The average urban unemployment in Latin America has reached levels (e.g., 7.7 in 1996) which are well above typical figures of the 1960s and 1970s.

In most countries, the existence of a serious unemployment problem has shifted policy concern away from measures aimed at protecting real wages toward addressing the employment problem, among them the attaining of higher levels of private investment and output.[14] In contrast, less attention than traditionally has been directed to the setting of a MW level compatible with social objectives; it was evident that, in the presence of many jobless people, wage policy could not be

[14] In countries such as Costa Rica or Mexico, a substantial underemployment (measured as those working less hours than a given norm, and willing to work additional time) must be added to the existing open unemployment. The rate of labor underutilization is at least twice or three times the observed unemployment rate.

considered an effective way to protect the poor. In fact, there has been increasing acceptance of the idea that a higher MW could significantly reduce employment prospects, particularly for youth and women, especially in the context of an open economy. Thus, due to its practical irrelevance as an income floor for poor people and the likelihood of harming more people than those actually benefitting from the policy, MWs are no longer used in an aggressive fashion in most countries. Evidence of the more conservative approach used in designing wage policies, is the significant drop seen in MWs relative to the per capita income in Latin America.

In addition to the open unemployment problem, there has been increasing recognition of the important informal segment of the labor market and its implications. The Latin American adjustment experience indicates that informal sector jobs are a common response to observed labor market pressures and imbalances, and help to avoid very high levels of open unemployment (PREALC). Policy makers have increasingly recognized that the informal sector is not only a transitory phenomenon, exclusively associated to times of macro adjustment, but rather a structural feature of developing economies which, in the typical Latin American economy constitutes up to 40-50% of urban employment. As a consequence, there has been growing agreement that traditional labor market policies do not really assist informal sector labor. The view that rising formal sector labor costs may lead to labor spillovers into the informal sector, thereby worsening the relative income situation of informal workers, has also gained substantial support.

The New Social Policy Approach

Traditionally, in the context of a closed economy with large state intervention, labor market policies have been considered paramount in the attainment of desired social outcomes. With state intervention deemed capable of keeping open unemployment at acceptable levels, wage intervention was considered the key instrument to raise the labor share and the per capita income of workers. Public policy influenced private wages both directly—i.e., through the nominal fixing of the MW and the introduction of binding guidelines regarding periodical wage adjustments (Riveros, 1994)—and indirectly—i.e., by means of public sector employment and wage policies (Stevenson, 1994). In turn, the MW policy was designed to fulfil a very important role in protecting the unskilled from poverty, and in keeping the very bottom of the wage structure under direct control of the authorities.

Several questions acquired new prominence during most adjustment episodes. One issue concerned the fact that the MW could not be manipulated in such a way as to provide comparable protection to families of differing demographic composition, since the specific monetary level mandated by the authority did not consider either family size or income. Further, since the poverty problem was concentrated among informal sector labor and among such partially overlapping groups as households headed by women and young workers, and these groups were typically mentioned as "victims" of MW policies, there was a growing consensus on the need to use the MW conservatively in order not to aggravate the incidence of poverty among these groups. Meanwhile, as the state increasingly ceded direct control of activities in which it could be efficiently substituted by the private sector, the social policy area stood out as an arena in which public policies would continue to fulfil a very important role. The idea that social problems should be addressed through specific and targeted social policies was the flip side of the view that social problems were not necessarily or systematically responsive to labor market policies.

9.4 Are MWs a Binding Constraint on the Competitiveness of Latin American Countries?

Real labor costs, expressed in dollars, have experienced wide swings in Latin American countries over the period 1975-1995.[15] In all these countries except Colombia real labor costs declined rather substantially in the mid-1980s, and recovered thereafter, reaching by the mid 1990s a level higher than that of 1975 (the only exception to this pattern being Peru). There are two explanations for these observed fluctuations in the dollar cost of labor: first, there was a significant depreciation of the real exchange rate in the mid-1980s in almost all Latin American countries followed by an appreciation at the beginning of the 1990s; second, institutional reforms have led to a relative drop in non-wage labor costs.[16] These observed changes in labor dollar costs are consistent with observed changes in real wages in the same countries (see Table 9.2).

No similar fluctuations in labor cost levels are observed in the case of the U.S. and Canada, or in the Asian NIEs. In Canada the constant real labor cost over the decade 1975-1985 was followed by an important increase during the 1985-1995 period, significantly increasing the gap vis-à-vis Latin America. European countries exhibited a real drop in labor costs during the early 1980s, but this was much more than offset by the dramatic increase of the late 1980s. Until about 1990, it was not only the fluctuating real level that distinguished Latin America from North America and Asia but also the smaller increase (in some cases decrease) in real labor costs, likely associated with a more unstable economic

[15] Labor costs correspond to the sum of wages and non-wage costs of labor. The latter are represented by employer outlays such as social security contributions, insurance, contributions to provident funds, paid vacations, and various bonuses.

[16] This is, for instance, the case of the Chilean privatization of social security funds, and reforms in Peru, Mexico and Argentina regarding non-wage benefits and payroll taxes.

climate, changing productive patterns and higher structural unemployment. As a result, the differences in total labor cost between the North and Latin America increased;[17] this would lead one to expect that, especially with new commercial trade agreements, Latin America would receive significant investment flows from industrial countries, as indeed it has in the 1990s. Over 1990-95, however, and in part due to that inflow of capital, there was a marked shrinking of the differential of Latin American labor costs with respect to both the industrial countries and the Asian NIEs, a possible warning sign of likely loss of international competitiveness of the former group of countries.

    The behavior of the MW was similar to that of labor costs in Latin America during the 1980s; real MWs fell4 sharply (Table 9.4). However, in contrast to the observed trend in labor costs, the recovery has either not been very noticeable or entirely absent, as in Mexico and Peru. In no country has the MW (in US$) reached the previous 1980 value, whereas in a number of countries average labor costs have done so (Table 9.5). The lack of a close correlation between MW increases and labor cost levels does not necessarily refute Paldam and Riveros's (1989) finding of a strong causality from MWs to average wages. It is probable that the structural change which has occurred in most labor markets, in combination with the actual low level of the MW seen in the 1980s, is responsible for the low observed correlation between Mws and labor cost trends. It is clear that the level

Table 9.4
Real Minimum Wages, Selected Latin American Countries, 1980-1993
(1992 U.S. Dollars Per Month)

Year	Argent.	Brazil	Colom.	Mexico	Chile	Peru	C. Rica	Ecuad.	Parag.	Urug.	Venez.
1980	231.8	113.1	133.9	259.1	175.6	106.8	170.0	225.2	245.0	170.2	295.3
1981	179.2	116.7	134.7	281.3	190.8	68.7	84.1	206.1	265.8	176.3	270.3
1982	104.7	110.1	141.4	164.0	149.6	86.1	76.7	167.2	234.1	158.7	256.6
1983	138.7	71.0	139.1	101.1	95.1	77.3	109.2	137.0	214.1	78.6	186.1
1984	165.8	58.6	127.3	120.6	75.3	56.9	115.3	120.0	175.3	73.3	138.6
1985	97.2	57.9	106.2	109.5	56.1	40.7	123.1	131.1	162.1	71.9	215.5
1986	114.6	64.9	99.5	92.1	55.8	58.2	135.2	101.4	193.3	82.5	226.9
1987	121.9	58.2	96.0	89.2	54.5	80.6	138.7	88.3	168.5	91.1	188.9
1988	90.6	65.3	94.5	99.6	58.2	56.0	131.1	66.3	186.1	84.5	198.7
1989	33.8	85.8	89.7	101.2	66.5	49.6	139.5	52.1	146.0	79.9	121.5
1990	57.3	72.0	83.2	96.1	75.7	55.6	146.2	42.5	169.0	74.4	86.9
1991	103.7	69.9	82.3	101.9	86.1	69.3	132.6	40.6	186.1	71.4	94.5
1992	99.7	148.7	88.6	108.8	99.7	61.9	152.8	45.5	170.1	82.8	106.9
1993	119.3	165.5	99.4	108.8	107.5	61.9	153.1	42.7	170.1	82.8	106.9

Source: ECLAC.

[17] This labor cost differential is, of course, partly explained by differences in labor productivity, as well as by exchange rate distortions. In the case of Chile-USA, for instance, it has been shown that the ratio of approximately 2 to 15 is reduced to 2 to 4 after correcting by purchasing power parity exchange rates, and discounting for the difference associated with the productivity of labor in manufacturing.

Table 9.5
Real Labor Cost, Selected Latin American Countries, Selected Years, 1975-1995[1]
(1990 U.S. Dollars Per Hour)

	1975	1980	1985	1990	1995
Argentina	2.98	2.96	2.25	2.00	4.00
Brazil	1.69	1.92	1.33	1.48	3.30
Colombia	0.87	1.56	1.51	2.04	4.40
Chile	0.85	2.00	0.87	1.28	2.46
Mexico	3.60	3.51	1.90	2.06	2.75
Peru	1.93	1.11	0.40	0.31	1.49
OECD	9.60	11.48	9.29	15.53	16.00
Europe	10.16	10.97	8.75	17.39	17.91
USA	12.64	13.63	14.23	14.91	15.36
Canada	11.85	11.98	11.97	15.83	16.30
Asian NIEs	1.03	1.62	1.80	3.73	3.84

Note: [1] The deflator used is the average Wholesale Price Index for industrial countries (IMF, *International Financial Statistics Yearbook*, 1994).

Sources: For industrial countries, NIEs's and Mexico, U.S. Department of Labor (1994). For other Latin American countries, Riveros (1989), and author estimates.

of open unemployment in Latin America has been not driven by the MW as much as it has been by the level of economic activity. For instance, in Argentina the increase in open unemployment rates has been accompanied by diminishing real MW levels. This is also observed in Chile and Mexico. In fact, statistical analysis in the case of all the six countries included in this study (Argentina, Brazil, Colombia, Chile, Mexico and Peru) indicates that unemployment bears a very low and positive correlation with the MW in the period 1980-1994, whereas during the same period it exhibits a significant negative relationship with per capita GDP, which can be taken as a measure of the level of economic activity.

Analyzing the information on MWs, average wages, labor costs and unemployment for the mentioned set of countries, three conclusions can be drawn: (1) as indicated by the low observed correlation, it does not appear that the MW has been causing any significant increase in observed labor costs; the MW level, expressed in terms of hourly earnings for a person working full time, is not more than 30% of observed average hourly labor costs (though it is true that the latter figure includes non-wage costs); (2) there does not seem to be a significant positive relationship between MWs and open unemployment, as one would expect from a simple neoclassical model; and (3) the strong correlation between changes in MWs and in the per capita GDP suggests that the use of this policy instrument has been guided by global economic circumstances. Nonetheless, the low relative importance of MWs in Latin America in the 1980s and 1990s notwithstanding, the tradition of more aggressive MW policies could return if fostered by changing economic circumstances.

9.5 Minimum Wages in a Model of Labor Market Segmentation

The Problem

The actual effects of MWs in an economy may be strongly linked to the prevailing labor market structure. In a simple, neoclassical model, the expected effects of minimum wage increases are some combination of higher open unemployment, higher average wages and greater inflation. Given that MW policies would tend to be binding for unskilled labor, the unemployment impact would be proportionately bigger in the case of women and youth.

Given the presence of labor market segmentation, the role of the MW is both more subtle and, probably, more important. Segmentation between a formal and an informal labor market is closely related to which activities are covered and which are uncovered by labor market regulations. Policies aimed at protecting the unskilled, the underemployed and the working poor cannot be expected to be effective, since these three categories are largely concentrated in the informal sector.

The Model

The model assumes a segmented labor market, with MWs being binding for the formal sector only.[18] The formal sector uses both skilled and unskilled labor, with MWs being binding for its unskilled segment. The informal sector is basically uncovered with regard to different labor market regulations, particularly the MW, and uses only unskilled labor.

The stock of skills is taken as given in the short-run. In the skilled sector of the formal market the labor supply is thus given, and the equilibrium wage is determined only on the basis of demand conditions. The formal sector is assumed to produce both tradeable and non-tradeable goods, but in general the labor demand from profit maximizing firms will be associated with changes in real wages, real output and the real cost of capital, the complementary factor. For unskilled labor in the formal market, though the labor demand is determined by similar factors, the MW determines the employment level. MWs may also indirectly affect the demand for skilled labor, either as a parameter which institutionally shifts the entire wage structure upwards (for instance, through wage bargaining based upon the objective of maintaining certain wage-skills differentials), or simply because there prevails substitution or complementarity

---

[18] This model includes the fundamental aspects included in that developed by López and Riveros (1989).

between skilled and unskilled labor.

The informal sector is a neoclassical market in which real wages are driven solely by prevailing demand-supply conditions. The total supply of unskilled labor is a positive function of the wage. Given that the employment level in the formal sector is determined by the MW, the effective labor supply to the informal market is equal to the total supply of unskilled labor minus the amount of formal sector employment corresponding to each MW level. In turn, the demand for labor in the informal sector is determined by the level of activity and the prevailing real wage in this sector, as well as by the real cost of capital to the establishments which operate there. In reduced form terms, the observed change in the equilibrium wage would depend upon changes in the MW, observed output prices, output levels and the cost of capital.

In this stylized labor market model, the MW may fulfil three related roles. First, it is the determinant of the level of unskilled labor employment in the formal sector. Second, it can be a determinant of the prevailing wage for the skilled labor in the formal sector, given its institutional role of determining the "bottom" of the wage scale and its effect upon the particular skilled-unskilled mix. Third, given that equilibrium wages in the informal sector will be below or equal to the MW (otherwise, the MW will not be binding and the segmentation problem would not exist from a wage perspective), there will be "quasi-voluntary" unemployment (Harberger, 1971). This will correspond to individuals with an opportunity cost above the equilibrium wage in the informal sector, but still below the prevailing MW.[19]

An Empirical Test

The simple model just described can be expressed in terms of the reduced form for the three sub-markets (formal skilled, formal unskilled and informal). Using the above assumptions, and in terms of nominal changes, the model would consist of three wage equations. In the case of the formal unskilled wage, the observed wage should correspond to the MW, a situation which can be empirically tested on the basis of a standard econometric model. The following will be the reduced form equations for observed changes in the nominal wage of skilled labor (W_s), unskilled (formal) labor (W_u) and unskilled informal sector labor (W_I):

$$W_s = W_s (P, Y_f, r, MW) \qquad (1)$$
$$W_u = W_u (P, Y_f, r, MW) \qquad (2)$$
$$W_I = W_I (P, q, r, u) \qquad (3)$$

[19] In practical terms, these can be considered unemployed given that they will be waiting for a job opening in the formal market. In other words, they could be considered unemployed from a classical viewpoint, i.e. as a result of relatively high (fixed) wages.

Where P is the wholesale price index, Y_f is the (real) output level of the formal sector; r is the relevant cost of capital, q is the real aggregate output (a determinant of the demand for labor in the informal sector), and u is the observed rate of open unemployment.

The model implies that, in the second equation, every other variable except the MW will be statistically insignificant. In the third equation, u should be statistically significant because it represents the effect of the MW upon the labor supply and the effective equilibrium wage in the informal sector. In this case, the effect of MW can also be directly tested by including it in the reduced form wage equation for the informal sector. The other important issue that can be addressed with this model concerns the effect of MW on the wage of skilled labor; it may be direct and significant (under the hypothesis that the MW can be considered a dynamic floor of the wage structure). Finally, the effect of inflation on the wage for skilled labor is also a primary aspect to be empirically assessed through the first equation.

The model has been empirically tested using Chilean data from the Greater Santiago area in the period 1980-95. Formal sector wages are measured through the prevailing wage for white collar (skilled) and blue collar (unskilled) workers in manufacturing. Informal sector wages are measured through the observed hourly incomes of self-employed workers with less than eight years of formal schooling. Formal sector production is measured through an index of industrial production, and aggregate activity through a GDP index. The cost of capital is proxied by the prevailing medium term real interest rate, and the unemployment rate corresponds to those declaring that they are actively seeking a job. The empirical results are shown in Table 9.6.

The econometric results indicate that changes in formal (skilled) wages are more closely correlated with the inflation rate than with the MW, until the real cost of capital is included in the regression. When it is, the inflation rate becomes insignificant, while activity level and the MW do become significant. The third equation estimated for this formal sector (with lagged MWs) indicates the prime role of this variable in determining formal sector wages, probably suggesting the effect of institutional factors. Changes in formal (unskilled) wages are fundamentally explained by changes in the minimum wage, the effect of other related variables being statistically zero. This is the result predicted by the model in the sense that MWs are indeed binding on the wage determination for unskilled labor employed in the formal sector. Changes in informal wages are determined by real output and capital cost, but not by inflation. The unemployment rate exerts a negative effect on equilibrium wages, which is also manifested in the negative impact associated with the MWs. These are, of course, expected results in the context of a neoclassical labor market.

Table 9.6
**Econometric Estimates of Percent Changes in Three Selected Wages
for the Period 1976-1994, Greater Santiago[1]**

1. Dependent Variable: Percent Change in the Formal (Skilled) Sector Wage

	a_0	$\dot{P}$	$\dot{y}$	$\dot{MW}$	$\dot{r}$	
OLS	-0.020	0.927	-0.061	0.389		$R^2 = 0.89$
	(-0.203)	(1.63)	(-0.05)	(0.99)		DW = 2.55
OLS	-0.138	-0.233	1.169	0.456	0.096	$R^2 = 0.97$
	(-1.75)	(-0.78)	(2.04)	(2.53)	(2.88)	DW = 2.61
				(MW-1)		
OLS	0.022	-0.039	0.509	0.313	0.004	$R^2 = 0.89$
	(0.15)	(-0.13)	(0.72)	(2.37)	(090)	DW = 2.09

2.Dependent Variable: Percent Change in the Formal (Unskilled) Sector Wage

	a_0	$\dot{P}$	$\dot{y}$	$\dot{MW}$	$\dot{r}$	
OLS	0.065	0.275	-0.012	0.657		R2 = 0.95
	(1.17)	(0.93)	(-0.018	(3.17)		DW = 2.54
OLS	-0.125	-0.104	0.985	0.435	0.009	R2 = 0.97
	(-1.35)	(-0.34)	(1.39)	(2.15)	(2.41)	DW = 2.55
2SLS	0.089	-0.019	-0.090	0.856		R2 = 0.95
	(0.14)	(-0.03)	(-0.13)	(-0.78)		DW = 2.81
2SLS	-0.109	0.104	0.877	0.366	0.007	R2 = 0.97
	(-1.06)	(0.16)	(1.13)	(1.69)	(1.44)	DW = 2.34

3. Dependent Variable: Percent Change in the Informal Sector Wage

	a_0	$\dot{P}$	u	$\dot{q}$	$\dot{MW}$	
OLS	0.127	0.464	-0.014	0.715		$R^2 = 0.95$
	(1.19)	(0.93)	(-1.74)	(1.63)		DW = 2.31
OLS	-0.003	-0.147		0.764	-0.373	$R^2 = 0.95$
	(-0.06)	(-0.30)		(1.74)	(-1.60)	DW = 2.16
2SLS	0.366	2.917	-0.030	1.438		$R^2 = 0.87$
	(0.73)	(0.92)	(-1.76)	(0.51)		DW = 2.24

Note: With the exception of the rate of unemployment (u), all variables expressed in percent changes.

Source: Author's estimates. For definition of variables, see the text.

REFERENCES

Bell, L. A. (1995). "The Impact of Minimum Wages in Mexico and Colombia." Policy Paper
    1514. Washington, D.C.: The World Bank, Policy Research Department, Poverty and
    Human Resources Division.

Bourguignon, F. (1988). *The Measurement of the Wage-Employment Relationship in Developed
    and Developing Countries*. Geneva: ILO.

Casar, M. A. and C. Márquez (1983). "La Política de Salarios Mínimos Legales: 1934-1982."
    Mimeo.

Castañeda, T. (1983). "Evolución del Empleo y Desempleo y el Impacto de Cambios Demográficos sobre la Tasa de Desempleo en Chile 1960-1983." Documento Serie de Investigación, No. 64. Santiago: Universidad de Chile.

Castañeda, T. (1984). "Salarios Mínimos y Empleo en el Gran Santiago: 1978-1981." *Cuadernos de Economía*, No. 61. Santiago: Universidad Católica de Chile.

Corbo, V. (1981). "The Impact of Minimum Wages on Industrial Employment." In *The Economics of Legal Minimum Wage*, S. Rottenberg, ed. Washington, D.C.: American Enterprise Institute.

Drobny, A. and J. Wells (1983). "Wages, Minimum Wages and Income Distribution in Brazil. Results from the Construction Industry." *Journal of Development Economics*, Vol. 13, No. 3, pp. 305-330.

Fox, M. L., E. Amadeo and J. C. Camargo (1994). "Brazil." In *Labor Markets in an Era of Adjustment*, S. Horton, R. Kanbur and D. Mazumdar, eds., Volume 2, Case Studies. Washington, D.C.: The World Bank.

García, N. E. (1992). "Formación de Salarios y Precios (Chile 1986-91)." *Investigaciones Sobre el Empleo*, No. 36. Santiago: PREALC.

Gregory, P. (1979). "Wage Policies in Chile." In *Country Economic Memorandum*, World Bank. Washington D.C.: The World Bank.

Harberger, A. (1971). "On Measuring the Opportunity Cost of Labor." *International Review*, No. 130.

Isbister, J. (1971). "Urban Employment and Wages in a Developing Economy: The Case of Mexico." *Economic Development and Cultural Change*, Vol. 18 (October).

Linneman, P. (1982). "The Econometric Impacts of Minimum Wage Laws: A New Look at an Old Question." *Journal of Political Economy*, Vol. 82.

López, R. (1987). "Unemployment and the Structure of Labor Market in Colombia." Mimeo

López, R. and L. Riveros (1989). "Macroeconomic Adjustment and the Labor Market in Four Latin American Countries." In *Towards Social Adjustment: Labor Market Concerns in Structural Adjustment*, G. Standing, ed. Geneva: ILO.

Macedo, R. (1977). "A Critical Review of the Relation Between the Post-1964 Wage Policy and the Worsening of Brazil's Size Income Distribution in the Sixties." *Explorations in Economic Research*, Vol. 4, No. 1.

Macedo, R. (1986). "The Brazilian Labor Market: An Overview." Washington D.C.: The World Bank, DRD Discussion Paper Series, DRD 151.

Marshall, A. (1980). "Labor Market and Wage Growth: The Case of Argentina." *Cambridge Journal of Economics*, Vol. 4, No. 1.

Márquez, C. (1982). "Nivel de Salario y Dispersión de la Estructura Salarial : 1965, 1970, 1975."

Economía Mexicana, Vol. 4. Mexico: CIDE.

Paldam, M. and L. Riveros (1987). "The Causal Role of Minimum Wage in Six Latin Labor Markets." Washington, D.C.: The World Bank, DRD Discussion Paper Series, DRD 270.

Paldam, M. and L. Riveros (1989). "Salarios Mínimos y Medios: Análisis de Causalidad. Los Casos de Argentina, Brasil y Chile." *Cuadernos de Economía*, No. 73. Santiago: Universidad Católica de Chile.

Paredes, R. and L. Riveros (1989). "Sesgo de Selección y el Efecto de los Salarios Mínimos." *Cuadernos de Economía* (December). Santiago: Universidad Católica de Chile.

Riveros, L. (1984). "Una Aproximación al Problema del Desempleo en Chile en la Década del 70." *Estudios de Economía*, No. 23. Santiago: Universidad de Chile.

Riveros, Luis (1989). *International Differences in Wage and Non Wage Labor Costs*. Washington, D.C.: The World Bank.

Riveros, L. (1994). "Chile." In *Labor Markets in an Era of Adjustment*, S. Horton, R. Kanbur and D. Mazumdar, eds., Volume 2, Case Studies. Washington, D.C.: The World Bank.

Riveros, L. and C. Sánchez (1994). "Argentina." In *Labor Markets in an Era of Adjustment*, S. Horton, R. Kanbur and D. Mazumdar, eds., Volume 2, Case Studies. Washington, D.C.: The World Bank.

Rottenberg, S. (1981). "The Economics of Legal Minimum Wages." Washington, D.C.: American Enterprise Institute for Policy Research.

Sánchez, C. (1987). "Characteristics and Operation of Labor Markets in Argentina." Washington D.C.: The World Bank, DRD Discussion Paper Series.

Santiago, E. (1989). *Minimum Wages in Puerto Rico*. San Juan: University of Puerto Rico.

Solimano, A. (1983). "Reducir Costos del Trabajo, Cuanto Empleo Genera." *Cuadernos de Economía*, No. 61. Santiago: Universidad de Chile.

Stevenson (1994). "Public Sector Employment and Wages under Adjustment Programas." Washington, D.C.: The World Bank, Working Draft.

Souza, P., and P. Baltar (1979). "Salario Minimo e Taxa Salarios no Brasil." *Pesquisa e Planeamiento Economico*, Vol. 9, No. 3.

Suárez, R. (1987). "Labor Markets in Peru: An Overview." Washington D.C.: The World Bank, DRD Discussion Paper Series.

Taylor, L., E. L. Bacha, E. A. Cardoso and F. J. Lysy (1980). *Models of Growth and Distribution for Brazil*. New York: Oxford University Press for the World Bank.

UDAPSO (1993). "Situación del Mercado del Trabajo en Bolivia." La Paz: Ministerio de Planificación, Publicación UDAPSO.

U.S. Department of Labor (1994). *International Comparisons of Hourly Compensation Costs for Production Workers in Manufacturing*. Washington, D.C.: Bureau of Labor Statistics.

Vargas, R. (1994). "Salarios Mínimos y Entorno Macroeconómico: La Evidencia Empírica en Costa Rica." *Estudios de Economía* (November). Santiago: Universidad de Chile.

Webb, R. (1977). "Wage Policy and Income Distribution in Developing Countries." In *Income Distribution and Growth in the Less Developed Countries*, Charles R. Frank and Richard C. Webb, (eds.). Washington D.C.: The Brookings Institution.

World Bank (1995). *World Development Review 1995: Workers in an Integrating World*. Washington, D.C.: The World Bank.

Chapter 10

TRAINING IN CANADA

by Morley Gunderson and W. Craig Riddell

10.1 Introduction

Training issues are at the forefront of concern for all major actors in the labor market in both developed and developing countries. For employers training is crucial to productivity and competitiveness. For employees it is a key ingredient of human capital formation to enhance wages and employability. For governments it is an important policy instrument to deal with adjustment consequences, productivity, growth,[1] unemployment, and other broader social issues including those pertaining to income maintenance as well as special equity assistance for particular groups. Training is of particular policy and practical relevance since it is subject to policy control with respect to various dimensions: how much training; what type of training; where it should occur; and who should pay for it. In Canada, the continued importance of training is highlighted by the fact that it has been examined in a wide range of reports and Task Forces.[2]

The purpose of this chapter is to outline the Canadian experience with labor market training, with particular emphasis on the lessons that can be learned from that experience. The importance of training as a policy issue is first discussed. This is followed by a description of the current picture in Canada with respect to

---

[1] The relationship between education and training on the one hand, and education and growth on the other hand, is discussed in Canadian Labour Market Productivity Centre (1989a and 1989b), with particular reference to Canada in the international context.

[2] These include the Macdonald Commission (1985), Gigantis (1987), the Ontario Premier's Council (1988, 1990), the Canadian Labour Market and Productivity Centre (1990), Employment and Immigration Canada (1989), Ontario Ministry of Skills Development (1988 and 1989), Grandpre (1989), Strand (1991), and the Economic Council of Canada (1991). Davies (1986) also reviews four reports of the early 1980s: the Dodge report; the Allman report; the Economic Council of Canada's report *In Short Supply*; and the Skill Development Leave Task Force report on *Earning a Living in Canada*.

training, as well as a discussion of the recent changes that are being emphasised. The role of employers, employees and governments is then analyzed, with particular emphasis on the appropriate role of governments. Evaluation results are briefly documented, emphasizing what we know and what we do not know in this area. The chapter concludes with a statement of the lessons that can be learned from the Canadian experience.

10.2 Importance of Training as a Policy Issue

As indicated, training issues are of concern for all major actors in the labor market—employers, employees and governments. This stems from the interaction of a variety of interrelated forces that are occurring in the labor market. In this section, these forces are outlined, as are their implications for training (see also Gunderson and Riddell, 1991; and Riddell, 1995).

Global Competition

For high-wage countries like Canada, there is general recognition that it is almost fruitless to try to compete on the basis of a low-wage, low labor-cost strategy. This is especially the case in competing with countries whose labor cost can easily be in the neighborhood of one-tenth or less than that of Canada, with the productivity differences being much less than the wage differences.

In such circumstances, the competitive advantage of high-wage countries will increasingly lie in a high-productivity, high value-added workforce that can produce quality products often for higher priced market niches. Quality and customer satisfaction are key, and in fact one market niche is to not just "sell" a product, but to sell a total package of services to the customer, with the product (often being produced in low-wage countries) being one component of that service. Organizations in high-wage countries are often becoming "virtual" organizations—essentially holding companies that co-ordinate the activities like financing, production, sales, distribution, and research and development, much of which is done "offshore."

For high-wage countries, comparative advantage is shifting from natural resources and heavy industry and more towards the strategic use of high-priced human resources. This has often meant more emphasis on managerial, professional, technical and administrative positions in the knowledge-based, business oriented services, as well as in research and development. It has also meant, however, a greater polarization into the low-end occupations that essentially service the consumption needs of the high-wage clientele. That portion of low-wage activity is produced domestically because it tends to be done in non-tradeable services that cannot be moved "offshore" to take advantage of low-wage labor in other countries.

These changes suggest that training needs are being redirected towards various different dimensions: high value-added activities often associated with the information-oriented sectors; quality and customer satisfaction; co-ordinating, managing and administrating rather than simply producing; and "people" skills as much as production skills. For the developing economies, this also means that the training needs are shifting towards the former middle-wage manufacturing and industrial jobs that are moving "offshore" from the higher-wage countries. It also means that their own training needs will shift "upscale" if they hope to move up the value-added chain away from low-wage assembling and manufacturing.

Adjustment Issues

Labor markets in developed economies are facing severe adjustment consequences emanating not only from global competition but also from interrelated forces like technological change, just-in-time delivery, trade liberalization, industrial restructuring (especially from manufacturing to services), privatization, deregulation and general downsizing. These have led to mass layoffs, plant closings and an increased demand for flexible and contingent workforces—a just-in-time workforce to meet the just-in-time delivery needs of employers.

These changes have profound implications for training. Training is necessary to facilitate the adjustment of labor from the declining to the expanding sectors. The problem is compounded by the fact that workers in the declining sectors often have industry-specific skills built up over a long period of time, and that are not transferable to the expanding sectors. They are often also older workers coming from high paying jobs, therefore finding it difficult to "start over" and accept low wages while retraining for new positions— positions that are also sought after by younger workers.

The fact that many of the demand shocks are industry specific also places a premium on each industry itself to develop its adjustment and training responses to deal with their own specific adjustment needs. While industry specific solutions are likely to be best crafted by those with the most knowledge of their particular industry, the challenge will be one of co-ordination between the expanding industries experiencing the upside adjustment consequences and the declining industries experiencing the downside adjustment consequences. Those in the declining industries may be most knowledgeable about the adjustment problems of their displaced workers, but they may not be knowledgeable about the training needs of other expanding sectors.

Training is necessary to deal with not only these "downside" adjustment consequences, but also the associated "upside" adjustment consequences since new and different jobs are also being created. Skill shortages and retraining needs obviously can arise in these new jobs, and a failure to meet these shortages can create severe bottlenecks that can result in a loss of customers and the associated jobs for other workers. In a just-in-time world with global competitors everywhere, customers will not wait for a slowly responding training system to fill skill shortages that are leading to production bottlenecks.

The importance of adjusting from declining to expanding sectors has also led to an emphasis on the part of policy makers towards adjustment assistance programs that facilitate the reallocation of labor from the declining to expanding sectors. This has led to a de-emphasis on passive income maintenance programs like unemployment insurance that can encourage workers to remain in declining high-unemployment sectors and regions, and towards more emphasis on active adjustment assistance programs like training, mobility and labor market information that encourage the reallocation towards emerging market opportunities (Gunderson and Riddell, Chapter 3).

Workplace and Human Resource Practices

The previously discussed pressures have affected not only the external labor market but also the internal labor market of firms, especially with respect to their workplace practices and human resource policies. These changes in turn have had important implications for training.

The number of job classifications have generally been reduced, with workers expected to do a wider range of tasks both horizontally at the same level of complexity (i.e., job enlargement) and vertically at different levels of complexity (i.e., job enrichment). This multi-tasking and job rotation has increased the demand for multi-skill training as well as for broad-based, generally usable training in generic skills. More emphasis is placed on "learning how to learn" as opposed to learning a particular task, given that the tasks change so frequently and a wide range of tasks are often involved. Furthermore, the greater number of tasks associated with job enrichment has led to reduced supervision; hence, greater emphasis is being placed on self-responsibility skills and decision making.

Employee involvement and empowerment have also increased, in part to enhance commitment as an important ingredient of quality control and customer service, and in part to tap into the knowledge of those closest to the process—employees "on the shop floor." This has taken a variety of forms: quality circles; team production; suggestion schemes; information sharing; and self-paced work with reduced supervision. This has led to a greater emphasis in training in "people skills" and interaction and communication as well as in self-responsibility and decision-making skills.

Greater use of contingent workers, subcontracting, temporary help agencies and part-time employment has also occurred. This has reduced the need for employers to train in some of these areas, since they now "buy the service" rather than produce it internally. However, it has enhanced the need to train their smaller core of internal employees to co-ordinate, monitor and interact with the contingent workforce.

Contingent compensation is also more prominent, with pay increasingly being linked to performance. This should enhance the private returns to training and it should provide an incentive for individuals to obtain more generic, generally usable training to diversify against the risk associated with more frequent job changing. To the extent that the greater wage flexibility leads to reduced layoffs in downturns, this can create an opportunity to expand the training time if the employees are otherwise underutilized.

Changing Nature of the Workforce

From the supply side of the labor market, the Canadian workforce itself is changing. Women have dramatically increased their participation in the labor market over the past several decades and the two-earner family is now the norm and not the exception. The baby-boom population (born shortly after World War II) is now middle-aged and approaching the years of early retirement. While the demographic population bulges once led to problems of youth unemployment, they now lead to problems of clogged promotion opportunities and an aging workforce that is expensive given seniority-based wage increases and the costs of pension benefit accruals and health care and other age-related expenses. The Canadian workforce is also becoming more ethnically diverse given the changing immigration patterns.

This changing nature of the workforce has important implications for training. Increased emphasis is being placed on "lifelong learning" involving recurring education and adult retraining. Again, this places greater emphasis on basic generic skills that can provide the foundations upon which to subsequently retrain—and retrain. Training for lateral transfers is more common given the clogged promotion opportunities. "Downtraining" may also be necessary as people are often relegated to less skilled tasks as an alternative to being laid off.

Given the smaller portion of youths in the labor market, there is less emphasis on training to deal with youth unemployment or the transition of youths into the labor market, albeit the bleak labor market prospects for many young entrants is an important social policy concern. Increased emphasis is being placed on the special training needs of older workers, especially those who permanently lose their jobs.

Human Rights and Diversity Issues

The Canadian labor market is becoming more diverse in various dimensions including ethnicity, gender and age. As well, human rights issues are becoming more prominent with regard to race, gender and age discrimination, as well as disability status. Increased pressure is being placed on employers to "reasonably accommodate" the needs of disabled workers at the workplace. Workers' compensation schemes are also more often emphasizing the importance of enabling injured workers to return to the workplace. Increased attention is also being paid to health and safety at the workplace.

These changes have implications for education and training. More significance is placed on the need to train and sensitize the workforce in areas of human rights and diversity. Vocational rehabilitation of injured workers is increasingly emphasized to facilitate their return to work. Training in health and safety is also being given more prominence. In each of these areas, there is increased need for training to deal with the technical aspects of administering and complying with the regulatory requirements, which are often technical and complex.

Workfare and Income Maintenance

Increased attention is being paid in income security programs to workfare—that is, compelling persons who are employable to be working or enrolled in a training program to be eligible for income support, notably welfare payments. Even if enrolment in a training program is not required as a condition of eligibility, there is often a strong emphasis on the provision of training to persons who are employable so as to enable them to move from income maintenance programs to gainful employment. As indicated previously, this is prompted in part by an emphasis on active adjustment assistance as opposed to passive income maintenance. It is also prompted by pressure to reduce the cost of income maintenance programs, as well as a recognition that recipients in general would prefer to be able to "earn their living" through gainful employment as opposed to the receipt of transfer programs that often have a social stigma.

This emphasis on gainful employment as opposed to income maintenance has important implications for training, since many of the trainees are otherwise disadvantaged workers who are not able to find a job—that is often their reason for relying on transfer payments in the first place. In some cases, they may be reluctant to take the training if it is imposed as a condition of employment, and this can have obvious implications on their ability to benefit from training. In other cases, the characteristics that make them unable to obtain or hold a job may also lead to their being unable to benefit from training. It may be the case, however, that they are at the early stages of the "learning curve" and can experience increasing returns to some basic training. The relevant measure of efficiency (for training as in any other activity) is value added, not final value, and it is distinctly possible that the value added is greater for more disadvantaged workers even if they do not emerge as high-productivity workers. Going from zero productivity to low productivity can involve greater gains than going from high productivity to marginally higher productivity.

Unemployment

The Canadian economy has been subject to lengthy periods of high unemployment, especially associated with the recessions of the early 1980s and early 1990s. Equally disconcerting is the fact that since the 1960s, each period of higher cyclical unemployment is followed by higher unemployment rates. There is a pronounced upward trend to unemployment rates, superimposed on the cyclical fluctuations. This is often taken as a sign of structural unemployment, reflecting a mismatch between job vacancies and the unemployed.

Training is an obviously important potential instrument for matching the skills of the unemployed with the skills required to fill the job vacancies. Furthermore, the (opportunity) cost of training is lowered by periods of unemployment since the income forgone is zero. The dilemma is that training is still expensive, and there is no guarantee that it will lead to a job or wage improvements, especially in periods when there is a large pool of unemployed available to take the scarce jobs. While skill mismatches are possible, it is also possible that there are simply insufficient jobs irrespective of the skills and training of the unemployed.

Wage Polarization

As with many other developed countries, the Canadian labor market has experienced increased wage polarization. This reflects a variety of inter-related forces: technological change that is biased towards skilled labor; import competition from low-wage countries that disproportionately affects low-wage workers in Canada; and de-industrialization away from middle-wage, blue-collar manufacturing jobs and towards jobs at the polar ends of the wage spectrum—high-wage professional, technical, managerial and administrative jobs on the one hand, and low-wage service jobs on the other.

Since wage polarization reflects an increasing skill premium, skill-based training should be economically more attractive. In essence, wage polarization should increase the private economic return to training. Furthermore, since the greater wage inequality is of some social concern, then training low-wage workers for the high-wage jobs is often regarded as a way of reducing the wage inequality.

Public Sector Restructuring

The previous discussion tended to emphasize changes in private sector labor markets and workplace practices. The public sector in Canada, however, has been under similar pressures. The pressures emanate from a concern with the public sector deficit and a reluctance to raise taxes to reduce the deficit. If taxes cannot be increased, the only option is to reduce expenditures, and a reduction of government expenditures quickly translates into reductions in the wages and employment of public sector employees, given that labor costs are usually a large component of total costs in providing public services. Where the government was once to be a model employer by providing high wages and good working conditions, it is now to be a model of restraint.

In Canada, the restraint tends to take the form of wage freezes, hiring restrictions, and increased use of limited-term contracts, subcontracting and privatization. Budget cuts are being imposed on elements of the broader public sector (health, education, social services) leading to pressures to restructure, to "reinvent government," and to base transfers to the broader public sector partially on performance measures. Since these pressures are relatively recent, it is difficult to determine the exact extent to which they have led to workplace changes similar to those occurring in the private sector (e.g., broader job classifications, employee involvement, pay for performance). To the extent that these workplace changes will occur in the public sector, then they will have the same implications for training as in the private sector (e.g., multi-skilling, broad-based training, emphasis on "people skills"). The civil servant of the future is less likely to be a producer of public services. Rather she or he will be more of a manager and co-ordinator—organizing, monitoring and co-ordinating those activities as they are provided by subcontractors, private producers and contingent workers hired for the life of a particular project. The skills required for these tasks imply different training needs, and retraining will be an issue as this restructuring occurs.

10.3 Role of Employer, Employee and Government

A key question in the training area is: who should pay for training? The answer in part depends on the distinction between company specific training that enhances productivity only in the sponsoring company, and general training that enhances productivity elsewhere. Employees will appropriate the benefits of general training, since their enhanced productivity will increase their market wages. The sponsoring employer will appropriate the benefits of company specific training since productivity in the sponsoring firm is enhanced, and the firm will not have to pay a higher wage since productivity is not enhanced elsewhere. Under these circumstances, there is general agreement that the employer should pay for company specific training and the employee should pay for generally usable training.

In such a world of easily identified specific and general training and competitive markets, there would be no rationale for government intervention since the private parties would have the economic incentive to invest in the training that benefits them, and the returns from that training provide the means to finance the training. There are, however, a number of possible market failures and other rationales for government intervention.[3]

Most training contains elements of both company specific and generally usable training and hence it may be exceedingly difficult to apportion the respective shares. Knowledge "spillovers" of the type envisioned in endogenous growth models may make it difficult for the private parties, be they employers or employees, to appropriate the full returns of their investment. Co-workers, may be reluctant to provide informal on-the-job training to fellow workers for fear they are training their own replacement! Structural bottlenecks or key skill shortages may affect the employment opportunities of other workers, as well as the business opportunities of other employers. In such circumstances, the social benefits of training can exceed the private benefits.

Even if they appropriate the full benefits of generally usable training, employees may find it difficult to borrow money to finance the training because they cannot use their human capital as collateral to finance the loan. If they default, their human capital cannot be appropriated by the lender because the borrower embodies the human capital—the lender cannot repossess the individual like they can a car or house. Even if employees can borrow the money, they may be extremely reluctant to do so, given the tremendous uncertainty that now exists about job security and market conditions. Since there is often an information asymmetry in this area, with employers possessing better information about market conditions, employees may be reluctant to engage in investments over which they may have little control. Institutional constraints, such as minimum wage or other wage fixing legislation, may make it difficult for employees to accept lower wages in return for the training.

Governments may also have an equity role to play by supporting training for certain target groups that are otherwise disadvantaged in the labor market: youths who are having difficulty making the transition from school to work; the long-term unemployed or persons affected by mass layoffs or plant closings in small communities; and persons in depressed industries or communities. In some

---

[3] These theoretical rationales are discussed in Gunderson (1974) and Gunderson and Riddell (1990).

circumstances, governments may prefer to provide assistance in the form of training since it may foster self-sufficiency. In other circumstances, governments may want to make enrolment in training a condition of income support. Governments may also feel pressured to provide subsidies to trainees to compensate for the fact that they tend to provide substantial subsidies to education. High school is provided free, and in higher education the tuition fees seldom cover the full cost.

The most frequently discussed case of "market failure" with respect to training is associated with the so-called "poaching" problem.[5] Employers may be reluctant to train because they may simply lose their trained workers to other firms that do not train but simply hire them away. To keep their trained workers, the sponsoring firms would have to pay the higher wages, in which case they paid for the training and are now "double paying" in the form of the higher market wage. In such circumstances, however, the employees have an incentive to pay for the training because they are appropriating the returns of what is obviously generally usable training. The poaching problem then reverts to the question of why employees do not pay for such training, perhaps by accepting a lower wage during the training program. Possible reasons for this were discussed previously.

The previous discussion highlighted a potential role for government when there are well-defined market failures or equity concerns. In general, however, these are not strong rationales, and at best provide an "uneasy case" for government subsidies. As stated by Riddell (1995, 154): "None of these mechanisms appear to provide a compelling case of private market failure; in each of these situations a case can be made that market forces operate at least to a degree, and in the appropriate direction. However, in each there may also be at least some failure of the market to address the problem adequately and the sum total of these 'uneasy cases' for government intervention may be a case for at least some intervention."

A more aggressive role for governments as part of an industrial strategy is envisioned by some. In that perspective, the government should be an active partner in developing the public infrastructure of the country, and training is part of that infrastructure to enhance competitiveness. Market failure is not a precondition for government intervention. Our perspective is that this is always a possibility, as with any industrial strategy, but that the potential for rent seeking and public subsidies that would crowd out and distort private decision making is too great. Government subsidies in this area should be directed more to areas of reasonably well-defined market failures, including broader equity and distributional concerns.

---

[5] This has been one rationale for the recommendations of a training tax or levy to be imposed on all firms, and then rebated for those that engage in training. This has been recommended in Adams (1979) and de Grandpre (1989), although it has not been implemented, presumably because of strong resistance of employers to further payroll taxes.

10.4 The Current Picture of Training in Canada

The constitutional division of powers in Canada is such that the federal government has responsibility for the state of the economy and the provincial governments have responsibility for education. Since training relates to both the state of the economy and education, it falls under both federal and provincial jurisdiction. This joint responsibility has given rise to federal-provincial disputes over how training should be administered, with each party often blaming the other for shortcomings in this area (Gaskell, 1991; Gunderson and Riddell, 1991; Meltz, 1990).

Federal Training Programs

Federal training programs are constantly being repackaged under different initiatives and legislative regimes.[6] The current structure involves five main programs, each with a number of components. They are administered by Human Resources Development Canada (HRDC), the government department responsible for employment services, social services, and labor issues. The five programs, and their main rationales are as follows:

(1)   Employability Improvement: To improve the employability and facilitate the successful integration into employment of selected individuals who require assistance to overcome labor market barriers.

(2)   *Labor Market Adjustment*: To induce employers, particularly in key adjustment situations, to meet changing skill needs.

(3)   Community Development: To support the development of local employment opportunities and to assist communities that are facing severe labor market problems.

(4)   Information and Special Initiatives: To provide information on the labor market and employment opportunities.

(5)   Program for Older Worker Adjustment (POWA): To provide long-term assistance until age 65 to older workers who have been permanently laid off, who have exhausted their unemployment insurance benefits, and who have

---

[6] The Technical and Vocational Training Act of 1960, the Adult Occupational Training Act of 1967, the National Training Act of 1982, the Canadian Jobs Strategy (CJS) of 1985, and the modification of the CJS through the Labor Force Development Strategy of 1990. Meltz (1990) provides a thorough discussion of many of these changes and the rationales behind them.

little prospect of finding new employment.

These programs are financed out of general tax revenues. A growing portion of employment programs are financed out of Unemployment Insurance (UI) funds and hence out of the payroll tax that pays for such funds. In most circumstances these programs allow for the receipt of UI benefits by groups who conventionally would not be covered by UI (e.g., persons engaged in worksharing, or in a job creation program, or training, or becoming self-employed). They also sometimes pay for some of the project costs. These UI development funded programs include:

(1)   *UI Worksharing*: UI benefits to persons on approved programs who agree to reduce hours to avoid layoffs.

(2)   *UI Job Creation*: UI benefits to qualified claimants participating in limited-term jobs on job-creation projects.

(3)   *UI Training Income Replacement*: UI benefits, training costs and supplementary allowances for persons taking full-time training in other HRDC programs.

(4)   *Self-Employment Assistance*: UI benefits and project costs to assist claimants to set up their own business.

Table 10.1 indicates the proportion of total program expenditures and of program participants in each of these programs,[7] distinguishing those supported out of general revenue and those supported by UI funds. It also gives the separate components of the general programs.

As the bottom panel of Table 10.1 illustrates, almost 60% of Canada's training and other employment programs are now funded out of UI funds, essentially involving a reallocation from conventional payment of UI for the unemployed, and towards paying UI (and sometimes additional project costs) to persons who are unemployed but who engage in one of the UI development funded programs—worksharing, job creation, training or self-employment. Such programs, however, cover only 8% of program participants. Within these UI-assisted programs, paying UI benefits to provide income support to persons in training accounts for 31% of total program expenditures, and training program costs account for an additional 20%. In essence, 50% of all employment program expenditures in Canada now involve UI benefits or training costs for unemployed persons in training programs.

Within the generally funded (i.e., non-UI) employment programs, the

---

[7] POWA and a few other small programs are not included in the figures provided by HRDC.

Table 10.1
Relative Importance of Training and Other Employment Programs, Canada, 1993-94

Program and Components	% Expenditure	% Persons
Employability improvement	**26.94**	**80.45**
Project-based training	6.24	8.06
Purchase of training	11.19	51.98
Job Opportunities	1.36	2.08
Employment assistance	1.52	8.53
Youth initiatives	5.05	9.10
Mobility assistance	0.19	0.72
Delivery assistance	1.39	n/a
Labor market adjustment	**3.38**	**4.18**
Workplace-based training	1.55	4.18
Human resources planning	0.66	n/a
Agriculture employment service	0.37	n/a
Industrial adjustment service	0.80	n/a
Community development	**8.74**	**7.30**
Local projects	4.97	6.08
Self-employment assistance	0.15	1.22
Community futures	3.62	n/a
Information and innovations	**1.28**	**n/a**
Sub-total general funding	**40.34**	**91.92**
UI development funded	**59.66**	**8.08**
UI Worksharing	1.32	n/a
UI Job creation	3.79	n/a
UI Training income support	31.21	n/a
UI Training program cost	19.66	n/a
UI Self-employment assistance	3.69	n/a
Total all programs	**100.00**	**100.00**
Total expenditures ($billions) and participants	**3.106**	**709,434**

Source: Calculations from data in Human Resources Development Canada (1993).

proportion of total expenditures that goes into training programs is 6% for project based training, 11% for the purchase of training spaces mainly in community colleges, and 2% for workplace-based training as part of the labor adjustment program. These training related components totaled 19% of program expenditures. When added to the 50% of training expenditures from UI assisted training, this implies that approximately 70% of employment program expenditures in Canada are on training related projects. While this is a large component, it is a large component of a small amount since such active labor market programs are not prominent in Canada. As indicated in Table 10.2, as of the mid-1990s Canada spent a little over 2% of its GDP on *all* labor market programs. However, 71% of this was on passive income maintenance programs, notably transfers from unemployment insurance[8] (the passive component would be much larger if social assistance were included). Only 29% of expenditures on labor market programs were on active programs, mainly training but also employment services, job

---

[8] The special development component of the UI benefits that includes training courses and supplementary allowances for training is less than 4% of such UI expenditures (HRDC 1994, 14).

Table 10.2
Public Expenditures on Training and Other Employment Programs, Canada, 1994-95

Program	% of GDP	% of Expenditures on Employment Programs
Training	0.37	16.7
Employment Services	0.21	9.5
Job Creation, Subsidized Employment	0.06	2.7
(Sub-Total Active)	(0.64)	(29.0)
UI and Other Passive	1.57	71.0
Total	2.21	100.0

Source: OECD (1994).

creation and subsidized employment.

Provincial Training Programs

Systematic and comparable information is not available on the different provincial training programs. In an attempt to compile such information, Meltz (1990, 300) concluded: "While the author had hoped to develop data on the provincial expenditures, on the basis of information available it is difficult to determine the precise amount of provincial spending on training. At the present time it appears that the federal government is still the major provider of funding for training in Canada."

Employer-Sponsored Industry Training

Systematic information is also difficult to compile on the extent of employer-sponsored training that occurs in industry. In Canada's largest and most industrial province, one survey (Ontario Manpower Commission, 1986) indicated that about 27% of establishments conducted some training, involving about 22% of their full-time permanent workers, but with only 2.7% being given formal training lasting two weeks or more. Based on these numbers, Meltz (1990, 300) calculates that the 2.7% in formal industry training programs is slightly higher than the approximately 2% that were in government sponsored programs. However, the government sponsored ones lasted much longer (median of 26 weeks compared to 3.5 weeks for private industry) so that total time spent in federal training was approximately five times that of employer sponsored training. Even if the short-term (i.e., less than two weeks) employer-sponsored training is included, federal training would be twice as extensive as private training. If provincial training were also included then total government training would exceed employer-sponsored training by more than these 5:1 or 2:1 ratios. Furthermore, since Ontario is

Canada's most industrial province where employer-sponsored training is most likely to occur, the dominance of government over industrial training is likely to be even greater in other provinces. This dominance may be offset to some degree by the fact that the employer-sponsored training does not include the informal, on-the-job training and "learning by doing" that may constantly be occurring at the workplace. This can include, for example, the time spent by an employee learning a computer software program at work, and time spent "learning the ropes" from a more skilled co-worker.

While a number of ad hoc surveys have been conducted on the extent of employer-sponsored training, differences in concepts, definitions and sample frames make generalizations difficult. With these caveats in mind, the following generalizations emerge from the surveys (Bennett, 1994; Betcherman, 1993; and Economic Council of Canada (1991).[9]

- About two-thirds of private firms provide some informal or formal training, with about one-third providing formal training.

- About 56% of employees indicated that they received some informal or formal training over the previous two years, although only 7% to 19% indicated that they received formal training.

- On average, firms spend about $250 per employee on formal training.

- Large firms are more likely to provide formal training, although their expenditure per employee is only slightly above average. Small firms also have above average expenditures per employee on training.

- Training is more prevalent in firms and industries experiencing rapid technological change.

- Formal training is more likely to be received by employees who are already more highly educated and well-paid.

- Unemployed workers are more likely to take training, but within the unemployed, those most likely to experience difficult adjustment problems are less likely to take training (Picot, 1987).

- There is no consensus on the extent to which firms are reluctant to provide training because they are afraid that they may simply lose their trainees to other firms that do not provide training (i.e., the poaching problem). The

[9] These results are based mainly on 14 surveys of employer-sponsored training in Canada, from 1963 to 1989.

proportion of firms indicating this to be a problem ranged from 1% to 58% across the different surveys!

International Comparisons

As indicated in Table 10.3, relative to the other major OECD nations, Canada is "in the middle" in terms of total *public* expenditures on *all* labor market programs as a percent of GDP. It tends to be at the lower end (ranked 6 out of 9) with respect to its expenditures on active as opposed to passive income measures and one of the lowest in terms of active measures (Riddell, 1995, 159). The change reflects the recent emphasis on reallocating from passive income maintenance programs like UI to more active measures, especially the use of UI funds for persons in training.

Table 10.3
Percent of GDP Spent on Training and Other Employment Programs,
Major OECD Countries, 1994-95

Country	Training (1)	Employment Service (2)	Other Active[1] (3)	Total Active (4) (1+2+3)	Total Passive (5)	Total (6) (4+5)
Australia	0.16	0.23	0.37	0.76	1.90	2.66
Canada	**0.37**	**0.21**	**0.06**	**0.64**	**1.57**	**2.21**
France	0.44	0.15	0.62	1.21	2.10	3.31
Germany	0.42	0.24	0.66	1.32	0.81	2.13
Italy	0.02	0.08	0.8	0.90	0.87	1.77
Japan	0.03	0.03	0.03	0.09	0.32	0.41
Sweden	0.8	0.27	1.89	2.96	2.48	5.44
U.K.	0.16	0.24	0.19	0.59	1.59	2.18
U.S.	0.07	0.08	0.10	0.25	0.45	0.70

Note: [1] Includes youth measures, subsidized employment, and measures for the disabled.

Source: OECD (1994). Where data was unavailable for 1994-95, the latest available figures were used.

This raises the question of the extent to which some of these changes are mainly cosmetic. The simple change of allowing persons to collect UI while on training, would provide a "double whammy" in terms of the appearance of shifting from passive income maintenance to active training expenditures since these expenditures would not only be removed from the passive UI expenditures but also they would be added to the active training expenditures.

With respect to combined employer and government support for training in industry, Canada is categorized by the OECD as one of the "weak" countries for training (Economic Council of Canada, 1991). Since it tends to be categorized as average or above for public support, this suggests that employer support is exceedingly weak by international standards. This has led tocomments that Canadian employers lack a "training culture." As stated by Betcherman (1993, 22) "available data offer a strong sense that Canadian firms do train less than their counterparts in other major industrialized countries." Extensive reliance on immigration as a source of skilled labor may have deterred the development of an indigenous training system (Meltz, 1990). The training system in Canada is also characterized as not well-linked to the education system (Gaskell, 1991), in part because of the low status attached to vocational education. Relative to other countries Canada appears to have missed opportunities for higher productivity and growth because of low investments in education and training (Canadian Labour Market and Productivity Centre, 1989a and 1989b).

Investment in human capital in countries like Canada us likely to be at least as large as, and probably substantially larger than, investment in physical capital.[10] Nevertheless, given the modest amount of funds devoted to training, as reported here, such formal training is not likely to account for a large share of accumulated human capital.

Evaluation Results

Riddell (1991, 1995) summarizes the results of a number of studies that have evaluated the federal training programs. Most have focused on the wage and employment gains in the first year or two after training. The main conclusions are:

- The effects ranged from zero to small to large. Basic skills training (maths, science and communications upgrading) had no impact; institutional, classroom training had a small positive impact; and industrial training at the workplace combined with work experience had the largest positive impact. The latter highlights the importance of public-private partnerships in the provision of such training, so as to use the private sector for the delivery of practical training.

- The largest impacts were found in training for skills and for occupations that were in short supply relative to demand.

- These larger impacts also tended to be at the higher skill levels, for persons who were not disadvantaged in the labor market. This suggests, unfortunately, that there may be a trade-off between efficiency and equity in that the higher returns were going to people who were already advantaged in the labor market.

[10] Gunderson and Thirsk (1994, 41) cite evidence of investment in human capital ranging from 48% to 96% of the total capital stock, with the upper figure also reflecting the value of human capital in non-market activities.

- Over time the impacts on earnings and employability have increased. This could be due to better program design (as worse programs were abandoned and better ones expanded) or because the returns to training simply increased—a distinct possibility given that the wage polarization that occurred should increase the skill premium.

- While institutional, classroom training only had modest effects, it tended to work best for youths and females re-entering the labor market.

- When earnings are increased, it tends to result more from increased employment (hours and weeks worked) rather than increased wages. Presumably this reflects the fact that wage structures are slow to respond to productivity increases from training, so that firms have an incentive to increase the hours of such persons.

- The gains from training are greatest in a more buoyant labor market, highlighting the importance of available employment opportunities.

These results seem to have had an impact on the re-orientation of training over time[11] since the changes tended to be in line with those suggested by the evaluation studies. That is, there has been a redirection from basic and institutional classroom training and towards training provided at the private sector workplace and combined with work experience. Increased emphasis has been placed on higher-level training for emerging skill shortages, and on the involvement of employers in the delivery of training. This is especially the case with respect to the recent re-orientation of UI from passive income maintenance and towards more active adjustment assistance, as UI funds are increasingly used to enable recipients to receive training at the workplace and to garner work experience.

While the evaluation results appear to have been useful, more information is needed on various aspects related to training in Canada.[12] Evidence is needed on the longer run impact of training as well as on the extent to which persons who receive government supported training may simply be displacing others or "crowding out" private sector training. There is the possibility that much of this training may have occurred even without the government support, especially given the high returns that resulted from the skill-based training. Furthermore, more evidence is needed on the characteristics of those who gain the most by training, including the extent to which disadvantaged workers gain, even if they do not gain the most. This would enable better targeting of increasingly scarce training dollars,

---

[11] See Meltz (1990), Economic Council of Canada (1991), Riddell (1995) and the various annual reports of HRDC, formerly Employment and Immigration Canada.

[12] Research needs in the training area in Canada are discussed in Betcherman (1993) and Riddell (1995).

and it would facilitate informed decision-making on the viability of training as an instrument to assist disadvantaged workers. Information is also needed on how training affects the performance and competitiveness of firms as well as on how training decisions are made within firms and how those decisions can be influenced by policy levers, if that turns out to be desirable.

10.5 Lessons from the Canadian Experience

The previous analysis highlighted a number of possible lessons that can be learned from the Canadian experience with training. At the risk of oversimplification, the following generalizations are advanced:

- The call for increased emphasis on training is linked to a wide range of recent inter-related changes and policy concerns: global competitiveness; labor market adjustment on both the downside and upside; new workplace and human resource practices; demographic and other changes in the workforce; human rights and diversity issues; workfare and income maintenance; unemployment; wage polarization; and public sector restructuring.

- While each of these are important, and they have crucial links to training, the precise nature of the links can be difficult to establish. It is easy to say that training has important potential implications for each of these areas; it is another matter to precisely establish that linkage and spell out the specifics of how training should be changed. Perhaps that is one of the reasons why training has been examined by so many different task forces and royal commissions in Canada. They usually recommend that more emphasis should be placed on training, but they are often short on the specifics of exactly how training should be altered and who should pay and how the precise roles of employers, employees and governments should be delineated.

- Rather than simply saying that "Canadian employers lack a training culture" or that "governments do not invest enough in training" or that "individuals have a bias against vocational education"— all of which have been said in the Canadian context—we need more information on why these biases or "mistakes" occur, if they do occur. More attention needs to be paid to the issue of the extent to which private unregulated markets will yield the optimal amount of training, and on the precise source of any market failure and how it can best be dealt with.

- Jurisdictional splits between the federal and provincial governments over responsibility for training has led to endless wrangling and blame-shifting in this area, highlighting that divided or ill-defined responsibility often leads to no responsibility.

- The web of training programs in Canada can be characterized as complex and difficult to understand. Neither employers nor employees usually have good information on their existence or nature. The program names and nature are constantly changing. While this may be a sign of flexibility and adaptability, it can also be a sign that they are used for political ends, as political capital is garnered by announcing new programs and reallocating to particular interest groups. Training can foster rent-seeking activities as well as being an important component of human capital formation.

- The development of indigenous training in Canada has likely been hampered by the fact that immigration has been a readily available source of skilled labor, and the training system is not well integrated with the education system.

- It is difficult to determine the extent to which firms are reluctant to train their employees for fear of losing them to firms that do not train (i.e., the poaching problem). While this has given rise to recommendations for a training tax, such a levy has not been implemented presumably because of employer resistance to increased payroll taxes. To the extent that poaching is a problem, one must ask why employees are reluctant or unable to pay for such generally usable training since they are appropriating the benefits. While there are plausible reasons for this, they are not usually clearly delineated in a fashion that can guide policy makers decide on the appropriate intervention, if any.

- The evaluation studies tend to find that training "pays" (usually in the form of greater employability as opposed to higher wages), although the benefits are sometimes small or even zero. The largest benefits tend to be associated with employer-based training when combined with work experience, rather than with basic and institutional training. Rapid technological change may make it difficult for institutional training to utilize the most up-to-date equipment—equipment which is more likely to be available at the employers' worksite. The largest benefits also go to already skilled persons who are upgrading their skills even further to meet emerging shortages—again raising the question of why they do not engage in such training without government support.

- Unfortunately, the strict monetary benefits from training tend to be smallest for more disadvantaged workers, suggesting that public support for their training has to be based more on equity rather than efficiency grounds. A legitimate trade-off can exist, however, since society may well deem it appropriate to use training to raise the earnings of its most disadvantaged members even if the training premium is low for such persons.

- Other policies and practices can have unintended effects on incentives to invest in training. Wage fixing policies, for example, may make it difficult to accept a lower wage in return for training, and subsidies to higher education may discourage vocational education.

- Active adjustment assistance measures like training are more likely to be effective in facilitating the reallocation of labor from declining to expanding sectors, than are passive income maintenance programs like unemployment insurance.

- Canada has been characterized as emphasizing passive income maintenance programs like UI as opposed to active adjustment assistance programs like training, although recent changes appear to have considerably redirected the emphasis away from UI and towards training.

- Before making final judgement calls on the Canadian system of training, however, more information is needed on various dimensions: the appropriate division of payments amongst employers, employees, and governments; the longer-run impacts of training; the extent to which successful trainees simply displace other workers; the extent to which government supported training simply displaces private training; the precise nature of any trade-off between efficiency and equity in training disadvantaged workers; the extent to which different persons benefit differently from training; the extent to which training affects the performance of firms; and the best policy levers for altering the amount of training, if that turns out to be desirable.

- These issues highlight that training will remain on the policy agenda for Canada, just as for other developed and developing countries.

REFERENCES

Adams, R. (Chairperson) (1979). *Education and Working Canadians*. Report of the Commission of Inquiry on Education Leave and Productivity. Ottawa: Labor Canada.

Bennett, K. (1994). "Recent Information on Training." *Perspectives on Labor and Income*, Vol. 6

(Spring), pp. 22-25.

Betcherman, G. (1993). "Research Gaps Facing Training Policy-Makers." *Canadian Public Policy*, Vol. 19, No. 1, pp. 18-28.

Canadian Labour Market and Productivity Centre (CLMPC) (1989a). *Focus on Adjustment*. Ottawa: CLMPC.

Canadian Labour Market and Productivity Centre (CLMPC) (1989b). "The Linkages Between Education and Training and Economic Performance." *Quarterly Labour Market and Productivity Review*. Ottawa: CLMPC.

Canadian Labour Market and Productivity Centre (CLMPC) (1990). *Report of the CLMPC Task Force on the Labor Market Development Strategy*. Ottawa: CLMPC.

Davies, J. (1986). "Training and Skill Development." In *Adapting to Change: Labor Market Adjustment in Canada*, W. C. Riddell, ed. Toronto: University of Toronto Press.

Economic Council of Canada (1991). *Employment in the Service Economy*. Ottawa: Supply and Services Canada.

Employment and Immigration Canada (1989). *Success in the Works*. Hull: CEIC.

Gaskell, J. (1991). "Education as Preparation for Work in Canada." In *Making Their Way: Education, Training and the Labour Market in Canada and Britain*, D. Ashton and G. Lowe, eds. Toronto: University of Toronto Press.

Gigantes, P. (1987). *In Training Only Work Works*. Report of the Sub-Committee on Training and Employment of the Standing Senate Committee on Social Affairs. Ottawa: Supply and Services Canada.

Granpre, A. de. (1989). *Adjusting to Win*. Report of the Advisory Council on Adjustment. Ottawa: Supply and Services Canada.

Gunderson, M. (1974). "The Case for Government Supported Training." *Relations Industrielles/Industrial Relations*, Vol. 29 (December), pp. 709-726.

Gunderson, M. and W. C. Riddell (1990). "Incentives for Undertaking On-the-Job Training." Victoria: B.C. Task Force on Employment and Training.

Gunderson, M. and W. C. Riddell (1991). "Labor Force Adaptability: Implications for Education and Training." Victoria: B. C. Task Force on Employment and Training.

Gunderson, M. and W. Thirsk (1994). "Tax Treatment of Human Capital." In *Taxes As Instruments of Public Policy*, A. Maslove, ed. Toronto: University of Toronto Press.

HRDC (1994). *Annual Report: 1993-1994*. Ottawa: Human Resources Development Canada.

Macdonald Commission) (1985). *Royal Commission on the Economic Union and Development Prospects for Canada*, Vol. 2. Ottawa: Supply and Services Canada.

Meltz, N. (1990). "The Evolution of Worker Training: The Canadian Experience." In *New Developments in Worker Training*, L. Ferman, M. Hoyman, J. Cutcher-Gershenfeld and E. Savoie, eds. Madison: Industrial Relations Research Association.

Ontario Manpower Commission (1986). *Training in Industry: A Survey of Employer-Sponsored Programs in Ontario*. Toronto: Queen's Printer.

Ontario Ministry of Skills Development (1988). *Adjusting to Change: An Overview of Labor Market Issues in Ontario*. Toronto: Queen's Printer.

Ontario Ministry of Skills Development (1989). *Building a Training System for the 1990's: A Shared Responsibility*. Toronto: Queen's Printer.

Ontario Premier's Council (1988). *Competing in the New Global Economy*. Toronto: Queen's Printer.

Ontario Premier's Council (1990). *People and Skills in the New Global Economy*. Toronto: Queen's Printer.

Organization for Economic Co-operation and Development (OECD) (1994). *The OECD Jobs Study: Taxation, Employment and Unemployment*. Paris: OECD.

Picot, G. (1987). *Unemployment and Training*. Ottawa: Social and Economic Studies Division, Statistics Canada.

Riddell, W. C. (1991). "Evaluation of Manpower and Training Programs: The North American Experience." In *Evaluating Labor Market and Social Programs: The State of a Complex Art*. Paris: OECD.

Riddell, W. C. (1995). "Human Capital Formation in Canada: Recent Developments and Policy Responses." In *Labor Market Polarization and Social Policy Reform*, K. Banting and C. Beach, eds. Kingston: Queen's University School of Policy Studies.

Strand, Kenneth (Chair) (1991). *B.C. Task Force on Employment and Training: Learning and Work*. Victoria: Task Force on Employment and Training.

Chapter 11

TRAINING AND RETRAINING IN LATIN AMERICA

by María Angélica Ducci

11.1 The Context for Training and Retraining in Latin America

The Challenges: Competitiveness and Equity

As Latin American countries enter the 21st century, their development strategy is becoming centered around two major challenges: on the one hand, to improve their competitiveness in a globalized economy; on the other, to consolidate and heighten equity and social cohesion. The key development issue is, therefore, to reconcile economic and social concerns at the national level, within a new international context.[1]

The current policies are based on a firm commitment to economic modernization and are defined around two major axes: one, the rationalization and restructuring of production, geared to the improvement of productivity and quality; the other, the liberalization of enterprise activity, and the reduction of state intervention in production.

On the economic scene, the internationalization of production and trade and the liberalization of markets are forcing developing countries to maximize their competitive advantages. Until now, most of the revealed comparative advantage of Latin American countries has been in primary products. Too often, this has been achieved by resorting to low wages and indiscriminate exploitation of natural resources.

From the social point of view, the countries of the region have witnessed a

---

[1] ECLAC (1990) provides a comprehensive approach to this issue.

considerable strengthening of their democratization processes. Expectations for economic, social and political participation have grown for all groups of the population. Nevertheless, deep inequalities persist and have even worsened in many countries as a consequence of development strategies incapable of successfully integrating vast social sectors into the growth process. According to the UNDP 1996 *Human Development Report,* "income distribution in Latin America improved only in Colombia, Costa Rica and Uruguay. It deteriorated in Argentina, Bolivia, Brazil, Peru and Venezuela"(UNDP, 1996).

The most recent figures for the region show that though urban unemployment was slightly reduced during 1990-93, it has risen since then in nearly all of the major countries , including a historic high in Argentina (1995) and a near high in Colombia (1998). The weighted regional average of 7.7% in 1996 is well above the 6% registered in 1980 (ECLAC, 1997). The relatively low unemployment, reflecting below average rates in Brazil and Mexico, was sustained basically by the upsurge of informal jobs, which came with a deterioration in job quality and productivity. In most countries industrial wages recovered during the 1990-94 period, but the level attained was still 5% lower than that of 1980, in real terms (ILO, 1995).

It is now recognized in the region that raising productivity and improving product quality are *sine qua non* conditions to compete successfully on the world market, and to create more and better jobs in the process. Consequently, the crucial challenge lies in the enhancement and efficient use of the productive capabilities and talents of the people. *"Intelligent labor"* based on knowledge, innovation and technology, is increasingly valued as the key factor for ensuring a genuine and progressive increase in the *intellectual value added* of production. This scenario inevitably compels every country to steadily raise the skill level of its work force, and to strengthen the entrepreneurial and management base of its productive units.[2] The development of human resources is, therefore, at the center of the policy debate in Latin American countries.

Among the many factors affecting the incorporation of technological innovation and the spread of technical progress, education and training appear central if that process is to contribute both to economic growth and to social equity. Besides boosting productivity, competitiveness and growth at the enterprise and national levels, education and training can contribute to the redistribution of income by equipping workers with the competencies that facilitate and improve their access to employment, income, job security, mobility and re-adaptation to occupational change. Simultaneously, education and training are a valuable instrument to foster the economic and social integration of disadvantaged and marginalized groups of the population.

Moreover, in the current international setting, investment in the education

---

[2] An in-depth analysis of the centrality of human resources to the development strategy of Latin American and Caribbean countries is presented in ECLAC-UNESCO (1992).

and training of the workforce is both strategic and cost-effective for developing countries: firstly, the gap between the countries of the region and the industrialized world is particularly wide in terms of the levels of education and training of their workforce; secondly, people are an abundant resource in the region, with clear prospects for improvement; and thirdly, despite noteworthy progress during the last decade, the starting point—the current skills base—is still relatively low.

An additional dimension that makes investment in the training and development of human resources a priority, is the drive towards economic integration among countries. In Latin America, commercial agreements and economic integration attempts at the regional level have failed for decades. Conversely, sub-regional trade agreements have flourished during the 1990s.[3] Economic integration is sought as a way to increase competitiveness, to better use resources and productive capacity, to raise national and foreign investment and, ultimately, to create jobs and increase welfare. It has direct and indirect implications for the workforce's skills requirements and utilization. In the first place, it is likely to accelerate technology transfer and innovation, economic restructuring and transformation in product composition, thus altering and increasing the demands for qualifications (Mercado, 1994). Secondly, it creates the need for exchange, cooperation and harmonization among countries in critical areas of human resources training and development.

Education and Training in Overall Human Resources Development

There has been much debate in recent years about the relative importance of general education as compared to vocational training to foster occupational skills and productivity. The debate has contributed to differences of views as to how developing countries should organize their overall human resource development effort and, most particularly, on the role that the state and the private sector should play in the finance and provision of the various levels and forms of education and training.[4]

It is broadly accepted that formal general education is essential to the development of the trainability and flexibility which allow workers to adapt to the constant changes in skills requirements which go with rapid technology change. It

---

[3] The North America Free Trade Agreement, NAFTA (Mexico, the US and Canada), the Andean Pact (Bolivia, Colombia, Ecuador and Venezuela), MERCOSUR (Argentina, Brazil, Paraguay and Uruguay), the Group of Three (Mexico, Colombia and Venezuela), the Central American Common Market, MCC (Costa Rica, El Salvador, Guatemala, Honduras and Nicaragua), the bilateral Chile-Mexico Economic Cooperation Agreement, and the open trade agreement between Central America and Venezuela, are some examples of economic integration attempts in the region.

[4] A detailed analysis of this subject can be found in Middleton *et al.* (1993).

is through this system that people acquire the basic mental abilities of reading and writing, arithmetic, and the scientific and technological foundations that enable the further understanding and learning of new technological processes throughout their working lives.

The evolution of the occupational profiles brought about by rapidly changing structures of production, work organization and job content, highlights the need for all workers to acquire a good breadth of knowledge, aptitudes and attitudes from a very early age, necessarily well in advance of their career choices. This situation underlines the importance of improving the coverage and quality of basic education; it is essential that the primary level be accessible to the whole population and desirable that the secondary level be. But this is not enough. For employment purposes, vocational training is the desirable and often necessary complement to general education, in particular for those who do not continue on to tertiary education.

Moreover, in Latin American countries a significant proportion of the population is illiterate or has only a few years of primary schooling. For some years to come, many of the new entrants to the labor force will have insufficient schooling, and it will be important that some form of vocational training be available to help them offset this disadvantage. Vocational training is still the main way—and often the only option available—for low-educated workers to acquire occupational skills through a structured learning process, geared to provide competencies valued on the labor market.

It must be recalled that in Latin America, enterprises have thus far played a very marginal role in training. This was the major reason for the government-led development of vocational training in the region (Ducci, 1980 and 1983). But it also helps to explain the slow progress made by enterprises in incorporating the discipline of training as a critical dimension of their economic performance. Except for the very large enterprises—and particularly the most dynamic ones—which have moved very recently to organize their own training strategies, programs and even infrastructure, small and medium size enterprises have depended heavily on training initiatives from the government.

Therefore, institutional vocational training has been a key determinant of skills development. For youngsters, and particularly for early school drop-outs, it has provided a path of transition from school to work. For the unemployed, vocational training facilitates reinsertion by providing opportunities for up-grading their skills, and/or for readjusting them to the real demands of the labor market.

Continuous training and retraining have increasingly become a must for the already employed. As a minimum it is needed to adjust to changes in the technological and operational contents of their job; additionally, it is important in facing the changes in jobs, occupations, enterprises and even economic sectors that workers are likely to confront throughout their professional lives. Life-long learning has become an imperative to succeed in adapting to the ever-changing world of work. Thus, general education constitutes the essential platform on which successive learning will be rooted, allowing for a continuous process of retraining in accordance with the evolution of working lives.

More and more, the objectives of formal education and vocational training have converged, and sharp distinctions between the two are hardly justified on conceptual grounds, in particular at the level of secondary education. While general education is increasingly attempting to provide teaching that can be meaningful and useful for work, vocational training is broadening its scope beyond the purely instrumental skills required for specific jobs. In fact, vocational training institutes (VTIs) are making a significant effort to introduce in their programs the ethical dimension of a *"culture of productive work"* aimed at forging the values, aptitudes and attitudes deemed necessary for competent performance of the labor force.

In Latin America, formal education and vocational training have traditionally been organized separately, with few links and/or transfer paths between them. This is now felt to be a shortcoming and several countries are considering the reorganization of the overall educational effort, emphasizing convergence, complementarity and coherence among its parts. Though the independence of the training system from regular education allowed for positive results in terms of its dynamism and flexibility to respond to the changes in the world of work, there are also a number of concerns that have come to the fore in the wake of new pressing demands.

11.2 Training and Retraining in Latin America

Training in Retrospect

A review of the performance of vocational training in Latin American countries is a necessary background to assess the key short and medium term policy issues related to skills development for external competitiveness and internal equity. This discussion will concentrate on the VTIs which, as noted, were assigned the responsibility for training the workforce to increase its productivity and income levels.

Since the 1950s Latin American countries have made a significant effort to develop national systems for education, training and technological and scientific research, as a fundamental support to the development strategy based on import substitution that most countries of the region had embraced by that time. The results of that effort have not been satisfactory. Though illiteracy was drastically reduced, from an average rate of 45% in 1950 to 13% in 1990, it remains high in some countries, particularly among rural and indigenous populations. Primary school is today accessible to practically all school-age children, but serious dropout problems exist. Of the children entering basic education, only 53% reach the fourth grade; here too there are broad variations between and within countries. As a result, the average educational level is barely six years of schooling, and almost half of the Latin American labor force has not completed primary education. Considerable progress is reflected by the fact that "between 1960 and 1990 secondary and tertiary enrolment taken together increased nearly eightfold. Nevertheless, nearly 20 million boys and girls are out of school at the secondary level (UNDP, 1996). In addition, deficiencies in the relevance, efficiency and equity of formal education have resulted in serious shortcomings in terms of response to the current needs of development in a globalized economy.

In the period beginning in the 1940s and extending into the 1960s, publicly sponsored VTIs were created in all countries of the region to train the skilled and semiskilled labor force as a parallel and complementary system to formal education. The saga started in 1942 with the creation of the National Industrial Apprenticeship Service (SENAI) in Brazil, followed in 1946 by the National Commercial Apprenticeship Service (SENAC) also in Brazil. Both Brazilian institutions were attached to the respective employer's federations in the industrial and commercial sectors, funded by a compulsory payroll levy of 1% paid by all enterprises, except the very small. Most other countries opted for the same type of VTI, independent from the regular educational system, financed by a training levy ranging from 1% to 2% of the payroll, or from the public national budget, but with one major difference: they all established VTIs directly administered by the government, with the participation of employers and workers taking the form of membership in the governing bodies. During the 1950s and 1960s, national VTIs were founded in six countries: SENA in Colombia (1957), INCE in Venezuela (1959), SENATI in Peru (1961), INA in Costa Rica (1963), INACAP in Chile (1966), and SECAP in Ecuador (1966). In the early seventies, a new generation of VTIs appeared: SNPP in Paraguay (1971), INFO in Honduras (1972), FOMO in Bolivia (1972), INTECAP in Guatemala (1972) and IFARHU in Panama (1973). The original purpose of all these training institutions was to make up for the lack of formal education, providing young workers—often from the countryside—with the occupational skills and work habits needed by industry. Their focus was on apprenticeship for the new entrants to the labor market. In practice, it became the educational alternative to early school dropouts, mostly from blue-collar workers' families.

The initial attributes and characteristics of these VTIs determined their evolution and adaptation to the changing requirements (Ducci, 1988). By and large, such attributes are still present to a greater or lesser degree in most Latin American VTIs: first of all, clear-cut independence from regular education systems, as a means of ensuring greater proximity to the world of work; second, solid and stable financing based on a compulsory contribution by firms and enterprises under the form of a tax on their payroll; and, third, participation of the key players involved in production—governments, employers and workers—in decision-making at the top.

Viewed in retrospect, there has been significant progress in the way these VTIs have approached their task. Roughly speaking, three stages can be identified. The first focused on the training of new workers, at skilled and semiskilled levels, to hold the jobs available or foreseeable in the formal labor market. Consequently, attention was focused on young people, through the apprenticeship formula, structured primarily for the so-called "universal" occupations in the manufacturing sector, and later expanded to cover major occupations in commerce and services and, to a lesser extent, agriculture. Adult workers also came to be included through programs which retrained them for activities and occupations in the modern sector of the economy, at times of rapid expansion.

The second stage, dating from the mid 1960s in the pioneer VTIs of the region, is marked by a stress on social concerns, as the result of the employment crisis and the marginalization of large contingents of the population not absorbed by the modern sector. This new challenge implied moving the focus away from the job towards the needs of the individual workers, as integral human beings. Training was geared to developing "human aptitudes" and not only vocational skills. A significant expansion to cater for the unemployed and for workers in the urban and rural informal sectors displaced the traditional axis of some VTIs, which in the process became an important social policy arm of governments.

The third and most recent stage, still emerging in several VTIs of the region, attempts at a new balance between economic and social concerns, and defines the task of VTIs as providing training to individuals and enterprises for "*productive work.*" This approach recognizes that the productive tissue of an economy is made up of a heterogeneous set of economic units that vary by size, levels of productivity and technology, dynamism and prospects for stability and growth, market orientation, and degrees of organization and permanence in production processes; and that workers move within and across these productive units. Therefore, the emphasis is put on the improvement of the competencies of workers against the background of the collective interest for upgrading the economic and social performance of enterprises, regardless of their size and degree of formality and organization.

Recent Trends in Vocational Training

A comprehensive study on changes and innovations in VTIs and vocational training systems was undertaken by CINTERFOR/ILO in 1991.[5] The study revealed that VTIs' in Latin America had been cautiously changing their traditional role, while exploring innovative ways of responding to the new demands stemming from economic restructuring. The six main strategic trends identified in their specific fields and forms of action confirmed that a significant transformation of VTIs was taking place.

1. Pre-employment training declines while in-service training takes the lead
Apprenticeship and other forms of initial training which had traditionally been the core activity of VTIs, diminished steadily over the 1980s, both in terms of enrolment and resources allocated. In 1987, for the nine large VTIs for which comparable statistics were available,[6] only 31.4% of the trainees were enrolled in initial training, while 67.5% were in complementary training. As noted below, these VTIs strongly emphasized retraining, implementing a wide variety of programs targeted in particular to employees of small and medium-sized enterprises, often with significant degrees of direct involvement of enterprises. Several factors contributed to this marked shift: a significant improvement in the general levels of education of new entrants to the labor market; the increasing difficulties in placing trainees, mainly due to the stagnation of formal employment; the high cost of initial training in times of decline of VTIs' financial resources; the pressure from enterprises for retraining of their workers to adapt to internal changes in job contents and work organization; and the demands from the labor market as a whole, to reconvert workers in times of restructuring of production.

2. Technical skills' levels move upwards VTIs initiated or strengthened programs for training technicians and technologists at post-secondary education levels. Although enrolment at this level is still very modest in institutions such as SENA (1.6%), SENAI (1.0%) and SENCICO (2.6%), it represents one third of the enrollment of INACAP, and the trend for most VTIs is towards slowly increasing this level of training. This is a significant move in spite of the often modest numbers of trainees involved since it means an important change in the resource allocation by VTIs: as shown by the case of SENA, training at this higher level can absorb as much as ten times more per hour/course/trainee than conventional courses. This new field of VTI action involves entering into a common area, and to some extent even in duplication, with formal education. The reasons argued by VTIs stress the need to open up a mobility track for skilled workers, and the

---

[5] CINTERFOR/ILO (1991) was undertaken with the financial support of the World Bank, the International Development Research Centre of Canada, the GTZ of Germany and the Inter-American Development Bank (IDB). The research was designed and conducted by María Angélica Ducci as an input to the preparation of World Bank (1991).

[6] SENAC and SENAI in Brazil, SENA in Colombia, INA in Costa Rica, INACAP in Chile, INFOTEP in Dominican Republic, SECAP in Ecuador, SENATI and SENCICO in Peru.

urgency to respond to the technological innovation in enterprises in ways which formal education is not doing. This new role of VTIs can be seen as attempting to fill the gap left by an excessively academic formal education which has not responded to the new technological skills requirements demanded by the modernization of production. It also has the effect of regaining legitimacy for VTIs among workers, and particularly among employers, by placing them as centers of excellence for training in high technological skills. The issue at stake, however, is the rationale for overlapping and duplication between VTIs and formal education.

3. Training activities are increasingly organized by economic sectors With the purpose of getting closer to the specific needs of the different economic activities, VTIs have progressively organized specialized training by economic sector, either through their internal compartmentalization or through breaking up into sectoral VTIs. In some countries, such as Brazil, Mexico and Peru, VTIs were organized by economic sector from the very beginning. Increasingly, multisectoral VTIs in the remaining countries of the region are breaking down into decentralized or independent units directly linked to specific sectors. The clearest example of this is INCE in Venezuela, which has created independent bodies linked to the corresponding employers' chambers or groups for the most important industries.

The trend towards a sectoral approach has called for strong alliances between VTIs and the business organizations of each sector. In order to maintain adequate contact and a permanent flow of information on innovations and demands arising in the corresponding sectors, VTIs have created intermediate consultative and advisory bodies at the sectoral level. These flexible bodies have helped to improve the relevance, efficiency and effectiveness of VTIs, and have spread throughout the region. While having some obvious advantages, the sectoral approach does raise the issue of whether excessive compartmentalization by sector, including budgetary allocations, could hinder the periodic need for reallocation of resources across the various sectors, according to their varying dynamism and needs, in a context of economic restructuring.

4. Training delivery is being progressively transferred to enterprises In the context of the increasing role of private enterprise in the strategy of economic development, the responsibility for training delivery has naturally shifted in the direction of firms. This trend has taken different forms and proceeded at varying paces within the region. In some countries, such as Chile, the transfer has occurred through legal measures that have changed the basic organization and mechanism of the financing of training. As early as 1976 Chile moved radically away from the still prevalent pattern by dismantling the government sponsored VTI and replacing it with a system of fiscal incentives to stimulate enterprise's demand for training services, which could be purchased in an open market.

In other countries, transfer of training from VTIs to enterprises operates through regulated agreements which allow enterprises to retain part of their compulsory financial contributions to VTIs, against direct delivery of training for their employees; Brazil, Venezuela, and to a lesser extent Guatemala, have made important inroads in using this mechanism. More frequently, VTIs resort to flexible arrangements with enterprises through a variety of partnerships that have extended significantly across the region.

The issue in transferring training from VTIs to enterprises highlights the limited capacity of the majority of firms to undertake training on their own. In particular, small- and medium-size enterprises, and very specially micro-enterprises, lack the motivation, the resources and the capacity to take over training responsibilities. Interesting solutions are being explored and put into practice to strengthen enterprises' training capacity and, therefore, to widen the scope of their role. In the case of SENA in Colombia, INA in Costa Rica and INCE in Venezuela, the strategy has been to extend technical assistance programs to small and medium size enterprises to develop and strengthen their own training units. In Chile, where training is under the responsibility of enterprises, based on tax incentives, the law provides for the establishment of intermediary associations of small enterprises belonging to the same economic sector to organize group training and jointly benefit from tax incentives.

5. Management training: the entry point for small enterprises The weakness and reluctance of small firms to give priority to training has often been a barrier to the effectiveness of VTIs. Moreover, such enterprises typically perceive their critical needs as being more in the areas of credit, markets, products and appropriate technology. On the other hand, a case-by-case response to the needs of small enterprises is too burdensome and expensive for VTIs. Therefore, efforts have focused increasingly on management training, preferably for groups of small enterprises and with emphasis on exchange of experiences and networking, both in urban and rural areas.

Thus far the results are promising: on the one hand, management skills cut across all decision-making areas that constitute the real bottlenecks for small units; secondly, management knowledge generates, among other things, the demand for technical skills' training; last but not least, this approach has allowed VTIs to achieve economies of scale in working with small productive units.

The application of this scheme to micro-enterprises, in particular those that operate in the informal sector, is less clear. For such a clientele, VTIs have opted for interventions in joint ventures with other institutions covering broader areas of social development, and insisting on the organization and association of micro-enterprises in order to constitute an accessible group. Under such approaches, training is just one component of promotional strategies, usually linked to credit. In this respect, a recent evaluation of the results of training programs for micro-enterprises executed by VTIs and NGOs in Colombia indicates that many micro entrepreneurs are lured by the credit facilities offered by these programs but not interested or aware of the need for training (Ramírez, 1996).

6. Technological assistance cum training VTIs, particularly the most advanced in the region, are entering the field of technological assistance to enterprises, going well beyond their traditional training role. Following the path opened by SENAI in Brazil, various VTIs are increasingly offering enterprises a span of services, including direct technological support, research and development, dissemination of information and demonstration of technologies and even productive services connected with industrial design, improvement of production processes, functional organization of work, quality control, and the like. VTIs have entered into this new area for two fundamental reasons: at root, training on its own was not solving the broader productivity problems of enterprises, and its results were being undermined, particularly in small- and medium-size enterprises, by bottlenecks in product-design, materials, technology, production management and quality control. Secondly, for financial reasons VTIs sought a fund-raising strategy to counterbalance the increasing scarcity of resources due to the fiscal stresses of governments, by selling non-conventional services to enterprises in areas complementary to training. What started as an integrated package to service small and medium enterprises in the more dynamic industrial sectors expanded rapidly, especially in the richest and oldest VTIs having sophisticated infrastructure, modern equipment and high technological standards.

This approach has been controversial. On the negative side, it has been argued that it distracts VTIs from their essential mission. On the positive side, it has demonstrated the higher impact of training on productivity when it is integrated into a broader strategy for technological improvement, and has contributed to significant improvements in the quality of training.

The progressive shift of VTIs' focus from individuals to enterprises is the most significant innovation in training in response to economic restructuring in the region. Though individuals continue to be the direct subject of training, training programs are increasingly organized around the needs of productive units. To a certain extent, VTIs are moving towards a new identity as *"training and productivity centers"* which offer services organized in two main areas: technological development and organizational development (Ducci, 1990).

In this endeavor, distinguishing the roles that VTIs play with respect to the different kinds of enterprises is essential. The bulk of VTIs' direct attention concerns, logically, the small and medium enterprises, where the biggest potential exists in terms of technological and organizational advance. VTIs maintain an indirect and supportive role towards the larger enterprises, which are usually capable of organizing training for their employees on their own. The most difficult and challenging area for VTIs continues to be the vast sector of productive units constituted by micro-enterprises and self-employment, where responses are still unsatisfactory. This is an urgent area for improvement.

The second most important trend is closely linked to the previous one. Again taking the needs of enterprises as the central reference, VTIs are opening their span of action in two main directions: vertically, by covering training for higher occupational levels (middle management, technicians and technologists), and horizontally, by providing non-training technical services to enterprises, as the complement of training. The former trend raises the question of the extent to which VTIs, that were precisely created to provide skills to the lower strata of the population, have abandoned that objective. Is someone else taking over their role?

The paths set by the recent evolution of the long-existing VTIs highlight both the innovative strategies that deserve consolidation and expansion, and the gaps and backlogs that need to be addressed. They lead naturally to a set of critical policy issues.

11.3 The Critical Issues to Be Resolved

Building a National Consensus on Human Resources Development

Most countries of the region are becoming aware of the need for a comprehensive public policy for human resource development (HRD), as a constructive framework for the development of all relevant public and private expressions, levels and forms of education and training aimed at responding to employment and labor market needs. One major concern is to ensure equitable access to education and training, as a means of integrating all sectors of the population into development.

An effective HRD policy calls for a national consensus involving a broad range of stakeholders. Building such a consensus starts from good public information and understanding of the importance of education and training; of its benefits for individuals, enterprises, sectors, groups, local communities and for the society at large; of its significance for workers and employers; of its effects on the country's regional and international prospects; of its potential impact on economic growth and on social equity. The awareness, support and commitment of the general public and its various groups and organizations will be decisive for its success.

The next step is dialogue and negotiation. The key players at the negotiating table will necessarily be the government and employers' and workers' organizations. Unless the initiative comes from the social partners, it will be up to the government to promote and create a favorable climate for dialogue around these issues, and to provide the background information and the knowledge base for discussions. It will be crucial that representatives of all three sectors come from the highest level of authority. Even more, efforts will have to be made to strengthen the technical capacity of the representatives of the social partners, and of the government, to pursue the increasingly complex decisions in the area of HRD policies.

Redefining the Role of the Public and Private Sectors

A hot debate continues in the region as to the relative roles and responsibilities that the state and the private sector should assume with regard to human resources development. In the area of general education, the major responsibility of the state is not questioned, especially at the primary school level. Nevertheless, there is room for discussion on the role that it should play at central and local levels, on its interaction and partnership with the private sector and the civic society, and on the management of schools.

Much more controversy surrounds the roles and responsibilities of the different social actors in the field of vocational training. Until very recently, training had been understood as the primary—and almost exclusive—responsibility of the state. The rationale prevailed for several decades: vocational training, though to a lesser extent than general education, was nonetheless perceived as a basic service to the population, with social objectives sometimes overriding the economic ones. The consequence, brought to the extreme, has been that the state became the principal agent of financing and provision of training, with little involvement from the private sector. Private enterprise, with its rather passive attitude towards undertaking training on its own, has tended to take the position that, since they contribute through a levy to the financing of public VTIs, they can expect the adequate level and quality of training to be provided by such VTIs.

Despite many positive contributions of VTIs in the region, the increasingly pressing skills needs have given rise to some dissatisfaction with their overall performance, in particular in employers' circles. This in turn has led to a strengthening support for private sector participation in the training and development of human resources, and a corresponding redefinition of the role of the state and of the various private agents (Ducci, 1995). Among the reasons for this significant policy shift are:

i)   the insufficient and rigid response by government-led VTIs and their lack of capacity to adjust quantitatively and qualitatively to the new social and economic demands;

ii)   the excessively supply-driven approach of institutionally-based training;

iii)   the increasing complexity and diversity of skills training management, and the need to differentiate and decentralize and, simultaneously, to coordinate and harmonize its various functions;

iv)   the willingness of the various stakeholders, and in particular of employers and workers, to have a say in training decisions, and to play a more active role in their implementation;

v)   the chronic and increasing shortage of public resources, and the relative inefficiency and lack of accountability in their use;

vi)   the existence of underutilized private capacity for training;

vii)   the growing confidence in the functioning of market forces for the efficient allocation of resources and factors;

viii) the key role of the private sector as the main engine of the new development strategy;

ix)   the conviction of the economic value of workforce skills in a globalized economy; and,

x)   the belief in substantial private returns to skills training for individual workers and enterprises.

From VTIs to National Training Systems

Modernization of training requires a collective effort involving all sectors having actual and potential capacity to contribute to its accomplishment. Moreover, if increased relevance, efficiency, effectiveness, equity and sustainability of the overall national training effort is to be achieved, scattered training initiatives need to be acknowledged, organized and coordinated, and related in an integrated manner to the labor market. This puts Latin American countries on the road towards the building of national training systems.

In Latin America, the existing capacity and know-how on training is, to a large extent, concentrated in government hands and, most particularly, in national VTIs. However, private capacity in enterprises themselves is growing fast, as is that in private providers, ranging from for-profit training firms to unions, NGOs and community organizations. Simultaneously, the public capacity is more and more dispersed among a number of government agencies and bodies, at central and decentralized levels. The picture further includes a number of private/public partnerships for training. A training market is emerging in varying degrees in all Latin American countries. Conventional wisdom coincides with the current widely accepted political support to stimulate and make the best possible use of the training market.

It is another matter, however, to guess the extent to which an open and free market for training can effectively satisfy the needs of the economy. In all countries, regardless of their level of development, training operates in an imperfect market; such imperfections are obviously more serious in developing countries. In Latin America, the demand for training is still weak. Neither enterprises nor individual workers are willing and able to invest in training up to the level required by society. Moreover, the interest, capacity and willingness to invest is unevenly distributed and, both among enterprises and individuals, the ones who need it most are those who either cannot afford it or (sometimes) do not recognize the need. Despite the general awareness of the value of knowledge and of the importance of professional qualifications, there is a lack of information and understanding of the routes and options available to acquire them. Too many expectations are put on higher formal education, which is accessible to only a minority of the population. Vocational training is less visible and, usually, the residual option. The needs, therefore, do not translate very accurately into expressed demand.

From the supply side, and despite the mushrooming of private providers, programs are not sufficiently diversified to cover the wide range of needs: they tend to concentrate on technical areas which require low fixed costs and limited technological investments, in metropolitan areas, in commerce and service trades. Private providers offer programs of varied quality and tend to suffer even more from some of the rigidities that have raised criticism against traditional public VTIs. Moreover, their services, presumably demand-driven, often follow a mis-informed clients' demand and their delivery tends to remain rather mechanical.

The major failure of the training market is in the area of equity. Unless a well-designed system with adequate financing is available to serve the training needs of the socially disadvantaged groups lacking a private capacity for accessing training, inequalities will grow dramatically. On the other hand, the disadvantaged groups, concentrated in unemployment or in low-quality and low-paid jobs, are precisely the ones upon which training, if adequately provided, should be able to make a major difference.

The Latin American experience has shown that, despite some efforts to cater to equity concerns, even public VTIs have failed to make a major impact on that front. The challenge is, therefore, to devise, adjust or reform the national training systems so as to enable them to more effectively balance and reconcile responsiveness to the economic needs of enterprises on the one hand and the social needs of individuals and groups on the other.

There is a growing consensus within the region to the effect that national training systems must be shaped by government, as representative of the collective interests of society; moreover, since the majority of the countries have strong and experienced public VTIs, it is natural that these should play the key role in shaping and strengthening a national training system. But it is also clear that national systems must make the best possible use of market forces, both in the training market and the labor market. The policy debate focuses on the degree and forms of government intervention in the training process which are needed to effectively guide, foster and unleash the capacity of the market, while at the same time compensating for its distortions.[7]

11.4 The New Role of the State in Training

The diverse organization, capacity and performance of existing training systems in the various Latin American countries, together with the different national needs, priorities and constraints they confront, imply that there can be no single blueprint for government intervention which would apply across the board. Instead, some suggestions are provided below concerning the possible roles that governments are likely to undertake in national training systems reformed along the lines stated above.

Defining a National Training Policy

Within the overall framework of a national consensus on human resources development as referred to earlier in this chapter, the government should promote the adoption of a national skills training policy. Preferably through the Ministry of Labor or its equivalent dealing with employment and labor matters, the government should convene the social partners to discuss and agree on the objectives to be achieved, the roles to be played by the government, enterprises, individuals, employers' and workers' organizations and other stakeholders, the strategies to be put into effect, the mechanisms for their financing, and the institutional and technical support for its implementation.

A sound and effective training policy needs to be founded on objective knowledge and information. Government's have a responsibility to ensure the availability of such information, in particular on the supply and demand for training, the evaluation of past experience, feasibility studies for new proposals, and assessment of their potential, in all of this drawing on the lessons of

---

[7] This view is based on discussions among the heads of VTIs of Latin American and Caribbean countries in the 1995 meeting of the Technical Committee of CINTERFOR/ILO in Jamaica.

international experience. The knowledge and experience of VTIs are important repository of information and should be fully tapped.

Organizing the System

Setting the stage for effective participation by the diverse institutions active in training is a difficult task. A good system should allow maximum flexibility for its components and for the relationships among them. Experience shows that excessive controls and sanctions may be counterproductive; an enabling environment and positive incentives get better results. The bottom line is to establish clear *"rules of the game"* for the different players, and to make them extensively known and understood. The institutional arrangements have to be defined, making adequate provisions for as much decentralization as possible, and emphasizing the coordination mechanisms that will facilitate communication within the system, and with its environment. Leadership and guidance from a national training authority are essential; leading a training system requires a sound technical base that is not built overnight. Again, the capacity of VTIs should be fully tapped.

A critical challenge involves the participatory mechanisms at the various levels of the system. There is a long-standing tradition of tripartite involvement in the governing bodies of most Latin American VTIs. However, in the wake of the moves towards decentralization and privatization of VTIs, and as the result of greater pressures from political and market forces, this participation has lost some of its impact and significance. A modernized training system should strengthen tripartite dialogue and participation formally structured at the top of the system; nevertheless, to be effective, the involvement of employers and workers needs to be complemented by additional forms of flexible participatory mechanisms at decentralized levels—regional, sectoral, enterprise and community.

Legislation and Standards

Appropriate legislation is one requirement of a good training system. The current legislative picture is, nonetheless, far from coherent in many Latin American countries. Legal provisions concerning training, education, labor and employment are sometimes contradictory. Moreover, even where it is coherent, the legislative framework may not be adequate to foster the needed policies. Governments should therefore proceed with a review and where necessary revision of the relevant legislation.

Minimum standards need to be set, in particular to ensure the quality of training to be delivered by providers, and the transparency of the overall system.

Registration and accreditation of training programs are essential if an effective system involving multiple providers is to be established. At a higher level, standards for certification of skills and competencies will add to the relevance, efficiency and effectiveness of the system.

A competencies standards system should aim at establishing and regulating the mechanisms for evaluation, testing and certification of the knowledge, qualifications and skills of individuals, regardless of the means through which they were acquired. An effective competencies standards system is a key tool to improve the quality of training and the transparency of the labor market, by providing a sound and objective base to hire workers and to facilitate their occupational mobility. Furthermore, it allows for avoiding wastage and overlapping, improving mobility within the training system and transfers across the training and the formal education systems. Finally, it capitalizes on competencies acquired informally or on the job, and even in other countries. Nevertheless, standards should be set at a sufficiently broad level so as not to constrain the flexibility of the overall system.

Financing

Public financing is probably the most controversial issue in the training reform arena. As noted earlier, private investment in training is well below the socially-optimal level in Latin American countries. Hence the volume and mechanisms of public financing of training remain the cornerstone for the effective national system. Among the array of sources and mechanisms of public financing of training used worldwide, Latin American countries opted for a fairly common pattern from the very early stages of organized training. Most of them continue to finance their training systems through a levy ranging from 0.5% to 2% of the payroll, allocated to one or several VTIs. The levy is paid by enterprises above a minimum number of employees and, with some exceptions, from all sectors of economic activity. In recent years, there have been attempts in some countries to abolish or modify this financing mechanism. In others, cuts and freezes have reduced the availability of funds collected through the levy. In practice, VTIs have reacted by trying to diversify their sources of income; they have had some success in this objective (Ducci, 1991).

Other countries have opted for different or complementary mechanisms for training financing. The Chilean case is of special interest. In 1976 the government enacted the first legal framework defining the public role in vocational training and labor market intermediation. The new Statute created a market oriented system where the state, instead of providing training services as it had done until then, would subsidize training activities and control the overall performance of the system. Private training agencies were free to sell their services to private firms and government-sponsored public training programs. On the other side of the market, private clients would decide the amount and kind of training they wanted to buy, with the government subsidizing firm-based training programs through tax rebates or financing public training programs for workers not covered by private activities.

The Chilean system has adjusted over the years, both to improve its performance and, notably, to increase its equity impact. In 1992, public expenditure on training was more than three times the former Chilean VTIs' budget, and its growth exceeded that of the GNP and employment; private expenditure on firm-based training activities accounted for 43% of public expenditure on firm-based training (Martínez, 1994).

While the optimum level of public investment in training is too much influenced by national conditions and circumstances to permit useful generalizations, the question of the best feasible financing mechanisms opens a wide range of possibilities that should be carefully scrutinized in accordance with the set of objectives to be achieved. As a general rule of thumb, flexible mechanisms should be encouraged, probably involving differentiated allocations and/or incentives aimed at balancing the two major purposes of any national training system: enhancing economic productivity and guaranteeing social equity.

Training Provision

It is in the area of training provision itself where the greatest transfer of activity from the state to the private sector has occurred, and where the biggest potential for further transfer is foreseeable in the near future. The degree of such a transfer depends to a large extent on the efficiency, quality, diversity and strength of the infrastructure and technical capacity of the existing public training facilities, and on the comparative capacity of the private sector. Moreover, a combination of public and private provision may be a good option, including the possibility for privatizing the management of public facilities, or the training facilities themselves.

The government should, in any case, reserve for itself a subsidiary role in direct provision, to ensure training for those activities, sectors, geographical areas, groups, categories or individuals that, being essential for the society's interest, are not and cannot be appropriately catered to by private initiative, even if publicly funded. Once more, VTIs would be the best placed institutions to guarantee high quality public provision.

Technical Support

As guarantor of the national training system and responsible for its smooth functioning, the state has to ensure important technical functions to support decision-making by the overall system and by its parts and beneficiaries. Such functions might be accomplished directly or through third parties. Among the most important are: information services on training, employment and the labor market; research and development; and technical assistance. The underlying criteria are to allow the system to take advantage of economies of scale and to make state intervention a facilitator for the improvement of the overall performance standards of the national training effort.

In all three functions, Latin American VTIs are naturally called upon to provide the backbone of the system's technical capacity. Deliberately or not, VTIs' contribution in transferring their know-how to external training operators has been remarkable. Within an organized national training system, their role in this regard should become central.

11.5 Creating the Climate for Training Reform

There is no doubt that the region is ready to go a step forward in promoting an increasing partnership for training between the public and private sectors. However, multiple difficulties and constraints need to be overcome. Amongst the measures that governments and other institutions could launch to prompt the process, the following are proposed:

a) Sensitize the public, opinion leaders and key players in economic and social life, as to the value of investing in training and its positive impact for economic growth and social equity. Information campaigns, open fora and the objective demonstration of the benefits for different groups could be organized by the governments and interested parties.

b) Stimulating the interest and active participation of the social partners in a national debate on training. Initiatives to strengthen the employers' and workers' organizations institutional, political and technical capacity to discuss, negotiate and decide on these issues are particularly important.

c) Promoting strategic alliances and giving room for collaboration, joint work, cost-sharing, complementarity, convergence and mutual reinforcement between governmental and private agents on the supply and demand sides.

d) Modernizing and making more flexible the operation of government structures and institutions, prioritizing technical over political criteria in discharging its functions, and establishing working habits and performance standards conducive to dialogue and mutual trust.

e)   Facilitating the exchange of information and experience among countries, and promoting collaboration links at regional and international levels on training issues. The regional network of information, research and technical cooperation that has been operating in the region for more than thirty years under the leadership of CINTERFOR/ILO has been instrumental in fostering and strengthening Latin American VTIs. In an increasingly dynamic international context, the role of such a network and of extended cooperation links among countries inside and outside the region becomes even more important to foster training reform.

REFERENCES

Centro Interamericano de Investigación y Documentación sobre Formación Profesional (CINTERFOR) (1995). "Training Horizons: A navigation chart for Latin America and the Caribbean." Reference paper presented at CINTERFOR, 32nd Meeting of the Technical Committee, Ocho Rios, Jamaica.

Centro Interamericano de Investigación y Documentación sobre Formación Profesional/ International Labor Office (CINTERFOR/ILO) (1991). "Vocational Training on the Threshold of the 1990s." *PHREE Background Paper Series*. Washington D.C.: The World Bank, Education and Employment Division, Population and Human Resources Department.

Economic Commission for Latin America and the Caribbean (ECLAC) (1990). "Changing Production Patterns with Social Equity." Santiago: ECLAC.

Economic Commission for Latin America and the Caribbean (ECLAC) (1997). *Preliminary Overview of the Economy of Latin America and the Caribbean 1997*. Santiago: ECLAC.

Economic Commission for Latin America and the Caribbean/United Nations Educational, Scientific and Cultural Organization (ECLAC/UNESCO) (1992). "Education and Knowledge: Basic Pillars of Changing Production Patterns with Social Equity." Santiago: ECLAC/UNESCO.

Ducci, M. A. (1980). "The Vocational Training Process in the Development of Latin America." *Studies and Monographs*, No. 47. Montevideo: CINTERFOR/OIT.

Ducci, M. A. (1983). "Vocational Training: An Open Way." *Studies and Monographs*, No. 62. Montevideo: CINTERFOR/OIT.

Ducci, M. A. (1988). "Equity and Productivity of Vocational Training - The Latin America Experience." *International Journal of Educational Development*, Vol.8, No. 3, pp. 175-187.

Ducci, M. A. (1990). *Formación Profesional y Ajuste Estructural.* Montevideo: CINTERFOR/OIT.

Ducci, M. A. (1991). "Financing of Vocational Training in Latin America." *Training Discussion Paper*, No. 71. Geneva: International Labor Office.

Ducci, M. A. (1995). "Rol del Estado y de los Sectores Privados en la Formación de Recursos Humanos." Mimeo.

Gitahy, L. (Coordinator) (1994). "Reestructuración Productiva, Trabajo y Educación en América Latina." *Lecturas de Educación y Trabajo*, No. 3. Red Latinoamericana de Educación y Trabajo. Montevideo: CIID-CENEP/CINTERFOR-OIT/IG-UNICAMP/UNESCO.

International Labor Office (ILO) (1995). "The Employment Challenge in Latin America and the Caribbean." *Working Papers*, No. 7. Lima: ILO Regional Office for Latin America and the Caribbean.

Martínez Espinoza, E. (1994). "Vocational Training in Chile: A Decentralized and Market Oriented System." *Training Policy Study*, No. 8. Geneva: International Labor Office.

Mercado, A. (1994). "Cambio Tecnológico, Calificación y Capacitación en un Contexto de Integración Económica." *Lecturas de Educación y Trabajo*, No. 3. Red Latinoamericana de Educación y Trabajo. Montevideo: CIID-CENEP/CINTERFOR-OIT/IG-UNICAMP/ UNESCO.

Middleton, J., A. Ziderman, and A. Van Adams (1993). *Skills for Productivity - Vocational Education and Training in Developing Countries.* Washington, D.C.: The World Bank.

Ramírez, Jaime (1996). "La Capacitación Laboral Como Instrumento de Lucha Contra la Pobreza." *Estudios de Políticas de Formación*, No. 26. Ginebra: Oficina Internacional del Trabajo.

United Nations Development Program (UNDP) (1996). *Human Development Report.* New York: Oxford University Press.

World Bank (1991). "Vocational and Technical Education and Training." World Bank Policy Paper. Washington, D.C.: The World Bank.

Chapter 12

CONCLUSIONS

by Albert Berry

Canada is noted for its relatively developed social safety net and the considerably lower incidence of poverty than found in the United States. Payroll taxes fund a substantial share of the social expenditures and unemployment insurance is a central feature of the system. Gradually rising costs and increasing concerns about possible efficiency loss due to distorted incentives have led to a reform process over the last few years. Meanwhile, minimum wages have also tended to be higher than in the U.S., but economists have not provided much endorsement of their impact on poverty reduction and have expressed some concern that they may be reducing employment. Training programs are numerous and complex, but taken together not a major component of social expenditures, in contrast to many European countries. Canada is sometimes described as a country which economizes on such expenditures by drawing on immigrants who bring human capital with them.

Currently the most obvious challenge in Canada involving the four policy issues discussed in this volume is the need to maintain a strong unemployment insurance system but one which is more efficient, less subject to distortions and disincentive effects, and hence less costly. While there may be no strong evidence that payroll taxes create major distortions or losses, the increasing integration with the U.S. economy could raise those losses in the future (e.g., by leading to emigration of enterprises). Minimum wages are probably a useful instrument in some contexts, but there is no persuasive evidence that they have a significant poverty-alleviation impact in Canada. Although it may be that Canada's limited investment in training in the past has not had significant growth costs, this may be changing; among the many possible factors in Canada's growth deceleration vis-à-vis the U.S. over the last three decades, one is inadequate investment of this sort at a time of rapid technological change.

Latin America's overall economic policy confronts a need to shift from halting, inegalitarian growth to faster and more equitable growth. Can labor market policy contribute more to these objectives than it has in the past? Judging from the statements of many Latin American governments they believe so (or want to persuade their citizens that they do). And, indeed, there is a strong argument that the job protection system which makes firing very difficult has to some degree reduced modern sector employment, while not benefitting many poor people. An alternative way to protect people against the costs of job loss is needed; experiments are currently going on in a number of countries. That new way should achieve wider coverage and involve less negative effects than the past systems.

As with job protection, minimum wage legislation may have had many fewer positive effects than its supporters argue, due to a combination of partial coverage (limited to the formal sector and to relatively larger firms in most countries) and, as in Canada, possibly negative effects on employment in the activities where it is applied. Payroll taxes have been high in these countries, and would only be justified at the past levels if the benefits were comparably large, which appears unlikely to have been the case. Most Latin American countries have large public vocational training systems and substantial enrolment in technical secondary school programs; overall benefits are hard to judge but it does seem clear that many programs are too distantly related to market needs to get close to their potential yields; hence improvement needs to be sought in this domain as well.

Canada's experience with *unemployment insurance* highlights the delicate challenge of providing a good level of protection against the welfare costs of unemployment and the fear of it, as well as contributing to overall income maintenance, while inducing as few negative side-effects as possible. The system has recently been undergoing reforms aimed at alleviating some of its major perceived weaknesses. Canada's system is interesting from the Latin American perspective, since it falls between the spare U.S. model and the more generous European ones (in terms of the income replacement rate, duration of benefits, conditions for benefits, etc.). Though the historically generous (since 1971) Canadian approach has indeed alleviated the social costs of unemployment, it has also contributed to a somewhat (perhaps 1-1.5 percentage points) higher unemployment rate; has helped to sustain chronically high levels of overall and (especially) seasonal unemployment in the Atlantic provinces; has deterred interregional movement; and may have had such other undesirable effects as discouraging human capital formation—though here the evidence gets fuzzier. If the system has slowed the regional convergence of income, as argued by some—also hard to judge from the evidence—that convergence has still been proceeding. Supporters give it credit for contributing to the smaller worsening of income distribution over the last couple of decades in Canada than in such countries as the United States and the United Kingdom, but this too remains open to debate.

Some of the negative side-effects of this federally-operated system have been related to the fact that it is in the narrow interests of provincial governments to shift as much of the overall burden of income maintenance to the national level and to "collaborate" with local business and workers in the development of a system which "milks" the federal government as much as possible. Its fiscal dimensions are significant; between 1966 and 1993 the effective payroll rate to fund the system rose from 1.11% to 5.15% of wages and from 0.54% to 2.57% of GDP (Lin, Picot and Beach, 1995). Whether this is excessive or not depends on the importance of the insurance function, on the distortion costs of the tax, and on whether, to the extent that it acts as an instrument of redistribution, it is effective in that regard. As a *de facto* part of the income maintenance system, the program must be judged in part by how much it contributes to that function relative to the other instruments in use or available. Similarly with regard to its insurance function, one must ask whether there are better instruments (or better types of UI systems) available. The central question in Canada now is whether politically feasible reforms can produce a system which does well on the support front but with less negative side effects and hence lower total costs than the previous one. On this point, only time will tell.

The traditional way to protect workers against the costs of job loss in most Latin American countries has been a combination of tight regulations on dismissal and high severance payments. It has thus provided strong protection against unemployment (at least when the legislation is vigorously enforced) for a usually relatively small "insider" group (though larger in the more developed countries of the region like Argentina and Uruguay) while providing none for what is usually the majority of workers who are outside the formal sector. This system has come under serious criticism for being regressive (protecting mainly the better off), reducing total employment in the modern sector (by increasing the employer's costs/risks in hiring), and reducing the mobility of the labor force, which may be especially damaging in middle income countries in the process of integrating themselves into the world economy. Few in depth studies have tried to quantify these negative effects, or even undertaken a careful assessment of the *de facto* coverage of this system. The allocation of much labor to the informal sector may or may not be inefficient from a static point of view, and if inefficient it may or may not be avoidable through labor market or other policies. Increasingly the evidence seems to suggest that not much efficiency loss results from barriers to movement between the formal and informal sectors. Such contrary evidence notwithstanding, a strong enough *prima facie* case has been made to send analysts and policymakers in search of something better than the existing set of institutions.

Since it is implausible that a worker-protection system can be very effective on behalf of a large number of workers by impeding firing, it seems clear that a system must be found which gives employers greater freedom, while still protecting workers against the full vagaries of the job market. Such unemployment insurance systems as have recently been introduced in a number of Latin American countries are attempts to confront this need. None has yet achieved a level of coverage anywhere near those of the countries of Western Europe, the U.S. or Canada. Cortázar's Chilean proposal (Chapter 4) is designed to get around the problems of implementing standard industrial country unemployment systems in lower income countries where informal sector employment is more the rule than the exception. This fact makes it difficult to avoid serious abuse of any system where there is a private incentive to claim unemployment while continuing to work. The proposed system avoids these negative incentives by making the worker pay for his/her own unemployment insurance through a fund which accumulates when the person is working and can be drawn on or borrowed from when unemployment strikes. It skirts the cheating problem by making the insurance personal, and in so doing foregoes the potential for risk-sharing across individuals. Various other proposals are on the table or in their trial phases at this time; most can be thought of as hybrids between the Cortázar plan and the standard industrial country model, in the degree to which they combine individual self-insurance against the risk of unemployment and risk-pooling insurance whose side-effects include incentives to abuse, and the allocation of too much labor and other resources to industries in which average unemployment rates are high.

The choices facing Latin American countries can be thought of as falling within a triangle of options defined by the three systems just described—the industrial country model, the Cortázar model and hybrids of the two. The first two have the potential to foster desirable labor mobility by reallocating the cost facing the displaced workers—either to society (in the industrial country model) or over time (in the Cortázar model). The industrial country model has the advantage of distributing the costs of unemployment more widely and/or acting as a progressive transfer system toward poorer workers, provided that it does not lead to too much moral hazard. In the context of labor markets with large informal sectors, it is implausible to assume that all workers can be covered, so a major issue is the extent to which a system can be selectively applied to a part of the labor force where it is useful to the workers as well as the firms. It is tempting to conclude that the industrial country model itself holds little interest in Latin America given the level of moral hazard and the low likelihood that it could act as an instrument to redistribute income to poorer groups. But since most of the Latin countries are more industrialized than the Third World average and hence structurally more similar to industrial countries, the planning of UI systems should take this into account. The best option would be one which can both serve a useful function at present but that with reasonable adjustments could in future take care of those worker needs which are more typical of an industrial economy. The Cortázar plan avoids most moral hazard problems, though there is a question of how much coverage could be extended under such a scheme.

The assessment of the performance of the social safety net—including the unemployment insurance system, the family welfare system, old-age pensions, etc.

involves not only the measurement of their social benefits but the recognition and assessment of their social costs and the indirect costs related to these. ***Payroll taxes*** are the source of about half of the income security benefits paid to Canadians (as of 1992-93) and have risen from 2.0% of GDP 1966 to 5.8% in 1993. Most of the controversy around these taxes involves their indirect costs through incentive effects, either on those who pay high overall marginal tax rates or on those who take advantage of the allegedly generous and easy-to-access public income support program including the UI and workers' compensation. There is little dispute that the programs do provide real benefits to many people. The impact of the taxes on hours of work for those working, whichever the direction may be, is agreed to be small, especially for men. Green and Riddell (1997) conclude that many workers would not be in the labor force at all but for the UI program and that it tends to increase the weeks of work by the more poorly qualified and unemployment-prone workers. As for the demand side, estimates of the labor cost elasticity of demand tend to fall mainly in the range -0.5 to -1.0 (OECD, 1994). To predict the impact of lowered labor taxes on the demand for labor, however, one must allow for the fact that labor costs will fall by less than the labor taxes do, so the labor tax elasticity of labor demand could be just a fraction of the above figure.

One of the trickier but nonetheless central aspects of the question of payroll taxes relates to their impacts relative to that of other ways of raising the funds used for pensions, UI, etc. Kesselman (Chapter 6) concludes that payroll taxes are well suited to financing social security, though benefit-tax linkages may need reform in some programs. The key point is that, though in the perception of the individual employer it appears that these taxes raise the total cost of labor, that impact is smaller (perhaps much smaller) than it appears. Payroll taxes are simple and easy to operate and are a relatively efficient form of taxation when compared to taxes on income or capital. When tied to benefits in a well-designed program of social security, they offer the additional advantage of posing minimal distortions to labor market and other economic behavior.

Payroll taxes have tended to be very high in most Latin American countries relative both to developed countries and to other LDCs. The context differs from that of Canada or other developed countries since the partial coverage has the effect of creating or widening a labor cost gap between the modern and the informal sectors. Thus much of the debate on the merit of such taxes reflects differing views as to the impact of that labor cost gap. Their value also depends, of course, on how large one believes the benefits from the social security systems to be. Current reforms in Latin America are lowering these taxes and, with respect to the pension component of them, creating the option for the funds to be invested in private sector institutions. To the extent that the switch from pay-as-you-go funding of pensions to the fully funded system raises national savings, this could be a major boon. Chile's fully funded system appears to have contributed importantly in this way and thus deserves some credit for the fast growth of the economy in recent years. The impact on modern sector employment is, as noted above, much harder to predict and in any case shifting employment from the informal to the modern sector may not raise overall economic efficiency if the modern sector continues to benefit from imperfections in the product and capital markets, imperfections which have been to date partially offset by the labor cost advantage of the informal sector.

As in Canada, the recent reforms in the social benefit area in Latin America have been designed to reduce fiscal strain and to encourage job creation. Unlike the Canadian situation, a relatively high share of Latin America's workers are not covered by the social benefits financed through payroll taxes; the challenge of broadening coverage has not been given much thought in these reforms and needs to be addressed seriously.

In today's integrating world one of the issues most frequently mooted about labor taxes is their impact on international competitiveness. The perspective of the individual business is that any cost increase lowers competitiveness; when other local firms face the same cost component (such as labor taxes) it is accepted that a firm's situation sub-à-vis these competitors may not be affected, but that all of them suffer sub-à-vis competitors from other countries. But this widespread perception is invalid in any situation where a country's balance of payments is kept in equilibrium by the usual mechanisms—the exchange rate where it is allowed to vary, or monetary/fiscal policy where the exchange rate is fixed. Where these mechanisms are operating as they should be, tax levels should have no long-run impact on a country's overall competitiveness in international markets, either in an industrial country like Canada or in developing ones like those of Latin America. As Kesselman points out (Chapter 6) higher taxes can cut competitiveness only in the short-run.

The main objective of *minimum wage legislation* in industrial countries like Canada is reduction of poverty by raising the labor incomes of relatively poor families. As with UI, there is also an issue of whether it generates negative side-effects, in particular whether it leads to fewer jobs (especially for poor family members) and slower economic growth through efficiency (deadweight) loss. At a second level of analysis is the question of whether a higher minimum wage has the effect of shifting the rest of the wage structure, or at least parts of it, up. In some countries of Latin America, wages which are not at the bottom of the structure are nonetheless denominated in terms of the minimum wage, which automatically gives it a more prominent role in affecting wages in general. And even where the link is not a formal one, it is known that bargaining often occurs with the MW as the benchmark unit, and that through this mechanism it may have a greater effect, at least on the overall nominal wage structure, than would at first glance appear to be the case. If all wages move up in line with the MW, however, the main final outcome may be inflation which at the limit can cancel out any initial increases in real wages—for the lower income workers and everyone else—while the fact that all wages rose means that there was no redistribution within the wage system either. Considerations such as these make it clear that identification of the effect of minimum wage legislation may be difficult.

Canada has experienced moderate levels of inflation and has a "modern" labor force structure—few workers in agriculture, nearly all *de facto* covered by legislation, a very small informal sector, and a considerable number of families with no income earners (related to unemployment, single parent families on welfare, etc.). Against this background, Benjamin (Chapter 8) finds that minimum wages have only limited scope for improving the welfare of the lowest income households, since most of these families have no full-time earners. Many of the benefits of higher minimum wages go to teenagers who are distributed relatively evenly across the income distribution though, among adults, such benefits do flow somewhat disproportionately to those with lower incomes. However, the estimated disemployment effects of minimum wages may be great enough to actually reduce the wage bill received by low wage workers as a group. Whether this extreme outcome holds or not, it is important that this instrument be compared with others whose objective is to improve income distribution, such as a negative income tax; too few attempts have been made along those lines.

The minimum wage (MW) has traditionally been considered an important poverty-reduction instrument in Latin America. But concerns have increasingly been expressed, somewhat similar to those in Canada and other industrial countries, that this instrument has few if any positive effects, especially as countries strive to consolidate their trade openings and value wages flexibility. The tendency of MW laws in Latin America has been to formally include all workers regardless of gender, age, geographical context, skill or occupation, in spite of the obvious existence of labor market segmentation, and the possibly negative effects of such laws on the less skilled, through job destruction. The complexity of sorting out the determinants of wages, employment and poverty make it a major challenge to understand how MWs have affected these variables accross Latin America. It is credible, as argued by López and Riveros (1989), that the MW has little capacity to protect the poor, given the context of labor market segmentation and the resulting modest level of coverage of the instrument. Still, it is not impossible that there is significant real coverage in some areas where the net effect of the legislation is likely to be positive (perhaps domestic servants in urban areas) while in other activities where the impact would be negative the legislation is simply circumvented. In addition, Morley (1995) suggests that a MW can be especially useful in conditions of recession, noting that during the 1980s in Latin America movements of the real minimum wage were correlated negatively to movements in poverty, after allowing for the growth of per capita income. Low coverage will probably become less an issue with time as labor market segmentation decreases and potential coverage of the MW rises. But this challenge may be replaced by a new one, as a common feature of industrial country structure emerges—the frequency of households with no earners. In that case, as noted for Canada, there are once again many poor families which cannot be assisted by MWs. One hopes that 1980s-style recessions will not recur, but macroeconomic instability remains a threat.

Unemployment insurance and minimum wages are passive labor market instruments in the sense that they do not entail direct action designed to improve labor productivity, in the expectation that this would in turn raise wages. *Training*, in contrast, is an "active" policy in this sense. Unfortunately, while its relevance and potential importance is obvious, gauging which types of training/retraining are really paying off is often much more difficult than might be expected. Training is recognized as crucial to employers, workers and any government aspiring to a strong performance from the economy and to avoiding the social consequences of serious mismatches between the supply of skills available and the needs of the economy. Globalization and the rapid pace of technological change are generally believed to make effective and lifelong training more important than before. In developed countries like Canada, labor markets are facing severe adjustment consequences of these and other phenomena, such as the implementation of just-in-time delivery, privatization, etc. Also necessitating an increased emphasis on training, are new workplace and human resource practices, together with demographic and other changes in the workforce. Despite this general recognition, it is hard to pinpoint just what needs to be done and by whom. There is logic to a certain amount of more general training being done in institutions, some more specific training at the firm level to take advantage of inside knowledge as to the needs, and some at the industry level, to respond both to knowledge of needs and economies of scale.

Canada's training system is, by most assessments, relatively small in terms of total resources expended, but at the same time rather complex. Canada is categorized by the OECD as one of the "weak" countries in terms of combined employer and government support for training in industry, with the weakness coming from the employer side. This has led to the view that Canadian employers lack a "training culture." Extensive reliance on immigration as a source of skilled labor may have deterred the development of the indigenous training system, and contributed to another alleged failing— the absence of good links to the educational system, which also owes something to the low status attached to vocational education, a quality shared with most countries of Latin America.

The measurement of benefits (whether gross or net) from training programs is notoriously difficult. Evaluation studies in Canada generally but not always find that training does pay, usually more in the form of greater employability than of higher wages. Measured impacts on earnings and employability have increased over time, perhaps due to better program design (as worse programs were abandoned and better ones expanded) or perhaps because the returns to training have increased for other reasons, such as the speed and character of technological change. The largest estimates usually relate to employer-based training combined with work experience, rather than from basic or institutional training. Gains from training are greatest in a more buoyant labor market, highlighting the importance of available employment opportunities. Among training options there is evidence of a tradeoff between efficiency in raising overall productivity of the labor force and the associated distributional effects. Most notable is the fact that formal training is more likely to be received by employees who are already more highly educated and well-paid. Also, though unemployed workers are more likely to undertake training than others, within the unemployed those most likely to experience difficult adjustment problems are less likely to do so.

Various of the cited study results may have had an impact on the re-orientation of training over time. There has been a redirection from basic and institutional classroom training toward training provided at the private sector workplace and combined with work experience. Increased emphasis has been placed on higher-level training for emerging skill shortages, and on the involvement of employers in the delivery of training. This is especially the case with respect to the recent re-orientation of UI from passive income maintenance and toward more active adjustment assistance, as UI funds are increasingly used to enable recipients to receive training at the workplace and to garner work experience.

In Latin America the training needs have also been changing significantly over recent decades, first as the economic crises—in most countries centered around the 1980s—slowed growth and cut the demand for many types of skills, then as the recovery tended to be accompanied by trade openings and a burst of imports of machinery/equipment and the associated technological change. By the onset of the crises, the majority of Latin countries had well-established and relatively large national training institutions which dominated much of the training scene. These shared the stage with the vocational secondary schools, technical institutes, a modest number of private training institutions, and a generally limited amount of in-house training carried out by firms. But overall coverage remained limited; most non-agricultural workers in blue collar activities had (and probably still have) received little if any training apart from informal on-the-job help from co-workers or supervisors. Probably the region's growth did suffer somewhat from its various weaknesses on the training front, even during the import substituting industrialization phase of the pre-crisis period. It is likely to suffer a good deal more under the new circumstances of 1990s and beyond, unless substantial improvements are undertaken. It now faces the challenge of recovering the growth performance of the pre-1980s decades in a context of increasingly complex technologies calling for a substantially improved human capital base. At the same time, the evidence of sharply worsening income distribution in most countries of Latin America—in the wake of the 1980s crisis and the economic reforms which accompanied or followed it—raises the challenge of assuring that the increases in human capital are broad-based enough to allow those who have been losing ground over the last decade or so to recover some of it or at the least not to lose more. On grounds both of productivity and of equality, it is pivotal that quality and access be improved at the primary level and that training systems play an increasing role in raising and maintaining productivity potential of as large a segment of the labor force as possible. As in Canada, the extent of training individuals receive in Latin America appears to be positively related to the level of their formal education. If this pattern is general (it has been clearly identified in Peru) the risk that unequal access to training will continue to be a significant source of earnings inequality is a very serious one.

Direct evidence of the low quality and incomplete coverage of primary schooling in a number of countries (most importantly Brazil) is complemented by the views of employers and the statistical evidence indicating that most vocational training is received by people with completed primary (probably good quality primary also). The increasing pace of technological change, together with the increasing need for worker flexibility, is raising the need for systematic training over the working career, which puts a new onus on training systems. Chile and various other countries have interesting experiments in the area of training programs for the poor, many or most of whom would normally be expected to wind up in the informal sector. Hopefully evaluations will soon begin to throw light on which of these offer the best promise.

The training picture in Latin America has been in a process of considerable change for some time, fueled by the macroeconomic problems and trends noted above, the increasing scarcity of public funds, and the increasing doubts about the competence of public institutions in general which have come with the neo-liberal wave of thinking about economic policy in Latin America and elsewhere. Alternative sources of training have been growing relatively fast. Varying policy responses have emerged across the region, with Chile pushing as much of the management and resource allocation decisions as reasonably possible into the private sector; other countries, though moving in the same direction, have not gone as far. As a result, there is within the region a useful range of experiments underway on the alternative ways of handling training. Taken together, the prevailing trends involve a shift of focus from the individual trainee to the firms, and a broadening of activities to include other productivity-related services as well as training. In terms of clientele there has been increasing recognition of the importance of small firms, though the question of just what package of services most benefits them and how it can be delivered remains to be resolved.

As Ducci (Chapter 11) argues, there is no doubt that substantial public sector involvement must be part of an effective training system in Latin America. The needs are changing with time and with shifts of macroeconomic context. The goal is a well thought-out, activist strategy, based on a continuing reevaluation of the skill needs of the economy with focus on the unmet needs. The extent to which the public sector should be a funder rather than a direct provider of training is under debate.

With respect both to the overall training systems and to their vocational training institution (VTI) component, a key issue is their capacity to meet the training needs of small and medium enterprises (SMEs). The training systems were historically built mainly to serve the larger scale sector and had their closest links to it. In the last decade or so most have begun to take seriously the challenge of shifting some of their attention to the needs of SMEs. It is clear that most training in this area must be subsidized, especially at the start. Whether VTIs, with extensive participation in their management by employers' associations will in most cases be the best option, or whether subsidized private provision (prevalent in Chile) will be superior remains to be seen. Though organized data are usually not available, it is likely and generally believed that private and NGO involvement in the training area has been rising rather rapidly. Certainly this is the case in Colombia, noted for the strong business involvement through associated NGOs in support of micro-enterprise.

The 1990s have been a difficult period both in Canada (except for the last few years) and in Latin America (except for a couple of countries). In Canada, income inequality has widened, a significant share of the population seems not to have seen any increase in income, and economic insecurity of various types has risen. In Latin America, although the "lost decade" of the 1980s is now history, the recovery of the 1990s has been much slower, more erratic and less satisfactory than hoped and expected. Income inequality, always a critical problem in most Latin American countries, has got even worse since the early 1980s. Reflecting these troubled settings, the decade has been a period of turmoil, reconsideration and reform of many labor market instruments in both Canada and Latin America. Many changes have now been implemented and more will be in the next few years. The more the accumulated understanding of these instruments can be incorporated in the design of the next round of reforms, the better, and the more monitoring and evaluation occurs in the early post-reform years the greater the chances will be of positive adjustments and refinements to improve on the inevitable weaknesses of any relatively novel approach.

The studies presented above suggest that developing (in the case of Latin America) and refining (in Canada's case) the system to protect workers against involuntary unemployment and more generally against income instability may be the highest priority item in both cases. Whereas in both Canada and Latin America the challenge is partly to get around political pressures against reform, in Latin America there is the additional complication that in the world of middle and higher income developing countries in general, there are no precedents to build on, so it is inevitable that whatever is tried will be in the nature of an experiment. Improving their training systems appears to be the second really important challenge in both parts of the world, partly because the existing ones have a number of weaknesses, and partly because with technological change increasingly central to growth, the needs are likely to be greater in the future than they have been in the past. Minimum wages appear to do much less to alleviate poverty in both contexts than might be expected. Though the need for a wage floor is not greatly in dispute, its level is. Finally, although payroll taxes are viewed as onerous by many employers, and have probably been unduly high relative to the benefits forthcoming in many Latin American countries, the use of moderate rates, like those in Canada, seems quite defensible *per se* as long as the funds collected are used reasonably well. In other words, the idea that resulting distortions are larger than would inevitably accompany the next best way of collecting the funds appears weak, as does the argument that such taxes have a significant effect on a country's overall competitiveness in international markets.

REFERENCES

Green, D. A. and W. C. Riddell (1997). "Qualifying for Unemployment Insurance: An Empirical Analysis." *Economic Journal,* Vol. 107 (January), pp. 67-84.

Lin, Zhengxi, Garnett Picot and Charles Beach (1995). "What Has Happened to Payroll Taxes in Canada over the Last Three Decades?" Ottawa: Statistics Canada, Business and Labor Market Analysis Division, mimeo.

López, R. and L. Riveros (1989). "Macroeconomic Adjustment and the Labor Market in Four Latin American Countries." In *Towards Social Adjustment: Labor Market Concerns in Structural Adjustment,* G. Standing, ed. Geneva: ILO.

Morley, Samuel A. (1995). *Poverty and Inequality in Latin America: The Impact of Adjustment and Recovery in the 1980s.* Washington, D.C.: John Hopkins University Press.

Organization for Economic Co-operation and Development (OECD) (1994). *The OECD Jobs Study: Taxation, Employment and Unemployment.* Paris: OECD.

INDEX